~ Purchased
with interest income
from the
library's trust fund ~

BRAVE
JOURNEYS

Also by David Mixner

STRANGER AMONG FRIENDS

BRAVE JOURNEYS

Profiles in Gay and Lesbian Courage

DAVID MIXNER
AND DENNIS BAILEY

BANTAM BOOKS
New York   Toronto   London   Sydney   Auckland

BRAVE JOURNEYS

A Bantam Book / August 2000

All rights reserved.
Copyright © 2000 by David Mixner.

Book design by Casey Hampton.

Library of Congress Cataloging-in-Publication Data

Brave journeys : profiles in gay and lesbian courage / [edited by] David Mixner and Dennis Bailey.
p. cm.
ISBN 0-553-10651-1
1. Gays—United States. 2. Homosexuality—United States. 3. Lesbians—United States. 4. Lesbianism—United States. I. Mixner, David B. II. Bailey, Dennis.
HQ76.3.U5 B688 2000
306.766'0973—dc21   00-023636

Published simultaneously in the United States and Canada

Bantam Books are published by Bantam Books, a division of Random House, Inc. Its trademark, consisting of the words "Bantam Books" and the portrayal of a rooster, is Registered in U.S. Patent and Trademark Office and in other countries. Marca Registrada. Bantam Books, 1540 Broadway, New York, New York 10036.

PRINTED IN THE UNITED STATES OF AMERICA

BVG   10   9   8   7   6   5   4   3   2   1

For Jeremy Bernard, Tony Leonhardt, Jeff Matchan, and Patrick Marston

For Beth Broderick and Gary Bankston

They know the joy is in the journey.

Contents

FOREWORD

Heroism is the brilliant triumph of the soul over the flesh—
that is to say, over fear: fear of poverty, of suffering, of calumny,
of sickness, of isolation, and of death. There is no serious piety
without heroism. Heroism is the dazzling and glorious con-
centration of courage.

— HENRI FREDERIC AMIEL

Over the last half-century, the gay and lesbian community has witnessed the advent of an unstoppable courage—courage rooted in the
fight for survival, tenacity born out of a community's determination to
be free. That bravery has sometimes been expressed in a roar; more often, it has manifested itself in a steady, unremitting rumble. It would not
let itself be daunted, and by this insistence, it has moved to open closed
minds. Those open minds have changed lives.

For us who are gays and lesbians, the journey to freedom has been
an arduous and often daunting pilgrimage. We have suffered rejection
by our families, friends, and home communities; been demonized by
religious bigots; been haunted by the fear of losing our jobs; seen many
among us succumb to suicide; and been decimated by violence and
AIDS. Yet along this difficult path, we also have witnessed incalculable
courage as brave individuals embraced the battle and taught the entire
world lessons in commitment and integrity. Without their leadership,

we would remain directionless; without their foresight, we would remain in darkness.

The dedicated trailblazers profiled in these pages never set out to be heroes. Rather, they felt that circumstances left them no choice but to stand up and be counted, to join selflessly in the fight against bigotry and discrimination. In espousing human dignity, championing the disenfranchised, and confronting injustice, these leaders embody the best of American values—honesty, compassion, and tolerance. Through this book, we hope to enshrine their stories in the lore not only of our community but of the world at large, so that from the telling and retelling of such stories, all can draw inspiration and strength.

The lives we recount here represent just a few of the countless stories that deserve documentation, for the effort to record gay and lesbian history has only recently begun. Lost and destroyed records, vague recollections, revisionism, societally imposed shame, and a desire to escape the past have made it difficult to uncover many of the histories that should be our legacy. Some to whom we spoke deny that homosexuality played any role in decisions that affected them, while others recall meetings where words like "queer," "faggot," and "pervert" echoed without protest throughout the halls of those then in power. Some with whom we have talked still hide in a suffocating closet, fearful of exposure. Others, for self-protection, have chosen to forget the pain and hatred they endured, finding denial the best way to soothe old wounds.

But we owe it to ourselves and to future generations to preserve the rich tapestry of our struggles, our contributions, and our experiences. When the remarkable lives of Del Martin and Phyllis Lyon, Elaine Noble, Sir Ian McKellen, Roberta Achtenberg, Tracy Thorne, and Dianne Hardy-Garcia are stitched together, they form a vivid quilt of the gay-rights movement over the last fifty years. These lives teach us that sexual orientation need not keep anyone from living a full life or fulfilling his or her dreams. The people we portray here have done both, and they did it in mainstream society. In the process, they changed the world for the better.

In his moving poem about the Irish Rebellion, "Easter 1916," William Butler Yeats wrote, "Too much suffering makes a stone of the heart." But the lives shared in this book celebrate the courageous journeys of individuals who never let their suffering—the oppression they endured—harden their hearts to stone. Their example tells all of us, gay and straight, that we too can summon the courage to live bravely as they have, and thereby help write a different history in the future.

—*David Mixner and Dennis Bailey*

BRAVE JOURNEYS

DEL   PHYLLIS

MARTIN & LYON

Wanting More

SEPTEMBER 21, 1955, WAS, SEEMINGLY, just another ordinary Friday evening in San Francisco. A cooling fog was settling in, and the last stragglers from the day's work were filtering into their homes, grateful that the weekend was finally at hand. Many San Franciscans were sitting down to their small-screen Philco television sets, flipping through the few available channels, wishing that the new season of the number-one show, *I Love Lucy,* would begin. Others were stepping out to the movies to see the new MGM musical *Love Me or Leave Me,* starring Jimmy Cagney and Doris Day. Adolescents were reading about teen idol James Dean in the latest *Photoplay* magazine, a mere week and a half before he would meet his untimely end in an automobile crash. The minimum wage had just been raised to one dollar; the Salk polio vaccine had been approved; and a new amusement park called Disneyland had opened down in southern California. Although globally the Cold War may have raged and open-air testing of nuclear weapons may have been commonplace, the majority of Americans found the fifties settling into a calm and uncomplicated decade. And for most, that balmy autumn night was typically uneventful.

However, it was anything but typical for eight brave women who had decided they had to change their lives, whatever the cost—even if it meant risking the loss of their jobs and the love of their families. They had come to the decision that they wanted something more than a life of shadows—something more than an existence of lies and loneliness.

They must have been frightened as they made their way to the small, quaint house just off Fillmore Street in San Francisco's Western Addition; and it is amazing, given the stakes, that they all found the nerve to climb the steps and enter the warm, inviting home. These women, who were literally taking their lives and their livelihoods in their hands, were lesbians—outcasts of society—seeking strength in numbers. If the world would not accept them, they would make a world of their own.

If only it could have been that simple.

For gays and lesbians in the late 1940's and early 1950's, life in America was perilous. Senator Joseph McCarthy, notorious head of the Senate Permanent Investigating Subcommittee, labeled homosexuals in government as "enemies within," second only to Communists, and launched vitriolic witch-hunts to expose and expel them. In 1953, President Dwight D. Eisenhower signed a directive banning gays from all federal employment. Police commonly raided places where homosexuals gathered, to harass them, or to haul them off in paddy wagons to the police station, where they were booked, photographed, and fingerprinted. Newspapers would print the names of those arrested and the notoriety could lose them their jobs or even their families; some were driven to suicide. Children were often taken away from a homosexual mother or father and never allowed to see that parent again. Loving families forcibly committed their homosexual children to mental institutions, allowing doctors to perform lobotomies in order to "cure" them. Beatings and killings were not uncommon, as the law looked the other way or declared publicly that the victims had gotten what they deserved. Given the dangers, the wisest homosexuals hid deep in the closet, praying that they would not be found out.

But that night, eight women in San Francisco were cracking open the closet door—just a little at first, but still enough to make history.

The group that met inside the nondescript neighborhood home was diverse, ranging in age from young adulthood to midlife. Vivacious redhead Phyllis Lyon, thirty, and her assured, earth-mother lover, Del Martin, thirty-four, fell roughly in the middle. Two of the women were mothers; four were white-collar, four working-class; and among them were a Filipina and a Chicana. None of them were revolutionaries promoting some profound social reform. Instead, what they were proposing was breathtakingly simple: a club, guaranteeing its members anonymity, where lesbians could meet others like themselves and escape the constant pressure of societally induced shame; a safe haven where women could come for a few hours a week to talk about their fears, goals, and frustrations, and how to cope in a hostile world; to laugh, play cards, dance freely, and gossip—that's all.

In 1955, however, when just inviting six lesbians over for coffee was a radical act, founding such a club was downright subversive—and indeed, what began as a little gathering of women would rock the social order in years to come. Christened the Daughters of Bilitis, it eventually blossomed into a nationwide movement that, for the first time, gave lesbians a political voice, and that became a powerful vanguard force in the struggle for gay rights.

Asked over forty years later what they had thought would emerge from that first meeting, Phyllis replies, "Well, I can tell you what we did not envision. We did not envision three homosexuals on the San Francisco Board of Supervisors. We did not envision the Gay Games. We did not envision a whole hell of a lot of stuff that has happened. Basically, Del and I got involved to meet other lesbians and broaden our circle of friends. We had no idea what the future held for us."

Roberta Achtenberg, one of those San Francisco supervisors, later the highest-ranking open lesbian ever to serve in the federal government, says, "Phyllis and Del are even better than their reputation. As younger women came up behind them, they were so encouraging and so helpful and so desirous of us to be everything that the times would allow us to be—times which, by the way, they helped to create. Everything that was possible for us was because of the battles they fought. They won them for us."

Phyllis Lyon was born in Tulsa, Oklahoma, in 1924, less than a decade before the catastrophic drought that rendered the state the Dustbowl. When she was very young, the family made the trek west to California, initially relocating in the San Francisco Bay Area. As the country was swirling into the vortex of the Great Depression, her father was fortunate enough to secure employment as a traveling salesman with the U.S. Gypsum Company, a job that led them to move from place to place around the Golden State. After living for a while with grandparents in Riverside, Phyllis finished grammar school in Berkeley, then attended junior high in Oakland and high school in Sacramento.

It was as a high-schooler that she learned her first hard lesson about the stigma of homosexuality, when a popular young boy in her drama class committed suicide. "Somehow it came out that he was gay," she recalls. The resonance of the desperate act reverberated through the school. "That was the first time I ever heard about homosexuals. And it didn't seem to make a lot of sense to me, really. Killing yourself over such a thing."

As a teenager, Phyllis knew what it was like to be different, but the realization had nothing to do with sexuality. She felt set apart because, unlike many women of those times, she was not drawn to marriage and homemaking but was determined to have a writing career. She had her sights set on a degree in journalism from the University of California at Berkeley. "My parents wanted me to go for another year to get a teaching certificate to fall back on," Phyllis recalls. "But I didn't want to be a teacher!"

At the university, an experience involving Lyon should have set red flags to waving, but she was, at the time, totally oblivious of its ramifications. She found herself in a deep and exclusive friendship with her roommate, "Jane." Inseparable, they would spend hours huddled together, sharing the most intimate details of their lives. Before long, other girls began to talk about them, and eventually the dean of women pronounced their friendship "too close" and asked them to leave the dormitory. It was not until years later that Lyon understood why—that the dean and their fellow students suspected them of being homosexuals.

Upon graduation from Berkeley, Lyon returned to San Francisco to look for a job as a journalist. "I was determined I was not going to be a society writer," she says vehemently, but for women the opportunities to do "hard" newspaper reporting were few. Disappointed and needing money, she decided to take a job in corporate America with the Burroughs Corporation, rather than write about teas and white gloves. But soon, she recalls, "I was bored to tears and decided, to hell with it!" She then heard of a dreaded "society editor" position at a newspaper in

Chico, California, a small town some 120 miles northeast of San Francisco. Swallowing her pride, she wrote to apply, but by the time the *Chico Enterprise* received her letter, the position was filled—and the only slot the paper had open was for a general reporter. Delighted with the happenstance, Phyllis could at last achieve her dream of doing some real news writing. Although she would have to trade the cosmopolitan atmosphere of San Francisco for the sleepiness of a little town—even the bus trip there was "the most boring ride in the world!" she says, laughing—she took the job for forty dollars a week.

Before long, she moved up to covering the police beat and city hall. Being extremely competitive, Lyon was hell-bent on scooping her rivals at *The Record,* Chico's other newspaper, and worked hard to establish a professional relationship with the police chief and his staff in order to get good stories. She alternated reporting on city government issues with stories on rural Chico's underbelly—covering minor break-ins, public drunkenness, bar brawls, and domestic quarrels.

A break from the ordinary occurred when Eleanor Roosevelt came to Chico to speak. Phyllis was given the job of covering her arrival, by train, at the nearby town of Durham. She was excited by the opportunity, because the former First Lady, a champion of the poor and disenfranchised, was a particular heroine to her. She and Matt, the staff photographer for the *Chico Enterprise,* arrived in Durham to find a small crowd awaiting the train. Excitement danced through the gathering as the locomotive chugged into the station—and then, suddenly, appearing on the platform was the imposing Mrs. Roosevelt.

Phyllis approached the First Lady, instantly feeling her famous charisma and graciousness. "I was stunned and amazed and in awe," she says. Initially breathless, she quickly realized she was first and foremost a reporter. "I went up to her, and I think I at least had enough sense to tell her who I was and why I was there," Phyllis recalls. "And she gave me an interview." She still treasures the photograph capturing the occasion. In it, Mrs. Roosevelt is bending down; Phyllis, hat perched on her head, is looking up, with her back to the camera. "The photographer, Matt, said later, 'I kept waiting for you to turn around! Finally I just had to take the picture!'"

After that inspiring meeting, Phyllis recognized that she was outgrowing Chico. Opportunity soon presented itself in a choice of two jobs: one in Washington state, near Seattle, the other in Fairbanks, Alaska. Alaska being a bit remote for her tastes, Lyon opted for Seattle. There, she accepted a position with a government naval shipyard on Bremerton Island, just offshore of the city, to write "man on the street" articles for its weekly newspaper. Although far from glamorous, at least the job had the fringe benefit of the ferry commute to work in the silence of the morning light and then back home in the mellow patina of dusk. Unfortunately, owing to a civil-service rules mix-up, the job was not to last. Since she liked Seattle, Lyon decided to stay and soon found employment on a periodical called *Pacific Builder and Engineer,* which would enable her to continue honing her journalistic skills.

Up to that time, Lyon was unaware of her true sexuality. Although she had always dated men, they were more often than not married. In retrospect, she admits that perhaps their unavailability was their most attractive feature. "It was safer," she realizes now. The one serious relationship with an available man resulted in an engagement. But her older fiancé's penchant for jealousy made her break off the relationship before long. This male-female business, it occurred to Lyon, was decidedly difficult. As she said in an interview with *The Advocate,* "Women had always seemed much more fun to be with, but it never occurred to me there was more I could have with them than friendships."

Then she met Del Martin.

Del was the new San Francisco–expatriate editor of a sister publication, the *Daily Construction Reports*—a woman and a "gay divorcée," as the boss described her. "He didn't know how gay," Del says with a laugh. "Well," says Phyllis, "the gay part came along a little later. . . ."

Del's path to Seattle was decidedly different from Phyllis Lyon's. Born Dorothy Taliaferro in San Francisco in 1921, Del knew from a very early age that there was something different about her. She could never relate to boys as easily as she could to other girls. When the neighborhood children would play "house," Del would seize the opportunity to portray the daddy and, sneaking into her parents' closets, would comically emerge in her stepfather's oversized pants and shirts to proclaim her dominance over the family. As described by Martin and Lyon in their influential book, *Lesbian/Woman,* "Wearing the pants in the family had a deep significance for Del. It meant playing boss, laying down the rules, making the decisions, being catered to . . . it meant being important, being master of the house. It meant being worldly and free to do what one chooses." Young Del even went so far as to fantasize about becoming a boy, reinforced by a notorious newspaper story about a female-to-male sex change in England.

But when she reached adolescence she recognized that the seemingly innocent role-playing had taken on a confusing sexual tone—something that should never be discussed—and that it had to do with other girls. "In our day, we didn't use the word 'homosexual' until the whole movement started—we didn't know about lesbians and gays; we didn't have that language either," Martin says. "So we had no way of identifying what we were feeling except that it wasn't like everyone else, so you kept it to yourself. You just knew instinctively that you shouldn't say anything about how you were feeling."

Sublimating those forbidden feelings, she buried herself in schoolwork and extracurricular activities that revolved around debating and writing for the school paper and yearbook. She had been encouraged by her parents to pursue college preparatory courses and had her sights set on Stanford University. But when she graduated from high school in 1937, Stanford, a private institution, was out of the question financially. Del's mother put her life insurance in hock so that her daughter could go to the University of California at Berkeley.

There, Del majored in journalism and worked nights on the college paper, the *Daily Californian*. But after a year, the long commute to Berkeley and its comparatively high tuition were proving taxing, so Del transferred to the closer, less expensive San Francisco State, which was located in the heart of the city. She became managing editor of the *Golden Gater*, the school paper; there she met Jim Martin, its business manager. Working together in the paper's shabby offices, they found a lot in common. As journalism students they were both fascinated by current events: union organizing, President Roosevelt's fireside chats on the radio, the frightening news of Nazi Germany's annexation of Austria and Czechoslovakia, and the first public exhibition of television at the 1939 World's Fair on Treasure Island in the city's bay. Together they helped organize a campaign to elect a woman student-body president, an unheard-of notion at the time. Yet, so imbued with the patriarchal/hierarchal model was the student body that even the women wouldn't support the female candidate. She didn't win, but Jim did in Del's eyes.

He had recognized that females should be able to aspire to leadership roles and not just settle for the status quo.

When Jim asked Del to marry him, she accepted. There wasn't a particular woman in her life at the time and she convinced herself she was in love with Jim. "I did it partially to get away from home, too," Del admits now. Marriage was also a decisive way to prove to herself that she could be just like every other girl in America.

They were husband and wife when Del got the chance to rise to the editorship of the school paper, but Jim convinced her not to apply, claiming that being married to him would create a conflict of interest. "And we needed the commissions he brought in as business manager," Del recalls. She strove not to resent taking the backseat; and then when she got pregnant in her third year of college, she was forced to quit school altogether. Amid all this upheaval in her personal life, World War II erupted.

With housing in the city constricted, the Martins found it difficult to find a larger apartment for them and their new daughter, Kendra. Soon they were forced to leave the high-priced Bay Area for San Mateo, a sleepy town seventy-five miles south, where they bought a two-bedroom house through the Federal Housing Authority for $4,500. There Del found herself settling into suburban life. Jim had a civilian job with the Army at Fort Mason up in San Francisco.

Over time, Del grew increasingly unhappy. While she genuinely cared for and respected Jim, terrifying doubts about her sexuality continually clouded her thoughts. To complicate matters, she found herself attracted to the straight married woman next door. Del was finding herself more and more confused, more and more depressed. Finally, she confronted her husband and asked for a divorce. She was shocked when Jim demanded to know whether her unhappiness was related to the cache of unsent love letters Del had written to the woman next door. Martin had never dreamed that Jim—or anyone else—knew of her secret dilemma.

Feeling he had the upper hand, Jim made it clear that he would use the letters in court if Del persisted with her divorce action. Terrified that he would then win custody and that she would lose access to her beloved daughter, Del wavered and temporized. But she knew in her heart that she could not go on living a lie forever. Finally she mustered the courage to stand her ground, challenge Jim, and call his bluff. And they went to trial.

Right up until their day in court, Del was too sick with fear and shame to tell her lawyer about the love letters. "I was scared spitless," she recalls. To make matters worse, the straight woman who had inspired them had shown up in court to offer Del moral support—never suspecting that Del's interest in her had been anything other than neighborly. But it was too late for Del to back down. She told Jim's lawyer to go ahead and submit the incriminating letters, leaving her own attorney frantically scrambling to lodge a protest. Mercifully, the judge, without disclosing their content or to whom the letters were written, ruled them irrelevant to the case. Without the letters, the divorce proceeding unfolded uneventfully. The marriage was dissolved and, to Del's relief, she was granted custody of her daughter, Kendra, while Jim was ordered to pay child support and alimony.

Later, ironically, the woman next door, who was also in the process of a divorce, asked Del for a place to stay and actually moved in with her and Kendra—strictly as a roommate. Furious at the thought of paying for a roof over the head of the object of his wife's unexpressed ardor, Jim withheld alimony. Del had to take him to court again, and again the judge ruled in her favor.

Although the obstacle of her unhappy marriage had been removed, Del remained deeply depressed. Her job as a bookkeeper for an advertising firm in San Francisco did not lead to copywriting as she had hoped; she had to conceal her attraction to her roommate; she had to endure Jim's animosity when he came by to claim his visitation rights to Kendra; and, most importantly, she had not yet begun, even tentatively, to come to terms with her homosexuality.

At that time, there were precious few places a lesbian could turn for solace, let alone self-enlightenment. She was all but absent in popular culture. Movies did not address her, nor did any periodicals. On Broadway, Lillian Hellman might have dared to explore the theme in her play *The Children's Hour,* but at the sensational climax, one of the leading characters, despairing at the thought that she might be a lesbian, shoots herself dead. Although riveting theater, it was not a story line that gave gay women much comfort. There was, however, one notorious novel, revered in the underground lesbian world, that dared to brave the subject: *The Well of Loneliness,* by Radclyffe Hall. Roundly scorned and vilified when first published in England in the 1920's, it survived a much-publicized obscenity trial to become a virtual primer for closeted lesbians. A book redolent with purple prose, wild emotions, and gushing sentimentality, it nonetheless spoke stirringly to a group of women hungry for acceptance.

Charting the relationship of two young women and their struggle to keep their love alive in a hostile society, it became a classic—possibly the most influential lesbian novel ever written—and Hall herself, a lesbian who dared to dress in tweedy mannish attire, became a patron saint to many. As noted feminist historian Esther Newton has said, "*The Well* has continued to have meaning to lesbians because it confronts the stigma of lesbianism—as most lesbians have had to live it."

At the advertising agency where Del was employed, an intuitive coworker quietly encouraged her to secure the book. Intrigued, she did, and as she delved further and further into the novel, the fog surrounding her personal life began to lift. Finally, she could utter the words and summon the courage to proclaim her true self—that she was a lesbian, a woman who loved other women. While Del could not relate to everything in the book, she did take comfort in knowing that she was not alone, that there were others like her. Hall's ending gave her hope:

> We are coming . . . we are still coming on, and our name is legion—you dare not disown us! . . . You, God, in Whom we, the outcast, believe; you, world, into which we are pitilessly born; you, who have drained our cups to the dregs—we have asked for bread; will you give us a stone? . . . give us also the right to our existence.

Frantic for more information, for more validation, she ran to the library to search for books about lesbianism. Hoping to find another *Well of Loneliness,* she was stunned to discover that there was nothing on the verboten subject on the library shelves. There were reference books available, but you had to look them all up in a card catalogue, write down the title and author and catalogue number, and request the librarian to obtain them for you. Of course, Del knew that in doing so, the librarian would know she was "one of them." But she finally worked up the nerve to ask. She had come too far; she had too much to learn to be reticent. When she got the books, she found to her chagrin that they were all diatribes on the evils of homosexuality, portraying gay people as pathetic misfits or as sick and depraved. They were an affront to her courage. "It was either people in prison or people who were in therapy," she says. "And all that was written about them was so awful—how could you identify with that?"

Del now swung back and forth between euphoric self-recognition and near-suicidal despair. She didn't know where to turn. There was no one in whom she could confide. Her professional life was faring no better: Tired of the commute up to San Francisco, she quit her advertising job and ran through a succession of unsatisfying jobs, ranging from cocktail waitress to racetrack ticket seller to supermarket checker. She felt as though she was atrophying—and drowning in her own well of loneliness.

When Kendra was three years old, she pleaded to join her playmate, the son of their neighborhood friends "Frances" and "Bob," at the private boarding school he was attending in Belmont. Unable to deny her daughter, Del agreed; Kendra would stay at the school during the week and live with her mother on weekends. Then Frances and Bob moved to the city, inviting Del to follow; they even found her an apartment in their building. Ready to reconsider her life, Del sold her house, bidding adieu to all its unhappy emotional connotations as well as to the straight roommate, to return to San Francisco. Finally her depression began to ebb.

She became quite friendly with Frances, a dancer, as well as with her sister-in-law. Frances's mother also welcomed Del, who had taken to writing poetry, as a fellow artist. Feeling secure enough with these women, Del could finally voice her sexual confusion. They listened sympathetically, though not actually believing that Del was a lesbian, and told her about the enclave of gay bars in North Beach. Too frightened to investigate them and perhaps settle her doubts, Del demurred. Then Frances's husband, Bob, was sent to Saudi Arabia for a year by his employer and asked Del to take care of his wife while he was gone. "I took it very seriously," Del says. Indeed, for a time her friend Frances became her first lesbian lover.

By now Del and Jim's relationship had reached an equilibrium. "I even helped him sort through his marriage options," Del says, laughing. When Jim remarried, he and his new wife thought they were unable to have children; coming from a big family himself, he yearned for the chance to raise his own child, Kendra. Gently he mounted a persuasive argument to Del that he could offer his daughter a stable, two-parent environment and, better yet, a chance to see the world, since his Army job now afforded him extensive travel. Deeply loving her only child and wanting the best for her, Del eventually came around to Jim's way of thinking. She acceded to Jim's plea and allowed Kendra to leave her home.

With Kendra gone, and Bob's return abruptly changing Del's intimate relationship with Frances to that of the ever-faithful friend, Martin felt herself bereft. She decided to explore the lesbian bars in North Beach. Mona's, on Broadway, with its male impersonator floor shows, proved to be the most popular—lesbians were admitted without paying the cover charge; the owners felt the gay women provided the mysterious ambiance. Del, however, found the bar scene forbidding. Even in the legendary establishments, "There was no one to talk to," she recalls. "I was so green. Everybody seemed to be in the know and I was this dummy—I felt like a tourist. I wasn't about to let them know I was dumb about all this stuff, so I would just listen and try to figure it out. I didn't ask a lot of questions. It was difficult trying to learn that way."

But it didn't take Del long to learn about harassment. One night she left a bar called the Chi Chi Club, planning to walk to her downtown apartment and enjoy the night breeze. Suddenly she heard footsteps behind her; and when a hand touched her shoulder, she whirled around, frightened. There stood a large policeman, who quickly dispelled her initial relief by demanding to know who she was, where she lived and worked, and what she was doing walking the streets at two A.M. Worried that he might have seen her leave the gay bar, Del refused to provide any identifying information. The cop was furious at her reticence and threatened to arrest her, but Del stood firm. "What am I being charged with?" she asked, striving to remain calm. "Is there a law against a woman walking alone on the streets at night?" Seeing that she wouldn't be intimidated, the frazzled policeman let her go, saying, "Get off my beat, lady."

Though nothing came of the incident, it rattled Del, for it revealed how complicated life as a homosexual could be. She had to ask herself just how far down this road she wanted to go, whether she could accept the challenges she would face if she followed her heart. As noted lesbian feminist and activist Ivy Bottini says, "Back then, it was physically, emotionally, and psychologically dangerous to come out of the closet. It just wasn't done. And those who did were truly courageous individuals." Del began to think that it might be easier to make the transition somewhere away from San Francisco, with its established gay circles, away from the people who knew her and the other vestiges of her old life. So when she was offered the job in Seattle as editor of *Daily Construction Reports,* she grabbed it.

Phyllis still recalls how assured Del seemed on her first day in the office, dressed in her smart dark suit and stylish open-toed shoes. "She was carrying a *briefcase,*" Lyon says, "and it was the first time in my life I had ever seen a woman carrying a briefcase." She smiles at the memory. "I was overwhelmed." Martin remembers it a little differently. "I was totally unprepared for the weather!" She laughs with a shiver. "I came down with an awful cold. It was two below zero and there I was in sling pumps with no money to buy warm clothes!"

Since they were both from San Francisco, Lyon threw a "Welcome to Seattle" party for her new coworker, inviting people from the office as well as her own Seattle friends to her tiny apartment near Puget Sound. She had to fold the Murphy bed up into the wall to create a living room, where she set out candles and chips and dip, and established a bar on a counter in the kitchen. It was there, by the bar, that she later found Del, surrounded by men smoking cigars, deep in discussion on how to configure a Windsor knot in a man's necktie. Impressed at how well Del was holding her own, she decided that she wanted to know more about this confident woman. They made a date for the next afternoon.

That afternoon stretched well into the evening as the two talked, warmly and without reservation. Somehow, their conversation rambled onto the subject of homosexuality. "Oh, I don't know what all the fuss is about," Phyllis said, to Del's surprise. "Why can't they do whatever they have to do?" She certainly couldn't understand why everyone was always getting so upset about it. Del noted her new friend's liberal attitude, but did not pursue the issue. Yet.

Nearly a year went by. Then, one Friday evening, when Phyllis and Del went out for drinks at the Seattle Press Club after work, again they found themselves on the topic of homosexuality—and this time, Del confronted the issue head-on, declaring that in fact she was a lesbian. Phyllis, far from being shocked or dismayed, was intrigued. Martin's confession, to her, seemed worldly and sophisticated. "I thought it was one of the most interesting things I had ever heard!" Phyllis recalls. "It was so exciting."

She could not contain her enthusiasm, and when she went home she wore out her dialing finger telephoning friend after friend, telling them the controversial news. Not having ever met any other lesbians, she was totally oblivious about the dire consequences that such broadcasting could have for her closeted friend. "She reacted okay at the time," Del says, shaking her head. "I had no idea she would go out and spill the beans all over the place! She 'outed' me before we even had the word 'outed.' " Fortunately for Martin, there was no fallout from Lyon's enthusiastic pronouncements, save for one friend's husband. "He said as long as I had anything to do with Del, she couldn't have anything to do with me," Phyllis says. "As far as I was concerned, it was her loss, not mine."

Although she had fallen in love, Del had endured unrequited crushes before, so she told herself that Phyllis could never be more to her than a sympathetic straight friend. Still, for nearly two years she wrestled with the question of whether to reveal her true feelings to Phyllis. It was not until Lyon began planning a lengthy coast-to-coast car trek with her married sister, Patricia, who was about to graduate from college, that Del finally worked up the courage. Then, as Martin likes to tell it, "I started a pass and she finished it!" Lyon, it turned out, had been ready all along.

After the trip, Phyllis stayed with her parents in San Francisco. It was a time for reflecting and soul-searching. She and Del kept in touch by phone and letter, but the long-distance romance was exhausting. Del wanted them to move in together, but Phyllis wasn't sure. She did love Del, but was reluctant to settle down.

Del's parents also lived in San Francisco, and she came down to visit several times. She and Phyllis played, loved, fought, and made up. During those heady early days of courtship, they even saw the great Judy Garland live in concert. With her outsized talent, her gamine quality, and the exquisite pain that came through in her songs—the longing, the loss, the hope, and the outrageous drama—Garland was becoming something of a gay icon. She was in her prime, fresh from her Palace Theater triumph in New York City, vibrant and spellbinding as she delivered her signature tunes—from "The Trolley Song" to "Get Happy" to "For Me and My Gal"—to a rapt and appreciative audience. "She wound up with 'Over the Rainbow' sitting on the edge of the stage," Del recalls. "We didn't notice anyone else in the theater. It was like she was singing to the two of us there. . . ."

As romantic as those times were, whenever Del would return to Seattle, their relationship would disintegrate into inevitable miscommunication. It got so bad that a frustrated Del was ready to give up—ironically, just when Phyllis was finally deciding that she did indeed want to live with her. Relieved to be on the same wavelength, each began to eagerly work on her end of the deal. Phyllis searched for an apartment they could afford and Del quit her job and prepared to move to San Francisco, her hometown.

Phyllis finally found an apartment for sixty-five dollars a month on the ground floor of a four-plex building between Nineteenth and Twentieth streets on San Francisco's Castro Street, which was not yet the gay mecca it would become in later decades. She moved in and waited anxiously for Del to arrive. "I got there at eleven P.M. on Valentine's Day, 1953," Del recalls. "I thought it would be an easy date to remember as an anniversary." Yet, almost immediately, Phyllis became concerned about what people would think. "I had been running up and down Castro Street for weeks in jeans and flannel shirts, sometimes even my father's white oxford shirts. But after Del got here, I thought, 'Oh, my God, everyone's going to know I'm a lesbian!'" While she felt in her heart that this relationship was exactly what she wanted and needed, she also was now aware of the severe stigma associated with same-sex relationships. "We didn't know what would happen," Lyon says, "but we knew people wouldn't approve."

Fortified by their commitment, though, they were determined to begin a life together of mutual respect, passion, and above all, fun. As Ivy Bottini says, "They refused to take themselves seriously. They had marvelous senses of humor."

Intent on making their relationship a true "marriage," Del took Phyllis down to the local bank to open up a joint checking account, and later a joint savings account. The notion was threatening to Lyon, who had controlled her own money for a long time, but Del insisted. "A lot of women get together still holding on to their own possessions, their own money, just so there won't be a hassle when they break up," Del says. "I think that sets them up for breaking up. A lasting relationship has a lot to do with how you start out. If you have the idea that you want to stay together, you've got a better chance than if you're 'iffy' about the whole thing."

Phyllis, in turn, demanded that Del deal with her recurrent jealousy. Recalling the difficulty she had experienced with her fiancé, Lyon was not going to allow the green-eyed monster to invade this commitment. "I did have some problems with it when we first got together," Martin admits, "but those gradually disappeared as I became more secure."

Still, the first year that the two headstrong, independent women spent together under one roof was thorny. Melding two lives into one is difficult enough in a heterosexual relationship; for lesbians in the mid-1950's, it was doubly complicated. At the time, the butch-femme paradigm was deeply entrenched in the lesbian community worldwide, and taking their cue from the standard heterosexual models, female couples often adopted the stereotypical roles. The butch partner was the dominant one, socially and sexually, and styled herself in mannish attire, right down to the neckties and argyle socks and short-cropped hair slicked back with Brylcreem. The femme dressed in typical women's clothing, dresses and stockings, and took on the traditional passive female persona. Two butches never dated; likewise, two femmes never coupled. Those who didn't follow the pattern were called "ki-ki." Sometimes the classic butch-femme couple would be so convincing that they would pass as heterosexual. It was as if lesbians determined that if the hostile heterosexual world was going to force them into hiding, they were going to become masters of subterfuge.

For Phyllis and Del, however, such a division of roles was not easy. Who was the more "masculine," who the more "feminine"? Since Del was the first to announce her sexuality to Phyllis, she assumed that made her the aggressor, the more masculine one, as did the fact that, when they moved in together, Del worked and Phyllis did not. Since Del had already assumed the butch role, that left Phyllis to play the femme; but they both consciously and constantly blurred the lines between the imposed designations. Phyllis liked boy-type shirts and suits; Del was sensitive, emotional, and romantic. Del didn't drive, Phyllis did; Phyllis knew her way around a tool kit, Del didn't even try. "My mother had served my father breakfast all her life, so I did the same thing for Del," Phyllis remembers with a chuckle. "For about three days. Maybe a week. A) I didn't like doing it, and B) Del didn't like getting it." They were two women. Why should they have to act like man and wife?

As Lyon explained later in a *Playboy* magazine interview, "This whole pattern of breaking down into butch and femme has really changed over the years. At the beginning of a relationship between two young women, often the only pattern they have on which to base their relationship is the masculine/feminine pattern of their mother and father. But pretty soon most lesbians find out that's not what they want."

An equally vexing problem was explaining their "marriage" to the families. The only family members Lyon and Martin confided in were their sisters, who were accepting but ultimately recommended that their parents not be told. Indeed, Lyon's mother was distinctly uncomfortable about the subject. "But I think that was because my mother was partly lesbian and didn't know it," Phyllis says, with a grin. And her father was ill at ease around Del, confiding to his wife that he thought Martin was "a queer." Del's family was no more tolerant. Once, when she tried to broach the subject of homosexuality, her opinionated mother proclaimed that such a lifestyle choice was the parents' fault. Del wisely decided not to use the moment to come out.

Estranged from their families, they could not look to the lesbian community for support either. The thriving gay population in the Bay Area at the time was deeply underground. "We were sitting in San Francisco without knowing any lesbians," Phyllis recalls. "It was very difficult," Del concurs. "There was no way to meet people." Doing their best to connect, they made the rounds of lesbian bars in North Beach, but had no luck in making friends. They went to The Black Cat, a bohemian outpost and haunt of the Beat writers Jack Kerouac, Lawrence

Ferlinghetti, and Allen Ginsberg. "It was in this narrow building," says Bob Ross, publisher of *The Bay Area Reporter*. "The back opened into a large room whose walls were covered from floor to ceiling with artwork done by the patrons." On Sunday afternoons, Bay Area drag legend José Sarria would perform parodies of famous operas, accompanied by a pianist on a rickety honky-tonk piano, for a packed house of knowledgeable opera devotees who would laugh and sing along. In between arias, Sarria functioned as a one-man community bulletin board, announcing events and often warning patrons of pockets of police entrapment in parks and bars. The evening would end with everyone clasping hands and singing "God Save Us Nelly Queens." Allen Ginsberg said, "It was the greatest bar in America . . . and everyone went there, heterosexual and homosexual." Phyllis and Del felt a sense of belonging, but they were disappointed to find that there were few lesbians there.

One night they chanced into the 299 Club located on Broadway at Montgomery Street. The diner at the back of the building was shuttered and empty, but the tavern was open—a big room with booths lining the wall opposite the bar and a few small tables scattered in between. Neon beer advertisements flickered in corners, and the jukebox was stocked with tunes by Elvis Presley, Eddie Fisher, and Billie Holiday. The two women struck up a conversation with the friendly bartender, Jerry, a darkly macho man, who, it turned out, lived with his female impersonator boyfriend, Rikki, just around the corner from the women on Twentieth Street. The four soon became fast friends. At last, Phyllis and Del had found a slight foothold in San Francisco's gay community.

Phyllis and Del grew so close to Jerry and Rikki that they decided to go into business with them. The bar owner offered the foursome the use of 299's small, abandoned dining room with tables, Naugahyde booths, and a service counter and kitchen, rent free. He thought the restaurant would bring in customers to the bar, and Jerry was sure the bar would bring in customers to the restaurant. The women were skeptical—none of the four had ever run a restaurant—but they decided to give it a try. Their menu would be limited to steaks and salad so they could charge rock-bottom prices. Del, who held a regular job, invested fifty dollars, Jerry did the cooking, and Phyllis, who had been unable to find work as a journalist, waited tables alongside Rikki.

Expecting 299 Club patrons to fill the diner, they never advertised, which was a distinct miscalculation. They soon discovered that there was a different cachet to drinking in a dark bar than there was in eating a meal in an adjacent brightly lit restaurant. Phyllis sighs, "We never had many customers." Then Tad's Steaks, founded on the same concept—cheap steak dinners—opened on nearby Powell Street and funneled off potential business. Within six months, Tad's, which eventually became a wildly profitable nationwide franchise, drove the 299 Diner into the ground. Fortunately, its demise didn't threaten the couples' friendship, and Martin and Lyon continued to make the 299 Club the center of their gay social life.

Becoming regulars meant that they had to confront the constant harassment that Del had only glimpsed on her first tentative forays into North Beach. Undercover vice officers, in tandem with the ABC (Alcohol Beverage Control Commission), would work the bars, posing as lesbians and gay men, to root out such illegal activities as dancing or displays of affection between members of the same sex, or carrying a drink from the bar to a table—under the law, that was cruising. If a woman wore slacks, she could be arrested for impersonating a man; to be a man in drag was even more dangerous. Although the ABC did not forbid physical contact or even kissing between men and women in straight bars, should same-sex kissing or touching be attempted in a gay bar, the owner's liquor license could be immediately revoked. Del recalls a time when she put a hand on the shoulder of a blind friend in a bar to guide her, and a waitress snapped, "Get your hands off her! You want to close us down?" When Del innocently replied that she was just leading her friend who was blind, the waitress countered with, "Yeah, well, the ABC isn't blind!"

Like the old speakeasies, gay bars installed a red light that would flash to signal a police raid, so patrons could make a mad dash to escape. In a raid, those unlucky enough to be caught even sitting in a gay bar would be hauled off to the police station, where they would have mug shots and fingerprints taken and be booked for "visiting a house of ill repute," "disorderly conduct," "lewd conduct," or even "conduct contrary to public welfare or morals." Then the police would observe the time-honored custom of slipping names to the *San Francisco Chronicle* or the *Examiner,* where they would be listed under the headline PERVERTS ARRESTED; they also phoned employers just in case they had missed seeing their disgraced staffers' names in the papers. Jobs were lost and lives were ruined.

Del and Phyllis themselves narrowly missed a couple of run-ins with the vice squad. "Hazel's was a really big raid," Del recalls vividly. "And we were there just the week before." Located just outside the city in Pacifica, Hazel's had seemed too out-of-the-way to attract attention. "It was a funny little place in the middle of nowhere," Bob Ross recalls. "A big barn of a bar out in the country surrounded by sand dunes. A type of beach hangout. But they also had after-hours." It was after hours when the police descended on the bar, cuffing its unsuspecting patrons like common criminals. "The police just swept everybody out," Phyllis says. "They had several patrol wagons there to take everyone to Redwood City."

When a lesbian bar closer to home, Kelly's on Fulton Street, was raided—a police sweep that Phyllis and Del missed by a night—the two women decided that it was time to find a way to fight back. In those days, most people who got swept up in the raids would plead guilty. Possibly, Lyon suggests, "They did feel guilty about being gay. So they wanted to get out. Pay the ten-buck fine and get the hell out." But spurred on by the legal advice of an attorney they had befriended, Del explains, "What we found was, they were really pleading guilty to being homosexual, which was not against the law. The ones that our attorney represented, he told them to plead no contest. So when the cops were on the stand and were asked, 'What did they do?' the cops didn't know—they had just rounded them up. And so those cases were dismissed."

The defiance following the Kelly's raid was one of the San Francisco gay and lesbian community's first small victories, but some were growing weary of the constant struggle. Attempting to avoid the embattled bar scene as well as other negative intrusions on their lives, Noni, a lesbian acquaintance of Jerry's, phoned Phyllis and Del to ask if they would be interested in joining her and five other women in a secret social club for lesbians. Del and Phyllis answered with a resounding "Yes!" "We were so eager," Del says. "We were finally going to meet some lesbians. Six of them!" "We had only met one of them," Phyllis adds, "so that meant five more lesbians!"

So on Friday, September 21, they gathered for the first time at Noni and her lover Mary's house off Fillmore Street—four couples, eight women in search of a haven where they could be themselves, far away from the police, the public, and prying family eyes. At their fourth meeting, one of the women suggested calling the group the Daughters of Bilitis, after a poem of love between women called "Songs of Bilitis." Written by Pierre Louys, the book purported that the poem had been found in a cave on the isle of Lesbos and that Bilitis was a contemporary of Sappho. It was, in fact, a literary hoax, but it was also a potent, passionate message of love. The women liked the idea—although most had not read the book; to them it sounded like a typical women's group, not unlike the Daughters of the Nile or the Daughters of the American Revolution (DAR).

Del was elected the first president of the Daughters of Bilitis, and Phyllis became its first secretary. As the group began to codify its philosophy and goals in its first set of bylaws, it was careful to avoid the inflammatory word "lesbian," opting instead for the quasi-clinical and more neutral terms "invert" and "variant." Its objectives were:

1. EDUCATION OF THE VARIANT: To enable her to understand herself and make her adjustment to society . . . this to be accomplished by establishing . . . a library . . . on the sex deviant theme; by sponsoring public discussions . . . to be conducted by leading members of the legal, psychiatric, religious, and other professions; by advocating a mode of behavior and dress acceptable to society.
2. EDUCATION OF THE PUBLIC: Leading to an eventual breakdown of erroneous taboos and prejudices.
3. PARTICIPATION IN RESEARCH PROJECTS: Duly authorized and responsible psychologists, sociologists, and other such experts will be directed toward further knowledge of the homosexual.
4. INVESTIGATION OF THE PENAL CODE: As it pertains to the homosexual, proposal of changes . . . and promotion of these changes through the due process of law in state legislatures.

It was further decided that the initiation fee would be five dollars for active members and two dollars and fifty cents for associate members, with monthly dues of one dollar for the former and fifty cents for the latter.

Armed with its mission statement, the DOB cautiously held its first official open meeting, which became more a reflection of rifts in the community than an auspicious debut. Noni and Mary had invited four very masculine-looking women whom they had met at bars and factories, and they strode into the gathering surly and defiant, challenging the DOB members to explain themselves and the club.

Del, as president, took the floor to describe the DOB as a social club that would hold parties and discussion groups in members' homes; and Phyllis chimed in to affirm that all members would remain anonymous. The hostile spokeswoman for the guests, clad in a man's full suit, announced she didn't care for the name Daughters of Bilitis. "I wouldn't want to carry a DOB membership card in my wallet!" she barked. "What if someone saw it? It's too obvious!" Del and Phyllis remember turning to each other incredulously, for the woman was so butch that they were tempted to test her for testosterone. Surely she would not have to offer a membership card to betray her sexuality!

But what the woman said echoed the sentiments of many homosexuals, who were still in the closet and felt that any exposure to mainstream society would place them in jeopardy. Some took umbrage at any sort of politicization of the gay and lesbian community, wanting only to create a secure social realm where they could meet others like themselves. Some had strong opinions on how gay people should present themselves in the heterosexual world, and wanted their peers to dress a certain way, or to avoid acting too "nelly" or too "butch," in order to gain approval. Others reacted with bitter anger that they had to change who they were in order to win societal acceptance. Many lesbians were opposed to working with male homosexuals; a disturbing number of gay men were unwilling to work with the women. Phyllis felt strongly that the Daughters of Bilitis should be fully inclusive, even to the point of welcoming straight women and friends and relatives. Lesbians had been hiding underground long enough and needed to find a place in the heterosexual world, she held, believing that assimilation could be accomplished without surrendering sexual identity.

Discussions of such issues were raging throughout the entire homosexual community, male and female, during the 1950's, when the so-called homophile movement was uniting homosexuals and bringing them more visibility than ever before. California, not surprisingly, was the center of the movement. Alongside the Daughters in San Francisco, a gay men's organization, the Mattachine Society, flourished under the leadership of Hal Call and Don Lucas. The society had replaced the Mattachine Foundation founded in Los Angeles by activist Harry Hay. Also in Los Angeles, ONE, Inc., another fledgling but nonmembership gay organization, had formed a corporation to publish a monthly magazine. While Mattachine and ONE welcomed DOB for bringing more lesbians into the movement, they chided the organization for limiting membership to women. It was a somewhat disingenuous argument; while professing to be coed, these groups were themselves mostly male. And what few women they had soon joined the DOB.

Before long, a division began to evolve among the DOB membership: Some members sought only a social structure—parties and picnics and coffee klatches (dubbed "gab 'n' javas")—while others wanted to take the risk of growing more publicly and politically involved. The debate created a crisis, splitting the founding members directly down white-collar and blue-collar lines. Frightened by the prospect of losing anonymity, the blue-collar members, including Noni and Mary, left to pursue a different agenda—a more secretive, strictly recreational "sorority type of thing," in Del's words, "like a women's lodge." The remaining white-collar members restructured the DOB, and, taking a giant step toward visibility, moved the organization's base from members' private homes to a tiny sublet room in the Mattachine Society's offices on Mission Street.

Now all they needed were more members.

To reach out more systematically to lesbians, the Daughters decided to publish a national newsletter, *The Ladder,* and appointed Phyllis Lyon as its editor. The first issue, released in October 1956 and leading off with the catchy phrase, "From the city of many moods, San Francisco," opened with a president's message from Del, who implored readers to support them in adding women's voices to the new homophile movement. She wrote:

The lesbian is a very elusive creature. She burrows underground in her fear of identification. She is cautious in her associations. Current modes in hairstyle and casual attire have enabled her to camouflage her existence. She claims she does not need help. And she will not risk her tight little fist of security to aid those who do not. . . . If lethargy is supplanted by an energized constructive program, if cowardice gives way to the solidarity of a cooperative front, if the "let Georgia do it" attitude is replaced by the realization of individual responsibility in thwarting the evils of intolerance, superstition, prejudice, and bigotry, then the lot of the lesbian can be changed. . . .

The first issue was an enormous success, but the letters that streamed into the DOB post office box all cited the same problem—the writers' fears of subscribing (at the rate of one dollar per year) to a homosexual publication. To address the issue, Lyon wrote an editorial entitled "Your Name Is Safe!" which began, "We have run up against the fear that names on our mailing list may fall into the wrong hands, or that by indicating interest in this magazine a person will automatically be labeled a homosexual. . . ." To assuage such fears, she cited the 1953 U.S. Supreme Court ruling stating that publishers cannot be forced to give up mailing list names to anyone. It was a compelling argument, although somewhat undercut by the fact that Lyon used the pseudonym "Ann Ferguson" for her byline—even the editor trying to empower lesbians was afraid to use her real name. Finally, in the fourth issue of *The Ladder,* Phyllis decided to publish an obituary:

> I confess. I killed Ann Ferguson—with premeditation and malice aforethought. Ann Ferguson wrote that article, "Your Name Is Safe!" Her words were true, her conclusions logical and documented—yet she was not practicing what she preached. . . . At the December public discussion meeting of the Daughters of Bilitis, we got up—Ann Ferguson and I—and did away with Ann. Now there is only Phyllis Lyon.

Slowly but steadily, the homosexual underground circulated *The Ladder* to lesbians across America. No longer just a newsletter, the magazine-sized periodical could be picked up by a gay woman visiting New York or San Francisco on business, be carefully hidden in her luggage, and taken home to Des Moines. There, it would be shared with a lesbian friend who would pass it on to another, then another. Some women even braved being on the mailing list and had it sent directly to their homes. Suddenly, *The Ladder* had a following in the heartland, and a lesbian in Omaha or Bismarck or Toledo finally had a place to confide her questions. "We had married women who were still with their husbands but didn't know what to do and were coming for information," Del recalls. "We had women thrown out of the armed forces," Phyllis says. "They'd show up and say, 'I just got kicked out of the Army. The guy said I was a butch. What is that?' " Speaking of this outreach effort, Billie Tallmij, who with her lover Shorty had joined the Daughters early on, told Eric Marcus in *Making History,* "My main drive was to educate the public, but foremost, to educate our girls, to give them the answers I had once needed and to give them some sense of who they were. We had to teach our people that it wasn't a crime to be a homosexual." Tallmij also addressed the problem of being perceived as a subculture of a subculture: "You see, no one knew that women could be this way. People seemed to know that guys did this, but people knew nothing about the lesbian."

Inevitably, *The Ladder* also became a forum for debate of the larger questions vexing the gay community. In one controversial issue, the president's message even addressed the sacrosanct butch-femme paradigm, condemning it: "Our organization had touched on that matter and has converted a few to remembering that they are women first and butch or femme second, so their attire should be that which society will accept." A letter to the editor was cited, which said, "I find that because now I am wearing woman's slacks and letting my hair grow long I am getting a wider variety of friends and I have neighbors instead of people next door. I no longer have the feeling that everyone is watching me. . . ."

To further its educational mission, the DOB began to convene public discussion meetings, at which sympathetic attorneys and other professionals would address the plight of the lesbian. Since the gatherings were officially open to the general population, women—and men, too—could convince themselves that they would not be labeled homosexual simply for sitting in the audience. DOB also had private sessions for lesbian mothers who were concerned about the effect their "deviant" relationships might have on their children. Del recalls, "We managed to get Eleanor van Leewen, specialist in parent education for the San Francisco Unified School District; suffragist Rhoda Kellogg, director of Golden Gate Nursery School, and therapist Faith Rossiter to talk to the mothers." The gist of the message was, if there was love and security in the home, the environment would be problem-free. "In the *fifties!*" Del remarks. "To get those kind of women to do that for us was amazing."

Within two years the Daughters of Bilitis had grown so much that it could afford offices of its own and, in 1957, it became an official non-profit corporation. The next year, a Los Angeles branch was founded, and there was a clamor for chapters on the East Coast. Barbara Gittings, visiting from Philadelphia, attended a DOB meeting. Initially un-impressed—she considered the name Daughters of Bilitis "too com-plicated, too long, too difficult to pronounce, and too difficult to spell"—she came away a convert, so inspired by the Daughters' work that Del and Phyllis asked her to found its first chapter on the East Coast. Assisted by Marion Glass, Gittings marshaled the New York chapter of the DOB into existence, becoming its first president. Shortly thereafter, another chapter was founded in Rhode Island. The organi-zation's realm of influence now stretched from coast to coast. Through the grit and sheer will of those early recruits, what had begun as a sim-ple gab-'n'-java club was on the cusp of a national movement with the potential power to press for real change.

The group's new visibility made it urgent for Del to explain her life to her daughter Kendra for the first time. Understandably, Del was ap-prehensive about the coming-out discussion, having seen firsthand how children could spurn their parents and parents reject their children over the issue. Yet, Del thought that Kendra, now an intelligent college girl already familiar with gay friends of her mother's, might have some inkling. When the moment of truth came, Del had to trust that her strong bond with her daughter would prevail.

Still, when Del sat her down and discussed not only the Daughters of Bilitis but also her "marriage" with Phyllis, Kendra was totally shocked. "I just thought you were friends!" she cried. "I certainly never thought of you as having sex together!" Kendra had, in fact, entertained the notion that if she never met "the right guy," she would love to have a warm and nurturing relationship with another woman, like that of her mother and Phyllis.

After her outburst Kendra asked if she could tell her steady boyfriend and soon-to-be-fiancé about Del's revelation. Del replied that certainly she could. Kendra and her young man then did what many of the relatives of gays did in postwar America: They went to the library to look up information as to whether homosexuality was hereditary. Even though the scientific and psychological views of the subject bordered on the Neanderthal in the 1950's, the "experts" had at least stopped claiming that homosexuality could be passed down from parents to children. Reassured on that score, Kendra and her fiancé accepted Del's way of life. In fact, after they married, Kendra's new husband was loose enough to quip that he was a lucky guy for having two mothers-in-law instead of one.

As the 1950's waned, the DOB, and with it Martin and Lyon, found itself nudged into the political arena through events beyond their control. At the Mattachine Society's national meeting in Denver in September of 1959, a man named William Brandhove pressed for a resolution praising San Francisco Mayor George Christopher and Police Chief Thomas Cahill for being tolerant in "sociological problem areas." Brandhove, a well-connected, moneyed newcomer to the San Francisco chapter, said the resolution he presented had been mailed to him by members of the police department.

Though present in Denver only as honorary Mattachine Society members, with no vote, Martin and Lyon immediately voiced their suspicion. Why would a mayor up for reelection seek the endorsement of a group as controversial as the Mattachine Society? Moreover, it was well known that both the mayor and police chief were anti-gay. But the women's arguments fell on deaf ears and the measure passed. Less than a month later the resolution exploded into front-page headlines in the weekly San Francisco Progress: SEX DEVIATES MAKE S.F. HEADQUARTERS, accompanied by the charges of Russell Wolden, Christopher's opponent, that the endorsement belied the mayor's claim that he was running a "clean city." The article went on to list the bars, steam baths, hotels, and after-hours spots frequented by homosexuals that, along with the national headquarters of the Mattachine Society and the DOB, were sullying the city. Though the San Francisco Chronicle exposed Brandhove as a Wolden plant "with a long police record," the damage had been done. The Mattachine Society slapped Wolden with a million-dollar lawsuit because the candidate had "wrongfully and maliciously" referred to the society as a homosexual organization that "exposed teenagers to contact with homosexuals." Mattachine had always carefully identified itself as an organization "interested in the problems of homosexuality."

Subsequently, the DOB was attacked in a mimeographed leaflet that was hand-distributed throughout San Francisco. It read, in part: "And you parents of daughters—do not sit back complacently feeling that because you have no boys in your family, everything is all right as far as you are concerned. To enlighten you as to the existence of a lesbian organization . . . whose purposes are the same as the Mattachine Society, make yourselves acquainted with the name 'Daughters of Bilitis'!"

Del Martin called an emergency meeting of the DOB, and a special edition of *The Ladder* was immediately released to denounce the leaflet and to calm the membership. Meanwhile, anticipating the possible arrival of the police (which did, in fact, occur the next morning), Del and Phyllis surreptitiously transported the DOB's mailing and membership lists to the back of their station wagon, covered with a blanket. For the next few weeks, that automobile was the DOB's operating address.

Ultimately, Wolden's smear tactics backfired. The Mattachine Society and DOB got the word out through word of mouth, fliers, publications, meetings, and some press coverage. Neither mayoral candidate was acceptable to the homosexual community. Interestingly, nine thousand people went to the polls and voted, but passed on the mayoralty race—presumably homosexuals and their allies who could not in good conscience vote for either candidate. Christopher, who could not even bring himself to utter the "H" word, was reelected.

After the exposé of Brandhove and Wolden, the announcement of Mattachine's lawsuit, and a few letters to the editor, the daily newspapers dropped any further coverage of the issue.

Nonetheless, the experience, the first foray into the political arena by San Francisco's growing gay and lesbian community, was an empowering lesson. It showed that, in times of crisis, the community could band together despite any differences. No one backed off out of fear of the consequences. And the nine thousand nonvotes gave impetus to a burgeoning homosexual voting bloc. It would be hard, if not impossible, for San Francisco politicians—or the media, which Wolden had exploited—to dismiss the community again.

While both Mattachine and DOB were in the forefront of the new political organizing, it was Mattachine that got most of the attention. To their anger and chagrin, some dismissed Martin and Lyon and the DOB as the "Mattachine women's auxiliary." This mischaracterization set off waves of muted grumblings within the core of the Daughters, and the relationship with Mattachine grew stormier. Although many of the members felt an allegiance with their homosexual brothers, others bristled. As future DOB national president Shirley Willer told historian Eric Marcus, "A lot of the women resented working with the men, because it was the men, not the women, who were cruising the tearooms and getting in trouble with the police. 'Why should we fight to help the men?' they'd say. And I'd say, 'What difference does it make whether they're men or women? They're homosexuals.' "

Yet many lesbians did begin to question whether gay men recognized—or understood at all—that lesbians had to fight on two fronts, both for acceptance by the straight world and for acceptance as women. Del Martin, speaking at the Denver Mattachine Society convention, had said angrily, "At every one of these conventions I attend, year after year, I find I must defend the Daughters of Bilitis as a separate and distinct women's organization. What do you men know about lesbians? In all your programs and your [Mattachine] *Review,* you speak of the male homosexual and follow this with Oh, yes, and incidentally there are some female homosexuals, too. . . . Lesbians are women, and this twentieth century is the era of emancipation of women. Lesbians are not satisfied to be auxiliary members or second-class homosexuals!"

Consequently, the DOB decided to organize its own annual national lesbian convention, the first ever, to be held in San Francisco in 1960. The fete was a decided success, boasting over two hundred in attendance—more than any previous homophile conference. Hal Call, Mattachine's president, felt compelled to write DOB a letter criticizing its publicity release for blatantly calling it a lesbian convention. He was concerned that most Mattachine members—99 percent of them gay men—might hesitate to attend. Jaye Bell, president of the DOB host chapter, tartly replied that if the members of Mattachine were to dress properly and act with decorum, she was sure no one would mistake them for lesbians. Indeed, the homosexual detail of the vice squad showed up, attempting to determine if the DOB was advocating women wearing the clothes of the opposite sex. They found no citations—this being DOB's first real public event, everyone was dressed to the nines.

The program featured a volatile discussion between Morris Lowenthal and Sidney Feinberg of the ABC, where the board's anti-gay policies—perceived and actual—were debated. Attorney Kenneth Zwerin gave lesbian couples financial advice about property, bank accounts, and inheritance taxes. And entertainer Lisa Ben (an anagram of "lesbian") topped off the banquet festivities with a round of gay songs and parodies as she accompanied herself on the guitar. Her first recording under the DOB label was available to convention-goers for a special price. Before the close of the event, the women were even gracious enough to remedy their omission of gay men by giving Sons of Bilitis awards to male individuals, straight and gay, who had been supportive. To this day, many prominent politicians and gay men are proud card-carrying members, although, perhaps, understandably hesitant to call themselves "SOBs."

The DOB was redefining the lesbian agenda as parallel but not identical to the political and cultural struggles of gay men. It was reaffirming its founding principles, for as Del wrote in *The Ladder,* "From the beginning, DOB was a self-help organization. Certainly no one else was concerned about the lesbians, not even the other homophile groups. We tried to redirect the self-pity, self-consciousness, and self-abasement that had always been the lesbian's lot through the paths of self-awareness, self-knowledge, and self-observation toward another self—that of self-acceptance, self-confidence, and self-esteem."

By 1961, an internal power struggle precipitated the dissolution of Mattachine's area councils in various cities across the country and reverted the society to a California corporation headquartered in Los Angeles. That left the Daughters of Bilitis as the only national organization in San Francisco. This distance eased the acrimony between the two organizations somewhat. Within a year, they were realigned in a common cause to fight the homosexual's most potent foe: the archaic and punitive sex laws that many states had on the books. At that time, all but two in the country still labeled sodomy as a felony. In California, oral sex (homosexual or heterosexual), for example, was punishable by up to fourteen years in prison. Anal intercourse (homosexual or heterosexual) was no different, under the law, from having sex with an animal; both were deemed sodomy. "We wanted to change the sex laws that made people felons," Lyon says. "We thought that there would come a time, hopefully, when there wouldn't be any laws against our sexuality and we'd be accepted as people by the outside community."

While the sex laws applied to both gays and straights, they were invoked far more often against homosexuals. Members from the DOB and Mattachine Society decided to attack the problem at the core and attempted a dialogue with some local governmental representatives. In 1962, Phillip Burton and John A. O'Connell, assemblymen in the California state legislature, were approached to solicit their support. Burton and O'Connell, being lawyers, could clearly see the injustice of the laws. But being public servants—and considering the prevailing social attitudes—they knew they didn't have even a remote chance to introduce a bill to revamp those laws. Their only suggestion to the homophile leaders was to get the church to support changing the laws. It was an inspired strategy—though it was almost impossible to imagine that it could work.

"We thought, 'That'll be the day,' " Del recalls. Believing that the church would be the last institution to turn around, the two women reasoned that they might have a better chance of enlisting the legal profession, where they could perhaps cite the American Law Institute's Model Penal Code (which stated that sexual activity between consenting adults in private was no concern of the law). But they were cognizant of the fact that a legal strategy would be a tough go at best. Indeed, even the nation's great champion of the underdog, the American Civil Liberties Union (ACLU), had refused to defend homosexuals until the late 1950's, when its national board passed the following rather equivocal resolution that nonetheless made it gay people's only ally in the legal world:

The American Civil Liberties Union is occasionally called upon to defend the civil liberties of homosexuals. It is not within the province of the Union to evaluate the social validity of laws aimed at the suppression or elimination of homosexuals. We recognize that overt acts of homosexuality constitute a common-law felony and that there is no constitutional prohibition against such state and local laws on this subject as are deemed by such states or communities to be socially necessary or beneficial. Any challenge of laws that prohibit and punish public acts of homosexuality or overt acts of solicitation for the purpose of committing a homosexual act is beyond the province of the Union.

In examining some of the cases that have come to our attention, however, we are aware that homosexuals, like members of some other socially heretical or deviant groups, are more vulnerable than others to official persecution, denial of due process in prosecution, and entrapment. As in the whole field of due process, these are matters of proper concern for the Union and we will support the defense of such cases that come to our attention.

Basically, the idea of a protracted and possibly hard-to-win court battle was not appealing. And the savvy women knew that the psychiatric community, with its decided homophobia, was also a dead end. The insistent O'Connell and Burton kept pressing for dialogue with the clergy, but Martin and Lyon resisted. For Del, "Christian brotherhood and love were nonexistent when it came to the homosexual." Even though (or perhaps because) Phyllis's maternal grandfather was a Southern Methodist preacher, she and Del were not fans of organized religion. As they were to write caustically in their book Lesbian/ Woman, "Our rejection of and antagonism toward the whole concept of organized religion has been reinforced over the years as we have witnessed the damage the church has done to the lesbian, to the male homosexual, and to many heterosexuals, especially women . . . the church forces people into following rigid rules which only oppress consciousness."

Two years earlier, after countless rejections, the DOB had managed to get San Francisco's Council of Churches to find a clergyman to speak at their 1960 convention, the Reverend Fordyce Eastburn of the California Episcopal Diocese. In his speech Eastburn had said that while homosexuals would always be accepted in the church, homosexual activity could never be accepted—hardly a ringing endorsement, but at that time, the best the church could come up with. It was the old, condescending "love the sinner, hate the sin" routine, but as Martin commented at the time, "We're all used to it. We've already been called every name there is to call us. We look at it this way: We've opened the door to communication with the church."

Now, spurred on by O'Connell and Burton, Martin and Lyon, despite their dim view of organized religion, agreed to embark on a formidable endeavor: educating the church. Searching this time for a less equivocal advocate than Eastburn, they first approached a Beverly Hills Baptist preacher who called them "unclean vessels." Their next target was Catholic Cardinal Francis McIntire, who said they were "broken reeds, not to be encouraged." As they made the rounds of the religious denominations, they were assailed by Bible thumping and ignorant invocations of Leviticus and Deuteronomy. Homosexuality was still an irredeemable sin to most of the clergy—and, indeed, to most of the country.

They were near despair when they finally encountered the Methodist minister Ted McIlvenna, a progressive thinker whose ministry at the Glide Foundation concentrated on alienated youth. Astonished to learn that there was no "meaningful counsel" available to homosexuals, he helped organize a "live-in" at the White Memorial Retreat Center in Mill Valley, just north of San Francisco in Marin County. There, in a historic confrontational weekend late in the spring of 1964, fifteen religious leaders from a host of Protestant denominations—including Methodist, Lutheran, Episcopalian, and United Church of Christ—met with fifteen members of the homophile movement. As usual, the Daughters of Bilitis had to protest vigorously to make certain seven of the homosexuals in attendance were women. Billie Tallmij and Del Martin specifically planned transportation that would drop off all the participants at the retreat. They didn't want anyone to be able to get in a car and leave should the discussion become uncomfortable. And the weekend did indeed begin uncomfortably with the men, the ministers, and the women staying separate, distrustfully eating the first meal in their own groups. Yet, over the three tumultuous days, barriers were broken down, stereotypes were addressed, communication was achieved, and a common cause was established. As theologian Richard Peddicord relates in his book *Gay and Lesbian Rights*:

The upshot was that a remarkable dialogue was initiated. Most of the ministers had never had someone say to them, "I am a homosexual"; most found that they needed more understanding of the reality of homosexuality. The eagerness of the church representatives is probably best explained by an admixture of evangelical outreach and the ambience of the burgeoning civil rights movement. The cause of racial justice in American society provided a ready-made paradigm for gay and lesbian liberation; society's complicity in injustice was the insight of the age.

As a result of that retreat, liberal ministers Robert Cromey, Charles Lewis, Lewis Durham, Fred Bird, Clarence Cowell, Cecil Williams, and McIlvenna formed the Council on Religion and the Homosexual (CRH) to create an opportunity for gay people to return to the comforting arms of the church. To fund the work of the CRH, the major homosexual groups in San Francisco decided to sponsor a large-scale benefit—a New Year's Day costume ball to usher in 1965.

A delegation of ministers, along with attorney Evander Smith, met with top officials in the San Francisco police department to lay plans for the event. "It confused the hell out of the police," Phyllis says, laughing, "because they were used to men in drag around Halloween, but not any other time. Plus, they were upset because seven organizations were coming together to put this on and that had not happened before. Someone suggested that there had been sort of an unwritten law that no more than fifty queers could get together without breaking them up somehow." The police accused the clergymen of being pawns of the homophile movement and, seeing wedding rings on their fingers, tauntingly asked if the ministers' wives knew that they were involved with queers. At one point, one officer even slammed his fist on the table, screaming, "If you aren't going to enforce God's law, we will!" Calmly resisting such provocations, the clergymen continued to detail their plans while the police officers kept arguing that they needed to protect the public from any untoward disturbance. By the end of the tense meeting, the police officials grudgingly agreed not to interfere and gave the go-ahead for the New Year's Ball.

The site chosen for the feel-good event was the neglected and rundown California Hall on Polk Avenue. Faded but still hinting of glamor—and cheap to rent—the Bavarian-style building boasted a ground-floor bowling alley and a second-story auditorium that could accommodate more than a thousand guests. With its theater seats replaced by cocktail tables and festive with New Year's streamers and balloons, it was transformed from shabby to gala, ready to welcome the five hundred or so revelers who had made donations to the CRH.

On that chilly New Year's night, "Del and I had gotten there early because we were supposed to take tickets," Lyon remembers. "The cops had been there by the time we got there . . . to make sure we had a liquor license, to make sure we weren't blocking doors, and all this kind of silly stuff. . . ." Bob Ross, one of the evening's organizers, says, "We had no inkling of any problems coming up. The event started smoothly enough."

When the first few outrageously costumed party-goers arrived, Martin and Lyon found them strangely subdued. "They seemed kind of breathless," Del says. "No one said a word to us." Before long, John Moore, one of the ministers, decided to see what was going on. "He opened the door and turned pale," Del recalls. Unbeknownst to the planners, the police had installed arc lamps at the entrance to the hall and were photographing and filming the "perverts" in attendance. Many of the arrivals were decked out in costumes elaborate enough to hide their identities; others defiantly braved the taunts and flashbulbs. When Moore reached the street, in the glare of huge police-installed klieg lights, he saw police cars barricading the intersections, paddy wagons stationed at the curb, and officers outfitted in full riot gear. Cars full of costumed people would pull up and, intimidated by the police presence, immediately speed off.

Soon the harassment spread from the street into the hall itself. The police swept through the ballroom at least seven separate times, claiming they were checking for fire hazards and other possible infractions. Phyllis recalls, "Evelyn Williams, who at that point was Cecil's wife—they're both African-Americans—said to us, 'This is just like it is in the South!' " Bob Ross says: "We had a whole group of us at the doors and we stopped people from leaving and confronting the police. That is exactly what the police wanted to happen, and we wouldn't allow that."

The lawyers for the event, Evander Smith and Herb Donaldson, were summoned to the hall to intervene. "At that point, Del and I had given up the ticket-taking table and Nancy May had taken over for us," Phyllis recalls. Nancy May, a feisty straight volunteer in the homophile movement who was married to a gay man, was tireless in her efforts to integrate the homosexual community with mainstream society; together, she and her husband, Bill, were among the founders of SIR, the Society for Individual Rights. As Nancy took tickets, Bill slipped surreptitiously in and out of the hall, taking pictures of the police taking pictures. He could feel a confrontation brewing and he wanted documentation. To supplement May's record, the Reverend Chuck Lewis also took photographs.

The confrontation came. As the police completed their seventh pass through the hall, Evander Smith and Herb Donaldson stood with Nancy May at the door and informed the officers that they were no longer welcome. The hall had been "inspected" to death, they declared, and warned that they'd tolerate no further incursions without a search warrant. Without missing a beat, the police grabbed the lawyers, citing them for obstruction of justice, and hauled them off into a waiting paddy wagon. Nancy was alone at the door half an hour later when a large plainclothes policeman turned up, announcing that he was going to inspect the premises again. May stood up to defy him. She announced in no uncertain terms that she was at the end of her rope with the harassment, that the police had no warrant and no business being there. Furious, she showed him the door.

The cop soon returned with three backup officers. Reverend Cecil Williams, on the staff of the Glide Urban Center, tried to intervene, but the towering policeman picked up Nancy and began dragging her down the stairs just as Elliott Leighton, the lawyer Donaldson and Smith had called to take over when they were arrested, was coming up. Never before associated with the homosexual community, Leighton got a crash course on what it meant to be gay. Shocked at the policemen's insensitivity and brutishness, he attempted to stand his ground and sputter his protestations, but the police grabbed him as well and shoved him into the paddy wagon. "At least I had some companionship," Nancy May later chuckled in *Making History*. Fortunately, she'd had the presence of mind to slip the film she'd been holding for her husband to a SIR member. "All I needed," she said, "was to have a bunch of film when they took me to jail." The Reverend Lewis's photos would later appear accompanying articles in *The Citizen's News*.

Donaldson and Smith were soon released and returned to California Hall, only to find the dance floor swarming with police. Chaos ensued and the officers ended up arresting two men, Konrad Osterreich and Jon Borset, on a charge of lewd conduct. According to witnesses, the alleged contact was in fact an innocent episode involving a folding chair that had collapsed: One of the men grabbed the other to break his fall. Yet the police had to demonstrate that their intervention had been legitimate. As usual, those arrested would have their names, addresses, and places of employment printed in the San Francisco newspapers.

The next morning, the seven infuriated clergymen called a press conference, lambasting the police department for their obstructive tactics and "deliberate harassment." ANGRY MINISTERS RIP POLICE, the *San Francisco Chronicle*'s headline blared; above it ran a photo of the ministers with folded arms and stern faces. The article began:

> Ministers of four Protestant denominations accused the Police Department yesterday of "intimidation, broken promises, and obvious hostility" in breaking up a private benefit for homosexuals at California Hall Friday night.
>
> The ministers co-sponsored the event. They charged that they, too, had been harassed by police officials and questioned at length about their theological concepts.

By contrast, the more conservative *San Francisco Examiner* reported:

> . . . Many males were in eye-dazzling evening gowns, and a policeman was heard to estimate that "out of a hundred women, half were the genuine article."
>
> . . . The fund-raising ball, the first of its kind locally, was to provide organizational expenses for the council. "But because of police harassment we probably won't even break even," Rev. McIlvenna added ruefully. The break-even point was $2,000.
>
> Yesterday, Police Chief Thomas Cahill said the ball was not a

private party because tickets were being sold at the door and since a liquor license had been issued to California Hall, "the police had a right and duty to police the place."

The New Year's Ball incident galvanized the gay community. The ACLU, at last finding a homosexual-related case they thought they could successfully defend, stepped up to represent the three lawyers and one housewife who were charged with "blocking entry of the police to California Hall." For the four days of the trial, the San Francisco courtroom was standing room only. The ministers' wives, dressed in Sunday church finery, were in constant attendance—knowing that their staid, reserved presence would greatly benefit the defendants. As the prosecution presented its side, it did not help the state's flimsy case when the six-foot-four-inch arresting officer stood next to the five-foot-two May to demonstrate how she wouldn't let him pass; the courtroom dissolved in incredulous laughter. Even before the ACLU team of attorneys began their defense, the judge ruled that the police had not been blocked from entering the premises, because they were already inside California Hall when they arrested the four. Instructing the jury to return a verdict of "not guilty," he then issued an official reprimand to the police department.

Later, Donaldson and Smith themselves defended the two men arrested on the dubious "lewd behavior" charge. Although Osterreich and Borset were convicted, the judge, saying he thought they had suffered enough, fined them only twenty-five dollars. Still, 647a, Lewd Conduct, was a registable offense, meaning that should either of the men move to a new city, he would have to register with the police within thirty days. Had they been teachers or lawyers they would have had their licenses revoked—just for dancing at a costume ball.

While the court cases turned out more favorably than expected— the first had been won on a technicality and the second lost, but with sentences tempered by a judge who later said he would not have found the defendants guilty—neither trial came down to a test of the basic civil rights issues, such as homosexuals' right to assemble. Nonetheless, the event at California Hall ultimately did the gay community a great service. In its wake, the major Protestant denominations wrestled to define their stances on homosexuality. Indeed, Reverend Robert Cromey wrote in his book, *In God's Image,* "My stomach turns when I hear Christian people condemn homosexuality as a sin and homosexual people as perverts. . . . I pray for the souls of my fellow church people who continue to block full freedom for God's children who were given the gift of being drawn in loving and sexual communion with people of the same gender. . . ." In some states, the attention drawn to the archaic sex laws led to calls for reform. Locally, the San Francisco police department now appointed a special liaison officer to the homosexual community and dropped its policy of disrupting gay and lesbian gatherings, instead helping with issuing permits and directing traffic. The New Year's Ball advanced the gay rights movement by a giant step.

Having now initiated dialogues with two of its longtime antagonists, religion and government, the gay and lesbian community was ready to tackle a third great foe—the psychiatric community.

Back in the dark ages of 1948, sexologist Dr. Alfred Kinsey had published *Sexual Behavior in the Human Male.* In this vastly influential book, he posited that thirty-seven percent of American men had at least one homosexual experience leading to orgasm, and that four percent were exclusively homosexual for their entire lives. He followed the book with a second volume in 1952 entitled *Sexual Behavior in the Human Female,* which stated that thirteen percent of American women had at least one homosexual experience leading to orgasm and that possibly three percent were exclusively homosexual for their entire lives. For those who had grown up thinking "I am the only one," the two volumes provided a big boost.

Kinsey speculated that were there no social restraints on homosexuality, "such activity would appear in the histories of a much larger portion of the population." Moreover, he held: "The capacity of an individual to respond erotically to any sort of stimulus, whether it is provided by another person of the same or of the opposite sex, is basic to the species." Kinsey's conclusion that homosexuality was far more extensive than ever imagined had horrified moralists around the world and garnered the wholesale condemnation of such ministers as the Reverend Billy Graham. Of *Sexual Behavior in the Human Male* he ranted, "It is impossible to estimate the damage this book will do to the already deteriorating morals of America." Still, Kinsey resolutely stood by his data, saying, "The only kind of abnormal sex acts are those which are impossible to perform."

Dr. Evelyn Hooker, a UCLA professor and researcher, took the daring next step. No one, not even Kinsey, had scientifically challenged the widely held belief of the American Psychiatric Association (APA) that homosexuality was pathological—that is, a disease. Spurred on by a cherished gay friend, and backed by a grant from the National Institute of Mental Health (NIMH), Hooker was the first to conduct controlled tests on male homosexuality. Comparing a group of thirty homosexual men and thirty heterosexual men over the course of three years, she meticulously charted and analyzed the responses. In an effort to remain totally objective, she then presented the data to three other psychological experts for their dissemination. Dumbfounded, they could not clinically tell the difference between the gay and straight subjects. Hooker was elated. In 1956, at a meeting of the American Psychological Association in Chicago, she presented the paper of her controversial findings, "The Adjustment of the Male Overt Homosexual," revealing the surprising hard evidence that gay men were as well adjusted as straight men—and some were even better adjusted. Armed with a particularly strong, expressive voice and a flair for the dramatic, Hooker held the large hotel ballroom spellbound. Indeed, the electricity was such that when the hour had ended, the gathering was adjourned to another ballroom for further heated discussion. In the end, most of those attending the conference dismissively rejected her paper and its findings. Nearly twenty years later, Hooker would have the lasting satisfaction of seeing her learned conclusions and insights prevail and her study forming the basis of the APA's about-face in its belief that homosexuality was a disease; at the time, however, like all visionaries, she was ridiculed and chastised.

Feeling understandably slighted, lesbians approached her to conduct similar studies for them, but Hooker demurred, concerned that some would think her gender might compromise the endeavor.

Kinsey and Hooker notwithstanding, the psychiatric world of the mid-1960's continued to see homosexuality as a sickness and mainstream opinion followed suit. *Time* magazine expressed the popular view in 1966:

[Homosexuality] is a pathetic little second-rate substitute for reality, a pitiable flight from life. As such it deserves fairness, compassion, understanding, and when possible, treatment. But it deserves no encouragement, no glamorization, no rationalization, no fake status as minority martyrdom, no sophistry about simple differences in taste—and above all, no pretense that it is anything but a pernicious sickness.

Recognizing how much the "illness model" of homosexuality validated such bigotry, the homophile movement, including the DOB, had always attempted to court the psychiatric community, even inviting noted professionals to address homosexual groups. At the time, homosexuals were so grateful just to have the attention of such experts that they accepted whatever was said—no matter how dismissive or derogatory. Del Martin complains of the lack of compassion of "the historians and the ones that came later, who said, 'Why weren't you on the street, why weren't you doing all these things, why did you have all of these professionals come to your meetings?' Because we needed validation and assurance. And what they kept saying is that we were illegal, immoral, and sick. And that's what we had to cope with."

Two respected physicians, Charles W. Socarides, associate professor of psychiatry at Albert Einstein College of Medicine, and Irving Bieber, associate clinical professor of psychiatry at New York Medical College, were leading proponents of the "gay is sick" theory. As Neil Miller notes in his book *Out of the Past,* Socarides held that heterosexual relationships were characterized by "cooperation, solace, stimulation, enrichment, healthy challenge and fulfillment," while gay relationships were "masquerades" of "destruction, mutual defeat, exploitation of the partner and the self, oral-sadistic incorporation, aggressive onslaughts, attempts to alleviate anxiety, and a pseudosolution to the aggressive and libidinal urges which dominate and torment the individual." And Bieber, especially keen on his notion that "every homosexual is a latent heterosexual," had been one of the most strident voices against Dr. Hooker's revolutionary findings the decade before. Speaking specifically of lesbians, Columbia University psychiatrist Cornelia Weber labeled their relationships as "unstable and often transient" and incapable of fulfilling "an individual's need for stability and love."

Through the 1960's, homosexuality was deemed so pernicious that mental health professionals still often treated it with shock therapy or, should that fail, even attempted the surgical "solution" of a prefrontal lobotomy. Compassionate therapists were few and far between. "It wasn't until the seventies when we began to get lesbian therapists who were available for lesbians to talk to," Lyon says. "Remember that woman who called you in the sixties and offered her services?" Martin asks. "She wouldn't give Phyllis her name!" "She wouldn't give her name, she wouldn't meet, she wouldn't do anything," Lyon says, shaking her head. "And I said, 'You expect me to send lesbians who are in trouble to you, and you won't even admit you're a lesbian?'" But such was the fear—and because of the fear, the ignorance.

Frank Kameny of the Washington, D.C., Mattachine Society and a brilliant former astronomer fired by the U.S. Army Map Service for being gay, posed a simple challenge: that the "experts" stop talking *about* the homosexual and start talking *with* the homosexual. Barbara Gittings, as editor of *The Ladder,* ran an article by Kameny, "Does Research into Homosexuality Matter?" He argued, "We are the true authorities on homosexuality, whether we are accepted as such or not." Influenced by the black civil rights movement's argument "that mere persuasion, information, and education are not going to do for us in actual practice the rights and equality which are ours in principle," Kameny decided that if "Black Is Beautiful," then "Gay Is Good." "We must say this and say it clearly and with no possible room for equivocation or ambiguity," he insisted. Gittings and her partner, Kay Lahusen, also of the New York DOB, aligned with Kameny, agreeing that the homophile movement needed to unite in proclaiming that homosexuals were not sick. But Florence Conrad, DOB's research director, took exception, and Del and Phyllis agreed with her, concerned that straight people would counter with, "Yes, you are!" They still contended that it was necessary to reach professional decision-makers in order to bring about change. Conrad responded to Kameny's article with "Research Is Here to Stay." Researchers, she said, would continue to investigate questions about homosexuality, "whether we help them or not. Their results will be far more distorted if we do not cooperate than if we do."

Although seeking the same result, the gay men and lesbians were on the cusp of another rift. But this time, the lines of allegiance were blurring.

In the summer of 1965, adopting the tactics of the civil rights and antiwar activists of the time, Kameny, Gittings, Lahusen, and other renegade members of the Mattachine Society and the DOB began taking a more confrontational stance toward the straight establishment. Organized by the East Coast Homophile Organizations (ECHO) to protest the government's "discrimination and hostility against its homosexual American citizens," gays and lesbians picketed the White House and the Pentagon in Washington and Independence Hall in Philadelphia. As Gittings remarked in *Making History,* "It was thrilling. You knew you were doing something momentous. People would stare at you. They had never seen self-declared homosexuals parading with signs." Yet these acts of defiance splintered the DOB into pro and con factions. As Kay Lahusen said to Eric Marcus: "Picketing was against DOB's philosophy. They wanted to hide behind the skirts of the professionals and have the professionals say we were OK. They thought we shouldn't run out in the streets and do this kind of thing. So we put the debate in *The Ladder.* Of course, that enraged the DOB, too." Lahusen overlooked Florence Conrad's concession: "There is no reason why we cannot support research and do other things at the same time, especially since the interests of persons in the homophile movement differ. . . ."

Undaunted by her critics, Conrad would continue with research projects on behalf of the DOB. Indeed, throughout the sixties, the DOB was instrumental in sponsoring no fewer than three research projects on lesbianism. The culmination would be 1968's revealing study, "Attitudes of Mental Health Professionals Toward Homosexuality and Its Treatment." In conjunction with Dr. Joel Fort and Claude Steiner of the Center for Special Problems, an agency of San Francisco's Public Health Department, a questionnaire was developed and sent to a sample of 163 scientifically selected Bay Area psychiatrists, psychologists, and social workers.

The high rate of return, 147, and its results were unprecedented. Nearly all (ninety-eight percent) felt it was possible for homosexuals to function in society effectively, opposed laws treating private homosexual acts between consenting adults as criminal, and opposed prohibitions against homosexuals in civil service. More than ninety percent said homosexuals should not be restricted from the teaching profession and that public misunderstanding arises when the terms "illness" and "disease" are applied to homosexuality. And ninety-seven percent said that the goal in working with a homosexual client would be self-acceptance, not change to a heterosexual orientation. Also, eighty-eight percent said homosexuals should not be disqualified from serving in the military, and seventy-three percent held they should not be barred from security-sensitive positions. The results were so prohomosexual that it took three years to find a professional journal willing to publish the data; they finally appeared in *Psychological Reports* in October 1971.

It was becoming very clear that in order to achieve more, in order to facilitate real movement, the gay and lesbian community had to fan the winds of change themselves. And a breeze that had begun on Friday, June 28, 1969, at a seedy gay bar on Christopher Street in New York City, blew those winds of change into a full-blown hurricane on the East Coast.

It was the day of Judy Garland's funeral, when thousands, gay and straight, had lined up outside the Frank E. Campbell Funeral Chapel on Manhattan's Upper East Side to bid farewell to the great performer. In the last few years of her turbulent life, Garland had been fully enshrined as a goddess by the gay community, so mourning continued well into the humid night. By then, the crowds had migrated downtown to the West Village and into the bars, which the police could not resist the opportunity to raid.

However, at one bar, the Stonewall Inn, the raid did not go as planned. When the plainclothes vice squad entered to shut down the establishment for an alleged lack of a proper liquor license, the eclectic patrons—students, drag queens, lesbians, hustlers, and business professionals—fought back. Although accounts differ, many, including the bar's waiter, claim a butch lesbian had resisted arrest and one of the policemen struck her. Enraged, the patrons revolted. After being herded onto the sidewalk, they massed, shouting epithets, refusing to disperse and resisting being herded into the waiting paddy wagon. A sympathetic, supportive crowd began to gather across the street in Sheridan Square Park. Knowing that the police had a reputation for taking kickbacks from bar owners, the patrons started throwing coins at the officers—pennies, nickels, dimes, and quarters. The crowd joined in. To escape the angry mob, the rattled cops barricaded themselves inside the bar, while outside the hurled projectiles segued to bottles and rocks. The plate-glass windows were shattered, parking meters uprooted. Soon, Fellini-style mayhem reigned. One memorable image, as described by historian Martin Duberman, was a chorus line of ragtag drag queens kicking up their heels and raucously chanting:

> We are the Stonewall girls, we wear our hair in curls;
> We wear no underwear, we show our pubic hair;
> We wear our dungarees above our nelly knees.

DOB activist Martha Shelley happened to pass the bar that night, along with some friends from Massachusetts who were in town to discuss opening a Boston chapter of the Daughters of Bilitis. As she told Eric Marcus in *Making History,* when they came upon the melee, she shrugged it off. "One of the women turned to me and said, 'What's going on here?' I said, 'Oh, it's a riot. These things happen in New York all the time. Let's toddle away and do something else.' "

But the standoff intensified. A metal city trashcan was set on fire and hurled through a broken plate-glass window. Using a fire hose inside, the police put out the trash fire and then turned the hose on the taunting crowd. A fire engine raced to the scene, followed by the NYPD Tactical Police Force, which came down the block wielding billy clubs. In a blue-shirted phalanx, they attacked the protesters, sending them beaten and bloody into side streets. It was only then that the vice squad could be rescued from the trashed Stonewall interior.

Word of the confrontation spread like wildfire through the Village. By the next morning, accounts had appeared on the television news as well as in all the major newspapers. Saturday night, when the police returned to the bar, they met an even larger throng of protesters (among them Martha Shelley), now outfitted with picket signs and with the media on alert. Homosexuals were coming out of the closet en masse. The last revolution of the sixties—the Gay Revolution—had officially begun.

Within a month, the Stonewall uprising gave birth to the Gay Liberation Front (GLF), through the efforts of Shelley and others. Its kick-off rally started in Washington Square Park, and from there gays and lesbians—four hundred strong—marched to the Stonewall bar, shouting "Gay power!" That night, after nearly twenty years of the homophile movement, only forty-odd organizations existed exclusively for homosexuals. By 1973, that number would balloon to over eight hundred.

As the revolution gained momentum, however, the old, familiar conflicts were reignited. Once again, men had seized control of the gay-rights debate and were giving lesbian concerns short shrift. Although lesbians had joined in common cause with male homosexuals and their issues—police harassment, solicitation, washroom sex, or transsexual attire—some of the women believed there was little evidence that the gay men had any intention of making common cause with lesbians and their issues, which pertained more to civil rights than to criminal law. Many had come to believe that their needs might be better served by the budding women's movement. Among them were Phyllis and Del, who had long recognized that sexual orientation was only one battleground for women, who at the time were denied equal pay for doing work identical to men's, protection under the law from abusive spouses, and other basic human needs. The male-dominated gay-rights movement was still refusing to make these critical women's issues a priority.

In its early days, however, the feminist movement was tremendously resistant to admitting lesbians. Its leaders were terrified that the credibility of their cause would be compromised by charges that female homosexuals were running rampant in their ranks. In fact, Betty Friedan, one of the original founders and the national president of the National Organization for Women (NOW) and author of the watershed *The Feminine Mystique,* dubbed lesbians "The Lavender Menace"—even telling *The New York Times* that she suspected lesbians had been sent by the CIA to infiltrate the movement and later intimating that the FBI was using the lesbians as pawns to discredit NOW.

Friedan's paranoia on this subject was legendary, but there was some truth in her fears. "In the early days of NOW a lot of lesbians were in leadership positions, but they weren't 'out,' " admits Ivy Bottini, who was the NOW New York chapter president in 1968. In fact, Bottini did not come out of the closet herself until a few months after her election. "Even before the lesbian issue, Betty held NOW in an iron fist," avers Bottini. Although Friedan launched an effective smear campaign to defeat the reelection of the then openly lesbian Bottini, Ivy says, "I happen to like Friedan, as much as she caused me pain. I think she was and is an incredible person. She was just too conservative. She created incredible dissension throughout the entire national organization."

Nevertheless, Del Martin and Phyllis Lyon became the first avowed lesbians to join NOW. Lest there be any question as to their sexual orientation, they joined as a couple, making clear their determination to use their considerable powers of persuasion to educate the feminists about their gay sisters—and to change minds. They were abetted by sympathetic NOW national treasurer Inka O'Hanrahan, who ran interference with the executive board in welcoming the couple. "It's good to have you with us," the straight O'Hanrahan said upon meeting them. "Surely there are more of you. I hope you'll bring them around." O'Hanrahan and Aileen Hernández, NOW's Western Region director, would become valued mentors to Phyllis and Del. Hernández, an African-American appointed to the first Equal Employment Opportunity Commission by President Lyndon Johnson and who had resigned because of the sexism she found on the Commission, would eventually become national president of NOW.

While the West Coast lesbians did not suffer the animosity their New York sisters endured, they were sympathetic to their plight. They joined them symbiotically in the rebellion that was brewing on the East Coast forged by authors and activists Rita Mae Brown, Kate Millet, Sidney Abbott, Barbara Love of New York, and Elaine Noble of the Boston DOB, who in a few years would become the nation's first openly gay elected state official. A slow, inexorable crack was being perceived in the NOW anti-gay stance, and by the time of its national convention in September 1971, with Aileen Hernandez as national president, the organization was ready to give its lesbian members an official welcome:

Be it resolved that NOW recognizes the double oppression of lesbians; Be it resolved that a woman's right to her own person includes the right to define and express her own sexuality; Be it resolved that NOW acknowledges the oppression of lesbians as a legitimate concern of feminism.

Once finally fully accepted into the ranks, Martin and Lyon found themselves in a peculiar position—sticking up for men. "All this rage against men came out of these women," Del recalls. "Those of us who didn't have to live with them were beginning to get a little defensive for the men." Phyllis concurs, "There was so much anger against them that I finally said, 'They can't be all that bad.' " Del laughs, adding, "And we were supposed to be the man-haters!"

In joining NOW, Phyllis and Del had not turned their backs on the gay-rights movement. Indeed, they had now achieved the status of elder stateswomen, revered by the entire homosexual community for devoting their lives to the struggle. "They made great sacrifices economically over the years," Bob Ross maintains. "They put every penny into the movement. They never developed careers for themselves." They were also, to their dismay, seen as paragons, exemplifying the ideal lesbian relationship. "Their love was right out there for everyone to see," Ivy Bottini says. "They acknowledged each other as a couple and as a result became these icons in the lesbian community. They became role models and beacons in the night." Chuckling, Del says, "Phyllis used to tell me we should break up for a while just to shake them all up."

But in those turbulent times, the movement itself was undergoing a sea change. On the East Coast especially, the new, more confrontational generation was pushing hard for recognition; as Barbara Gittings reported in *Making History*, "They found that they could not blow their noses without permission from national headquarters of DOB. Women from Philadelphia, who were brainy women, finally said, 'What do we need Daughters of Bilitis for? We can't move in this organization. . . .' So they broke off . . . and founded a new organization for both men and women, called the Homophile Action League, that was dedicated to political action."

In New York, Gittings herself, along with Kay Lahusen, was coming under fire as a rebel. "Certainly we had our differences with Del Martin and Phyllis Lyon at DOB," Gittings admitted. "We had said to them, 'You're over the hill. Your thinking is out-of-date.' " Lahusen elaborated: "We took their magazine [*The Ladder*] in a totally different direction, and they weren't happy with that. We thumbed our noses at them—almost." Gittings and Lahusen would soon leave the DOB for the more radical and politically in-your-face Gay Liberation Force.

Ironically, before long, the GLF would label the one-time rabble-rousers as out-of-date as well.

When the Daughters held its last convention in the summer of 1970, it voted to make each chapter autonomous. Concurrently, the editor of *The Ladder,* Barbara Grier, and Rita Laporte, DOB national president, took the magazine away from the Daughters to publish it privately. In 1972, after fifteen-odd years as the rallying ground for the nation's lesbians, *The Ladder* ceased publication. Grier discovered too late that the magazine could not survive without the financial backing of the organization. And symbiotically, with *The Ladder* gone, the DOB lost its nationwide outreach and its superstructure began to crumble. Infighting tore at the very fabric of the freed entities, and soon, chapter after chapter collapsed. Ruth Simpson, New York DOB president in the early seventies, believed that the radical disruption within the chapters that abetted in bringing down the DOB was not only the work of "pseudo-militants." In her book, *From the Closets to the Courts,* Simpson wrote that to believe that the dissolution of DOB was "caused exclusively by people who are ill-advised and unintentionally disruptive is a serious error. DOB, we know, was infiltrated by at least two governmental agencies." Del and Phyllis learned also that DOB in California had been infiltrated by both the FBI and the CIA, but did not believe the agencies were instrumental in the organization's ultimate demise. They were more inclined to agree with Simpson's other assertion—that the disrupters who called the doers "leaders, elitists, or superstars" were forced to become the doers and then ended up as the elitists.

When the smoke cleared, only the Boston chapter was left standing.

Phyllis and Del, who had eased themselves out of leadership roles, had seen this finale coming: "What these radical women failed to understand was that DOB was a coming-out place, a self-help organization, and a safety net for women who were struggling with their new identity, hoping to meet other lesbians and learn survival skills," Phyllis says. "Women at that point in their lives need a chance to express and sort out their feelings and fears," Del insists. "Radical politics scare them away."

To some extent, the DOB had already fulfilled its mission, rescuing lesbians from the invisibility and utter isolation of the 1950's and ushering them to a seat at society's table. Eventually, many out lesbians felt fortified—and in some ways, disenchanted—enough to leave the feminist movement and return, invigorated—and a bit angry—to the front-lines of the lesbian cause. "The feminist movement allowed the lesbians to really become their own movement," Ivy Bottini states firmly. "Out of pain, sadness, disappointment, and anger."

Then, in 1973, another wall separating the gay and lesbian community from society fell in a crumbling heap. In the face of mounting overwhelming evidence and unassailable studies, the APA finally dropped homosexuality from its list of mental disorders—and with it, the stigma of pathology. Dr. Charles Socarides, writing in *Psychiatric News,* decried the decision, claiming that it caused "severe damage to the image of American psychiatry . . . impeding research and therapy for homosexuals. . . ." But that was a last hurrah. Another critical battle in the gay-rights struggle had been won.*

It is a measure of the hard-won progress homosexuals had made that, in the mid-1970's, the liberal San Francisco mayor, George Moscone, named Phyllis to the city's Human Rights Commission and Del to the Commission on the Status of Women. Then, in 1977, a gay Castro-district activist, Harvey Milk, was elected to the San Francisco Board of Supervisors—a historic first for the gay community. Phyllis and Del, who had known him for years, didn't back his candidacy. "Oh, Harvey was an ass at first," Del explains. "He had a ponytail and would say things like, 'Drag queens are more feminine than real women.' Well, as you can imagine, remarks like that didn't go over well with us." Then Milk cut his hair and began to soften his approach, starting to listen to his constituents. When he won his board seat, Phyllis and Del confronted him: "We hope you appoint yourself a woman aide, Harvey." Milk smiled. "Hey, I'm way ahead of you," he said, having already tapped Ann Kronenberg for the spot. He was becoming a champion, as well as a symbol, for the gay and lesbian community. Along with supervisors Carol Ruth Silver and Elizabeth Hill, Milk even sponsored a

---

* Ironically, Socarides's son Richard is an acknowledged homosexual activist, who in the mid-1990's was President Bill Clinton's official liaison to the gay and lesbian community. Today, Richard will only diplomatically say that he and his father have "agreed to disagree" on the touchy subject of homosexuality.

board resolution officially honoring Phyllis and Del on the occasion of their twenty-fifth anniversary together.

Milk's gay advocacy put him at odds with Dan White, a conservative former fireman who had also been elected to the board. At first, Milk and White strove to cooperate, but when White was the sole board member to vote against a gay-rights bill Milk had proposed, outlawing discrimination in housing, a serious rift developed between them. In 1978, White resigned from the board, and a week and a half later asked Mayor Moscone to reinstate him. Moscone refused. On November 27, Dan White returned to City Hall, this time armed with a .38-caliber revolver, entered Moscone's office, and shot him four times, killing him. Then White walked down the hallway to find Harvey Milk, who he was certain had convinced the mayor to deny his request. White shot Milk point-blank five times, the last shot at close range to the head.

San Francisco was in shock.

"It was unbelievable," Del recalls with a shudder. A friend had called her at work with the news, which Del refused to accept until the woman put the receiver up to the radio, so she could hear it for her-self—that Milk and the mayor, a dear friend to the gay and lesbian community, were gone, senselessly cut down in a gangster-style execu-tion.

Then came the jarring aftershock: the trial. Using the now infamous "Twinkie defense," White's lawyers argued that their client was de-pressed by personal matters and, fueled by junk food, had propelled himself into a state where he was not responsible for his actions. The gambit worked. For killing two people in cold blood, Dan White was convicted only of manslaughter and sentenced to a mere seven years and eight months in prison.

When the unconscionable verdict was announced, the city erupted. In what became known as the "White Night Riots," gays and lesbians marched on City Hall, storming the building and setting police cars on fire. The media was partly to blame for the rampage, according to Del. "They went up to people with microphones to interview them, asking, 'Is there going to be a riot? Is there going to be a backlash?' " When the microphone was shoved in front of her, Martin said calmly, "There shouldn't be if people would follow what Harvey did." Unfortunately, the community was too enraged to think, too hurt to remember. Phyllis and Del were deeply saddened to see gays and lesbians—though justifiably angry—running riot in the city as a primal, collective cry of pain. Milk and Moscone's courage and commitment had come at a terrible price indeed. But what was equally disheartening was that such an inspiring and celebrated gay victory as Milk's could be so suddenly and savagely reversed—that what seemed like progress could be instantly snatched away.

It was the end of an era. And the beginning of another.

Although the community was no stranger to subliminal violence— harassment, beatings, derision, and hatred were, and always had been, part of the unending struggle—murder was a horrifying new development. It was clear that some segments of society were becoming more and more threatened by the progress of homosexuals. But gays and lesbians knew there was no turning back. Determined to never be ruled by fear again, and holding fast to what they had achieved in the past two decades, they steadfastly insisted on more: More recognition. More tolerance. More acceptance. More clout. More visibility. More results.

And that, in truth, was all Phyllis Lyon and Del Martin, the mothers of the movement, had wanted from the beginning: More.

In recent decades Lyon and Martin have continued to fight for progress, though in an interview with *The Advocate,* Del lamented the fact that, being older, they need a little more rest than they used to. Not that they feel burned out: "I've honestly never felt that exhausted," Del said. "I've always wanted to be involved. I get off on it. In fact, I think the movement has gotten more and more intriguing to me over the years."

Martin's well-received book, *Battered Wives,* a catalyst for the battered women's shelter movement, had been published by the Glide Foundation in 1976. Lyon took on a new career in sex education. She became codirector of the national Sex Forum and played a prominent role in the founding of the Institute for the Advanced Study of Human Sexuality.

In 1995, both women were delegates to the White House Conference on Aging. They were successful in getting sexual orientation into the nondiscrimination resolution, along with other recommendations to meet the needs of older lesbians and gay men. It was the first time in the thirty-five-year history of the conference that sexual orientation was mentioned.

Today Del and Phyllis are passionately involved in Old Lesbians Organizing for Change (OLOC), a movement they helped found. "The whole point of OLOC is to be who you are," Del says. "And to struggle against ageism, which is rampant in the gay community as well as in society overall."

Given their hallowed place in homosexual history, the two still get called upon to lecture on gay subjects. "Changing minds takes persistence," Del declares. "You have to hang in and keep building more and more support. And it means you have to—every year—educate more people around the issue. I think part of the problem that we've had in the movement is that we poured our energy into electoral politics, and the need to educate people was forgotten." She shrugs. "So we did the educating."

"They have always been an enormous influence," Roberta Achtenberg says. "They were always there, rooting for us, encouraging us. They wanted the young women to be everything they could possibly be—things that they could never imagine. There are people who do great things, but they don't help the movement grow. Not them. Not Phyllis and Del." Ivy Bottini agrees. "I look at them and see this couple that has seen so much happen over the years with gays and lesbians," she says. "What is amazing to me is that their relationship has still maintained that old loving relationship they had at the beginning. And they are still organizing, still putting it out there for everyone to see. Talk about courage. Talk about bravery."

ELAINE
NOBLE

Moxie

S HE DOESN'T SIT; she perches, almost like a runner at the blocks, impatiently waiting for the next chapter to begin. Under the thick bangs of a tapered, shag haircut, her eyes have a friendly but sharp clarity; they are eyes that take in everything and everyone, that miss nothing. This woman of undeniable intelligence and assessable warmth is led to her desk in the statehouse chamber where she will spend the next two years. Radiating an insouciant confidence, she stakes out her territory in the crowded, ornate Beacon Hill room. She grabs a hand, pats a shoulder, and engages in an animated conversation; her full-throated laugh echoes off the walls. Before long, a concerned statehouse officer approaches. "Honey," he says to her, kindly but firmly, "these seats are reserved for the representatives. You'll have to move somewhere else." A wry smile comes to her lips, but before she can reply, an Assembly member steps forward. "She *is* a representative," he assures the guard. "This is Elaine Noble."

It is New Year's Day, 1975, in Boston, Massachusetts, and Elaine Noble is about to be sworn in as a representative in the state legislature from Suffolk 6, a district known as the Fenway. Joining the heaviest Democratic legislature in the state's history, thirty-year-old Noble is making a notable bit of history herself; this former teacher and neighborhood activist—one of only nineteen women in the 280-seat General Court (the Senate and House)—is the first openly gay person elected to a state office not only in Massachusetts, but in all of America.

In the mid-1970's, amid the aftermath of Watergate and the Vietnam War, the gay revolution had begun, but it was still in its infancy. While not quite the dark ages of the 1950's, the landscape was nevertheless a decidedly fearful one for many homosexuals. Most lived deep in the closets of shame and denial. Few were "out" to their friends and family; almost none were out to their coworkers. And here was an attractive, bright, aggressive woman who was not only out at home, with her family, and at work; she was going to be out in the Massachusetts House of Representatives.

At eleven-thirty A.M., Elaine Noble raises her hand and, along with the other recently elected representatives, is officially sworn into the Massachusetts state legislature by newly elected governor Michael Dukakis. Immediately following the short ceremony, she looks up and smiles to the gallery above, where her busload of friends and supporters sit. Still bundled in their coats, they beam back at her, some waving.

Exhilarated, Noble focuses back on the chamber floor, where several Assembly members circle around her to welcome her to the Hill. They speak of change; they speak of history. Others stand to the side, shooting curious looks, speaking in low tones.

Noble knows instinctively that she will be walking the fine line between the two camps for her entire term of office. She also knows that she is entirely up to the challenge. She will not be quiet. She will speak her mind. "The last thing that will die in me is my mouth," she says.

It is that uncompromising nature that has landed her in the Beacon Hill statehouse on this New Year's Day.

Just how did Elaine Noble accomplish such an unprecedented, trailblazing feat? How did she buck two hundred years of tradition and bias and bigotry and not only survive, but thrive? In Boston, they have a term for it: moxie.

Born in New Kensington, Pennsylvania, in 1944, Elaine Noble grew up in Natrona, one of the small, working-class steel mill and coal mine towns along the Allegheny River north of Pittsburgh. The grimy neighborhood was in an economically depressed valley; at the top of Elaine's street was a salt factory that continually rained down debris. As she told the magazine *The Advocate,* "When you walked outside your house you had to walk with an umbrella or babushka on your head because the fallout was so incredible you could see your footprints." She recalled power plants that emitted so much radiation that technicians were killed, and the rate of stillborn babies that climbed higher and higher in direct proportion to the nearness of the facility. For as long as she could remember, swimming was banned in the Allegheny River because of the waste and detergents that were discharged into it. "By the time I was twelve," she says, "I was aware of that."

Her mother's family was German-Jewish; they had emigrated to America early in the 1700's. Noted shippers in colonial Philadelphia, they made a point of changing their name from Solamon to escape anti-Semitism. "They changed it to Prager," Elaine says with a laugh. "You'd've thought they'd change it to Smith or something!" Two centuries later, Ruth Prager would see swastikas scribbled on the walls in her Wheeling, West Virginia, neighborhood. When she married Ronald Noble, of Irish-English descent, she decided to raise her children as Methodists, believing that assimilation was necessary to live safely in America. None of this escaped young Elaine's eye.

A conscientious objector during World War II, her father was required to serve in the Merchant Marine. "It was a rough time for my family," Elaine recalls. "My mother had to work; she had three little kids. But we were very close." Elaine was the youngest of the children, with a sister four years older and a brother sandwiched in between. "Poor Jim," Elaine says, laughing, "stuck between two aggressive women. It's a wonder he survived." Her paternal grandparents lived in the house with them, and there was a sizable contingent of relatives nearby. When young Elaine had trouble learning to read—she would later be diagnosed as slightly dyslexic—there was always an aunt or uncle or grandparent to read to her and assist with remedial exercises. "It was one of the good things about an extended family," she says. "Someone was always around to help."

After the war, Elaine's father became a grievance man for the unions, as well as one of the first organizers of the NAACP in the Pittsburgh region. "He was sort of an old lefty," Noble says with pride. "Not quite a card-carrying Communist, but most of his friends were." Elaine remembers a house full of her dad's flamboyant, left-leaning, and memorable cronies, many of them artists and performers. Against the backdrop of this neo-bohemia, the Noble children learned at an early age that diversity was a good thing, a distinct asset as opposed to an unwelcome liability. "Differences make for a richer pattern," Elaine says. "It's a recipe of life."

School would teach them some harder lessons about the ways of the world. When the poor children from the lowlands were integrated with the more affluent children from the surrounding ridge—the Heights—there were sometimes explosive results. Elaine and her siblings found themselves "the marked kids from the valley." Scrappy by nature, she soon learned that when her quickness of mind couldn't save her, she could use her fists. She wasn't only fighting her own battles, but also defending her brother, who, painfully shy and slowed by corrective eye surgeries, was a constant target of bullies. She warmed to the role of champion of the underdog.

Many of the Nobles' neighbors were recent immigrants, Polish and southern and Eastern European families who had come to America after the war. "Some," Elaine recalls, "had literally just gotten off the boat." On the block where she lived, for a long time her family was the only one that spoke English. Ruth Noble understood Polish and Czech and some Italian, so she could converse fitfully with the other women in the neighborhood. Although the Nobles were Methodist, a pervasive old-country Roman Catholic sensibility pervaded the valley, bringing with it, among other things, strict sexual taboos. "My little Catholic friends were so afraid that something would fall off their bodies! Sex itself was something you didn't talk about."

In high school, Noble encountered difficulty relating to the opposite sex. To her, girls seemed more giving and gentle, while "there was something about boys that was brutal," she recalls, "something different and distant—and threatening." For adolescent girls in the 1950's, decked out in bobby socks and ponytails, the biggest fear was getting pregnant, a concern young Elaine used in an attempt to justify her reluctance to connect emotionally with boys. She told herself at the time that she just felt more comfortable with members of her own sex. Social interaction was easier with girls. It was more fun. When she did date, she gravitated toward military men, who were always off in the service, away from home. "I had the legitimacy of having a boyfriend while I hung out with these wonderful cheerleaders." It all seemed perfectly harmless until the feelings changed from emotional to sexual. "I really thought it was a phase I was going through," she says, "and that I'd outgrow it. Or, I *hoped* that I'd outgrow it. It scared the hell out of me, because I didn't want to be known as queer. I didn't want to admit to *myself* that I was queer." All she'd ever heard about homosexuality came through her giggling schoolmates' derision. Moreover, there were no role models for Elaine to look up to, to talk to, to help her feel good about herself and her confused feelings. "There weren't any gay people that I knew of in my high school," she says, "even though I'm sure there were. Still, nobody talked about being lesbian or gay. It just wasn't an option."

After graduating from high school at seventeen, Elaine worked in a ceramics factory to earn tuition money for college. There she met her first true lesbian, Kelly. "I'd played around with women a little bit, but she was my first real bona fide affair," Noble recalls. "Before that, it was always something that I did when I got drunk—that type of thing." After some coy back-and-forth flirting, the two girls found themselves in a parked car in the woods. "She claimed that I threw the car keys out of the window so we couldn't drive away," Elaine says. That night, the adolescent affair began in earnest. "I came out with Kelly. I thought it was absolutely wonderful, but it also terrified me." Kelly was diminutive, cocky, and full of fire. "People mistook her for a boy—she had the short hair, the motorcycle, and everything. She was a hot little dyke. She really was *fun*." Elaine, however, felt extremely isolated during the brief but significant relationship. She had not come out to anyone else, nor was she prepared to. Her parents were wonderful to Kelly, Noble says, but she was not ready to discuss her sexuality with them, although she says in retrospect, "I'm sure they realized that something was going on."

Leaving Kelly behind, Elaine went to Clarion College in Pennsylvania for a year, then transferred north to Boston University, where she had gotten a coveted Trustee scholarship. She enrolled in the School of Education, then switched to the School of Fine Arts; perhaps because of her mild dyslexia, Elaine was always more drawn to the spoken word than the written. Her major, consequently, carried a decided emphasis on speech and communications. Her scholarship required that she maintain a B+ average, which she easily did.

While in school, she worked a variety of jobs, including cocktail waitressing and social work. Settling in the Fenway section of the city, where Boston University is located, she became friendly with the diverse groups of people who resided there. It reminded her of home. "It is a wonderful place to live," Elaine recalls. "A lot of working-class people, a lot of artists. And very mixed racially. As I changed schools and places of employment, the Fenway always stayed my nucleus. It was near the park, which I love. When I get very troubled, I still go over and walk through the park. It's one of my favorite places."

Through most of those university years, Elaine recalls, "Even though I hung around with lesbians, I didn't dare do anything. I dated men. And I just repressed it." When she graduated from BU with a Bachelor of Fine Arts degree and went on to Emerson College for graduate study, however, she met a talented artist, Renee Ware. Elaine could no longer hold back her natural inclinations and the two became lovers. On one school break, an emboldened Elaine brought Renee along on a visit to her parents' house in Natrona. At one point in the vacation, they were in the midst of an angry and loud lovers' quarrel when Noble's mother walked in. "I think you better turn around and walk out, Ma," Elaine said tersely. Renee fled to the bathroom, but Ruth Noble was not going anywhere. Sensing something, she demanded, "Has Renee taken advantage of you?" Elaine rolled her eyes and replied, "Mother, have you ever known anyone to take advantage of me?" She turned to pursue Renee, but Ruth pressed on, saying outright, "Your father wants to know if you're a lesbian." Elaine stopped in her tracks and shot back, "Then why doesn't my father ask me?" The remark hung in the air for a second until her mother replied, "Good question!" Although tension remained high for the rest of the weekend, Ruth Noble did not ask her daughter again about her sexuality. Soon afterward, the two young women split up and Noble returned to dating men exclusively. As a woman about to gear up for a career in the world, hopefully as a teacher, she knew she couldn't afford to give in to an "aberrant" sexual lifestyle. So, as her family had done years before with their Jewishness, she sublimated it. She assimilated. She pretended it wasn't there. "I had no place for it. It was too scary."

Armed with her master's degree from Emerson, Noble secured a teaching position at all-women Colby Junior College in New Hampshire. The totally female environment was like an oasis in the desert, bringing her a greater sense of comfort and ease than she had ever known before. She reveled in the experience, and for a blissful year, the outside world did not intrude. But then a corporate job offer came along with the promise of prestige, money, and opportunity. Although she hated to leave Colby, the offer was too good to refuse. She took the job.

As assistant vice president of advertising at Sweetheart Plastics, Elaine was transformed into a high-powered, smartly coiffed, go-for-the-throat executive. The ten-hour days of high-pressure creative challenges were exhilarating at first, and her coworkers were bright and compelling. Though still dating men, she began seeing women again too, and for a time, she resigned herself to walking the line of bisexuality. "Finally, I had to be honest with myself and say, 'What the hell are you doing?' " She decided to follow her natural inclination toward women, but remain in the closet. "It didn't come easily; it was something I really struggled with," she recalls. Before long, she met a "nice Jewish girl" named Ellen, also deeply closeted, who became her lover, and for a while, everything seemed to be working out well. She had her high-profile job; she had her clandestine relationship. And although the pressures of juggling the two made her edgy, she was able to manage the stress. For a time. Then, suddenly, it exploded and Elaine found herself in the emergency ward of Massachusetts General Hospital with a dangerous case of bleeding ulcers.

While recovering there, she subjected herself to some intense soul-searching about the lifestyle that had precipitated her health crisis. Getting back in balance, with the aid of an aggressive but compassionate therapist, would cost her the job at Sweetheart Plastics, her relationship with Ellen, and, for a while, a bit of her equilibrium.

It would also force her to accept, once and for all, her true sexual orientation. "It wasn't that I disliked men; it's just that my love of women increased," she says. "I'm sure there are a lot of gay men that care about women, but it just doesn't do it for them emotionally, spiritually, and sexually on an intimate level. It just doesn't work. With men, it was always like I was standing behind a plate-glass door; I could see them, but it didn't work for me. I didn't relate. It was like having a conversation and not really hearing it." Still, aligning that personal discovery with the reality of the outside world was daunting, and sometimes demoralizing. As she explained in an interview with *The Boston Globe Magazine,* "The world perceives lesbians one way, and when you realize that you are a lesbian, you can lose your feelings of self. You have to spend a lot of energy to get your self-perception back. You're just beginning to think, 'But I'm a nice person, I'm not a bad person, I'm okay. . . .' "

Luckily, she was soon offered a faculty position at Emerson College through one of her former professors, with the assurance that she would be accepted as a lesbian. Noble was elated that she could return to her old love, teaching, and finally come fully out of the closet. All that remained was the inevitable conversation with her family.

Ruth Noble declared that she was not surprised with her daughter's news. "I knew," she said. "I was just waiting for you to tell me." But however accepting, she cautioned Elaine, "Don't tell your father!" Her brother, Jim, also received the news fully and lovingly. "Of all the people in my family, he processed it and handled it better than anyone else," Elaine says. Remembering how his little sister had stuck up for him all those years ago, Jim was determined to do the same for her now. He sat down with his own young children and unflinchingly explained it to them. "This is what your aunt is," he said. "Don't let *anyone* say anything bad about her." Their sister, however, did not take it as well. "She was afraid she'd catch it or something," Noble recalls with a smile.

Having cautioned Elaine not to tell her father, Ruth broke the news to her husband herself. A big, burly, and sometimes remote man, Ron Noble was so upset at the revelation that he cried, which devastated Elaine. "It was a killer," she recalls, shaking her head. "*Such* a killer. But he came to terms with it. He came along very quickly." Ron Noble was always very protective of his girls, and perhaps more intuitive than even he would admit. After high school, when Elaine was briefly engaged to a boy, her father had taken her aside—possibly sensing that his younger daughter was not cut out for matrimony—to say, "You don't have to do this. He's kind of an ass, you know. You don't have to do any of this." Relieved, she kissed and thanked him. "But when my sister got married, all the way down the aisle he kept saying to *her,* 'You don't have to do this, you know. . . .' By the time my sister got to the altar she was so furious she wanted to kill him!" The fatherly advice that time, however, probably had more to do with his new son-in-law being a conservative Republican than anything else.

Freed from the constraints of the closet, Noble regained her center. And, like her father, she found herself drawn to community activism. "I just sort of fell into it," she says. Her love of her neighborhood, the Fenway, pulled her into the fray—lobbying for the elderly, organizing for rent control, battling with Fenway Park over its proposed use of a school parking lot for game overflow, curtailing neighborhood liquor licenses, building support for alcohol and drug centers, petitioning for better street lighting—and in one memorable escapade, even getting herself involved in the messy business of garbage collection.

"Dump It on City Hall" was the watchword for citizens fed up with Boston's inadequate refuse-removal system. With the aid of an agency in the South End and some Jesuit priests from the town of Weston, Elaine helped the neighborhood fight back by orchestrating clandestine dumps of garbage on the steps of City Hall. "My crazy Jesuit friends were in training. I called them 'Priests with Training Wheels,' " Elaine says. "They didn't want any publicity." The Catholic Church, perhaps the most potent force in Boston, was not inclined to sanction civil disobedience. "The guys were always missing their curfew," she says with a laugh. "I would drive them back to Weston, and when we'd hit their driveway, they'd go, 'Duck down, duck down,' because they didn't want to be seen with a young woman. And there is something about a priest telling you to do something, even a priest with training wheels—you do it." Years later she asked one of the Jesuits if anyone had ever seen him heading home in a driverless car. What would he have done if anyone had noticed that nobody seemed to be behind the wheel? The priest replied with a grin, "I just would have said it was a miracle." Elaine laughs raucously at the memory. "The *arrogance* of the Jesuits! But they were the ones who egged me on to do the garbage thing."

Through such interventions, Noble became known as an area problem solver. "It was all neighborhood-based," Elaine says. "A sort of working-class comrade kind of thing. Boston's a series of little villages. It's not like San Francisco. It's not like New York. It's a unique, wonderful place that is frozen in time. For better or worse. People really know each other." Indeed, it was a personal connection that helped heal a rift that had developed between the neighborhood and a popular gay bar, 1270. A large, two-story building that began life as a parking garage, it sat in the heart of the Fenway, not far from the ballpark. There was a bar up front and a dance floor in the back, with the same configuration on the second floor. Like many gay bars in those days, 1270 was more than just a local saloon; it was a cherished community center for homosexuals in the neighborhood. Noble herself was a regular there and a good friend of Bob White, its owner. But, determined to stamp out the noise and public drunkenness that had been plaguing the area, an outspoken neighborhood advocate and teetotaler named Virginia Hurley had marshaled an effort to shut down the bar. Hurley, a rotund woman with a mass of curly hair and a volatile Irish temper, had the reputation of being as tenacious as a terrier, never backing off until she got her way. She was a formidable opponent. However, having known Hurley since she first moved to the Fenway, Elaine could approach her as a friend. She was able to prove—and to convince Hurley—that the source of the problem was the liquor department in the nearby grocery store, rather than the 1270.

Noble's community interests extended naturally to the fledgling gay-rights movement. After the Stonewall uprising in 1969, pockets of militant homosexuals, for the first time in history, were demanding the inalienable rights conveyed in the Constitution; and Elaine, along with her sister "out" lesbians Gail King and Ann Maguire, began to look for activist groups to join. They investigated the Homophile Union of Boston. "But we couldn't vote in HUB," Elaine says, shaking her head. "We could be members, but couldn't vote because we were women." She also recalls a meeting at which a group of gay men and lesbians lodged protests with the Mayor's Office of Human Rights. They were told by a sympathetic City Hall spokesman, "The office understands your plight. It is important for men to be able to hold their heads high and walk proud. . . ." All the lesbians in the group could do was look at each other in wonderment—it was as if they were invisible. The lesson wasn't lost on them. "We decided we weren't going to be the brownie-baking auxiliary of any gay movement," she says, "so we joined the DOB."

The Daughters of Bilitis, the first lesbian organization in America, had been formed in San Francisco in 1955; by the early 1970's, chapters had sprung up all over the country. Gail King, though burdened with incipient multiple sclerosis, would rise to the presidency of the Boston chapter. "Gail was a force to behold," Noble says. "She's one of my heroes." King believed that reform could be best achieved by organizing the scattered pockets of the disenfranchised into one force. "You organize the oppressed when they realize they have something in common," she says. That strategy would prove invaluable to Noble in years to come.

With the Daughters, Noble found welcome solidarity until she witnessed a troubling episode of reverse discrimination. According to the bylaws, meetings of the Boston chapter of the DOB were open to anyone who wished to attend. Yet at one meeting, Noble explains, "There was a guy who was a transsexual, and the women were so unkind to him that it just freaked me out. Here's this cross-dresser who comes to a place to be with women. And I was so furious with them I said, 'Why are we being such jerks?' It really pissed me off." Noble viewed the distasteful incident as a classic case of one alienated group vying for validation by looking down on another. "It was like people looking for little scraps at the table, revealing that they didn't really feel that they deep down deserved a place at the table," she says. "It's either for all of us or for none of us."

Although she still believed in the purpose of the DOB, such incidents caused Elaine to distance herself from some of the women at the chapter. Before long, she and her friends, along with other disillusioned lesbians, decided to take a leave from the male-dominated gay revolution altogether and investigate the newly formed National Organization for Women.

Even Del Martin and Phyllis Lyon, cofounders of the DOB, had suspected that sisterhood might offer a stronger bond than sexual orientation. The issues confronting lesbians in the gay-rights movement were analogous to those feminists were raising in the straight world. As Noble said to the *Gay Community News,* "I think that some gay males can be just as piggy as straight males, in terms of viewing women as second-class citizens. And gay men can objectify other gay men just as badly as straight men do to women. When they refer to another man as a 'nelly queen,' what they're saying is that women are viewed so low that they use womanhood to put people down."

However, as Martin and Lyon had also discovered, lesbians were not exactly welcomed into NOW's bosom with open arms. Many feminists and even some lesbians were fearful that the commingling of the two factions would sink the women's movement. Elaine witnessed this fear firsthand when the National Organization for Women held its Massachusetts inaugural speakout on the Boston Common in 1970. There, in the leafy green meadow in the center of the city, a stage was set with an open mike and women in the audience were encouraged to come up and speak. Gail King wanted to address the crowd on behalf of lesbians. When she climbed the stairs, the president of the Boston chapter of NOW barred her way. "You're not getting near this mike," she snarled, and then struck King in the mouth. "She just cold-cocked her!" Elaine recalls. "And I remember picking her up and thinking, 'They're friendly, these women. . . .'" King was stunned, but would not leave the stage. Astonished by the hostility in the woman's eyes, she attempted to reason with her attacker. "You're a sister," she said. "I really do not understand why you hate me. I'm just you in another form. . . ." But the president pushed King away in full view of the disbelieving audience and stomped off the stage, declaring, "I'm not going to share this platform with you." Gail took the mike and continued addressing her and the entire audience. "We have so much in common, all the women here," she called out. "We're all oppressed." By the time she was finished, the crowd—straight and gay—was clapping and cheering.

That isolated victory notwithstanding, the initial animosity of NOW toward lesbians was a hurtful and unproductive distraction from the real challenges of the women's movement. And it was extremely difficult to combat, because the intolerance filtered directly down from the head of NOW, Betty Friedan. Friedan was convinced that lesbians were government plants sent to discredit feminism. Ivy Bottini, who came out of the closet during her tenure as New York NOW president in 1970, recalls the historic women's march down Fifth Avenue that year. From the back of a flatbed truck, Bottini was tossing out lavender armbands. "I have armbands here!" she called out. "Whoever wants to be in solidarity with our lesbian sisters, put on an armband." Women along the march route grabbed the symbolic bands and slipped them on their arms. As they turned a corner, Bottini spotted Betty Friedan. "Here, Betty!" she called, "Have an armband!" Friedan snatched the spinning purple armband as it flew toward her, then threw it in disgust to the street and stamped on it. "Well," Bottini remembers saying to herself, "I guess that lets me know where Betty stands."

Attempting to address the issue head-on, Elaine, MarDee Xifaras, a potent Democratic party activist from New Bedford, and some other NOW members had a meeting with Friedan in a private room at the Harvard Club. Before the gathering, Noble's champions told her, "You keep quiet. We're going to handle this." Away from the press, they cornered Betty, and as Elaine recalls it, basically said, "We want you to stop this because it's divisive. Elaine Noble, who's sitting right over there, is a lesbian and we care about her and we respect her and we want you to respect her." Xifaras, eight months pregnant at the time, looked at Friedan and said, "You know, Betty, there's a little lesbianism in all of us."

Friedan did not take the confrontation well. She pointed to Noble and shouted, "That woman is a CIA agent! If she's not a CIA agent, there's one close behind her!" Noble calmly replied, "Betty, the only person close behind me is a waiter who's running down the hall to see what you're yelling about!"

Elaine was deeply moved by her friends' support. "Such wonderful women—the political gals in the Democratic party and some of the more progressive Republicans—*wonderful* women." And, eventually, the volatile Friedan would come around. "She sort of recanted and tried to make amends, but she did a lot of damage," Noble maintains. "Again, it's for all of us or it's for none of us." As she said in an interview with the *Dayton Daily News,* "Women as a group have to get power. I want power not just for me, but for myself and my sisters. Women must learn to seek approval for themselves, rather than from men. You have to offend people. By your very presence, you offend them. But that's their problem, not yours."

Robert Dow, then president of the Homophile Union of Boston, said unequivocally, "Elaine is directly responsible for the stand that the National Organization for Women took on gay rights."

Still, NOW, like the DOB, didn't quite feel like home to Noble.

Consequently, when a new activist group, the Women's Political Caucus, was forming in early 1972, she and Gail King decided to get involved. Almost immediately, the membership found itself impressed with Elaine's acumen and integrity. "We had a whole bloc of votes from DOB members we had brought with us," she says, "and Gail wanted me to run as one of the WPC cochairs." Terrified by her lack of political expertise but invigorated at the prospect, Noble turned to another member of the WPC, Ann Lewis, for advice. The brilliant Lewis, a formidable heterosexual Boston politico who was later to become an adviser and chief White House spokesperson for President Bill Clinton, was a fierce proponent of women's rights, straight and gay. Lewis, who would also become a personal and political mentor to Noble, agreed with King and convinced Elaine to let herself be nominated for one of the three director's positions. Lewis felt she knew what the outcome of the election would be: "I thought I would be elected, I thought they would elect a person of color, and I thought that since Boston was a college town, the last one would be a 'graduate-granola type.' " She was right on two of the counts; she and Lena Saunders, a local black activist and police liaison, were chosen. But to her surprise and pleasure, the third was Elaine Noble. The WPC would be Noble's first real venture into electoral politics.

Being the first avowed lesbian many of the WPC members had ever met, Noble knew that she had a herculean job ahead of her—to win over the straight feminists and to coax the gay ones out of the closet so they could join the debate. Gradually, her cool intellect and warm manner brought the rank and file around, and the WPC steadily established enough clout to become an important force in the local political arena.

Energized with her success, in late 1972 Elaine made her first foray into state politics by campaigning for Ann Lewis's brother, Barney Frank, in his run for a seat in the Massachusetts Assembly. Frank won, in part because of the efforts of Noble to deliver the gay and lesbian vote. She was also making headway in her personal life. Her new lover, Kay Longcope, an attractive blonde with a colorful Texas drawl, had moved north to write for the religion section of *The Boston Globe*. Before long, the two women set up housekeeping at Noble's Marlborough Street apartment.

The one trouble spot in her life was her job at Emerson. With a friend, Diane Travis, Elaine had taped two half-hour special radio programs for WBUR-FM, a station owned by Boston University, highlighting the gay experience in Boston. The segments were so successful that the women had been contracted to produce an hour-long weekly show, called *Gayway*, featuring an eclectic mix of interviews, news, and music aimed at gay listeners. Soon, their audience extended up and down the New England coast; for some rural homosexuals, it was their only bridge to the gay community, allowing them to feel less isolated and fearful. But as Elaine became well known as *Gayway*'s unflappable moderator, her fellow faculty members at Emerson College began to regard her as "too gay." Before long, she was being passed over for promotions.

What finally brought matters to a head, Elaine recalls, was going to City Hall to obtain her first gay pride parade permit. "My student, Peter Meade [who would later become political himself, running for State Auditor], was so shocked to see a teacher from Emerson applying for a coordinating permit for a gay pride parade that he typed in Emerson College's name." When the permit with Elaine's name attached was mailed to the president of Emerson College, he was furious. "He sent me this hysterical, homophobic four-page letter," she recalls. "He was out of his mind, telling me I was jeopardizing their academic status, not to mention their tax-exempt status, and how *dare* I?" Stung, Elaine refused to back down. She would not, could not slip back into any closet. But she also knew that if she pushed too hard, her job might be in jeopardy. She went to close friend Ann Lewis, who advised, "Send the letter to Barney. He'll smooth things over." Assemblyman Frank, in turn, put in a call that calmed the irate president.

The crisis drove the fact home to Noble that homosexuals would be unable to live and speak openly unless those rights were guaranteed by law—and that the most direct way to effect that change was to become a lawmaker. "I think people consider politics when they're on the short end of the political stick," Elaine muses. "And I sort of moved up to politics when I found myself in a political situation."

Around that time, the Boston voting grids had been redivided, creating a new district, Suffolk 6, in the middle of the Fenway. The reconfiguring opened up a new seat on the legislature, and Ann Lewis, who was then an advisor to Boston mayor Kevin White, excitedly told a City

Hall group, "I've got the person to run. And she'll win." Intrigued, the roomful of men asked who. "Elaine Noble," she replied. There was silence in the room. "Isn't she gay?" one of the pols asked in a small voice. Lewis, adamant, repeated, "She's going to win." Lewis remembers more stunned silence, then a single muttered "Jesus Christ."

Undeterred by the response, Lewis now set about convincing Elaine. Inviting her to the Parker House, Lewis sat her down and unfurled a district map, pointing to the red circles around the Fenway. "They've drawn this new district for you," she declared. Although flattered, Elaine expressed doubt that the district would ever elect a gay person. Only one other openly homosexual candidate had ever been elected to public office in the United States—two years earlier, Nancy Wechsler had won a city council seat in Ann Arbor, Michigan. But Lewis insisted, "That's why you have to do it." Fortified by the fact that there was no incumbent to beat, Lewis began counting off Noble's strengths, not her liabilities. "They all know you in this area. You went to school here. You live here. You teach here. Just make a list of the things you have done in this area. They will elect you." Activist Ann Maguire, later Noble's campaign manager, concurs: "I look at other lesbians and gay men who had run at that time, like Frank Kameny in D.C.—they ran in races they never could have won. Elaine's was a small district, a liberal district with lots of students—a manageable area. If I was to pick a district, this was the kind of district I would have picked. It was winnable." Compatriot Gail King knew just how to build Noble a constituency. "I thought, 'Oh, goody, goody, goody!' " she recalls with glee. "We'd organize the whole gay community behind her—and the black community and even the Jewish community. Because Elaine would be dealing with a government that was not really friendly toward most of us. We'd get everybody organized! Team up together!" As Ann Lewis says succinctly: "She was just a natural fit for the Fenway—politically, personally, and geographically."

With all this notably strong public support—and with the encouragement of her lover, Kay—Noble seriously considered for the first time a career in electoral politics. "I thought it would do some good for people if a lesbian got elected. I thought it would be like breaking through a color line." Not everybody was as enthusiastic about the prospect, though. Weighing in among the naysayers opposing her candidacy was her father, Ron Noble. "My dad thought being a politician was like being a streetwalker—not an honest way to make a living," she told the *Boston Herald*. "You're a good schoolteacher," her father said. "Why do you want to go into a dirty business like politics?"

Still somewhat hesitant, a wary Noble was finally worn down by Lewis's dogged insistence. "She was really the architect of the campaign. It was her idea, she laid out the strategy, she was the brains behind the whole thing," Noble recalls. "She had run Barney's campaign, brilliantly. She loves politics. Maybe even more than Barney."

In the waning months of 1973, Noble met with friends and advisors, attempting to come up with a skeleton campaign committee. Friend Ann Maguire, a producer and moderator on *Gayway* and co-owner of the gay and lesbian bar Somewhere, was approached to be campaign manager. "There weren't too many people in the community in those days who were 'out' and doing things," recalls Maguire. "I thought it took a lot of courage for Elaine to run, because you are going from what you think is 'out' to *'out'*! A lot of us are 'out'—maybe we talk to our friends or our parents but we don't tell the world. It was a giant step for the community. So when she asked me to be her campaign manager, I said yes." Joe Martin, a local activist and later an aide to Barney Frank in the U.S. House of Representatives in the 1980's, was chosen to be media director. Neither Martin nor Maguire had ever conducted a political campaign before, but that fact didn't faze Noble. "No one in my campaign was politically astute and most of them had never been in any other campaign," Noble admitted to *The Advocate*. "We went to the library and took out books on how to run a campaign."

On a bitterly cold Saturday afternoon, January 25, 1974, nearly three hundred people filled Bob White's 1270 bar for what was ostensibly a thirtieth birthday bash for Elaine Noble. From three to seven P.M., drinks and a light buffet were served and a popular women's band, Whitch, performed. Then Assemblyman Barney Frank, who represented the heavily gay Beacon Hill district, introduced the radiant candidate-to-be. The boisterous crowd quieted when Noble rose to speak, then roared its approval when she unofficially announced her candidacy. She vowed she would not be a one-issue candidate. She was running for all her constituents in the Fenway—the students, the elderly, the immigrants, the transients, the disenfranchised, and, yes, the gays.

Joe Martin remembers the moment vividly as "the first time the community came together to celebrate the prospects of this woman getting elected. It was very exciting. It electrified the gay community in Boston, or certainly a large part of it, in a way that nothing I had seen until then had." He adds with a smile, "We can look back on it now and say it wasn't such a big deal. But it *was* a big deal."

In the months before the June deadline for filing candidacy papers for the September primary, Elaine was busy with a myriad of other concerns. She was named to the Governor's Commission on the Status of Women and sat on the boards of both the Homophile Community Health Service of Boston and the ACLU. In addition to teaching her class at Emerson, she finished a second master's degree, in education, at Harvard. And most importantly, she took a front-row position in the volatile battle Boston was having trying to desegregate its schools.

Federal judge W. Arthur Garrity, Jr., had ruled that the Boston School Committee was in violation of the Fourteenth Amendment with its nonintegrated school system. Blacks and whites, he argued, were entitled under the law to the same quality of education. He ordered that buses redistribute the children to equalize the level of learning.

The busing decision polarized the city, setting neighborhood against neighborhood in violent confrontations that made front-page headlines and the TV nightly news. Suddenly, to the rest of the country, the Boston of the early 1970's looked disturbingly like Selma, Alabama, in the early 1960's. The television screens were crowded with images of screaming, hate-filled faces, and of rocks and beer cans being hurled at black students bused to white schools. The people from lower-working-class South Boston, dubbed "Southies," were especially vitriolic. Buses were set on fire, innocent children were terrorized, and gunplay filled the streets.

Sensitive to the issue from her own childhood experience of school integration in Pennsylvania, and as one who had benefited greatly from the experience, Elaine came down firmly on the side of desegregation. Investigating the issue in Boston, she found that the black students who had already participated in Metco—a voluntary busing program that shipped urbanites to affluent suburban schools—had benefited greatly.

Furthermore, "When you looked at the reading averages before busing, the reading averages and rate of going off to college were higher in the black community than they were in the white community," she explains, "so there was something for the white kids to gain. But the powers that be couldn't admit that. So they created this incredible mess—a dirty, filthy little lie—that somehow black kids, black being synonymous with change, would mean less for the white kids. When in fact, what we found was just the *opposite*. But a lot of people were making a lot of money on busing. This one had the bus contract, this one had the milk contract, the cops were making a lot of money on overtime. It was a horrible time—the seams of Boston's old garment really came loose."

Noble did her best to try to help defuse the powder keg. She even positioned many of her campaign workers at the bus stops to ensure that the children got on and off the buses safely. "I told the volunteers that if they didn't want to do it, they didn't have to," Elaine says, "but, God bless them, they were there." Ann Lewis recalls seeing Noble speak before a group of angry parents during an open meeting on busing. The gathering was not only rowdy, but getting dangerous. Threats flew, and several people were close to throwing punches. Elaine expertly calmed the crowd, urging for more communication and less confrontation. Impressed, Lewis says, "She single-handedly defused an ugly situation." She left the meeting reassured that Noble had the moxie to be in electoral politics.

Elaine also helped form the Citywide Education Coalition, a group of parents, teachers, and former teachers who went out every morning as a kind of safety net, armed with coffee, to calm irate mothers from the South End who did not want their children bused to black schools. "They'd yell at us, scream at us. They didn't know what was going on," Elaine says, laying much of the blame for the ignorance at the feet of the Catholic Church. "There was no leadership from the predominant religious force in the city," Noble says. "If Cardinal Cushing had been alive during busing, we would not have had the problems that we had." The current cardinal, Humberto Medieros, was of Portuguese descent, not Irish, so the people in South Boston would not listen to him—even deriding him, because of his ethnicity, as "the nigger priest." At a loss after months of attempting to defuse the explosive situation, he said publicly that he was doomed to failure because he could not discipline the people in South Boston. "All the Southies went nuts and made him apologize," Elaine recalls. "I can't tell you how I felt when I had to hear the cardinal apologize. He had to apologize for telling the *truth*. I knew we were in terrible trouble. If they drove this poor Portuguese cardinal to his knees, imagine what they'd do to the children! It was a profound moment for me."

The rancor escalated almost daily as the city foundered. Elaine found herself facing the brunt of it one terrifying day as she stood amid a small group outside Roslindale High School and a fifteen-year-old boy pointed a loaded rifle down at her. "I froze," Elaine recalls. "It was the first time in my life when fear immobilized me." Directly across the street from the school, his mother leaned on a fence in her front yard as the boy aimed the gun out of an upstairs window. "It was so surreal. Everyone ducked under the squad car, and it was like my eyes were telescopes and they zoomed right into his eyes and I remember thinking, 'Please don't do it. Please don't do it.' I couldn't even speak." At that point, Joe Jordan, then the Assistant Police Commissioner, pulled up on the sidewalk. "All of you, get in the car!" he shouted to the gathering. Gratefully, they followed his directive. Just then, a policeman on the beat walked down the street, saw the armed boy, and called up to the window, "Put that away." And the boy did. "I had never known terror like that before," Noble admits. "I was frozen in my spot. You see things like that in the movies and you yell, 'Run, fool, run!' But I stood there. I could not move."

Still, the episode would not dissuade her from her vocal public stance. Later, in a particularly chilling but telling exchange, she had a quiet moment with Larry Quailley, a head of the Citywide Education Coalition, who was retiring. As they stood there looking out of a window in City Hall over the expanse of a shattered Boston, Elaine asked him what was going to happen to all the children of busing. Quailley shook his head and answered sadly, "We have to write them off." Dire, hopeless predictions like that made her more determined than ever to win her seat in the House. She knew she had to be on the inside to facilitate lasting change.

So on June 25, 1974, just days before the deadline, Elaine filed the required primary nomination papers at the statehouse. She would be one of five candidates seeking the Democratic nomination in September.

Noble headquarters, in the heart of the Fenway district at 78 Queensbury Street, was a simple storefront with a long, narrow room running the length of the building. It was to be a truly grassroots campaign, managed by a hodgepodge of committed volunteers—gay, straight, male, female, young, and old. "Given who Elaine was and the fact she was running, she didn't have to do much to draw a lot of attention," Joe Martin says. "My sense was that the excitement that she generated would be enough to carry her through. I thought she had a clear shot at it. I believed that in my gut from the start." Donations came in little increments, most less than fifteen dollars. Small but effective fund-raisers were planned, such as an all-night movie extravaganza at the Kenmore Cinema, where *Women in Love* and *Fortune and Men's Eyes* were screened; a gay dance at the Charles Street Meetinghouse where the donation was a mere two dollars; and a neighborhood cleanup that was organized to show concern for the area as well as support for Noble's campaign. Even an "Elaine Noble Design-A-Campaign-Button" contest was announced. The winner designed a button featuring Elaine's name in the form of a fluttering flag and received a home-cooked gourmet meal prepared by the candidate herself. Martin remembers collecting signatures in Back Bay and having total strangers come up to him, introducing themselves and asking how they could help. The gay community was especially engaged. "The historical factor was a big thing for the gay people who worked for her," he says. "I don't know how much it really meant to the greater public, but it certainly meant a lot to us. It certainly helped fuel her with volunteers and with campaign funds from the gay community." By the end of the campaign, Noble was to raise nearly thirteen thousand dollars, an impressive sum for such a small district.

Noble's support from the gay community was hugely enthusiastic. Among others, Gail King, now stiffened with MS, stumped furiously for her friend. "I got as many lesbians as I could to realize that we all had something in common with this brave, gutsy lady. We had so many things to gain politically by supporting her." In a particularly memorable occasion she was invited to speak at a local synagogue as an open lesbian. "God has us all as His children whether we are straight or gay," she said to the congregation. Then, deftly swerving to the practical, she said, "We all have civil rights. We'll help you with your civil rights, you'll help us with our civil rights." She then got them all to link hands. "We joined because we had the same oppressors."

According to Ann Maguire, "Most of the fund-raising came from gay people who weren't 'out-out.' But Elaine emphatically insisted that she was more than just a gay candidate. With Elaine, we focused on 'Yes, I happen to be a lesbian, but this is why I'm running . . .' We focused on the issues." The platform was fundamental in thrust:

1. *Decent Housing*—with Noble supporting rent control and the development of low- and moderate-income housing.
2. *Neighborhood Security*—with better lighting and stronger preventative law enforcement.
3. *Better Schools*—a passion for Noble as a teacher and as an ardent proponent of desegregation.
4. *Better Services*—with improved transit, parking conditions, and garbage removal.
5. *Health Care*—with a strong pro-choice stance.
6. *People's Rights*—a centerpiece of the platform.

Suffolk 6, a back-end section culled from Barney Frank's larger district, was just south of the Charles River and spanned Massachusetts Avenue, over to Hereford Street, and through the Upper Back Bay to Huntington Avenue. "It was not a rich or affluent district," Noble says. "Very diverse—a lot of students, a lot of poor people. A lot of nationalities, a lot of old people. Some were in the country illegally—living twenty in one room." According to the information available at the time, the Fenway contained twenty-four nationalities and was 84 percent white (including Spanish speakers), 16 percent black, Indian, and Asian, 57 percent women, and over 73 percent single persons living alone. Interestingly enough, the gay community, mostly college students, was not large—less than 10 percent. Determined to make good on her announcement back at the 1270 bar, although gay issues were always part of the agenda, Elaine Noble would not be a one-issue candidate.

To win the primary, Noble had to establish credibility with the straight citizens of the Fenway—particularly with the senior citizens. One of the first seniors to join the cause was an influential neighborhood Irishwoman, Mrs. Mullen, whose husband had worked for years as the maître d' at the Ritz Hotel. "I don't even remember her first name," Elaine says. "She was just 'Mrs. Mullen' to everyone." A plucky and irascible character who approved of Elaine's activist efforts in the Fenway, she arranged for her daughter Mary to host a "get to know the candidate" tea in her home. Then neighborhood watchdog Virginia Hurley, with whom Noble had resolved the 1270 and market clash back in the late sixties, joined the camp. Hurley's endorsement was crucial, according to Joe Martin: "Virginia was a longtime resident of the Fenway. She had ties, it seemed, to everyone and ties to the mayor's office. She had a reputation for being a persistent activist and was trusted by the old people in the neighborhood."

That senior support proved vital later in the campaign itself, when one of Elaine's opponents got a Catholic priest to sponsor an edict that stated that anybody who worked or voted for Noble would be excommunicated. In a heavily Roman Catholic town, "that is a pretty heavy-duty thing to have circulated two weeks before the election," Noble notes. Father Tom Oddo, a progressive priest and friend to the gay community, immediately came to the rescue. He personally handwrote a letter saying what a fine person Elaine was and gave it to the maven of Newbury Street, Mrs. Mullen. Armed with a large pocketbook, Mrs. Mullen canvassed the neighborhood in her sensible shoes, making sure everyone saw the letter. She even tracked down the priest who had instigated the excommunication edict; collaring him on Commonwealth Avenue, she stuck Father Oddo's missive directly in his face. "What do you think of this, Father?" she asked in her lilting brogue. Then, to twist the knife a bit, she added mischievously, "When we first came over from County Cork, we used to sleep six or seven lassies in the bed! What do you think of *that*, Father?"

The senior citizen bloc began leaning heavily toward Noble, which confounded many of the political pundits—but not Ann Lewis. "The seniors were wise enough not to care about her sexual orientation," she says. "It just wasn't an issue." Joe Martin agrees. "People just warmed up to Elaine," he says. "That was her strength. She ran for that election with a determination to win and she worked her butt off. She got in touch with as many people as she could in that district and built her base up as solidly as she could."

Eventually, Elaine's mother, Ruth, came up from Pennsylvania to help her daughter's campaign. Tentative and deferring to others at first, before long Mrs. Noble was up giving speeches on behalf of her daughter. "I was so proud of her," Elaine says now, still awed, "and it was very helpful. It made me less of a monster."

As the September primary approached, Elaine's competition began to thin. Three of the five candidates—Robert Kahn, a public relations consultant, Victor Themo, who claimed to be the only candidate born and raised in the Fenway, and William Foley, who was currently on trial for prostitution-related charges—failed to muster any real momentum. The field narrowed to Noble and Helene Johnson, a community activist. Ann Lewis, perhaps in an attempt to defuse the gay-versus-straight aspect of the race, commented to the press, "For the first time, the degree to which a candidate has acted on her feminist principles becomes a reason for choice in the political arena." Noble notes in retrospect, "Helene was to be the more acceptable neighborhood candidate, straight, with a liberal Back Bay tie-in." But Joe Martin was not particularly impressed or particularly worried. "I had seen Helene speak a few times and I didn't think she had the dynamic pull and the passion or perseverance of Elaine." Noble recalls rallies where she and the tall, thin, preppy-ish Johnson occupied the same stage. "She would always stand up with her two daughters. It drove me crazy." Noble chuckles at the memory. "So I would go to candidates' night and she would introduce her daughters and I would introduce my dog, Dylan. And the audience would laugh like hell."

September 10 dawned rainy and miserable. Noble's staff worked frantically, ferrying the elderly to the polls and walking the neighborhoods in the driving rain to get out the vote. Once the polls closed, they all gathered, wet and jittery, in the campaign office on Queensbury Street to wait for the returns. "Someone was filling out the numbers on the chalk board—it might have been Ann Maguire—and as the numbers were looking better and better, the excitement was reaching a fever pitch," Martin recalls. "When we knew, when we were over the top, the room was full of screams and hollers. And the calls started coming in from the press. There was this sleazy character, William Foley, a perennial candidate who was always jumping into the races just before the primary. It came over the AP wire and we got a copy from a Thai paper that went, 'LESBIAN DEFEATS PIMP IN BOSTON LEG-ISLATIVE RACE.' It made it seem like it was a district from hell! We got clips from newspapers around the world. That was another reminder for me of the importance of the race." In the end, Elaine Noble carried every precinct in the Suffolk 6 district, winning a 60 percent majority over the four other candidates.

The primary night victory party spilled out onto the street and over to 1270, the site of Elaine's announcement nearly eight months earlier. It seemed only fitting; Bob White, besides being a dear friend, had been one of the first people to give money to the campaign. Staffers, volunteers, supporters, and neighborhood residents joined in the impromptu festivities. Even Ruth Noble was there, beaming with motherly pride. "We got separated, but I always made sure someone was with her," Elaine remembers. All of a sudden, a voice from up front yelled out, "Hey, everybody! Stand up for Elaine Noble's mother!" Before a concerned Elaine could intercede, a confident Ruth Noble walked up to the microphone, and said to the room, "I want to thank you all for being here for my daughter." The crowd applauded warmly. "It was so sweet," Elaine says, still moved at the recollection. "She really rose to the occasion."

When the opposing camp called to concede, Noble expressed a firm desire to work with Johnson's supporters on neighborhood issues in the future. As she told her own jubilant crowd, the race was "first a victory for the neighborhood, and secondly, for people's rights." On the gay issue, she later told the press, "The real story is not that I may be the first gay to win a primary; but I'm the first one to have admitted it." The remark may have been a veiled reference to her friend and supporter, the still-closeted Barney Frank. Noble recalls sitting with mentor Ann Lewis back before she committed to running and asking her, "What's with Barney?" Ann replied, "My mother and I think he's gay. And your campaign will help him in a way." Frank, a popular liberal legislator who had unsuccessfully introduced several gay-friendly bills in the statehouse, was deeply closeted. He would not come out until 1987, when he was a member of the U.S. House of Representatives, and from then on would operate effectively as an openly homosexual senior congressman.

Noble's real test—the general election, to be held on November 5—now loomed large. Her opponent was Assistant District Attorney Joseph Cimino, thirty-one, running as an independent. Cimino, a handsome man fond of Italian suits and vivid ties, was also co-owner of a popular disco in Back Bay, Daisy Buchanan's. "He owned a lot of property and knew a lot of property owners," remembers Ann Maguire. "And everybody who was a Republican, although there weren't that many, backed him. We felt he was going to be a formidable candidate." Cimino even won the endorsement of Democratic Mayor Kevin White. Party loyalty notwithstanding, White was apparently hesitant to back an openly lesbian politician—even if the chief strategist of that politician was his own trusted aide, Ann Lewis.

Cimino had sworn that his campaign would be issue-oriented, rather than anti-gay. But then one of his backers, well-known politico Patrick (Sonny) McDonough, a relic from the "last hurrah" school of politics and a former assemblyman who was on the Governor's Council, held a press conference to announce that if Elaine Noble were elected, he would demand that the Governor's Council deny her seating because of her lesbianism. Nancy Gertner, Noble's attorney, held her own press conference in response, listing for the media all the gay organizations that would share in the spoils Noble would win when she sued Sonny McDonough for violating her civil rights. "They bought it, and Sonny backed off a bit," Elaine says. "Such a brilliant move on Nancy's part!"

As Elaine recalls, clearly "the gay issue was a major one. Probably at every campaign stop, someone would bring it up. And I'd say, 'When you wanted that streetlight and I went to City Hall and I got this paved or did that . . . did my lesbianism interfere with getting that streetlight? If you think it did, then don't vote for me. But if you can find your way clear to vote for me, then I would be very proud to represent you.' What I was basically doing was saying I could do the job and I could do a lot of good for people by being open about my gayness."

As election day drew near, Ann Lewis met some influential politicians in City Hall, one of whom took her aside to say, "I really don't think Noble is, you know, 'that way.' " Lewis just smiled, shrugged, and said, "You can't prove it by me. I just know what she tells me." Then she walked away chuckling, knowing that her friend must be on the road to victory. "They couldn't admit that a lesbian could possibly win!"

Then, only days before the election, the *Gay Community News* got a scoop:

> Cimino, Independent candidate for State Representative running against Elaine Noble, approached Democratic gubernatorial candidate Michael Dukakis recently, and reportedly offered to donate $1,000 to the Dukakis campaign if he would endorse Cimino over Noble. The conversation, according to a little bug, went something like this:
>
> "But don't you know she's a lesbian?" said Cimino.
>
> "Did she win the primary fair and square?" asked Mike.
>
> "Yes."
>
> "Well," Dukakis said, "if that's the only thing you have against her, then you have no business running."
>
> Dukakis obviously declined the offer and is supporting the Democratic nominee, Elaine Noble.

Cimino immediately took out a full-page political advertisement in the *Boston Ledger* to deny the story, labeling it a "cheap smear," and then threatened to sue the *Gay Community News* for libel. Unfortunately for Cimino, the Dukakis headquarters confirmed the same day that the offer had indeed been made and refused, and that Dukakis unequivocally supported Noble. Yet Noble harbors no animosity toward Cimino. "He had some class. He was a Sonny McDonough sort of guy—you fight like hell and then afterward you move on. But he also made a strategic error. . . . They used my lesbianism in a way—it was like, 'look at the green horse.' They kept the lesbianism issue going. What it did was create a sympathy factor. They thought it would scare the elderly, but what it did was piss them off. It backfired."

Coming down to the wire, a series of worrisome harassments bedeviled Noble and her staff. Obscene phone calls began coming in, both to Elaine's home on Marlborough Street and to headquarters, along with bomb scares and anonymous threats. Her apartment was broken into twice. The windows of her car, a nondescript Chevrolet Vega, were smashed; sugar was poured into the gas tank. Once, someone surreptitiously loosened the lug nuts on one of the wheels and then replaced the hubcap. Luckily, Noble heard the rattling and pulled off the road before the tire could separate from the axle. Needless to say, the episodes unnerved her: "I remember lying awake and thinking, 'What have I done? This is so crazy! Who *lives* in this world?' " Her partner, who had encouraged Elaine's political run, did her best to weather the storm too, but even as a seasoned journalist, Kay Longcope could not help but find the incidents very frightening.

The animosity and vandalism were not directed only at the candidate. Ann Maguire recalls, "I never saw anything like it. These crazy people would drive around all night from pay phone to pay phone and make threatening phone calls. The first message I got from them was, 'Ann Maguire. You don't know who we are, but we just air-conditioned your car.' "

Concerned, Maguire ran outside to find her automobile's windows smashed.

Finally, election day came. By early afternoon, the staff grew very concerned because the senior citizens in Noble's camp, most of whom did not drive, were not calling campaign headquarters for rides to the polls. Without the elderly, the candidate could not win. "I thought I had lost the election," Noble says, "until my precinct workers came in and told me that the seniors were taking rides from Cimino! They were saying, 'Tell her we're taking rides from him. Save her gas!' "

When the polls closed on November 5, the Democrats had succeeded in a near sweep. Not only had Dukakis been elected governor, but in the House, they would enjoy an unprecedented five-to-one majority over the Republicans. And joining them would be Elaine Noble, who had decisively beaten Joseph Cimino 1,730 to 1,201, again winning every precinct.

Now it wasn't just the newspapers calling. Reporters from all the major media jammed into Noble's headquarters. "ABC, CBS, NBC, *Time* magazine, they were all there," Ann Maguire recalls. With the cameras rolling, the elated Maguire got up before the crowd to introduce Noble, yelling, "All right, all you faggots and dykes. Here is Nixon's nightmare come true!" Barney Frank told *The New York Times,*

"She's going to walk around this place [the statehouse] breaking stereo-types by just her own style and intelligence. . . . You could not have a better individual to be the first openly gay person in office." The most poignant congratulatory message of the evening came from Elaine's fa-ther, who was too debilitated by cancer to travel from Pennsylvania. When he called, Elaine asked how he had known she had won. Ron Noble said simply, "I would expect nothing less."

Then, the next morning, a group of Elaine's elderly supporters, armed with wide smiles, called on her at the campaign office. Sur-prised, Elaine asked why they were up so early. The leader replied, "We came over to thank you." Touched, Elaine said, "Thank me for what? I should thank you!" And the women said, "Thank you for letting us be this big." Elaine swallowed back tears.

Nationwide, the gay community was elated by Noble's win, hailing her as a conquering hero. Unfortunately, the exultation had a flip side: As her fame grew, the anonymous harassment intensified; her offices were burglarized and five hundred dollars' worth of Christmas toys, destined for poor children in the Fenway, were stolen. Gay organiza-tions came under attack as well. On December 17, the offices of the Daughters of Bilitis, the Homophile Union of Boston, and the *Gay Community News* were all hit with break-ins.

On New Year's Day, 1975, Noble would be sworn in. Bob White rented a bus from the Gray Line and blocked out the "r" so that the ve-hicle was named "Gay Line." He picked up a small group of gay peo-ple who had met in front of his bar, then traversed the Fenway, gathering elderly supporters until the bus was full. Finally, he picked up the representative-elect, Elaine Noble. When they reached Beacon Hill, as the jubilant riders exited from the bus, Elaine looked up to the state-house windows and noticed faces pressed against the panes. Once in-side, she spotted people peeking out of doorways. Asking a court officer about them, she learned that a rumor had gone through the halls that Noble was bringing a busload of "faggots and queers" to the swearing-in ceremony—and everyone was curious to see what they looked like. "Here they were," Elaine says, laughing. "They were Rus-sian, they were Polish, they were Irish, they were over *sixty-five!* People were like, 'Is that one? Are those real old ladies or faggots dressed in drag?' It was very funny."

Just before noon, Noble was officially sworn into the Massachusetts State Legislature by the newly elected governor, Michael Dukakis. Her nervousness was supplanted by the excitement of seeing her elderly supporters in the gallery above her beaming with pride. "They finally had someone to represent them," she remembers. "It was very moving." She didn't feel like a figurehead for the gay and lesbian community. It was the people of Fenway who had elected her; they were the ones to whom she owed her allegiance. "It wasn't until the first four-o'clock-in-the-morning phone call from some poor, lost gay soul in South Carolina or somewhere that made me realize I was some gay people's only champion." That call came within days of her swearing-in, and they continued through her entire stay in office. But Noble refused to get an unlisted number. "I felt it was all part of the responsibility of being an elected official. You had to be there for people. Even if it was in the middle of the night, when people felt—I don't know—less afraid and more determined."

At the Inaugural Gala dinner held on January 11 in the elegant rococo ballroom of the Somerset Hotel, three hundred invited guests—from neighbors to gay activists to Noble's beloved senior supporters—toasted the history that the election had made and the groundbreaking yet to be done. Alongside the politicians attending was a particular favorite of Noble's—Joe Jordan, now Police Superintendent-in-Chief. Not only was he the man who had intervened in the terrifying busing incident with the boy and the rifle the year before, but he had known Elaine since back in the days when he was a foot patrolman in the Fenway and she was a college student. "I was eighteen or nineteen and he'd yell up and tell me my record player was too loud," Noble recalls. Following the dinner, Elaine rose to speak of the importance of committing to the political system and encouraged those present to become involved in community affairs. When the speeches were done, the all-woman rock band Lilith played and the theme of the evening—togetherness—was borne out by dancing until dawn. Scattered incidents of same-sex dancing barely raised an eyebrow, even among the elderly. "It was no big deal. They *knew* me. It wasn't anything new. And besides," Noble adds with a grin, "they were seniors. Most didn't stay past midnight."

Noble moved into her statehouse office with a modest staff comprised of Linda Lachman, her chief aide, and Linda's assistants, two eager and competent students, Linda Ray, a pre-law student in charge of legislative research, and Candy Frank, an Emerson student in charge of public relations. Elaine chose to be a member of the Education Committee, whose office was a bustling, congested, and often cacophonous workplace shared by the other committee members and their staffs. In their corner of the office, Elaine hung a sign above her desk: "Trust in God—She Will Provide."

And God would indeed have to provide, considering the status of the Education Committee, which was not a very popular place to be. But Elaine was never one to shy away from controversy. "People were *leaping* off of it," she recalls. "This was the committee that brought desegregation and 766." Chapter 766 was a law concerning the education of children with special needs. Considered very liberal and far-reaching, it had been blamed for decreasing overall quality of schools because of its expensive and energy-demanding agenda. Barney Frank tried to steer her away from the beleaguered committee, suggesting, "Why don't you get Transportation or something?" Noble, however, was adamant. "I'm an educator," she told him. "That's where I should be." From the beginning, she thought it wise to face her challenges head-on. She says today, "I felt that's what politics was about."

Her first few days in the House were an eye-opening initiation. "It was bizarre," Noble says. "Here were all these predominantly white males freaking out over this little lesbian. If I had a nickel for every time they said to me that I was the first lesbian they'd ever met. And I would say to them, 'No, I'm not the first one you ever met. I'm probably the only one that ever *admitted* it, but I'm not the first one you ever met.' Then I would have to go through the litany of 'You look so normal.' And 'You don't hate men.' It was like being the first black person in an all-white school." Her gayness, however, did not deter some pols from engaging in the occasional proposition. One colleague came right out and asked Noble if she "fooled around." Recounting the episode to *The Advocate,* she stared the man down, telling him, "Representative, if you really feel that is an appropriate question to ask me, then I will go straight to the press room and quote you on that." The man withdrew. Noble was clearly in uncharted waters. "It was an enlightening experience," she says.

The first major issue that the legislature would vote on was a controversial referendum concerning the Governor's Council. The new Democratic governor, Michael Dukakis, was intent upon abolishing the council, which approved pardons and judgeships. Elaine's old nemesis, Sonny McDonough, who had vowed to use the council to prevent her from holding office, now had to come to Noble to ask for her vote to keep it alive. "It was so close," Elaine recalls, "one or two votes." McDonough approached her saying, "I know we probably have bad blood, but . . ." Elaine looked him in the eye. "You know, Mr. McD, you ran a candidate against me," she said flatly. "I can't vote for you. But I do want to get along with you and all of your friends here. So this is what I'm going to do for you: I'm going to vote against you, but this is my friend Peter McCarthy; he's going to vote for you. So he cancels my vote out. And I have another gift for you—" and she called up another representative who pledged McDonough his vote. Impressed and grateful, McDonough said, "I want you to know, the door swings both ways." The news of Noble's solution spread through the House in record time, establishing her as a canny negotiator. "It was a great PR bit for me; I wasn't a monster, I wasn't a narrow-minded liberal, I was someone who understood what was going on there. So we started from scratch, me and Sonny."

In fact, against all odds, the two became friends. When Sonny was in Massachusetts General Hospital a few months later, she telephoned him and found him desperate for gossip. "Come on over here," he pleaded, "I want to hear what's going on!" Noble jokingly replied, "What if someone finds me at midnight in your room?" He gruffly countered, "I'll tell 'em you're my night nurse. Get the hell over here!"

Every freshman representative had to endure the ritual of hazing, and Elaine was no exception. "Even though the Sonny McDonough incident got me a lot of clout—maybe she's not so crazy, maybe she's not so bad—I still got probably two or three times the usual hazing," she recalls. "Someone put shit in my desk, there were a lot of fake constituent calls, that kind of stuff. A lot of asshole behavior. They were jerks—but I'd give it right back to them. One guy was very obnoxious and I got someone to go into the men's room and write, '—— GIVES GOOD HEAD.' And he got hysterical. He flew into the Speaker's office and demanded that someone be sent in there to scrub the wall off."

David Bartley, the Speaker, calmly informed the representative that if he was so upset about the scribbling, he should go in the men's room with a bucket and take it off himself. "I'll get around to it," Bartley said, "but it's not a priority." Noble readily admits that such behavior was border-line adolescent, but it served a purpose. "It showed people that I had moxie," she says. "It showed them that I would strike back."

As an elected official, Elaine grew even more outspoken in her sup-port of desegregation and made a practice of riding to school with the black children each morning before she went to work at the statehouse. When she ushered them from the bus, she was always startled by the hatred on the faces of the waiting white adults. Many of them drunk, they would hurl beer cans and epithets. "They hated me all the more because I looked like them," she says. "I looked Irish. Thank God they didn't know I was also Jewish!" She found no less opposition on the floor of the statehouse, for most of her colleagues were against forced busing. "Usually party members stand together," Elaine says, "but I veered from the pack." And some even tried to make her pay for it—like the time Representative Dickie Finnigan (D-Dorchester), speaking of a nonbusing-related issue, told the House, "This is a Noble bill. She supports busing. Let's give Noble a message and help us defeat this bill." Ironically, when Finnigan lost his seat due to redistricting, it was Noble he came to for help. Knowing she had the ear of the mayor, Kevin White, he asked if she would put in a good word for a job. "It was a tough thing for him to do, but he knew I had a soft heart. So I let by-gones be bygones and went to Kevin." The mayor, who had also taken a beating because of his support of busing, was incredulous. "Look, he has a wife and five kids," Noble said. "He needs a job." "He not only kicked the crap out of you," White exclaimed, "he kicked the crap out of me!" But Noble was insistent. "Mr. Mayor," she said, "it's a new day." White threw up his hands. "All right, I'll give him a job because you asked me. But I'm not making it permanent!"

In the midst of Noble's political baptism by fire, her personal life was foundering. Her relationship with Kay Longcope had been unraveling ever since the election campaign pressures began; then Kay committed what Elaine felt was an inexcusable breach of trust. Noble's lawyer, Nancy Gertner, represented the fugitive Susan Saxe, an antiwar radical lesbian accused of a bank robbery during which a policeman was killed. The FBI had put out a dragnet for Saxe and was harassing the lesbian community for information. Longcope was present at a confidential meeting about the situation, but, reporter that she was, she could not resist writing it up for the *Globe*. Elaine, who felt betrayed, was furious. "We broke up over this. Kay didn't get it for a real long time. She had no boundaries." Not long after their split, Elaine caught the eye of Rita Mae Brown, the Southern novelist famous for her 1973 breakthrough lesbian novel, *Rubyfruit Jungle*. Brown expressed interest in meeting the controversial assemblywoman from Massachusetts, and after encountering each other at a political dinner in New York, the two became romantically involved. Rita Mae would be there when the terrain really got rough.

Nearing the end of February 1975, Noble got the chance to fight for the gay-rights initiatives that had originally drawn her into politics. Several bills affecting the gay community were before committees that would decide whether to submit them to the House for a full vote. House Bill 2944, repealing the prohibitions of fornication, lascivious cohabitation, sodomy, and unnatural and lascivious acts—the punitive laws that criminalized homosexuality—was being introduced in committee for the fifth consecutive year. House Bill 2849, prohibiting state civil service job discrimination on the basis of sexual orientation, was being strongly promoted by Barney Frank, who told his fellow legislators that passing this bill would provide "a chance to expiate our sins at the Salem witch trials." He ended his plea by saying, "What conceivable reason could anyone have for saying to your fellow citizens, 'No, you can't work, you can't live where you want'? I cannot understand how any member of the legislature in 1975 wants to make that statement." Although one oblivious representative, Andrew Card (R-Holbrook) objected, saying, "I wonder where the misconception comes from that gays are discriminated against?" both bills, with some revisions, were sent to the House.

When the amended bill banning discrimination against gays in public employment, now relabeled House Bill 5868, was brought before the full legislature, Elaine, in her maiden speech, introduced it to the Assembly. Rising, she acknowledged the rows of gays in the gallery behind her, saying, "I brought my relatives with me today." Then she turned to her colleagues. "It is with great pride," she said, "that I stand before you to discuss two personal principles of mine: public service and personal freedom. Only you can put those principles into action." Elaine went on to describe the plight of homosexuals in America, the discriminations that are endured, the rights that are denied. Her voice rising, she ended by warning her colleagues, "Thousands are watching this bill today." When she finished speaking, many members of the House rose from their seats to accord her a long, standing ovation.

The House debate, however, quickly grew ugly. Democrat William A. Connell of Weymouth, no friend to the gay community, engaged in a startling harangue on the floor, crying that the bill would "give these people the right to recruit!" He jabbed at the air, shouting, "These people are predatory! These lesbians, these faggots and queers, are after your sons and daughters!!" When Speaker Bartley reprimanded him, Democrat Thomas Lopes of New Bedford rose to agree with Connell. "These people are like the emotionally disturbed and mentally retarded," he claimed. "They should not be given such rights. This bill would water down civil rights for all of us." Heartened by Lopes's support, Connell circulated an inflammatory letter in an all-out attempt to kill the bill:

With due regard to chivalry, I doubt that we should do this just to accommodate an aggressive and persuasive lesbian-legislator. The motivation of those who want this needless "special" legislation comes from a desire to give the impression to the citizens of the Commonwealth that the homosexual/lesbian lifestyle has the approval of the Massachusetts legislature!

Incensed, Republican state senator Robert A. Hall fired off a reply:

I find your memo on the gay-rights bill, as well as your reported comments on the House floor, both personally repulsive and degrading to the already shabby image of the Legislature . . . I also note your direct reference to Rep. Noble, and "due regard to chivalry." The code of chivalry included courage, courtesy, protection, and aid for the weak and unfortunate clearly beyond your "due regard" . . . While it is true that I find Rep. Noble's professed sexual attraction personally very unappealing, it is both private and far less distasteful than your lack of common decency toward a colleague. You need not worry about being like the Representative, for you are far from Noble in most respects. I found her an intelligent, warm, compassionate human being.

Nonetheless, the antidiscrimination bill was defeated.

At the end of March, Elaine attended the New England Gay Conference in Provincetown, where she spoke of community unity and political involvement. "We can never become a political power without getting rid of self-hate," she said. Soon she had a reason to invoke that principle on behalf of the Speaker of the Minnesota state legislature, Allan Spear. Spear had written to Noble just after her election and, inspired by her courage, decided to come out himself. They then met at a gay conference in Ann Arbor, Michigan, where, as Noble told *The Boston Phoenix,* "Allan, who has only been out now for a couple of months, got up to speak and it was so apparent that he was having difficulty. He was saying the same sort of things I would have said, but they started hissing him because he said something like, 'I don't mind wearing a shirt and tie to go to work.' Meaning working within the system. For anyone to get booed and hissed by an entire auditorium full of people is a real freak-out. They were just crushing this man who was being honest and up front with them just because he doesn't look groovy. I went up and grabbed the microphone and I said, 'You hiss me, you fuckers, and you'll get this up your ass!' I thought I was in for boos, but instead they started applauding." She ended her time at the podium pleading once again for unity. She still shakes her head sadly at the episode. "It was this meanness that I never understood in the gay community. We are so quick to devour our own. It always took my breath away when it happened to me or to other people. I could face a lot of things, but that I found devastating."

When the summer break arrived, Noble took a much needed breather from the political rat race. Not only had she cosponsored seventy-three bills, her office was always deluged with mail—nearly 250 letters a week from the gay community demanded her attention— as well as the innumerable late-night, desperate phone calls and disturbing hate letters and death threats. Her car had been vandalized so continuously that no insurance company would cover it, and Elaine had to settle for getting around town on a motor scooter. Besides the personal toll, the tension was beginning to wear on her relationship with Rita Mae Brown.

Not only a renowned writer, Brown was also one of the premier radical lesbian-feminists in the country. Mixing a bit of Southern humor with the usual stridency of activism, she averred that the only way to short-circuit the male-dominated society was for all women to become lesbians. She had dealt with intimidations from her detractors for years, countering them with an in-your-face sensibility. But, even though she was a seasoned veteran, she was troubled by the increasingly hostile atmosphere building around Elaine and herself. The stress was beginning to affect her work, and she was having problems finishing her new book, *Six of One.* Feeling her relationship and livelihood were in peril, she begged Elaine to consider leaving Boston. But Noble insisted she had a constituency that depended on her. She couldn't leave. She wouldn't leave.

When the fall term began, Noble threw herself with renewed vigor into gay initiatives, protesting the dismissal of alleged lesbians from the armed services and petitioning the Welfare Department to revise its archaic and sometimes hostile policy on gay parents and the placement of gay youth. She lobbied support for Project Lambda, a gay youth advocacy program, when the organization came under attack with unsubstantiated and ultimately false allegations of misconduct. Ever cognizant of her pledge not to be a one-issue politician, she also worked indefatigably to get services for the Fenway. She fought for gun- and rent-control measures; she lobbied for day-care facilities and food co-ops; she continued her drive to curtail the number of new liquor licenses in the neighborhood. She also cosponsored so much legislation for the Black Caucus that they were tempted to name her an honorary member. She came out in support of Mayor Kevin White's run for a third term, even though he had refused to endorse her in her race the previous year. In truth, once in office, Noble had found her relationship with the mayor to be "a good and healthy one," she said in a press release. "I have no problem in getting what I want out of City Hall." When the mayor approved a $52,000 grant to the beleaguered Project Lambda, it confirmed

Noble's belief in White's own brand of moxie. "If Kevin were really concerned about his reelection, he wouldn't have funded Project Lambda," she confided to the *Gay Community News.*

Elaine gave more than lip service to supporting the mayor's reelection; she supplied the White campaign with a large number of volunteers and vigorously encouraged the voters of her Fenway district to turn out for White, which they did in margins of two and three to one. The bloc of votes White received in the Suffolk districts helped counteract losses elsewhere around the city, and pushed him to a squeaker victory in November. Noble's efforts gained her much gratitude, as well as political clout with the mayor's office.

In the national arena, she organized an ERA study committee with a $30,000 budget after the measure was defeated in New York and New Jersey, and she began to actively support Senator Birch Bayh (D-Indiana) for president. The year ended publicly for Noble with the filing of three gay-rights bills (almost identical to those not passed earlier in the year) for the 1976 Massachusetts legislative session; it ended privately with her taking out a full-page ad in the *Gay Community News* saying:

> *Dear Rita: As you have said,*
> *"An army of lovers cannot fail."*
> *Lead on, my beloved. Happy Birthday—Elaine*

In turn, the *Gay Community News,* for its tongue-in-cheek Third Annual Bouquets & Brickbats Awards, gave the General Patton/Susan B. Anthony Medal to Noble and Rita Mae Brown "for leading an army of lovers in 1975."

But as 1976 began, the two leaders of that army found themselves under attack when the harassment directed toward them escalated. Since Elaine was often at the statehouse late into the night, Rita Mae would be alone at home, so it was she who bore the brunt of the terrorism. As many as forty threatening phone calls a day came into the Marlborough Street apartment, warning, "We're going to get you." Many times the callers identified what Rita was wearing or where she was standing, indicating that the apartment was under surveillance. An ominous telegram arrived saying, "Dear Rita, We'll be contacting you soon in person." One evening, a car drove by, its lights off, and shot out the windows in the apartment with a pellet gun. Terrified, Brown phoned Noble. By the time Elaine got home, the police were there, even though, curiously, they had not been called. The boys in blue claimed they were responding to an anonymous tip. When they left, the phone rang again. "I see the cops are gone," a voice said. "Too bad about your friend's car." Outside, Brown's Audi was riddled with bullet holes.

In desperation, Elaine called Massachusetts Attorney General Frank Bellotti for help. He immediately sent over private investigator Gil Lewis. "Gil still swears it's the weirdest case he's ever worked on," Noble remarks. Indeed, the shadowy events were later chronicled as "The Lewis Files" in Boston's *The Real Paper*. Lewis met with Elaine and Rita Mae to try to figure out who might be behind the terrorism. Forced-busing protestors? Some anti-gay hate group? Noble's lawyer's connection with the fugitive Susan Saxe? Lewis assured the women he would find out. That night, he, too, received a threatening phone call: "We saw you at Elaine's today. Stay out of this or else we'll take care of you."

In spite of that warning, Gil Lewis collected enough evidence to document that a lesbian woman, her lover, and a male accomplice had been harassing Noble and Brown. He presented his findings to Assistant District Attorney Peter McCray, and the three were scheduled to appear in court in a matter of weeks.

On the morning of the hearing, *The Real Paper* reported, Rita Mae was upstairs writing when she heard a crash of glass down below. When she summoned the nerve to investigate, she found that someone had broken through the front door and through the locked door of Noble's home office. The filing cabinet had been rifled, and all the records and evidence accumulated on the case were gone. Nothing else was stolen, not even valuables that lay in plain sight. "It was like they were delivering me a message," Elaine says. She was convinced that the three accused harassers had hired a professional. "Two locked doors," she pointed out, "and it only took fifteen minutes to clear the office out."

The episode had a surreal coda later that afternoon when the judge, after hearing the case against the defendants, simply ordered the accused to pack up and leave town. Gil Lewis couldn't believe it. "It was like something out of the Wild West," he exclaimed. Noble had a darker interpretation of the events. "I think the FBI was somehow involved," she says today. "I really do."

The break-in was the last straw for Rita Mae. When Elaine arrived home that night, she found a moving van in front of the apartment. "I'm out of here, honey," Rita Mae said. Deeply saddened by the abrupt dissolution of the relationship, Elaine was nonetheless not surprised. "I think Rita thought it would be tough, but I don't think she ever signed on for anything like that," she says today. "She wasn't a politician, she's a writer. And she had as much right as anybody else to say, 'I can't handle it! I can't work here! I don't feel safe here!' If you're a creative person, that studio, that place where you create must be a safe haven. And it wasn't. When bullets fly through your windows, it doesn't help your concentration much." She is doubtful that anyone could have handled a partnership with her at that time. "It was dangerous. I had gotten myself into this situation and it was unfair to ask other people to jump in. It's like, 'I'm swimming in this boiling water. Why don't you jump into it too and watch your skin peel off?' It wasn't a life that was conducive to stability."

Elaine was determined to continue with her professional life. With her old friend Ann Lewis now Birch Bayh's deputy national campaign director, Noble doubled her own efforts on behalf of Bayh's presidential effort, eventually becoming a Bayh delegate. If Bayh got more than nine percent of the vote in the Massachusetts primary, Noble would become the first gay delegate to a national political convention. Unfortunately, when primary day arrived, he finished a dismal seventh, with less than five percent of the vote. He withdrew from the race and Elaine's delegate hopes vanished.

News was discouraging closer to home, too. The Massachusetts Senate killed a bill that would have outlawed discrimination against gays under the Civil Service Law, and the House killed a bill that would have revised the archaic sex laws in the state. The only bright spot at the half-year mark was Mayor Kevin White's decision to issue an executive order adding "sexual preference" to the city's antidiscrimination policies. The order was a distinct and notable victory for Noble; indeed, it was direct payback for all the support she had given the mayor in his last election. Boston became only the second city in the United States to issue such an order, the first being New York City.

Yet despite the frustrations of the job and the toll on her personal life, Noble decided to seek reelection in 1976. "There were plenty of times when I just didn't want to go back into the legislature, but I had to run again," Noble recounts. "I didn't want people to think it was a fluke. I wanted to get reelected and then get out. It was very hard, but I had an agenda." One of the deciding factors that propelled Elaine into the grind of another campaign came from a surprising source: a new personal relationship.

Santa Fareri, a young, attractive, and feisty public relations consultant from Quincy, Massachusetts, was introduced to Elaine by their mutual friend, Peter O'Neill, assistant to the state Speaker of the House. Fareri had been raised in a political family; her mother was a Democratic state committeewoman who ran Attorney General Frank Bellotti's campaign. "Most kids went out and played stickball, I did brochure drops," she says, laughing. "I didn't have a lot of choice. I was like a sponge as a kid; I just took it all in. And I loved it." In Fareri, Noble believed that she finally had a partner who could accept—and even enjoy—the pressures and challenges of political life. Not long after they moved in together, Fareri would even become Noble's campaign manager. "I got involved because I believed she was a good state rep. She represented the district. She had what it took. She had an incredible way of making people look at her, past her sexuality. Actually, after meeting her, I believe people wanted to look past it because she was engaging, she was good, she was a fighter for all people."

Mixing the personal and the professional, though, was problematical. "It was very difficult," Elaine admits. "And ultimately a bad idea." Fareri concurs. "I think my credibility was skewed because we were lovers. I don't think I was taken as seriously as I should have been."

Unopposed in the Democratic primary, Noble would face Independent candidate Victor Themo in the November 2 general election. Although she had become a popular legislator in her first term, nothing was taken for granted. The new campaign offices at 475 Commonwealth Avenue were always bustling. Previous contributors were contacted, political favors were called in, and fund-raising benefits were announced. Unlike the button-designing contest and movie showings of the first campaign, Fareri went for more high-profile events, including a very successful concert given by popular comedienne Lily Tomlin. Noble would end up amassing nearly twenty thousand dollars in contributions.

In November, she handily won reelection to her House seat, with an impressive 3,373 votes to Themo's 852. However, in that same election the voters passed a referendum that would reduce the size of the Massachusetts House from 240 to 160 members in the next election in 1978. This redistricting would affect Noble directly; her Suffolk 6 would be reconfigured back into Barney Frank's Suffolk 5, so that in the next race, Noble and Frank would ostensibly be vying for the same district. Frank wondered whether he should consider stepping aside to let Noble run for the seat—a notion his advisors thought gallant but misguided. They insisted he was more powerful than she, and a more likely candidate to continue the leadership of the liberal cause. Noble, for her own part, felt that certain issues—ERA and gay rights included—would be better represented by her. Acknowledging that it would be like running against a sibling, neither was willing to get involved in playing political what-if games, pledging instead to take a wait-and-see attitude. That did not keep some members of the press, however, from depicting the situation as a knock-down, drag-out competition. As David Brill wrote in the *Gay Community News:*

> Noble is sticking to her original plans—to run for the new seat no matter what. The problem, however, is that the new district contains only two precincts of her present district; by next year, Frank will have represented almost 90 percent of the new district for six years. She is clearly very vulnerable . . . Noble does not want to appear weak, Frank does not want to look foolish. An intense psychological game seems to be transpiring. . . .

The Boston gay community began to grow polarized on the issue, taking sides in bars, in debates, and, of course, in letters to the gay press.

While striving to represent the interests of the Fenway, Noble, as the highest-ranking openly gay elected official in the United States, had to fight for gay rights not only on the state but also on the city and some-

times even on the national level. The gay community, considering Noble their one champion, believed that she belonged to them. Now some
were grumbling that she was not loud enough, not vocal enough, not
relentless enough. "It's true with a lot of people who feel they've not
had representation that once they feel they've got a voice, they demand
everything from that one voice," a frustrated Noble said to the *Gay
Community News*. "I just can't deliver that, and I never said I could."

Even some old staffers complained of thwarted expectations. Longtime friend and campaign manager Ann Maguire claimed, "Winning
really took a toll on her. After the election, she was very much in demand. She didn't know how to handle the new person that she became."

Joe Martin says that although she was very helpful in increasing the
bases of support for gay legislation, Noble "didn't become the kind of
legislator I had hoped for on a personal level." Santa Fareri blames the
gay community itself. "They weren't sophisticated enough to accept a
leader. They claimed Elaine for their own long enough to destroy her."

However, Noble's expanded influence also had its upside. Having
been appointed by the Carter/Mondale ticket to its national advisory
committee for women's issues the year before, she now found herself
being courted by the new Carter administration. On March 26, 1977,
she was invited to join a delegation of fourteen lesbians and gay men to
meet with the President's advisor for public relations, Midge Costanza,
at the White House. The group, assembled by the National Gay and Lesbian Task Force's codirectors, Jean O'Leary and Bruce Voeller, was the
first official gathering of homosexuals ever to be invited to 1600 Pennsylvania Avenue. For nearly three hours, they were able to dialogue with
federal agency leaders about such concerns as witch-hunts of homosexuals in the military, funding for gay community services, discriminatory
hiring practices in the U.S. Civil Service, and the lack of protection for
homosexuals under the federal employment laws. At one point, Frank
Kameny, the Washington activist who had himself been fired from the
Department of Defense for being gay, leaned over to Elaine and whis-
pered, "This is such a wonderful moment for me." Noble, who knew
Kameny's journey well, was deeply touched by his full-circle experience. "It *was* a very special moment," she says. After the discussion, the
group was given a special tour of the White House, including a visit to

the Oval Office, but the President never did join them. "We were all a little disappointed, but I was enough of a pro to understand that it probably was smart of him not to be there," Noble says. "That would make a great headline—'Carter Meets with Queers.'"

The day ended with a press conference in the sun-drenched rose garden, where the elated gay contingent reflected on the history that had been made that day. Standing toward the back, Noble was shaken from her reverie when Hamilton Jordan, Carter's chief of staff, walked by Midge Costanza. "I'll never forget it," Noble says. "Midge said to him, 'Hi, you stupid asshole,' and he said, 'Hi, you fucking bitch. . . .' And I thought, '*Whoooaaaa!* This President isn't going to get reelected. These people are too busy fighting with each other to look at what's really going on.'"

Regardless of the in-house fighting, the White House seemed serious about its new policy of inclusion. Not a month later, *The Boston Globe* reported that Elaine Noble was a leading contender for the job of director of Domestic Operations for ACTION, the government volunteer organization that oversees the Peace Corps and VISTA, as well as initiating beneficial programs for senior citizens. If Noble got the job, she would earn $48,600, nearly four times her salary as a legislator—and would set a new benchmark for the gay community, becoming the first open homosexual to occupy a high federal government post. In the end, Noble was offered a choice of three positions in ACTION—head of Domestic Operations, head of the Elders Affairs Department, or head of a new service that would conduct annual evaluations of the Peace Corps. Friends and advisors urged her to take one of the positions, but after a month of deliberation, she turned down all three, saying to the press, "It would be five to eight years of orchestrating the same programs that I'm in the middle of here. . . . Going to Washington is not something I want to do. I feel that I'm most effective where I am." Elaine believed that she owed her allegiance to the people who had elected her, and many agreed. Linda Lachman, her trusted chief aide, said, "Boston would have really felt the loss." On the other side, people like Joe Martin were worried what effect the decision might have on the upcoming House race. "If this means that Barney and Elaine are running against each other," he mused, "I think I'll go live on a kibbutz for a year."

Inevitably, the Carter administration's outreach to homosexuals brought the bigots out of the woodwork. The president of Save Our Children, Inc., former Miss America finalist and Florida orange juice spokeswoman Anita Bryant, stated, "I protest the action of the White House staff in dignifying these activists for special privilege with a serious discussion of their alleged 'human rights.' They are really asking to be blessed in their abnormal lifestyle by the office of the President of the United States!" With the backing of religious fundamentalists, Bryant had launched a well-financed campaign to overturn a Dade County, Florida, civil rights ordinance that protected sexual orientation.

Under the aegis of the Boston Advocates for Human Rights (BAHR), a press conference was convened at the Boston statehouse to oppose Bryant's initiative and the vitriol that surrounded it. Noble said, "These hate groups move from cause to cause. Unfortunately many of them are in positions of power. It's frightening. If Dade County goes down, these people have said they will move on to the big ones: New York, Massachusetts, California." Barney Frank was even more combative in his statement: "These weirdos are getting out of hand. It's time to crack down on these people who have an obsession with other people's sex lives. . . . Because Anita Bryant disapproves of certain people's sexual actions—which are by no stretch of anyone's imagination any of her business—they are to be denied equal opportunity."

That very week, Bryant claimed in *Miami Magazine* that a current California drought was linked to the passage of a gay-rights bill in Los Angeles, and that there was overwhelming evidence that God punished civilizations that showed tolerance for homosexuality. "Do you know why God hates homosexuality?" she asked. "Because the male homosexual eats another man's sperm. Sperm is the most concentrated form of life. The homosexual is eating life. That's why God calls homosexuality an abomination." The magazine, restraining itself from pointing out the "abomination" of such empty-headed logic, asked instead if women who performed the same act on men would incur similar condemnation from the Almighty. "Absolutely," was Bryant's resolute reply. "And that includes lesbians!"

Though her remarks were widely derided, Bryant's campaign prevailed and Dade County dropped the sexual orientation provisions from its civil rights ordinance. Soon voters in Eugene, Oregon, St. Paul, Minnesota, and Wichita, Kansas, also pushed through anti-gay initiatives. But on Boston Gay Pride Day, June 18, Noble focused on the positive. Taking the stage to thunderous applause, she called out, "This is a day of celebration! We are proud. We are beautiful. We are strong. I want you to remember, we have a lifetime of struggle." Then, looking out over the ocean of euphoric faces, she added, "When I think of quitting, I think of days like this, and I go on."

Every year, the same gay-rights bills were trotted out before the Massachusetts state legislature, and every year—due in large measure to Noble's tireless efforts—the bills came closer to being voted into law. "I wouldn't quit," Elaine professes. "I just literally wouldn't quit. I wouldn't go away. It was like a marathon. If they would screw one bill, I'd write another. Tenacity! Tenacity and trying to use humor went a long way." Near the end of 1977, House Bill 3676, banning discrimination in public employment on the basis of sexual orientation—which had cleared the Senate, albeit narrowly—once again came before the House.

The bill was debated for three endless, acrimonious days. At the close of the first day, a roll call was taken and the bill went down, 120–101. With the tallies so close, Noble officially moved for reconsideration of the vote. All that night, Elaine and Joe Martin, now the director of Gay Legislation, twisted arms and cashed in favors over the phone to convince the twenty or so representatives who were on the fence to vote for reconsideration. Their exhausting hours paid off, and the motion passed. This prompted a new spate of venom. At one point, Thomas Lopes shouted that should the bill be put into law, the state would become "the national headquarters of the Gay Liberation movement!" Tensions were so high that two of the legislators came to actual blows. Melrose representative William Robinson charged, "There is a sickness in the House. We are hating each other!" To allow the ill will to abate, Noble moved for a postponement of the vote until the next day, and the motion was accepted.

The final day began with William Galvin of Brighton proposing that the bill be amended to exclude police officers, firefighters, and corrections officers—changes that would allow many on-the-fence legislators to accept it. But Gay Legislation leaders rejected the watered-down version, and Noble and Frank reluctantly concurred. Weary of the battle and seeing no other way out, Noble rose to be recognized. She announced sadly that she and her gay advisers could not support Galvin's version. The bill went back to its original form and was roundly defeated, 129–93.

Many community leaders agreed that the Galvin amendments were an unacceptable compromise. "Elaine initially seemed willing to accept the amendments," Joe Martin says, "and I had strong reservations about accepting that kind of compromise. In the end, Elaine did what we wanted her to. I think we were right, and in the end, she took the right position." Others, however, including Santa Fareri, were severely disappointed. "I watched the leaders of the community force Elaine to go down on the floor of the House and kill a bill that would have been the first gay-rights bill," she says angrily. "The only people left out of the bill were the civil servants. Because of that, they wanted to kill the bill. They wanted it all or they didn't want anything. And it was God knows how long—ten years, eleven years—before another one was passed."

Noble attempted to put a positive spin on the loss, telling the press: "We were swimming upstream against the political climate. But we won in many ways, we made major inroads, we broke down many stereotypes." However, the defeat was a crushing blow for her, and the gay-rights struggle was coming to seem futile and overwhelming. "You can't sustain that kind of thing by yourself," she laments. "I did what I could. I really wish I could have gotten the gay-rights bill through. If people hadn't been paranoid, I think we could have pulled it off. But people weren't very sophisticated."

The defeat crystallized her doubts about running for reelection, especially in a race against Barney Frank; so she announced that she would not seek a third term. Venting her frustrations in an interview with *The Advocate,* she said, "Basically, what I have experienced in the last three years is that because I was considered the gay politician, I had not only more work, but got more flak, more criticism, more heartache from the gay community than from the people who elected me. I guess more than anything, I'm just exhausted and very, very tired and probably disillusioned, because I really tried the best I could and it wasn't good enough for the gay community. To be honest, I don't know what 'good enough' is."

Indeed, following the collapse of the gay-rights bill, writer David Brill took Noble to task in the *Gay Community News:*

Representative Elaine Noble . . . was hoping to make the passage of the bill the highlight of her legislative career. But some of her own strategy was flawed, and some of her actions were clearly inimical to the bill's success. . . .

Noble frequently contradicts herself by urging gay people to become involved in the political process, but then discredits and insults them because she doesn't want to share the limelight.

So in a way, it's not surprising that most of the men and women actively involved in her first campaign in 1974 (including Joe Martin) are no longer considered Noble loyalists. While no one should be expected to never make any enemies, it is rare that a political figure incurs the substantial erosion of support that Noble has.

Santa Fareri is Noble's lover and 1976 campaign manager, and she must, to be sure, share some blame for Noble's miscalculations. Fareri has done such an effective job at turning people against Noble that some people have jokingly suggested that she is an agent for either Anita Bryant or the FBI.

Noble was stunned by the virulence of an attack that would go so far as to out Fareri and their personal relationship. Although out to her close circle of family and friends, Fareri was rightly furious. Given the fact that she worked for the only gay elected state legislator in the country, lived with her, and spent every waking moment with her, she realized it didn't take a genius to figure out the relationship she and Noble had. "But it was my personal business," she insists. "It was not cool."

Many readers agreed, and for months, the *Gay Community News* was deluged with letters debating the issue. Even Noble's ex-lover Rita Mae Brown offered her opinion, saying, "I have profound differences with Elaine Noble, but I think the way she was treated was appalling and I'll always stand by her on that particular issue. Number one, she never deserved the adulation she got, and she never deserved the flip side of it, which was hatred. Everybody was at her and nobody wanted to give anything back. . . . If she went to Lincoln, Nebraska, every gay person showed up saying, 'Do this for me!' Well, how could she? She served a tiny district in the state of Massachusetts! . . . It's a miserable life. I lived with Elaine. I saw what she had to go through."

Finally, Noble herself felt compelled to respond with an angry and ultimately heartbreakingly sad open letter to Brill, detailing the misrepresentations she found in his article, deploring his unethical outing of Fareri, and then—referring to her decision to end her tenure in the statehouse—closing with a bequest:

To you, David Brill, I leave the following legacy: I will refer to you all the calls I receive at home and at the statehouse from local gays as well as those across the country. I wonder how you will answer a weekly average of two hundred pieces of mail from gays as far away as London, Germany, and Bangkok. I leave it to you to tell them what to do about immigration problems, custody problems, legal problems, licensing problems for a gay restaurant, gallery, or bar.

I wonder if you will become weary of answering the phone at two or three A.M. on an average of four nights a week to listen to a gay person who just needs to know that there is someone out there and understands?

How will you cope with obscene phone calls and persons threatening your life and those of the people who work and associate with you?

I wonder how you will mentally sort out, as I had to do, the realization that someone you never met has a compulsion about shooting through your apartment windows and car windows?

Will you choose to respond to gays who face losing their children in a custody case? Will you try to raise some money to defray legal expenses? Will you tell all who call, write, or ring your door at any hour of the day or night that it's okay to cry and that it will be all right in the end? Will you tell them not to give up hope, David?

This is my legacy to you. It is all the "limelight" I have to give you, David. Take it. It's yours. . . .

With that caustic adieu, she was ready to pack up her statehouse office and consider where next to place her trademark sign "Trust in God—She Will Provide." She instinctively knew that she was suffering from severe burnout. In her tempestuous time on Beacon Hill, she had been assistant majority leader, vice chair of the ERA Study Committee, member of the Rules and Education committees, a prominent member of the Ethics Committee, and a tireless advocate for the gay and lesbian community. "You can't be the first of anything and sustain it for very long," she says. "I did what I could. But it was so hard. It was so hard to be the only one of anything."

If she felt a little shaky about leaving, she also experienced a sense of relief. In the private sector, though, she realized that being a high-profile political lesbian limited her choices for employment. "I don't have a whole lot of options," she told *The Advocate*, "so I'm going to have to take what I can get." After four months of weighing the options, she recognized that what she could get was most likely to be in the political arena. "My adviser, Eddie McCormick, who was a former attorney general, and I came up with this wild plan," she says. "We knew it was impossible, but we thought 'what a way to go out!' If you're going to leave the banquet table, get a little dessert!" The dessert was a race coming up for the U.S. Senate against an incumbent who seemed unbeatable: Edward Brooke, a Republican and, at the time, the only black senator on Capitol Hill. On April 25, 1978, at the Park Plaza Hotel, surrounded by nearly three hundred old friends and supporters, including Ann Maguire, Linda Lachman, and Barney Frank, Noble, deliberately omitting the word "gay," announced her candidacy for the Democratic nomination.

Immediately focusing her attention on Brooke, Noble claimed that the Republican senator was out of touch—that even though the office itself was in Washington, D.C., it was imperative that a United States senator continue working "in the neighborhoods and in the cities and towns." She soon received several important endorsements, including the Massachusetts lieutenant governor, the House Speaker, the attorney general, and—of course—Barney Frank. In Washington, Tip O'Neill, Speaker of the House of Representatives, announced, "She'll make a tremendous senator. If she's the nominee, I'll support her."

Santa Fareri, who once again served as Noble's campaign manager, has a more jaundiced view. "We had a lot of support in the beginning," she says, "because they all looked at Elaine and thought, 'Yeah, all right, the lesbian's going to take on the only black United States senator. Let her go for it, she's cute, smart, tenacious.' No one thought Brooke was vulnerable. In our campaign we came out of the blocs punching at him and I think it dawned on a lot of people like Tom O'Neill and Paul Tsongas that he indeed was vulnerable." Brooke was in the middle of a messy divorce; allegations of marital indiscretions soon surfaced, along with an alienated daughter who was happy to supply the press with personal dirt on her father. Sensing blood in the water, candidates flocked to register for the primary; five would actually run. "That was the one political regret in my life," Fareri admits. "We made Brooke too vulnerable too quickly. We should have played it closer to the vest."

The broader field, and a gay community that was surprisingly unmotivated, made it hard to raise the $300,000 Elaine believed was needed to fuel her run. In the end, the campaign was able to raise only $38,000. Then, on September 6, two weeks before the primary, Elaine's father lost his long battle with cancer. It was an extremely painful loss for Elaine. Away for the funeral, unable to attend last-minute rallies and state canvassing, Noble returned to Boston to find that she had slipped further in the polls. When primary day ended on September 19, the final tally was: U.S. Representative Paul Tsongas, 35 percent, Massachusetts Secretary of State Paul Guzzi, 31 percent, Boston School Committee member Kathleen Alioto, 20 percent, former Conservative Caucus director Howard Phillips, 8 percent, and Elaine Noble, 6 percent.

Although she had known almost from the onset that she could not win, Noble was still stunned by her poor showing. But she conceded with grace and went on to Paul Tsongas's victory celebration at Faneuil Hall, where she pledged him her support. Tsongas was to go on to defeat the wounded Brooke in the general election.

Soon afterward, she and Santa split up, though they worked hard to remain friendly. "Elaine affected the course of my life as she had for an awful lot of people," Fareri says. "She gave me an entrée into an entirely different life. If it weren't for her, I don't know where I would be now."

Noble did not leave the political realm, for as she said to *Boston Magazine*, "Politics is a form of folk art in Boston," and she remained one of the city's premier artisans. As the decade neared its end, she went to work as a lobbyist for Mayor Kevin White, chairing the Democratic City Committee.

After a productive and successful tenure in the mayor's office, Elaine sought new challenges. She started a corporate lobbying enterprise, one of whose projects was a gay and lesbian substance-abuse treatment facility. In 1993, she stepped into politics again to run for City Council across the Charles River in Cambridge, where she was now living. Calling the campaign "a riot," she enjoyed the fact that she was the most qualified person running. But she ran into some fierce resistance from the local liberals. "Only in Cambridge could the liberal fascists make me look like a right-wing conservative," she says ironically. Their lack of support, however, left Elaine without a firm base and she lost the election.

Undaunted, Noble next turned her considerable talents to the corporate world of investments. Meyers Capital Management hired her to comanage Meyers Pride Value Fund, the first mutual fund to focus on companies with explicit antidiscrimination policies protecting gay and lesbian employees. "As I looked back over the years, it was clear to me that we had really made great gains in the national political arena," she says. "Change in the religious arena is quite active now, too. The next arena that needed social change was Wall Street—the last male bastion of power. For those of us who still consider it a great honor to serve the gay and lesbian community, this was the next natural step."

In June 1998, BankBoston Development Company, a division of the country's oldest bank, BankBoston, announced that it would become an equity investor in the Pride Value Fund, allotting $250,000 to market the plan. The bank may have been displaying admirable social consciousness, but it was also aware that by the millennium, the estimated tangible assets of the gay and lesbian community in America would exceed $800 billion. Like many pioneering plans, however, the Pride Value Fund had initial difficulty catching on, and toward the end of 1999, Meyers Capital Management amended its mandate and no longer focused solely on the homosexual community. Grateful for the experience—"it was like politics but without the slimy part," she says—Noble took what she had learned to another job with Funds Distributors, a financial institution specializing in marketing and communications.

Now surrounded by a growing coterie of animals, Elaine decided she had to relocate her home outside of the city. Looking in the wooded countryside thirty minutes from downtown, she found a defunct railroad station. "I just fell in love with it," she says. "I'm a train nut. And I think buildings have souls—and these are disappearing from our landscape. They're significant. They're part of America's history." Although most of her friends "thought I should be committed," she painstakingly restored the thatched-roof wooden building, adding a bedroom loft. An old-fashioned potbellied stove was tucked in one corner to warm the room and the comfortable living room below. Commuter trains whiz by daily, and on winter mornings Noble, ever a creature of service, sometimes will pass hot coffee through a window to passengers waiting outside on the platform. She lives there with a dog, a Missouri fox-trotter horse, an African pygmy goat, a hive of bees, and four Polish chickens. "It's a very international place," she says. After all these years, "diversity" remains more than just a buzzword. It's a lifetime commitment.

With the moxie to back it up.

Today, thanks in no small part to Elaine Noble's pioneering efforts, diversity reigns on the American political landscape. As of this writing, there are nearly two hundred openly gay and lesbian elected officials currently holding office on local, state, and national levels. Brian Bond, executive director of the National Gay and Lesbian Victory Fund, says, "Elaine Noble will always have a special place in the hearts and minds of gays and lesbians everywhere. Against all odds, she made a lie of the myth that people would not elect gays and lesbians to public office. She took the forces of hatred and turned them into victory. She faced death threats, violence, the fear of the unknown, to show that for us, anything was possible in politics. From her moment of courage sprung a whole well of possibilities."

Although officially out of politics, she remains active in assisting other people who want to run for office, especially women and minorities. "I feel like everyone's grandmother," she says. She calls the current gay visibility in the arts, in business, and yes, in politics, "wonderful. The more the merrier—the better off we all are." As for any future political ambitions, "I gave at the office," she jokes. "I'm all done. I'm happy I did what I did. It was exciting and I'm glad it helped people. It helped me. But I believe that everybody takes a turn." She likens the journey to a conga line on the floor of a roller rink. "You go around the floor and you do the conga line. The best spot is to be in the front. But the person who's in the front then is in the middle. And the worst place to be, where everybody ends up at some point in the conga line, is on the end. And you get whipped around and the trick is to keep your balance and try not to smash into the wall. Well, life is like that. I call it the Great Conga Line of Life.

"And I really have no desire to be on the end again."

SIR IAN
MCKELLEN

Playing a Part

H E STANDS ALONE ON A BARE STAGE. There is a wash of what appears to be an ochre curtain behind him, and a faint wood parquet pattern at his feet. In the light from a "special" above, he is luminescent in the inky darkness. Matching the simplicity of the setting, he wears a pale blue silk shirt open at the neck, light gray slacks, and plain black shoes. He holds just one prop, a volume of the plays of William Shakespeare, the greatest playwright in the English language. Although there have been other playwrights and other masterly plays for Ian McKellen, the actor keeps returning to the Bard of Stratford-upon-Avon—for the inspiration, for the challenge, and for the solace.

" 'All the world's a stage, and all the men and women merely players,' " he recites from *As You Like It*. " 'They have their exits and their entrances; and one man in his time plays many parts. His acts being seven ages. . . .' "

As he runs trippingly through the life list contained in Jaques' famous speech, the noted actor could just as well be speaking of his own ages. As of this night, very early in 1988, McKellen would seem to be departing his fourth age: " 'seeking the bubble reputation even in the cannon's mouth.' " His reputation won, he is standing at the pinnacle of his profession, arguably one of the finest stage actors of his generation—commanding the British theater as Laurence Olivier did before him—and a foremost interpreter of Shakespeare.

" 'And then the justice, in fair, round belly with good capon lin'd, with eyes severe and beard of formal cut, full of wise saws and modern instances; and so he plays his part.' " McKellen's fifth age will be ushered in by a "modern instance"—the need to be true to himself, to stand up to injustice, to lend his name and his eminence to a cause that he has not yet fully made his own, for he is still living in the shadows.

In his resonant, faintly Lancashire-accented voice, he invests the words of the remaining ages with their full majesty as he completes the magnificent litany: " 'Last scene of all, that ends this strange eventful history, is second childishness, and mere oblivion, sans teeth, sans eyes, sans taste, sans everything.' " Triumphantly, he snaps shut the book and breaks the spell that has held his audience rapt. "Welcome," he says, "to *Acting Shakespeare.*"

Standing at the edge of the stage of the Playhouse Theatre in the West End of London as he begins the bare-bones, modern-dress one-man show that he has developed to honor the Bard, McKellen is a riveting paradox of energy and serenity. At forty-nine years of age, a full head of tousled hair crowns his head; his face, apart from a slight puffiness under the eyes, is smooth and lineless. His trim, lithe body stands under the proscenium arch. "I've been acting in the plays of Shakespeare very happily for twenty years or so. I want to celebrate him with you now." As the curtain behind him opens, he continues, "And so, with your help, I want to share this bare stage with some of his characters and summon up the spirits of his kings, drunkards, princes, lovers, murderers, and magicians." He is now framed dead center of a blank white screen, and he says, "Always there will be actors on a bare stage in praise of a man of the theater, acting Shakespeare."

For the next hour and a half, he conjures up the hallowed characters: the demonic and misshapen Richard III, the fatally indecisive Hamlet, both Romeo and Juliet, the young, feisty Prince Hal, the corpulent Falstaff, and the others, reprising not only his own interpretations of the roles but also impersonating the legendary Shakespearean actors performing their most celebrated parts. "What is it, do you suppose, which connects Richard Burbage, David Garrick, Donald Wolfitt, John Gielgud, and actors like me who manage to make a living acting in Shakespeare's plays?" he asks the audience, and answers. "I think it's an undying affection and belief that Shakespeare, more than any other writer who ever lived, understood the complexity of human life, the variety of human beings, and the subtleties that go to make up our existence."

The evening is not only an entertainment, it is a veritable master class as McKellen dissects and analyzes the texts word by word, line by line, image by image, nuance by nuance. A persuasive teacher, he not only makes us see the inner workings of the verse, he challenges us to witness the foundations of creating a character. It is a speed-course in acting. He leavens the performance with theater tales, Shakespearean lore, and, in one memorable bit, an impersonation of the acerbic critic Samuel Pepys, who at the time lambasted what would become some of the most celebrated plays in the English language:"Saw *Romeo and Juliet* which is a play, of itself, the worst I ever heard in my life. . . . Saw *A Midsummer Night's Dream,* which I had never seen before. Nor shall ever again. . . ." He winds up the evening by quoting from Shakespeare's last play, *The Tempest.* " 'We are such stuff as dreams are made on, and our little life is rounded with a sleep.' "

The ensuing applause is deafening.

After his curtain call, McKellen stands at the theater door with a bucket to collect cash. Not only is he donating the proceeds of this entire eleven-week run of *Acting Shakespeare* to the Lighthouse, an AIDS hospice in London, he is still soliciting whatever additional monies the audience can spare to support the cause. In the line of fans eager to meet him he spots arts lobbyist Carole Woddis, who compliments him on the show and hands him a small parcel of information."I think you might find this of interest," she says. "It's about Clause Twenty-eight."

McKellen, half hearing, smiles and nods and puts the parcel in his pocket. He had known vaguely about the section of a bill that is going to be debated in Parliament; the newspapers have been full of it.

What Ian McKellen did not know, what he could not know, was that from that night forward, he would be catapulted not only into the forefront of the debate, but fully out of the closet as well. He would become spokesman for a movement; he would be a lightning rod for criticism. He would be denounced and derided; he would be acclaimed and commended. And his life would be inexorably, utterly transformed.

• • •

Ian Murray McKellen was born on May 25, 1939, in the industrial mill town of Burnley, Lancashire, in the northwest of England. His father, Denis Murray, was a civil engineer, and his mother, Margery Lois, stayed home to care for baby Ian and his five-year-old sister, Jean. Both of their parents were ministers' children, who expressed their Christianity by voting Labour, espousing socialism, and promoting worthy causes. "My father helped to run a pacifist organization and had connections with an international group called Christian Endeavor," McKellen says. "My family believed you were in the world to make it a better place and not just for yourself."

At the time, the steel- and coal-producing north of England was churning out armaments for defense against Hitler's threatened march across Europe, and once the war broke out later that year, the region seemed a likely target for Nazi attacks. By then the McKellen family had resettled in the dingy coal-mining town of Wigan—"the butt of many comedians' jokes at the time," McKellen says. Their four-bedroom house with a back garden sat midway between the grime of Wigan proper and the outlying rolling hills of the more affluent suburbs. When German bombs began to fall to the south in London, Margery insisted that baby Ian sleep in the safest place in the house—under an iron table in the dining room. Yet despite the war, Ian led a fairly ordinary childhood in Wigan, attending nursery school and making his theatrical debut at a Christmas pageant at the Hope Street Congregational Church, where he recited the story of the Nativity. He was immediately, unabashedly stagestruck. As he said years later to *Out* magazine, "There you are on the stage, free with your feelings, with people sitting there admiring you."

He was not yet four when he saw his first professional play, *Peter Pan,* on a family outing to the Manchester Opera House. "I wasn't overly impressed," McKellen wrote later. "For one thing, it wasn't a real crocodile, and I could see the wires. And I was terribly confused as to why the 'boy who wouldn't grow up' was played by a girl." When he was seven, he received a cherished Christmas present: a cardboard foldout Victorian theater, complete with scenery and cutout characters. Fascinated by the bigger-than-life personalities and ragtag appearance of the visiting repertory actors who traveled through town, Ian would fashion his own band of players on the miniature set. His introduction to Shakespeare came through his sister Jean, who not only took him to see *Twelfth Night* at the Wigan Little Theater, but, to her brother's delight, also played Bottom in a high school production of *A Midsummer Night's Dream*.

The other art form that colored McKellen's childhood was music, for his father was a gifted pianist. Running his beefy fingers up and down the keys of the upright piano, Denis McKellen would play his children to sleep with melodies from Beethoven, Chopin, Tchaikovsky, and Liszt. Unfortunately, it was a talent that was not passed down from father to son. "I inherited the hands," Ian says, "but not the musician-ship."

His parents' charitable works brought a parade of interesting guests into the McKellen home: "Among the first visitors to our house in Wigan were evacuees from London who'd escaped the blitz. After they left, there was a German prisoner of war, who was in a local camp. Shortly after that, the next visitor was a black man. A black man had never been seen in our town, and as he walked down the street, it was like the Pied Piper—just scores of children wanting to touch him."

McKellen was nine when he first found himself drawn to other boys. "I used to seek out the company of specific boys in my class whom I found attractive," he recalls. "Then I had my first little fumblings with my best friend when we were about eleven. That was at Sunday school. But even then, I was terribly aware that I couldn't talk about the feel-ings." Apart from two men who kept a local shop in town, who were the objects of occasional elbow-nudging and sniggering, homosexual-ity was an unknown subject. "I don't know how I would have *begun* to talk to my parents about it," he says, so he kept it to himself.

In 1951, when his father became borough engineer and surveyor of the somewhat larger city of Bolton, McKellen was enrolled in a new school, where he would thrive. "Achievement was regarded as estimable at Bolton School," he recalls, "but it didn't matter at what." Besides aca-demics, the school offered a wide array of extracurricular activities— debating, cricket, field trips—in which Ian participated. There was also an especially lively drama group that nourished his fascination with the theater. One of the first plays he was in was *The Beauty Contest,* written by a Bolton teacher, Leonard Roe, in which he donned a dress for the role of Rosie Meadows, a mill girl who cheats her way to the finale of a beauty pageant. Before long, Frank Greene, the senior English master at Bolton, recognized Ian's dramatic gifts and cast him as the lead in Shakespeare's *Henry V,* the major production of the spring term. Since it was to be staged in the school's huge main hall, "This required experimenting with being audible above the constant squeal of eight hundred bottoms shifting on eight hundred rush-bottomed chairs," McKellen recalls. "Frank Greene was right: if you can't be heard, you can't act on stage." But according to the school paper, he rose to the challenge:

> In the part of Henry, Ian McKellen amply fulfilled our expectations. His conviction and poise, timing, modulation, gesture, and demeanour were rarely at fault. If the pointing of some lines appeared rather odd, let me not cavil: His originality was like a breath of fresh air. Youthfully majestic, he always dominated the stage.

Ian had been at Bolton barely a year when a boy in his class was found dead, hanging from the doorway of an outside lavatory, partially dressed in his mother's underwear. "A twelve-year-old suicide," Ian wrote many years later, "and it seemed to me something to do with obsession and sex and misery." The incident was never fully discussed with the student body, leaving many, including young McKellen, "bewildered and nervous." Not long afterward, a sex-change operation, complete with before and after pictures, hit the front pages of the British tabloids. The two events deepened Ian's sexual confusion and anxiety. "As I entered my teens, I thought I, too, might be changing sex, and I waited for my breasts to grow," he says. "I fumbled and flirted my way through puberty and no one helped me to understand myself."

That same year, McKellen suffered the devastating loss of his beloved mother, Margery. Heartbroken, he delved deeper into the make-believe world of the stage, both at school and at a nearby old Edwardian house that two of his teachers had converted into the Hopefield Miniature Theatre. It had a tiny stage and only fifty seats, but there students could experiment with constructing scenery and hanging lighting, as well as with writing and directing their own plays.

Before long, his father remarried, and while Ian and Jean got along well enough with their new stepmother, Gladys, Denis McKellen recognized perceptively that his children still needed his comforting. To reach out to Ian, he began to take him to the Grand Theatre in Bolton, where he knew the owner, David Curnow. The affable Curnow would allow star-struck Ian to stand backstage for hours: "There, silent and ignored among the dust, I marveled as comics and magicians, the chorus girls and the acrobats, disguised the grinding hard work as glamour onstage," he wrote years later. "Their sweat shone like stardust. . . ."

Each summer, Ian eagerly took part in his school's annual pilgrimage to Stratford-upon-Avon. The students would camp in tents in Tiddington, half an hour upstream from the Royal Shakespeare Theatre site, and row down the river to attend plays. Night after night, he would sit in the audience, mesmerized by such legendary actors as Laurence Olivier, Vivien Leigh, Charles Laughton, Edith Evans, Peggy Ashcroft, and John Gielgud; then row back upstream with his classmates to discuss and dissect the productions around the campfire. The brilliance of the performances he witnessed there so overwhelmed the boy that he experienced a momentary lapse of confidence about his own talent. Other possible career choices began swimming in his head: "I started in my teens to think I might train as a chef or a journalist."

One challenge any actor raised in Lancashire faces, as Ian McKellen was to write later in *The Sunday Times* magazine, "is what to do with the accent which God and the environment and your parents have landed you with." He recalls his father proudly telling a friend, "Ian had two accents: one that he used at school and one that he used at home, and I remember thinking how clever he was to be able to sound different in different situations." He was also somewhat gangly and physically awkward. "People always used to ask me what I wanted to be when I grew up. I said an actor and they always laughed," he says. "I laughed with them because I never thought of it as a serious ambition."

But he took it seriously enough to apply to St. Catherine's College at Cambridge University, alma mater to many theatrical notables, including directors Peter Hall and Toby Robertson. McKellen was interviewed by Tom Henn, the Shakespeare and Yeats scholar at St. Catherine's, who always insisted that applicants read a bit of poetry so he could gauge their sensitivity to the written word. When asked to recite, the rambunctious young man immediately leaped onto a leather-upholstered chair to become Henry V, the character he had just played at the Bolton School. " 'Once more unto the breach, dear friends, once more!' " he cried, to Henn's astonishment. " 'Or close the wall up with our English dead!' " Reaching the rousing climax of the speech, he planted one foot on each arm of the chair and let his voice soar: " 'The game's afoot! Follow your spirit; and upon this charge cry, "God for Harry! England and Saint Geooorge!" ' " Duly impressed, Henn informed McKellen that he was now a Cambridge scholarship student—and requested that he kindly step off the chair.

He started at Cambridge in 1958, among such classmates as Derek Jacobi, Corin Redgrave, Clive Swift, Margaret Drabble, David Frost, Peter Cook, and Trevor Nunn. Mentoring them were three distinguished men of letters: George Rylands, F. R. Leavis, and John Barton, the triumvirate that had trained some of the finest actors in the world. From Rylands they learned a deep respect for text; from Leavis they learned nuance, the social context of words; from the indefatigable, larger-than-life Barton they learned all of the above, plus passion.

Within the university, there were several drama entities—the Marlowe Society; the Amateur Drama Club (ADC), which had its own theater; the Cambridge Mummers; the Fletcher Society; and the revue group, Footlights. McKellen found himself most involved in the ADC. Through it he came to realize that, despite being the best actor at the Bolton School, "What I was hopeless at was stepping onto the stage without any aids and just behaving in the style of the play as myself," he said in an interview. His best work was usually done when he was under layers of makeup and padding. When he had to be real, when he had to be simple, he was less surefooted. "I did not know how to release and reveal my inner life," he confesses. "My acting was all gestures and no heart." Nonetheless, from the start of his university years, he received excellent reviews for his performances in such plays as Shakespeare's *Henry IV* and *Twelfth Night* and Anton Chekhov's *Three Sisters;* and with each production, he grew more secure. By his third term in college, he had played twenty-one roles and had been elected president of the Marlowe Society.

With such devotion to the theater, McKellen, not surprisingly, tended to neglect his academic course work and so wound up achieving only a 2:2 Bachelor of Arts degree in English. As his friend Clive Swift, who would go on to act with the Royal Shakespeare Company, told McKellen's biographer, Joy Leslie Gibson, "None of us would have thought that, of all of us, Ian would be the one to have become the great actor he has, a star. Not then—he was the reticent one." Swift added that initially, McKellen had been very quiet, and kept very much to himself. "He seemed to have no girlfriends, and if he talked about his family, I seem to remember that it was in a jokey way."

In college, McKellen was deep in the closet. As for most gay men of a certain age, "When I started having sex, it was illegal," he says. "The message that one got growing up in that atmosphere was that if you felt yourself to be gay, you were thinking, 'I am potentially behaving like a criminal.' That was the situation. With our sort of upbringing, lower-middle-class evangelical Christian—good people—an eighteen-year-old wouldn't be expected to be talking about his sex life, whatever it happened to be. He would just turn up one day, age twenty-five, with a girlfriend, and they'd be married by the time they were thirty, and there wouldn't be any conversation about it." He admits frustration at not having been allowed to experiment sexually, as straight adolescents did. "The teens are a good time to be wondering about things and trying things out and discovering you like certain things and don't like others," he says. "And I was denied all that. There just wasn't the possibility."

McKellen recalls no talk of homosexuality except sporadically in the scandal sheets, "and very occasionally, and very influentially in my case, lawsuits that hit the broadsheets, such as Lord Montague and the writer Peter Wildblood." In this infamous case, Montague and Wildblood were convicted of having sexual relations with some underage Scouts who were camping on Montague's estate. The allegations and ensuing trial dominated the newspapers for months, and when the sensationalized ordeal was over, Wildblood wrote a wrenching book about his imprisonment, entitled *Beyond the Law.* The notion of homosexuality as criminal was also reinforced by the arrest of actor John Gielgud for "opportuning" a young man in the early 1950's. It wasn't until years later, McKellen says, "that I heard the story of the first performance after his arrest. He was very, very nervous about going onstage. The play was *Day by the Sea,* where he played a semigay character. Well, when he went onstage, the audience just clapped and clapped and clapped. Either they didn't believe the story and thought he'd been unjustly treated, or they didn't care."

In addition to living in such an atmosphere, McKellen, like many young actors, had self-image difficulties. "I felt when I was growing up that I wasn't pretty," he said years later to *Out* magazine. "There wasn't a day between fifteen and twenty-five that there wasn't something scabrous growing on my skin. And I felt that no one would find me attractive." Yet, when he now looks back at photographs from that period, he says with surprise, "I was cute!" The reticence about his appearance, coupled with the forbidden nature of homosexuality, disinclined McKellen to explore many relationships. "Apart from masturbation," he says with a chuckle, "I don't think I was very interested in sex. I would be sexually roused by men and women in my teens, but mainly men. I've never been truly attracted to the female form; it seems such a pity to cut myself off, but there it is. . . . I did begin to have an affair at university with a girl, despite myself. But that was the only time. And then I fell in love with a young man."

The young man was Curt Dawson, a strikingly handsome, blond, blue-eyed actor from Russell, Kansas, who had come to England to study at the Royal Academy of Dramatic Art. Warm and sharp-tongued at the same time, not only was the American dazzling to look at and fun to be with, but he could keep up with the quickness of McKellen's mind. With Dawson, Ian embarked on an exuberant journey of sexual discovery that convinced him that he was gay—and glad to be gay, for he fell deeply and fully in love. Like most first loves, however, the relationship did not last. Later, McKellen would jokingly attribute his decision to become an actor to the breakup with Curt Dawson. For one thing, it left him feeling that he was "not fit for anything else," and for another, he says, in the theater, "I'd heard that I might meet a few queers. And I did!"

Within a month of leaving Cambridge, McKellen had offers of employment from three acting companies and settled on the Belgrade Theatre Company in Coventry, twenty miles north of Stratford-upon-Avon. Not only did the company have a reputation for mounting impressive productions, it also offered the highest salaries. "I don't think I realized at the time how lucky I was," he later said. "I don't think you could do it so easily these days." From 1961 to 1963, he appeared in major productions of Robert Bolt's *A Man for All Seasons,* George Bernard Shaw's *You Never Can Tell,* and Shakespeare's *Much Ado About Nothing,* among others, doing such good work that the company soon began to build its season around him, selecting plays that would showcase him. It was then that noted talent agent Elspeth Cochrane decided that she wanted to represent him. "But I didn't ask him right away," she told McKellen's biographer. "Young actors, at the stage he was then, don't need agents, which is exactly what Ian said when I did approach him. But I knew other people were or soon would be after him, so I made my bid."

Cochrane then brought her client, Robert Chetwyn, head of the Ipswich Repertory Company, to see Ian perform. Chetwyn promptly asked McKellen to join his company. Chetwyn would become a mentor of sorts, not only directing Ian in many productions but also helping him develop as an actor. It was from Chetwyn that he learned to find the laughs in Shakespeare—even in the tragedies—which would become his theatrical trademark. On Chetwyn's advice, he eventually signed with Elspeth Cochrane, who would not only guide his career choices for more than two decades, but also sometimes act as a surrogate mother.

But by the time he was twenty-five, McKellen was outgrowing Ipswich, and with Chetwyn's blessing he moved up one more rung, to the Playhouse Theatre in Nottingham. Although he received slightly less money than at Ipswich, the Playhouse was new, and boasted an exciting array of actors, including John Neville, Leo McKern, and a young Michael Crawford. Another attraction was that it was a repertory company—which meant rehearsing future plays by day while performing the troupe's current offering each night. Although it was a grueling cycle, the experience sharpened his craft—as did the direction of the legendary man of the theater, Sir Tyrone Guthrie. The first production McKellen appeared in was Shakespeare's *Coriolanus,* in which Guthrie boldly chose to present the relationship between Coriolanus, played by John Neville, and his enemy Aufidius (McKellen) as repressed homosexuality. Inspired as the two leads were by Guthrie's revitalizing interpretation, Ian nonetheless kept stumbling over the anguished final speech he was to deliver over the body of Coriolanus. The epiphany, as he calls it, came when Guthrie took him aside and told him, "Aufidius is a man, but he can grow, as we all can, to behave like a god. His rage can turn to sorrow. Fill your mind, your imagination, with your feelings and let your heart wail. If you can't do it, it's all a waste." Then Guthrie looked squarely at McKellen and said, "You can."

When he performed the role, McKellen felt for the first time that he had truly connected with the essence of acting: revealing inner feelings to the audience and making them empathize completely with the character, no matter how vile his actions. Indeed, reviewing the production, *The Nottingham Evening Post* would say: "Ian McKellen gives a depth to the Volscian commander, Aufidius, that is twitching in intensity."

McKellen had garnered enough critical praise to try his luck in London and now won a role in a new play, *A Scent of Flowers* by James Saunders, at the Duke of York Theatre. His father, stepmother, and sister Jean all attended to celebrate his London debut. A disturbing drama about suicide that would be dismissed by critics, the play was nonetheless a tremendous success with the opening-night audience, who gave it fifteen curtain calls. Then, shortly after witnessing his son's London triumph, Denis McKellen was killed in an accident. Ian was shattered. His grief was compounded not only by the unresolved feelings about the distance he had kept from his father—knowing that he had never truly revealed himself to him—but also by having to perform, night after night, in a play about death.

During this time, actress Maggie Smith, who was working with Laurence Olivier at the National Theatre, caught one of McKellen's performances and pressured Olivier into attending a matinee of *A Scent of Flowers*. The day Olivier came to watch him, Ian was out with the flu, but trusting the brilliant Smith's instincts, he offered him a contract anyway—and the chance to join the ranks of such esteemed actors as Smith, Michael York, Albert Finney, and Derek Jacobi at the National. McKellen enthusiastically accepted.

With his professional life seemingly secure, Ian could begin to build a personal life in London and soon made a commitment to his first long-term lover, Brian Taylor, a history teacher from his old school, Bolton, moving with him and their two Scottish terriers to a house on Earl's Terrace in Kensington. With Taylor, McKellen was finally able to recover the sense of family that he had lost with his parents' deaths. Although not "out" to his blood family or the outside world, he never concealed his relationship with Taylor from his inner circle. "Everybody knew at work, my employers knew, the employees knew," he says. "There was no hiding it." But he kept a low profile. "The generally accepted behavior—even in show business, where, of course, there have always been gay people—was a sense of 'Yes, be gay, but be quiet about it.' You might be put in prison."

He also made a great friend in London, Edward Petherbridge, an actor who would gain fame in *Rosencrantz and Guildenstern Are Dead,* Tom Stoppard's remarkable reworking of *Hamlet.* The two actors would not only become lifelong friends but would twice be business partners. In an interview with the London *Times,* Petherbridge said of McKellen, "We make each other laugh a lot. We are aware of the eccentricities in each other's makeup. I suppose we are a lesson to each other."

By 1966, McKellen felt secure enough, personally and professionally, to risk going freelance as an actor. His first major job was a role in *The Promise* by Alexey Arbuzov, with Judi Dench and Ian McShane. The play was a tremendous success, and McKellen was singled out for praise by *The Sunday Times* critic: "There are moments in Mr. McKellen's performance . . . which must rank with as high achievements of acting as I have ever seen . . . his style, his panache, his vulnerable but never broken gentleness and pride are to be savoured." The play later moved to the Henry Miller Theater in New York, and Ian traveled to America for the first time to make his Broadway debut. Unfortunately, most of the attention the play received focused on the protests mounted by Actors' Equity Association, the stage actors' union. Objecting to an entire cast of British actors with no Americans in any of the roles, representatives from the union picketed the theater nightly. Unable to continue a run under such circumstances, the show closed after only ten days.

In 1967, during the time he was abroad, Great Britain repealed the 1885 Labouchere Amendment and decriminalized private, consensual homosexual sex, over the objections of the sitting Lord Chief Justice, who deemed the new act "a bugger's license." However, sex between two men—lesbians had never been subject to the law—was still forbidden in Scotland, Northern Ireland, Wales, and the Isle of Man. Furthermore, the new British law had typically curious stipulations. "There could not be a third party present," McKellen says, "or *potentially* present. The door, in other words, had to be locked and nobody else could have the key. So that meant, as is still the case, that it would be illegal for two men to make love in a hotel, because the manager of the hotel would have the key. You couldn't make love in your parents' home at Christmas with your boyfriend because that was technically not a private place. And although this seemed a big breakthrough in 1967, the age of consent was fixed at the age of majority, which was then twenty-one, while for straights, of course, the age of consent was sixteen. So there was this odd disparity that wasn't resolved in 1967, but for my generation—for me—I was twenty-eight before it was legal." Changing the law, of course, could not change public opinion. "For most people in England," McKellen says, "sex is a tricky topic." The majority of homosexuals continued to live quietly underground. "If you didn't feel ashamed, you just decided to be discreet and make what you could of it," he continues. "Which for a lot of people was the excitement of doing something secret—going to clubs and bars where you had to knock three times, that sort of thing. . . ." Being in a long-term relationship with Taylor, McKellen did not have that mindset, or need to resort to those venues. Still, there was relief that love could be physically expressed in the privacy of their home without being felons in the Realm.

Early in 1968, McKellen was approached by an old Cambridge classmate, Richard Cottrell, who was now an assistant director for the Prospect Company. Prospect was a touring troupe that played small towns all over the country that would not otherwise be able to enjoy professional theater. Cottrell had been assigned to direct Shakespeare's *Richard II,* a difficult and seldom-produced play that nonetheless featured a spectacular lead role, which he offered to Ian. McKellen loved touring, and recalling the joy he had felt as a child when such companies would perform in Wigan and Bolton, he accepted. The play, which proved a rousing critical and financial success, wound up at the Edinburgh Festival in Scotland, at which Prospect was also scheduled to present Christopher Marlowe's *Edward II*. Derek Jacobi was cast as the homosexual king and Ian as his lover, Gaveston. When Jacobi had to back out at the last minute, director Toby Robertson asked McKellen to switch over to the lead role. "He was very, very nervous about doing the two parts," Robertson told Joy Leslie Gibson, "but he worked tremendously hard. It was a tremendous effort to have the double yoke of playing two kings, but it was the making of Ian. He was a terrific success."

McKellen almost lost the chance to deliver that bravura hat-trick performance. When the Edinburgh City Council discovered the content of the Marlowe play—that it depicted King Edward's homosexuality and fatal disemboweling and, worse, that McKellen would actually be kissing another man onstage—they threatened to close down the production. "It is shocking and filthy," Councillor John Kidd told the press. "Can you blame me when I see two men kissing one another? I think it is the sort of play that Edinburgh does not want!" Robertson, although delighted with the publicity, had to take up the matter with the chief constable, who sent two uniformed policemen to screen the performance. "They sat with their knees wide open until Edward's painful death," Ian recalls with a laugh, "when in sympathy, they crossed their manly legs tight against any intrusion. At the end of the show, they started the standing ovation—and that's the last we heard of any censorship." It was Ian's first brush with censorship, and he would not forget it.

The two plays were the resounding hits of the festival, and when they began a triumphant run in London at the Piccadilly Theatre, the critic for the London *Times* wrote a paean in his review:

Since his prodigious debut in Guthrie's *Coriolanus* in 1963, Mr. McKellen had been widely credited with star quality. Reviewers are inclined to treat that term as indefinable; actors have either got it or not. In Mr. McKellen's case, one can go a bit further than that, as he is a star of a very special kind. Beyond sheer animal magnetism, he also raised acting from a secondary thing, a reflection of life, into a primary position. He seems not to work with the actor's usual tools of memory and observation, but to build a performance directly from the task in hand. It would not surprise me to learn that he has no private life and no need of close friends, as he appears to be drawing vital experience straight from the stage with no need for outside nourishment. . . .

From this impossibly high point, for Ian McKellen, the only thing to do next was to tackle the most famous role in all of English literature—Shakespeare's Hamlet.

He wanted no one to direct him but his old friend Robert Chetwyn; indeed, they had talked about doing the play back at the Ipswich company years earlier. In the late fall of 1970, they examined the play line by line for nearly four months. Re-creating Hamlet is always a watershed for an actor, and McKellen wanted to offer a new perspective on the play. Avoiding the pitfalls of striving to psychologically reconfigure the lead role, he and Chetwyn made the decision to play Hamlet as it was written, with fresh insights added through inventive staging and new interpretations of other characters. For example, the set was constructed entirely of mirrors, some of them two-way, and Hamlet's father's ghost was reimagined as a disembodied voice in Hamlet's head—not a real character at all. By the time he finished rehearsing, Ian was convinced that the play was the best thing he had ever done.

The critics, however, were not as rhapsodic. The review in *The Guardian* was fairly typical. It started off promisingly enough, saying, "People wait nowadays for an Ian McKellen performance with that breathless anticipation usually reserved for moon landings," but then went on to take McKellen to task for being too flashy and superficial: "What he lacks is anything that seems natural, truly felt, interpreted. His is the triumph of artifice over everything else." *The Times* agreed: "Despite his fire and passion, Mr. McKellen appears to lack any compulsive conception in his performance." However, audiences were much more receptive to McKellen's very accessible, modern-feeling, almost hippielike Hamlet than the critics, and the production toured the United Kingdom and Holland, Belgium, Germany, and Italy, playing to packed houses for nearly a year.

When he returned to London in 1972, McKellen discovered that his time on the road had put a serious strain on his relationship with his lover, Brian Taylor. Tension permeated the household, and began to spill over into the couple's social life. At a party at the home of Jeremy Conway, a noted and prestigious agent, Ian and Brian met actor Michael Cashman. Cashman, an intensely handsome man, was a rising star about to be admitted into the Royal Shakespeare Company. Ian misinterpreted his intentions. "About three months later, I joined the RSC and saw Ian in the canteen," Cashman recalls. "I went up to reintroduce myself and he was quite cool and I couldn't work out why." It was not until years later that McKellen would admit to Cashman, "I thought you were after my boyfriend!" The belated accusation startled Cashman. "Indeed," he says, "I wasn't."

Nevertheless, the Taylor-McKellen relationship proved beyond repair. Three weeks after the Conway party, Ian moved out of Earl Terrace and purchased his first home, on Camberwell Grove, where he would live alone for the next eight years. In his professional life, too, he decided that it was time to strive for self-sufficiency, for he was weary of being subject to others. As Ian would later explain to *Guardian* critic Michael Billington, he had "the feeling that we ought to be doing more as actors . . . to help change things, particularly the conditions under which we work. The physical conditions are not very good. And the psychological conditions are often worse, partly because of the difficulty of knowing what one's position is within the organization that puts on a play." With his old friend Edward Petherbridge, he came up with a plan to found a new kind of theater troupe, with actors in charge—selecting the plays, performing the full range of roles from leads to walk-ons, and voting on management and business issues. Richard Cottrell, then director of the Cambridge Theatre Company, offered the new company a home and seed money; and when they got primary funding from the Arts Council, McKellen and Petherbridge started rounding up actors they wanted to work with, including Margery Mason, Robert Eddison, Robin Ellis, and Felicity Kendal. They christened the new troupe the Actors' Company.

The Actors' Company caught on immediately with theatergoers, who were especially eager to see the well-known McKellen and Petherbridge perform. It toured the country for the next two years with such productions as John Ford's *'Tis Pity She's a Whore,* Chekhov's *The Wood Demon,* and Shakespeare's *King Lear,* gaining such renown that it was invited to appear at New York's Brooklyn Academy of

Music. By opening night, the company's *King Lear* sets had still not ar-rived from England, but rather than disappoint the sold-out house, the actors decided to perform the play with all they had—on a bare stage and in modern dress. When the final curtain fell, neither the audience nor the critics felt shortchanged. Clive Barnes of *The New York Times* wrote, "The company is a joy to welcome . . . the production is stuffed with good, unobtrusive performances. . . ." Singling out McKellen from the ensemble, Barnes declared, "He has a natural blaze to him that no amount of democracy can douse. . . . He is that rare bird—an in-tellectual actor with incandescence, so not only does he know what to do, he also seems to know why he is doing it."

But reviews like Barnes's were starting to sow dissension in the com-pany, for inevitably some of the members resented the attention that McKellen and Petherbridge were getting. In fact, one of the directors, David Giles, echoed Barnes when discussing the rifts in the company with the London *Times:* "There was a feeling of creative energy about them [McKellen and Petherbridge] which no amount of democracy could change." As Margery Mason said to McKellen's biographer, "It was all lovely at first; then people began wheeling and dealing to get parts, the atmosphere was spoilt, and we all had to spend too much time on administration." Agreeing with Mason's characterization, Ian re-signed from the Actors' Company at the end of 1974 and Petherbridge soon joined him, but the troupe had established such a fine reputation that it continued to attract audiences for several more years even with-out its major stars.

At the beginning of 1975, Ian received an offer from his old mentor at Cambridge, John Barton, now an *éminence grise* at the Royal Shake-speare Company, to play the lead in Marlowe's *Dr. Faustus.* McKellen had always been wary of joining the large, star-dominated RSC; his tenure at the National had not been all that happy. But the RSC was, after all, the premiere repertory company in the world; and McKellen was at a point in his career when he would not get lost in the shuffle even at a large company. He decided to accept, and his *Dr. Faustus* was a rousing success, as were the other plays he did for the RSC that year, one of them a felicitous reunion with Judi Dench in Shaw's *Too True to Be Good.* Besides the good work being done, Ian was delighted to dis-cover that the company was not an unwieldy monolith, as he had feared, but a flurry of smaller entities under the RSC banner. He was so enthusiastic about his season that he phoned his old schoolmate, Trevor Nunn, who had just taken over directorship of the RSC, to ask if there were any slots for him in the company's upcoming roster of plays at Stratford. As it happened, Nunn was just working out the new season, and was happy to come up with some roles that would spotlight McKellen: leads in *Romeo and Juliet, Macbeth,* and *A Winter's Tale.*

Although all the plays were successful, it was *Macbeth,* staged in a tiny Stratford shed called the Other Space, that created the biggest stir. Mounted on practically no budget, with a minimum of props and secondhand costumes, the play was stripped down to its basic skeletal structure. *Macbeth* has such a reputation among theater people for being unlucky that it is referred to not by its title but as "the Scottish play." However, in the hands of McKellen, Judi Dench as Lady Macbeth, and director Trevor Nunn, it became an astonishing, unparalleled triumph. "I have never seen the play come across with such throat-grabbing power," wrote Michael Billington in *The Guardian.* Robert Cushman of *The Observer* called it "the best Shakespeare production I have ever seen." The production was such an overwhelming success that it would be transferred to Stratford's main stage and from there to the Young Vic in London, where it continued to enthrall audiences and completely sold out its run.

The last two plays of the season, Henrik Ibsen's *Pillars of the Community* and Ben Jonson's *The Alchemist,* provided a spectacular finish for McKellen. Of *Pillars, The Sunday Times* critic wrote, "This is the finest performance I've seen Ian McKellen give." When *The Alchemist* came on its heels, the critics grew dizzy with praise for Ian's virtuosity. The one-two punch won him his first two Society of West End Theatres (SWET) awards as Best Actor of 1977 *and* 1978. But, for all his awards and acclaim, it was the intimate, scaled-down, small-theater experience he had in *Macbeth* that stayed with McKellen; and he now persuaded Nunn to produce versions of *Twelfth Night* and *The Three Sisters* designed for theaters seating no more than a hundred. Nunn did so, sending McKellen and Petherbridge on the road as the stars of the newly formed RSC Touring Group. Their success established the touring company as an important new wing of the RSC.

In 1978, when the tour stopped at the Edinburgh Festival, McKellen met a young Welsh actor, Sean Mathias, who was also appearing at the festival. Mathias, handsome, slender, bright, and seventeen years Mc-Kellen's junior, was on his way to a party for the RSC as the guest of his friend, actress Suzanne Bertish. "We stopped off in Ian's dressing room, and gave him a lift in my Beetle." Although put at separate tables for the rather grand dinner, Mathias recalls, "We made eyes at each other all through the meal. There was an immediate chemistry between us." Following their respective tours, when they returned to London, they began to date. "It was quite a while before we got into bed," Mathias says. "There was this whole courting period, which Ian held out for. I was hungry to get into bed. He made me wait."

His personal life again on track, McKellen cast about for a new professional challenge and found one, surprisingly, in the commercial theater. Gay Sweatshop, a theater cooperative specializing in plays with homosexual themes, had done a piece by American playwright Martin Sherman but felt honor-bound to reject his second submission, *Bent,* because it was, in their words, "too good," deserving to reach a broader audience than the Sweatshop could readily attract. Having written the lead, Max, with Ian McKellen in mind, Sherman then sent the play to director Robert Chetwyn, who enthusiastically recommended it to his old friend. McKellen loved it, and immediately gave it to Mathias to get his reaction. "I remember we stayed up all night talking about it," Mathias says. Armed with Ian's assent, Chetwyn took it to producer Eddie Kulukundis. Undaunted by the play's dark theme of homosexuality in a Nazi concentration camp, Kulukundis persuaded the Royal Court Theatre to mount *Bent.*

The play would prove to be another triumph for McKellen. Although some critics considered it "vulgar," others saw *Bent* as an eloquent plea for tolerance, and all concurred that Ian McKellen was breathtaking in the lead role. To play Max, he had transformed his appearance, shaving off his full, wavy hair and losing so much weight that his face and body took on an ashen pallor. Inwardly, he touched a nerve so raw and tapped into a reserve of emotion so full that he surprised even himself. Perhaps because the play dealt with a subject that Ian could relate to on a deeply personal level—homosexuality that had to be repressed—his simplicity and tenderness in the performance were noted again and again. The second act, set entirely in the concentration camp, contains a now famous scene where, standing on opposite sides of the stage, McKellen as Max and Tom Bell as his lover, Horst, unable to physically touch, make verbal love to each other to the point of climax. It was a dicey maneuver to pull off, but the two actors soared, earning standing ovations and bouquets of flowers tossed at the curtain calls. For his portrayal, McKellen won the SWET Best Actor award, his third in three years, setting a record that is still unbroken. Max remains to this day his favorite role.

In June of 1979, while he was performing in *Bent,* he received Commander of the British Empire (CBE) honors in recognition of his body of work. "I received a letter from Ten Downing Street ten days after the Tories won the election," Ian said later. "The first two things that Mrs. Thatcher did were to give me a CBE and to knock one and a half million off the Arts Council Grant." The following January, after the Tories had engineered even further cuts in arts funding, McKellen condemned the action in a blistering speech at the *Evening Standard*'s twenty-fifth Drama Awards. It would not be the last time McKellen would take the prime minister to task; the next time he did so, eight years later, it would be a full frontal assault.

When *Bent* finished its run, McKellen experienced an unusual three-month period of unemployment. During that time, he devised and wrote a one-man show, highlighting his work as an actor and interpreting his favorite playwright. Entitled *Acting Shakespeare,* the piece was directed by Mathias and designed to be performed in small, intimate theaters—now the actor's favorite venue. It toured the country, then the world, delighting audiences with a repertoire of characterizations from the pen of the Bard. Whenever he was between jobs, McKellen would tour *Acting Shakespeare,* which became both a popular and critical success, enhancing his reputation even further.

McKellen was now approached by Sir Peter Hall, head of the National Theatre, to take on one of the meatiest leads in modern drama—the role of Salieri, the refined court musician who has an insanely jealous relationship with the wildly undisciplined but brilliant Wolfgang Amadeus Mozart, in *Amadeus* by Peter Shaffer. Originally the inestimable Paul Scofield had played the part, but Shaffer and Hall had decided that they wanted a younger, more vibrant Salieri to appear in the New York production of the play. Shaffer expanded and extensively rewrote the part for McKellen, who opened on Broadway to a much different reception from the one that had greeted his New York debut in the truncated run of *The Promise*. He and the play were the toast of the 1981 Broadway season. "This month [September] marks my twentieth anniversary as a professional actor," Ian told *The New York Times* during the run. "Looking back, I realize that I always wanted to be on Broadway, right from the beginning."

"It was a very, very exciting time, because *Amadeus* was such a huge hit," Mathias recalls. "There were so many major celebrities always in the dressing room every night. And New York was very hedonistic at the time—lots of parties and lots of drugs and drink." McKellen also had a limousine at his disposal as well as a per diem and a hefty salary. The two men lived in a large apartment in Union Square, "which was still a bit risky. And people suggested, 'You really shouldn't live there, it's too dangerous, there's too many drug dealers down there. . . .' But we had a great time. Ian worked very hard in the show and sustained the performance eight times a week, but we did a lot of partying as well. A lot of friends and family came over from abroad and we were always sort of guiding them around and doing touristy things."

Yet, despite all the glamor and headiness, it was a trying time for Mathias. Although he was able to use the time to write a novel, *Manhattan Mourning,* which was published six years later, he felt dwarfed in McKellen's shadow. "I was a much younger man and a person who didn't have a career and who didn't have the same financial independence," he says. "All the scripts that arrived were for Ian and all the phone calls were for Ian. It was a very difficult aspect of our relationship."

Amadeus won the Drama Desk and New York Critics' Circle awards, and then was nominated for a string of Tony Awards, including a nod for Ian McKellen. Continuing his practice of not hiding yet not flaunting his personal life, he took Sean as his date to the ceremony. "A Tony Award is obviously a big commercial award and not only would it be a jewel in the crown for Ian's performance as Salieri, it would certainly mean something to his career," Mathias says. "I remember when his name was called, the first thing he did was hand me an envelope. When he got up and read his acceptance speech, I opened the envelope and

inside there was a personal note of thanks to me—which was lovely."
Mathias was also acutely aware that the two of them showing up as a
couple for the fete was also a big gesture. "Those were very early days
to be going around as a gay couple. There weren't many examples of
people 'out' at that point. So I think Ian was very courageous." Although McKellen admits that they weren't fully "out," he believes that
"there are gradations of being 'out.' I was never apprehensive about taking my boyfriend anywhere, yet I did not consciously kiss him in public. We did not consciously walk down the street holding hands." Yet,
Mathias's presence at his side did not go unnoticed. "I got a number of
letters from people saying that it was the first time anyone's taken their
boyfriend to the Tonys," he says. "But it wasn't true, because Peter Shaffer was sitting behind me with his boyfriend."

After performing in *Amadeus* for a year, Ian turned down the chance
to tour America with the play, opting instead to take time off and vacation with Sean. When the two reached San Francisco, they met with
the writer Armistead Maupin, who had been recommended to them as
a good tour guide by a mutual friend, journalist Adam Block. "We'd
met Adam at a D. H. Lawrence festival in Santa Fe, New Mexico, before *Amadeus* had started," Mathias says. "He was very cute and sexy and
I recall flirting with him a bit. It made Ian jealous and crotchety, but it
was through this guy that the relationship with Armistead was formed."
Maupin had gained fame as the author of *Tales of the City,* a novel about
gay life in San Francisco that had begun as popular stories in the *San
Francisco Chronicle.* But, that first day, when McKellen and Mathias
climbed into Maupin's Volkswagen, along with his lover, gay activist
Terry Anderson, the two couples knew very little about each other.
"We weren't sycophantic about each other's work at all," Maupin says,
laughing. "He hadn't read any of my books and I hadn't seen any of his
performances. All I knew was that he was a distinguished British actor."
Maupin was much more of a cinema buff than a theatergoer, and as he
drove his guests around the city, he kept pointing out sites where films
had been shot—the base of the Golden Gate Bridge for *Vertigo,* Lom-
bard Street for the comical chase scene in *What's Up, Doc?,* Alcatraz
Island for *Escape from Alcatraz,* and so on—to the annoyance of Mc-
Kellen, who did not have a catalogue of movie scenes in his head.

Finally, when Maupin pointed out one more site and simply described it as "beautiful," Ian dryly remarked, "What, no movie filmed here? Pity."

Nonetheless, the two men felt a strong rapport. "I think from the beginning, we both recognized that laughter had been our savior many times over the course of our lives," Maupin says. "To this day we enjoy finding humor in catastrophe. It's a big rescuer. We laugh a *lot*." One thing they had to laugh about was an amazing coincidence they discovered when McKellen, quite out of the blue, mentioned that his first love, Curt, had been an American actor. "Curt *Dawson?*" Maupin asked, astonished. "Oh, my God! He was my first, too!" The writer told the tale of how, when he had just returned from Vietnam and was living in Charleston, South Carolina, the extremely attractive actor and his friend, Barbara Caruso, came through on a break from performing a Chekhov play in Atlanta. "I struck up a conversation with them and he was very clearly coming on to me, but I was just a baby homo and didn't recognize the signals," Maupin says. "Actually I was picking up the signals, but they made no sense to me, because he was traveling with a woman. I didn't have the concept that there was such a thing as a straight woman and a gay man." Nevertheless, Dawson eventually got through to Maupin and the two had a short but delightful affair. "Something that he had in common with Ian—which attracted me to both of them—was the way he would take such pleasure in small things in the moment. Such a wonderful quality. He was the first time I really lost my heart to someone." From then on, Ian and Armistead fondly referred to Dawson as "Lover Zero." And also from then on, McKellen would regard Maupin as a close friend and confidant. He went out and bought the *Tales of the City* novels. Maupin, in turn, attends every one of McKellen's plays.

Maupin was one of the first successful writers to come out publicly. "It hugely improved my art," he says. "I learned how to write. I learned how to get into the deepest parts of myself after I was able to be honest about myself." Inspired by his example, Ian began to ponder the idea of coming out himself. "It seemed to me a rather ridiculous situation," he recalls. "Everyone but the press and my family knew—so I discussed it with Sean." Mathias now says, "I wasn't out to my family, but absolutely everyone else knew I was gay. I didn't feel particularly worried about being gay, but it was a problem being a young actor and being Ian McKellen's boyfriend. People were inclined to think you weren't going to be much good yourself."

But even McKellen, at the top of his profession, fell prey to prejudice. He was up for a role in the film version of Harold Pinter's play *Betrayal* and, at one point in his discussions with the producer, felt relaxed enough to mention that he was gay. Weeks later Pinter called to tell Ian that he would have gotten the part had he not admitted his sexual orientation. McKellen was stunned. "I hadn't really known that I had gotten the part, so I thought, 'Oh, what a lucky escape,'" he recalls. " 'Who wants to work with someone who thinks like that anyway?' " Still, the experience showed Ian that, even in the tolerant world of the cinema, there could be harsh consequences if one confessed to being homosexual. As Michael Cashman says, "Anyone who says you have nothing to lose in coming out doesn't understand that you just don't come out once—you come out for the rest of your life." So, for a time, McKellen put his plan to come out publicly on hold. Indeed, Joy Leslie Gibson's biography *Ian McKellen,* published in 1986, made no mention of his homosexuality.

He and Sean were living together, nonetheless. With his savings from the *Amadeus* run, Ian bought a three-story converted wooden Victorian warehouse on Narrow Street in Limehouse, on the banks of the Thames River. Its large airy living room featured a huge picture window with views of Canary Wharf and the Tower Bridge; just off it was a commodious country kitchen where Ian delighted in preparing gourmet meals. On the balcony overlooking the river, as a sort of household god, McKellen stationed a bust of Shakespeare, his inspiration for so much of his life.

Sean Mathias, deciding to fully move from being an actor, wrote a play of his own, *Cowardice,* and Ian, "bless his copper socks," Mathias says, "insisted on being in it." Although he would have done anything to help his boyfriend's career, McKellen was also cognizant that he was the one who was holding the young man back. "He wanted to redress the imbalance," Mathias recounts, "but in a funny sort of way it went on to do me more damage. It was as if I had written a vehicle for my boyfriend, which actually wasn't the case. Some of the critics attacked me for that." *Cowardice,* costarring Janet Suzman—wife of Trevor Nunn—made its

debut in 1983 and was not well received. In time Mathias came to believe that he would never achieve anything as an artist unless he escaped
McKellen's long shadow. "Eventually, I'm afraid I left the relationship—
simply speaking—for that reason."

Around the same time, McKellen suffered another disappointment
when he was denied the chance to play Salieri in Milos Forman's film
version of *Amadeus*; F. Murray Abraham would go on to win an Oscar
for the role. But as he would later say, perhaps a bit defensively, "I have
no desire to be a token British actor in Hollywood. And I've never had
any ambition to be a film star." One of his early films, *A Priest of Love,*
in which he played D. H. Lawrence alongside Janet Suzman and one of
his childhood heroes, John Gielgud, had proved unsuccessful; he also
would go on to play a small but pivotal role in the film of David Hare's
Plenty, with Meryl Streep and, again, John Gielgud. Still, he told *Ms
London* at the time: "I'm now forty-six, and I am under no illusion that
the time to make your name in movies is really in your early thirties—
as Tony Hopkins did. . . . If you are in demand as a theatre actor, it's not
that easy suddenly to pick up the offer of a film."

On the stage, McKellen was in great demand indeed. In 1984, Sir Peter Hall decided to split the lumbering National Theatre into five companies and asked McKellen to head one of them. He agreed to go back
to the National on the condition that his old friend Edward Petherbridge be brought in to share the leadership. Together they launched a
notable season presenting John Webster's *The Duchess of Malfi,* a double
bill of Stoppard's *The Real Inspector Hound* and Richard Brinsley Sheridan's *The Critic,* and Chekhov's *The Cherry Orchard.*

Then McKellen set out to tour *Acting Shakespeare* in the United
States, where it would be filmed for television. When the play made its
way to the West Coast, settling in for an extended stay in San Francisco,
his great friends Armistead Maupin and Terry Anderson brought a third
man, Steve Berry, to see Ian perform. Afterward the three joined Mc-
Kellen at his apartment. "It was one of those dreary rental units that
theaters provide for visiting actors," Maupin recalls. "I remember it being pea green and ugly," Anderson concurs. "And we had at least a couple bottles of champagne—and knowing Ian, maybe more." The
conversation drifted over a range of topics—the show; the rising tide of
conservatism in both England and America; the AIDS epidemic, to

which Ian and Armistead's long-ago lover-in-common, Curt Dawson, had succumbed; as well as McKellen's recent breakup with Mathias. Now that Ian no longer had to consider the effect on Sean, he asked his friends, "Do you think I should come out?" There was dead silence in the room. "They couldn't believe their luck!" McKellen says, laughing. "That anyone would be daft enough to say such a thing." Maupin remembers being shocked. "I was very jarred because people in the closet almost *never* ask that question. In fact, that's the only time it's happened in my life. The subject is usually avoided at any cost." McKellen was not likely to get an objective opinion that night: "One of the things that united the three of us was a deep hatred of the closet," Maupin says, "and the flip side of that, which was the importance of urging people to come out whenever we were in a position to do so." Anderson was the first to reply to Ian's query. "I gulped, looked him in the eye, and said, 'Well, yeah, I do think you should come out.'" Anderson believes that McKellen expected this. "It was on his mind when he came here. Sometimes people ask questions that they already know the answers to."

The three men laid out their reasons to McKellen, and Maupin made a deep impression when he spoke of the effect such honesty would have upon his profession. "I did not believe it would hurt his career," he says. "I felt that he would be reclaiming his life for the first time. And in doing so, he would hugely improve his art. I think it applies to almost every creative artist, including actors. It also boils down to an issue of character—I simply can't sustain admiration for anyone who lives that life for any length of time. I can admire and respect their work, but I end up losing respect for them as human beings."

Finally, McKellen said, "You've convinced me. I'm going to use the next opportunity that arises naturally to come out." Armistead Maupin had heard such professions before: "I remember thinking, 'This is either a first for me, or he is the most charming bullshitter I've ever met.' I knew him fairly well at that point, but not well enough to know if it would actually ever happen."

When McKellen returned to England, fired with his new determination to tell the truth, he found the climate inhospitable, due to the increasingly conservative Tory government under Margaret Thatcher. According to Chris Smith, the only openly gay member of Parliament,

Mrs. Thatcher's administration, then in its third term, was "off the leash." Deep cuts had been made in Social Security; property tax was abolished in favor of a uniform poll tax; an attempt was made to sabotage the National Health Service; and the Greater London Council—a Labour bastion and the largest of the local councils that were the only check of the prime minister's power—was abolished by Thatcher. In addition, not-so-subtle anti-gay sentiments were wafting through the halls of power. In October of 1987, Mrs. Thatcher gave a speech to the Conservative Party Conference in which she said, "Children who need to be taught to respect traditional values are being taught that they have an unalienable right to be *gay!*" The rancor finally erupted openly during the fall 1987 controversy over a picture book from Denmark, *Jenny Lives with Eric and Martin*. The story of a girl who lives with her father and his lover, it drew the ire of Conservatives who charged that the book promoted homosexuality; the tabloids immediately took up the cry under such inflammatory headlines as the *Sun's* VILE BOOK IN SCHOOL and *Today's* SCANDAL OF GAY PORN BOOKS READ IN SCHOOLS. Some outraged parents removed their children in protest. The fact that the book had appeared only in one teacher resource library—not available to children—and was checked out only once by a teacher, never to be seen by a single student, did not assuage the fury. In December, a Conservative backbencher in the House of Lords, Dame Jill Knight, appended a clause to the Local Government Bill, providing that:

A local authority shall not (a) promote homosexuality or publish material for the promotion of homosexuality, (b) promote the teaching in any maintained school of the acceptability of homosexuality as a pretended family relationship by the publication of such material or otherwise, (c) give financial or other assistance to any person for either of the purposes referred to under (a) or (b).

"The major point of the bill," Knight said, "is to protect children in schools from having homosexuality thrust upon them." Initially the Labour party did not oppose the measure, which came to be known as Clause 28, for they had suffered a bruising defeat in the last election and attributed the loss to their pro-gay policies. But Labour Leader Neil

Kinnock, alerted by Smith and other liberal politicians as well as concerned gay activists, soon realized the insidious bill's grave implications. Beneath its vague language lay the real possibility of censorship, not only in schools but also in the arts. Should the bill pass, any play, book, magazine article, or film with gay content could be banned. Kinnock labeled the measure a "pink triangle clause produced and supported by a bunch of bigots."

At the time the bill was proposed, McKellen was doing an eleven-week run of *Acting Shakespeare* at the Playhouse in the West End. He had pledged the full proceeds of the run to the Lighthouse, an AIDS hospice in London for which the Thatcher government had just cut off funding; and after each performance he personally stood in the lobby to collect any additional donations the audience could muster. It was at the theater door that he was approached by arts lobbyist Carole Woddis, who asked him to lend his name to the fight against the bill. He immediately agreed to help, and began by getting the arts lobby entrée to other very high-profile, sympathetic people who pledged their support.

Then, at the World AIDS Day celebration, Ian reencountered actor and activist Michael Cashman, at the time playing a gay character on the popular British soap opera, *EastEnders,* who told him that he had just come out publicly to protest Clause 28. The faulty accusations of Michael having "hit on" former boyfriend Brian Taylor laughed off and forgotten, McKellen found a kindred spirit in Cashman. "He became my mentor," McKellen says. That very night, when he appeared on live television as a presenter for the Society of West End Theatre Awards, McKellen made his move. Just as he was about to disclose an award winner's name, he turned to the television cameras and declared, "Before I make this announcement, I must warn you all of the dangers of Clause Twenty-eight of the Local Government Bill." The audience in the theater burst into cheers, giving the actor a lengthy ovation. Watching in his home, Michael Cashman was astounded. "The hair on the back of my neck was just standing on end," he recalls. "I screamed and yelled. I couldn't believe it! All the time we had been attempting to get more and more debate and publicity on this issue and it had been difficult. But suddenly Ian put it back there on the front pages—it sent a brushfire around the country."

Not long afterward, a press conference was staged at the Playhouse to lodge the arts community's official protest against Clause 28. "We bused some of the MPs from the Houses of Parliament," Michael Cashman recalls. "In the audience sat every imaginable major star, art administrator, writer, and painter in the UK." McKellen opened the session, and one by one, the illustrious supporters rose from their seats and joined him on the empty stage, denouncing Clause 28 and describing the impact it would have on their work. "It was a very, very impressive outing," Ian says.

Thereafter, he threw himself fully into the fray. "We would meet in the drill room of a small theatre in the West End and plan how we would get things written in the newspapers. I think I probably wrote something," he says. "Clause Twenty-eight became a focus for the media—censorship." Of the outcry against Clause 28, Stephen Jeffrey-Poulter would maintain in his book *Peers, Queers and Commons:* "It could be argued that the gay and lesbian community in Great Britain had finally been faced with their own equivalent of the Stonewall riot."

The press had begun to take sides in the debate. Peregrine Worsthorne, editor of the conservative *Sunday Telegraph,* insisted that the gay community only had itself to blame for the proposed legislation. Homosexuals, he wrote, had become "a bold and brazen proselytizing cult."

Journalist Ben Pimlott offered a contrary cautionary editorial in the London *Times:*

> Tolerance has constituted a tiny episode in our legal history, and in the face of the AIDS panic and a growing tide of illiberalism, it is vulnerable. In the future, to claim a work as a classic may be no protection, least of all in schools. . . . It may be that many people, conditioned by press stories of the excesses of gay activists, share the emotion behind Clause 28. If so, that fact is to be combatted. It also requires legislative courage. . . . Seldom, indeed, has the duty to make a stand for common sense and justice been more clear cut.

"Out" actor Simon Callow, to become famous for his roles in such films as *A Room with a View* and *Four Weddings and a Funeral,* held that

Clause 28 "seeks to reverse the open and unashamed self-image that homosexual people have projected since the repeal of the Labouchere amendment, to return homosexuality to the shadows. . . ."

The promoters of the anti-gay clause had hoped that the measure would be slipped into the government bill without catching attention. That was not to be the case. The Arts Council drafted a revision of the bill that would exclude material serving a bona fide "literary, artistic, scientific, or educational purpose" and proposed it to the Houses. As the battle lines were drawn in the media, and the debate began to take shape in the Palace of Westminster, Ian placed a call to lesbian activist Lisa Power, who had been involved in the Organization for Lesbian and Gay Action (OLGA) and was editor of the new gay newspaper in the UK, *The Pink Paper*.

"This beautiful voice said, 'Hello, I'm Ian McKellen and I've been told I ought to talk to you,' " Power recalls. "I thought someone was having a joke, because Ian has been a hero of mine for a long time as an actor." McKellen had agreed to appear on the BBC radio program *The Third Ear* to debate Clause 28 with editor Peregrine Worsthorne. "I think this is very important," he said to Power, "and I want to check out some of the issues with you." She and Ian ran through the specifics of the bill—the flaws, the misconceptions, and the maddening vague generalities—and prepared a strategy for an effective debate.

However, aside from the facts, Ian had decided to arm himself with something else, as well. "It crossed my mind that it would be a good debating ploy," he says, "and it was nothing more than that." It was, to be sure, much more than that. *The Third Ear* would provide the opportunity for the occasion Ian had promised months before to Terry Anderson and Armistead Maupin: He was going to come out. And in pure McKellen style, he was going to make it a grand, unequivocal statement—not in print, not at a news conference, but live before the entire BBC radio audience.

Beforehand, he called his sister Jean, with whom he had never been especially close because of his reluctance to discuss his personal life with her. She replied, "I'm glad you've told me, because I've often wanted to talk about it myself with you." Her only concern was her son's reaction, but all Ian's nephew said was: "Oh, well, I'm glad I didn't know at school because I don't know what my friends would have thought." Ian observed that everyone focused on how someone else would respond. "The converse of that ought to be, of course, that when you come out, there could be a good, positive chain reaction . . . as people discover that it doesn't bother them—and that it doesn't bother their friends, either."

He made a special journey to northern England to tell his eighty-two-year-old stepmother, Gladys, in person. When he broke the news, she gave a sigh of relief. "Oh, thank goodness!" she said. "I thought you were going to tell me something really dreadful! I've known that for about thirty-five years!" But there was a different reaction from David Curnow, the theater owner who had let him stand backstage as a child. "Oh, how could he do that to Gladys? Doesn't he realize she'll have to leave the village now?" he announced to friends. "That—from a very, very civilized man who really should have known better," McKellen says, shaking his head at the idea that his stepmother should be dunned out of her home because of his sexual orientation. As it proved, Gladys McKellen not only stayed on in the village but became something of an armchair expert on gay questions. "She follows them, and is often in advance of me on certain issues," Ian says.

The Third Ear aired on January 27, 1988. The host opened with an overview of the controversy surrounding Clause 28. "The clause is principally aimed at local authorities' responsibility for education," he said, "but there are fears, shared by the Arts Council, that Clause Twenty-eight could be applied to local-authority funding of the arts—in other words, that this is a back-door reintroduction of censorship." Then he addressed his first question to Ian: "The Minister for the Arts, Richard Luce, has specifically stated that Clause Twenty-eight is not meant to apply to the arts. Aren't you overreacting?"

"Well," McKellen replied, "if I am overreacting, I'm doing it in good company. I quote the QC [Queen's Counsel] employed by the Arts Council [who] says the result is likely to be that local authorities will curtail their support for the arts in a way that would be unacceptable in a democratic society."

Peregrine Worsthorne chimed in, "I don't think for a *minute* that it's aimed at the arts. I would be very surprised if it wasn't amended to exclude the arts and to concentrate on the proper aim of the clause, which is education."

Ian countered that censorship in the schools was also troubling. When the host replied, "So you would just like to see Clause Twenty-eight disappear altogether?" McKellen, not even pausing for emphasis, dropped the bomb: "Oh, yes. I certainly would. I think it's offensive to anyone who's, like myself, homosexual—apart from the business of what can or cannot be taught to children."

At first, perhaps because of the casual way he presented it, no one reacted to the fact that the leading Shakespearean actor in the world had just announced that he was a homosexual. Without missing a beat, McKellen continued: "The first part of this clause is that a local authority shall not promote homosexuality. Nothing about schools. It's a very vague—"

"And I would entirely agree that local authorities should not promote homosexuality," Worsthorne interrupted. "By promoting it, I mean advocating it and actually having the likelihood of turning more people into homosexuals that otherwise might not be. I don't think that reading Oscar Wilde, I don't think that reading E. M. Forster—I would say that anybody that reads *Maurice*, Forster's only homosexual novel, would be more likely to be turned *away* from homosexuality . . ."

Ian took up the question and broadcast his news once again. "Mr. Worsthorne thinks that a *book* can turn somebody into a homosexual," he said. "I don't believe that, any more than a book could have turned *me* into a heterosexual. I'd like to know what book might do that."

"I think it's an interesting question," Worsthorne said. "There was this famous book—and this has fairly triggered off this whole clause controversy—called *Jenny Lives with Eric and . . .* Tommy or something. This was a book which was introduced into schools by a particular local council with a view of teaching the young—the impressionable young—that homosexuality was a perfectly normal and desirable condition. . . . I think the aims of the people who are pushing that book are thoroughly deplorable. . . . It's absolutely understandable that parents should strongly object to having that kind of book, that kind of homosexual propaganda, put to children who are at an extremely impressionable age. I do believe that—I don't know what the exact ages would be, between, say, ten and sixteen—it is possible to push people in one direction or the other; that most people are very impressionable about these things. You can, therefore, have the effect of turning more people into homosexuals than would otherwise be the case. And I think this is very unfortunate—and antisocial."

Ian countered: "I would have to challenge you to quote the medical authority which supports you in assuming that people can be pushed into homosexuality as a teenager. Or indeed pushed into heterosexuality. It didn't work with *me*. I wasn't pushed into heterosexuality and you clearly have not been pushed into homosexuality. You must tell me, what is your basis for believing that?!"

The incredulity in McKellen's voice triggered a defensive story from Worsthorne about boys experimenting with homosexuality in his boarding school. "It was touch-and-go for a number of people whether they continued to be homosexual or ceased. This could very much be affected by a glamorous headmaster or by a particular teaching. I think you can be affected in this way. . . ."

"That is at the heart of the matter," Ian said. "Whether homosexuality can be promoted and taught and people can be converted to it. It is *just not true* what has been asserted. Of course, during teenage years, children experiment. According to Kinsey, which are the only reliable figures that we have, thirty percent of the population have homosexual experiences before they decide whether they are homosexual or not. That's perfectly natural and normal, and I don't think it necessarily should be discouraged. It is certainly not going to be caused by a *book!*"

The all-but-forgotten moderator, trying desperately to regain control of the discussion, now asked Worsthorne, "Surely there is a case, Mr. Worsthorne, to be made in a democracy such as ours that we have a responsibility to respect and indeed protect the rights of a minority such as homosexuals. Now you don't seem to be in favor of doing that."

"I supported the legalization of homosexuality between consenting adults in 1967 and still do so," Worsthorne snapped. "But I think that anything that would increase—I . . . I . . ." He began to stumble. "I regard homosexuality as being a great misfortune. I see it as something which is—the less frequent it is in any society, the better for that society. . . ." He went into a long ramble about the ancient Greeks and the Socratic dialogues, saying that even the Greeks "saw homosexuality as something which was practiced side by side with heterosexuality" and that they would be appalled by the "really rather disgusting homosexual practices" in which people engage today.

At this point, McKellen threw up his hands, and after a few more hostile parries back and forth, the moderator interjected, "I think this is a blind alley, quite frankly. What is going to happen, let us say, to the works of Wilde, to the works of Rattigan, to the works of Coward—people who are now in the perfectly acceptable middle-class canon?"

"Name me anything in the works of Wilde or Forster or Rattigan which promotes homosexuality," Worsthorne insisted.

"This is why we come back to the loose wording of the bill," the moderator said.

"You see, in 1988, of course, it is against the mores of the times to promote your homosexuality in the sense of to advertise it—" McKellen began.

"You've just done it," Worsthorne declared—finally acknowledging McKellen's self-outing.

"Indeed," McKellen said, deliberately.

He would drive the point home one last time as the debate drew to a close: "I think this country would be a healthier place if people in public life who are gay announced that they were gay and left it at that, so that the majority of society would understand that homosexuals are their friends, their supporters, and major [contributors] to the cultural life of this nation."

Then it was over.

The first people Ian called were Armistead Maupin and Terry Anderson. "He was very proud," Maupin recalls. "He wanted to share it with us because there aren't a whole lot of people who can cheer you on when you do something like that. I was very surprised and delighted." But Ian's current theatrical agent James Sharkey was not at all delighted when the news of his coming out flashed around the globe. "My agent said it would cut down on my jobs and it really wasn't something I should talk about in a lot of interviews," McKellen recalls. "Having done it, he thought that should be enough and it should never be mentioned again." Ian disagreed. "If I were twenty or thirty years younger, playing a sexy young blood in a movie, it might be different," he admits. "But my career was so settled that if someone said, 'Well, McKellen can't play King Lear because he's gay,' people would just laugh. The truth is, if somebody doesn't want to employ me because I'm gay, then I really don't want to work with them."

He did, though, purposely choose to play decidedly heterosexual characters in his next two roles. In the film *Scandal* he portrayed British cabinet minister John Profumo, who had had a much-publicized career-ending liaison with showgirl Christine Keeler; on stage he took the part of a perplexed married man in Alan Ayckbourne's romantic comedy *Henceforward* in the West End. "So there I was doing mainstream straight parts, getting good reviews for both," he says. "And if anybody thought that somehow Ian McKellen's career was going to be limited in some way, maybe choosing to play those two parts was rather a help to that."

But at the same time, Ian threw himself into the Arts Council's fight to weaken Clause 28 as much as possible, since it had not been able to prevent Parliament from taking it up. "Ian could have easily stood back in the closet and made a few phone calls, as some of the other closet cases did to worry their MP's," Michael Cashman maintains. "But what he did, along with others—including myself—was to give an example to other gays, lesbians, and bisexuals around the country. Now we had elegant, intelligent, passionate, and reasonable people who could stand up and really fight the good fight to promote our issues."

In the meantime, more militant gays and lesbians were taking to the streets. Cashman was present at the rally in Albert Square that drew twenty thousand protesters—the largest homosexual demonstration ever staged in Great Britain. When Clause 28 passed through its second reading in the House of Commons, more than one hundred protesters disrupted the proceedings by shouting antigovernment slogans until they were forcibly ejected from the Strangers' Gallery. A kiss-in was staged in Piccadilly Circus, where Gay Sweatshop activist Richard Sandells, clad in sexily torn jeans, gained immortality by climbing onto the statue of Eros and kissing it—which yielded a remarkable photo that wound up in wide circulation as an erotic postcard. McKellen and Cashman both attended a ten-thousand-strong march, sponsored by OLGA, that strode past the prime minister's house at 10 Downing Street. "As we walked down Whitehall, just passing Downing Street, there were some crash barriers there," Cashman recalls. "People broke away from the march in their deep anger and they jumped over the crash barriers and ran toward Ten Downing Street. It was the last time Downing Street was ever invaded by a group of demonstrators."

Thirty-four people were arrested, but Cashman says, "Every time I look at the gates of Ten Downing Street, I look at them as a monument in the fight for gay and lesbian liberation."

But as Lisa Power would acknowledge: "The arts lobby was the only part of the campaign against Clause Twenty-eight that had an impact. They were the major contact in the House of Lords and actually got a lot of people briefed in order to actually make some central arguments and to make major changes to the clause." The Arts Council was effective, in part, because of its "mole" in the House of Lords, Douglas Slater, a gay clerk who was also a deputy theater critic for one of the newspapers. "I made arrangements to make sure that people were briefed on how they could lobby the House of Lords," Slater recalls. "I wasn't giving any secrets away. I was just telling them how to do it." According to McKellen, Slater was invaluable. "He always knew a day before what the government was going to do, and he used to call me up at two in the morning to tell me. Then I would pass it on to activists, who were more proficient than I was in dealing with this information."

To raise much-needed funds to continue the fight against Clause 28, McKellen, Cashman, playwright Martin Sherman, and Sean Mathias joined with a lesbian production company, 20th Century Vixens, to mount a benefit entitled *Against the Act* at the Piccadilly Theatre. The exceptionally successful evening featured a star-studded cast performing pieces that had been either written or composed by a homosexual.

By now the government was growing concerned at the furor over the clause, as well as its bad press not only in England but also around the world. It was prepared to negotiate and decided that the most responsible body it could approach was the Arts Council. "And who were they prepared to talk to?" McKellen asks. "Me! Well, I didn't know what I was talking about! I don't understand the law, I'm not a lawyer, I didn't understand the reverberative issues, but who else was there to represent the gay point of view? I'd met bureaucrats, I'd been invited to meet politicians, ministers of the arts and so on, so it wasn't an entirely strange world. But it was an embarrassment to me that I had become an official spokesman when I didn't feel qualified to do the job."

However, those around him quickly recognized what an effective spokesman McKellen was. "Ian knew all these people in the establishment," Lisa Power says. "He was a gay man who all these respected people wanted to know and be seen with. For instance, he could sit and talk with Princess Diana at dinner and tell her what the problem was. He could phone up the editor of the newspaper and ask to talk to him. They all had enormous respect for him and they all were in awe of him. So he was very important in that sense." Michael Cashman agrees. "Ian, to perhaps give secrets away, is filled with self-doubt," he says. "I have seen him wracked with doubt before going out to give a speech or an interview, and he comes away having done the most wonderful interview, saying, 'I am crap at these kinds of things!' Those of us who have lived with the nervousness and paranoia in the hour before we do the interview want to kill him, because, of course, he brings it off brilliantly."

McKellen was soon called in for a personal meeting with the Home Secretary to discuss the language of the clause. The Arts Council's emendation proposing the exclusion of the arts had been voted down, and the Home Secretary proposed a slight, conciliatory change—adding the words "shall not intentionally" to the phrase "promote homosexuality." Michael Cashman, among others, claimed the new wording helped dampen the clause's impact. "And it was directly because of Ian's intervention," he insists. Still, McKellen recalls, "Lawyer after lawyer came forward and said, 'This law is totally unworkable, it doesn't make sense, it doesn't define its terms.' "

When the bill was passed out of committee, Viscount Falkland of the Liberal Democratic party warned: "The clause is putting the clock back by creating fear, and encouraging discrimination and violence." The Conservatives in the House of Lords paid his words no heed as, standing in their red gowns and powdered wigs, they squared off against the Labour party. Lord Beloff vowed that he would vote for the clause because, in his view, "Homosexuality played a critical role in the early Nazi movement." The Earl of Caithness, Minister of State, insisted that the clause did not discriminate against homosexuals. "Those attacking the clause are attacking a dummy which bears little or no relation to the clause," he said. "Their arguments are wide of the mark." Dame Elaine Kellett-Bowman justified an arson attack on the newspaper *Capital Gay,* claiming, "There *should* be the intolerance of evil."

On the other side, Liberal party member Lord Soper cried that he smelled fascism in the clause: "The country would be in a perilous state if it isolated homosexuals as if they belonged in a category of evil." Lord Willis agreed: "This is the first breath of a chilling wind of intolerance. It is the first page of a charter for bigots." Lord Rea made the most personal statement when he admitted, "I was brought up by two women, one of whom was my mother, in an actual family relationship. There was no pretense there. It was a good family and I maintain that there is nothing intrinsically wrong with a homosexual couple bringing up a child. I consider that I had as rich and happy a childhood as most children who are reared by heterosexual couples."

The Conservative majority, however, was unmoved, and when the vote was called, Clause 28 passed, 202–122. Suddenly, just before the tally was announced, five women and one man who had been sitting in an upper side gallery began to shout, "It's our lives you're dealing with!" Then three of the women hurled knotted nylon ropes over the balcony rail and rappelled down into the chambers, roaring, "Lesbians are angry!" One woman managed to drop into the Strangers' Gallery, while the other two swung over the chambers, shouting, "Don't worry, we won't hurt you," until the doorkeepers pulled them up. Douglas Slater, who was working on the floor, recalls that while some lords, especially Conservatives, were aghast, others began to chuckle. "Actually, most of the House was rather amused by it," Slater says. "It was a fabulous gesture of sorts and has become one of the legends of the House of Lords."

None of the protesters was ever formally charged.

On March 9, 1988, when Clause 28 passed in the House of Commons as well, 254–201, to become Section 28, the same plucky lesbians who had invaded the House of Lords on ropes talked their way past security guards and disrupted the BBC's nightly news. Just as the staid anchorwoman, Sue Lawley, began to read the day's headlines, the women burst onto the set screaming, "Stop Section Twenty-eight! Stop Thatcher!" One protester handcuffed herself to a camera, while another, in full view of the television audience of eight million, handcuffed herself to the desk at Lawley's side. "I do apologize if you are hearing quite a lot of noise in the studio at the moment," said the unflappable anchor to the cameras. "I am afraid that we have rather been invaded by some people whom we hope to be removing very shortly. In the meantime, if you can avoid the background noise, we will bring the news to you if we can." As she spoke, her coanchor, Nicholas Witchell, attempted to sit on the lesbian anchored to the desk, covering her mouth and hissing, "Shut up! Shut up!" The control booth switched from live coverage of the newsroom to taped footage of a nurses' strike. As it aired, burly staffers stormed the set and pulled the protesting women out of the studio. "The shameful thing is that the media just didn't cover it," McKellen says. "That *never* happens on the BBC news—but they never mentioned it again. I suppose they didn't want to encourage anyone else to try it in the future. But the other television companies didn't cover it either. The thought was 'Just don't give them any publicity.' "

Once again released without being charged, the same intrepid women would chain themselves to the gates of Buckingham Palace as a final assault on Section 28—inspiring the *Star* to brand them, in a memorable string of epithets, a "gaggle of screeching, lesbian harridans, hirsute hippies, loony lezzies, and dotty dykes."

Because of the barrage of bad publicity, the Thatcher government officially distanced itself from Section 28, disingenuously labeling it the work of radical backbenchers. However, *The Guardian* insisted that Mrs. Thatcher herself was "the driving force" behind the clause. According to Michael Hodges, writing in *The Nation,* the Thatcher government even "sent out whips to drag in the 'backwoodsmen'—the hereditary peers who rarely come to London, much less participate in Parliamentary votes—from the far corners of the realm."

How surprising it must have been when, after all the acrimony and posturing, Britain's Environment Department—analogous to the U.S.'s Department of the Interior—pronounced that sex education, by law, came under the jurisdiction of school governors, so that: "Section Twenty-eight does not affect the activities of school governors nor of teachers. It will not prevent the objective discussion of homosexuality in the classroom, nor the counseling of pupils concerned about their sexuality." Sponsor Dame Jill Knight was outraged. "This has got to be a mistake!" she proclaimed. "The major point of it was to protect children in schools from having homosexuality thrust upon them!"

"They knew this would happen all along," McKellen insists. "Schools are run by local authority. This was a national parliament telling schools what they could or could not do. It was part of a general movement to take over the running of local government. This fit right in with Mrs. Thatcher's overall philosophy." One of the Conservative Tory whips went so far as to tell Ian, "Section Twenty-eight is a piece of red meat which we have to throw to our right-wing wolves every once in a while."

Even though it had been defanged, Section 28 stayed on the books and proved intimidating: "Every teacher I've talked to and read about has said that it has had a devastating effect because everyone's frightened of it," McKellen says. "And it's been very good at just stopping people talking in the classroom. In public libraries, although they haven't removed the lesbian and gay books, they've removed the sign that says they *exist*. So now you've got to go up to the counter and say, 'Have you got a book on my problem?' And certainly there's been self-censorship in local theaters about programming. It's had an impact."

In the wake of the debacle of Section 28, the gay community in the UK began to rethink its strategies. As Lisa Power explains, "We had a couple of organizations that saw themselves as a political lobby, but weren't actually doing the work and didn't have the contacts." Michael Cashman says, "I woke up one morning and thought, 'Why are we in the streets demonstrating? Ian and I have contacts into government and into all the political parties. We should have an organization that is out there proactively campaigning and lobbying to prevent something like Section Twenty-eight happening again.' " Doug Slater had the same inspiration—and, moreover, was being promoted to business manager in the House of Lords, with the role of advising the government on the technical aspects of getting legislation through the House. "The power actually rests with all the ministers," Slater says with a grin, "but I would be the person who knew where all the bodies were buried." He knew that once his promotion went through, he would have to distance himself from the gay community; he wanted to leave it with the foundation for a first-rate homosexual lobbying group. He telephoned Ian McKellen to say, "Look, we don't know each other very well, but I think we ought to discuss fighting professionally." Immediately receptive, McKellen replied, "Can you come around and see me?"

The next Sunday morning, Slater met with McKellen and Cashman to start hammering out the structure for Stonewall—named for the famous riot that launched the gay-rights movement in America—which would become the premiere homosexual lobbying unit in Great Britain. Lisa Power and actor Simon Callow were among the first activists to join. "We agreed that it had to be an equal number of men and women," Slater says. "We needed to have some women involved." Michael Cashman concurs: "Lisa was absolutely pivotal. I think the early involvement of women was crucial. Often gay men really forget the woman side of the issues—the double discrimination that lesbians face." Once Slater assumed his business manager duties and could be involved in Stonewall only as a secret partner, Cashman and McKellen took up the reins. "He and Ian were 'the pair' in the early days of Stonewall," Power says. "They were like twins." Indeed, though they had been close before, "Ian and I became two halves of one mind," Cashman says. "He would come up with some passionate idea or some passionate reason of why something was wrong, and I would say, 'Yes, but the way *politically* we have to challenge this, or how we would have to play the political parties off one another or use the media is *this*. . . .' We were a very productive symbiotic partnership, questioning one another every step of the way." They would spend hours sharing ideas, sitting on McKellen's terrace overlooking the Thames. "He has taught me so much about how you stick to your ideas and you pursue them relentlessly and nobody ever should be allowed to undermine your principles," Cashman says. "That can only come from a relationship that allows one partner to challenge the other." Very quickly, Stonewall came together. "Most of the people involved had been gay activists for a long time and had tried various methods of organization which they'd found failing. They felt it was time for a change forward," McKellen explains. "Ian and I really used some muscle with his access," Douglas Slater says, and Lisa Power concurs, "Ian is very sensible about celebrityhood. His whole attitude is that if people want to be impressed by that, then it is something that should be used for the good of the gay and lesbian community."

One of the first uses they made of his celebrity was to stage another theatrical fund-raiser—this one for Stonewall. Martin Sherman offered them use of his play *Bent*. Ian, reprising his role as Max, was joined by Cashman, Ralph Fiennes, Ian Charleston, Richard E. Grant, Alex Jennings, and nearly one hundred extras portraying concentration camp victims, all under the direction of Sean Mathias. "It was important to us both that our friendship should survive the split," Ian said of his former boyfriend. "Sean is one of the three most helpful directors I've worked with—alongside Trevor Nunn and Tyrone Guthrie." Mathias recalls a grueling rehearsal period. "We rehearsed for four or five weeks," he says, "and were still rehearsing at seven twenty-five when the doors were due to open at seven." Outside the Adelphi theater, London's entire theater district became gridlocked. "It was like Judy Garland in the 1960's," Cashman says, laughing. "We literally stopped the traffic in the West End! There were so many people, they couldn't get in. There were all these queens yelling, 'I want to get inside to buy a drink,' as they waved their tickets." Onstage, trying to concentrate on the rehearsal, McKellen angrily demanded to know what the ruckus outside was about. Mathias replied, "Ian, they are literally breaking down the doors to get in, we've overrun on time so long. We just have to stop."

When the curtain finally rose, the performance was an unmitigated triumph—"Overwhelming on every level," Mathias remembers. "The ovation went on for nearly twenty minutes." It was an especially moving moment for Ian Charleston—famous for his starring role in the 1981 film *Chariots of Fire*—who was then in the final stages of AIDS. "Ian Charleston got an absolutely breathtaking ovation," Mathias says, not only for his "quite brilliant" performance as Greta, the drag queen, but also "because I think a lot of people knew that he had AIDS at that point even though it wasn't publicly acknowledged." Backstage was a veritable mob scene. "People were saying it was the most thrilling piece of theater. They were literally sobbing," the proud director says. "We were all knocked sideways by the response." Indeed, the production was such a success that it was moved to the Royal National Theatre for an extended run. In a single night, the sellout crowd endowed the new organization with thirty thousand pounds—enough to hire Stonewall's first director, Tim Barnett.

Stonewall's first office was a single tiny room at the back of a member's house in Eddington, outfitted with begged and borrowed secondhand office furniture—"battered chairs, battered desk, and a filing cabinet," according to Michael Cashman. Before long, the group managed to procure two rooms in Victoria that measured six feet by four feet and four feet by four feet—barely big enough for desks—but soon took over the entire floor and eventually moved to a modern office building. "When I think of where we have gone from those tiny beginnings it is quite amazing," Cashman says. "It is amazing how ideas coupled with determination can change the world."

Fueled by donations and a charitable arm called the Iris Trust, of which McKellen is a chair, Stonewall soon became the authority on gay issues. With its developing database and bank of research materials, it was an important source for newspapers in Great Britain, as well as the nexus for a growing body of sympathetic politicians and gay-rights groups. It worked tirelessly to push for change not only in Parliament, but also through the media, with employers, and with a wide range of social organizations. Inevitably, it also drew negative attention, and both Cashman and McKellen, being its most visible spokesmen, were singled out for harassment. Michael and his partner, Paul Cottingham, had bricks thrown through their windows; Cashman and McKellen were bombarded with hate mail. "Just vile things from people who profess to be Christians," Cashman says. "There was one from a man who said he wanted to run a hot poker up Ian's ass." McKellen adds, "Yes, it's shocking when you get anonymous letters that say I'm too good for death and those sort of things. Clearly they're from disturbed and cowardly people, because they never leave an address. I wish they would." The hatred had the effect of propelling Cashman forward; but in McKellen it roused great sorrow. He told Cashman, "Such hatred and anger are being directed at other less fortunate people every single day of their lives, and if they come out that is what they have to put up with."

For all his activist work, McKellen continued to tour, this time with an inventive reworking of Shakespeare's *Richard III* set in Nazi Germany. While resting between shows in a hotel room in Paris, he saw on television that Margaret Thatcher had been voted out by the Tories, her own party, and replaced by the more moderate John Major. "I was watching Mrs. Thatcher leave Ten Downing Street, and the phone suddenly rang," he recalls. The woman on the other end of the line said, "Mr. McKellen, this is Downing Street." Thinking that it was a friend playing a joke, McKellen said, "Yes! I'm watching it on the TV! Isn't it marvelous!" When the woman insisted that the call was indeed official, Ian said, "Look, I think you better give me your telephone number and I'll call you back." He rang back and was stunned to discover that the call had indeed come from 10 Downing Street—and that before Mrs. Thatcher had left office, she had conferred a knighthood on McKellen.

He was certainly a logical choice. "You don't get a knighthood if you're a movie star," he says. "Sean Connery, Michael Caine, Richard Burton, Peter O'Toole—no. It's theater people who work for very little money in subsidized theater, preferably in the classics. And I was down-the-line obvious for that. As far as the gay stuff goes—they just had to lump it." Douglas Slater concurred: "Everybody knew that with the tradition of theatrical knighthood in the country, it would be impossible not to give Ian his knighthood. He is so much the leading classical actor in this country, if not the world. He had done so much work for the National Theatre Company for no money, and he had done so much work abroad doing the British Council–arranged tours. He was an ambassador for the country. For anyone else to have received a knighthood and Ian McKellen not to receive one—people would have rightly claimed he hadn't been given one because he was gay." He adds: "It was not my place to say yes or no, but I was rather worried he might turn it down. I felt it would be a pity if he did, because it was another stage of recognition for us. People in England always hid the fact that they were gay in order to get a knighthood. This would make the gay issue kind of ordinary."

McKellen immediately got on the phone to his friends, inquiring if he should accept the honor. Mathias said, "That's amazing! You should definitely take it because you're the sort of person who would use it for the things you believe in." Cashman agreed: "Ian, you take it. Because if the Labour party had given it to you, the British establishment would dismiss it and would say, 'Of course, they would do that.' " Cashman held that, by conferring the knighthood on McKellen after he had campaigned against Section 28 and formed Stonewall, Thatcher was nearly acknowledging the justness of his cause. Ian also called Lisa Power: "I remember he said to me, 'If this is useful, if I can use this, then of course I should accept it.' " Armistead Maupin and Terry Anderson were at their winter home in New Zealand celebrating New Year's Eve when he reached them. Both were thrilled for their friend. "I think one of the most courageous things he ever did was to accept the knighthood and use it for political gains," Anderson says. Maupin adds, "I did feel that the one drawback about Ian's coming out might be that he would never receive a knighthood—so I was flabbergasted when he called. Utterly amazed. And he was *so* excited. He was having his cake and eating it, too."

Ultimately, McKellen decided to accept the honor, to be bestowed by Queen Elizabeth II, cognizant of the fact that some members of the gay community might consider it unseemly for him to receive such recognition from an administration known for its intolerance. Indeed, there was immediate backlash in the form of a vitriolic letter to *The Guardian* from gay filmmaker Derek Jarman, who denounced McKellen as a turncoat and called for a wave of protest against his acceptance of the knighthood. McKellen suggests, "His motive was that for so long, he'd been openly gay, and people like me arrived out of nowhere and seemed to him to be holding themselves up to be representatives of the gay movement, of which he was a crucial part." Jarman was also an outspoken critic of Stonewall, being more of the Act-Up school and believing that confrontation, not negotiation, would yield change. Although McKellen was sympathetic to any kind of heartfelt expression of protest, he himself felt uncomfortable about provocative acts. "I spend my life professionally showing off," he says with a smile. "I don't want to go do it in the streets."

Activist Angela Mason, later to become head of Stonewall, recalls, "The controversy was quite sharp. People like Derek Jarman—for whom we had a great deal of respect—were very critical, but I think that criticism, though I understood it, was completely misplaced." Lisa Power says, "Ian was terribly hurt . . . because he didn't understand why anyone could be like that when he was doing his best and clearly having an impact." Before long, McKellen learned what was behind the attack when he got a personal phone call from Jarman. "I hear you're upset about what I wrote," Ian remembers Jarman saying. "Look, it's nothing personal. I'm only trying to stir it up. I only want it to get into the newspapers. I think it's something worth debating." Shaking his head, McKellen now says, "You want to stir it up, you get a paragraph in the paper? Come on! We can do better than that. We can get the lead article in our favor. We can write a whole page, we can provide the information, we can do it properly, we can be efficient, we can be authoritative, and that's what Stonewall is all about. And Derek didn't like that." Indeed, Jarman ended the conversation indignant, accusing Ian of having "the facade of a gay man but the soul of a straight man."

Ian was saddened by Jarman's assault, but Michael Cashman was furious. "The right wing jumped on the letter and used it to denounce all lesbians and gay men, saying that the likes of Michael Cashman and Ian McKellen were in the minority, that we did not represent the wider lesbian and gay community," he explains. "It gave our enemies a field day. Both Ian and I believe we all are fighting the same fight and there is no singular way to do it. A multiplicity of approaches is the best way—direct action, campaigning, lobbying, working through your political parties and outside your political parties, through the church, through the media, through the police. Use every way possible, but make sure we are taking on our enemies and not burning up our own resources, our own energies, by fighting an internal fight."

Two days after Jarman's controversial letter appeared in the newspaper, a statement was issued in support of McKellen's knighthood by a score of his show business colleagues, including Martin Sherman, Simon Callow, Michael Cashman, and such previously undeclared gay celebrities as director John Schlesinger, actor Anthony Sher, and producer Cameron Mackintosh. Ian was very grateful for the gesture, which in time did seem to stem the controversy.

He chose his niece Cathy and Sean Mathias to accompany him to the knighting ceremony at Buckingham Palace. They were ushered into the great hall where an organ was blaring, as Mathias recalls, "popular tunes." Queen Elizabeth II entered, "and the tune played was [pop singer Billy Joel's] 'Just the Way You Are'—talk about getting the giggles. We were howling!" Without a speech from Her Majesty, or fanfare, the nearly two hundred honorees, men and women, marched single-file up to the front of the Throne Room, where each had a medal draped around the neck and was tapped with a sword on each shoulder by the queen, who then asked a question or two. "She asked me if I was working, and were people still going to the theater," McKellen recalls. "Then she nodded, held out her hand, and pushed me away." As he turned, his mispronounced name rang through the hall: "Sir Yon McLelland." Although thrilled to be there, Mathias admits, "It was fairly perfunctory and rather daft—the pomp and ceremony of England at its absolute worst." McKellen concurs: "It doesn't have much style to it. You don't even get a glass of champagne or a cup of tea. Then you're all thrown out."

Still, it was a momentous occasion both for Ian and for the homosexual community. He was not the first openly gay man to receive a knighthood, for writer Angus Wilson had been honored a few years before, but as Michael Cashman says, "Ian had the clear-sightedness to use the title as he wanted, to promote the good fight—the fight that was on behalf of lesbians and gay men not only in this country, but also around the world." As McKellen explains, "A knighthood does give you just a little bit more, I don't know, 'power' in the UK. Not *power* really, but I remain one of those people that journalists call up—my being 'sir' makes it look better in their newspaper; that's how it works." He adds, "It's dreadful that this should be necessary, but my knighthood has been a small symbol to young people who, when coming out to their parents, are able to point to me and increasingly to others in British public life such as Cameron Mackintosh and John Schlesinger and can say, 'Don't worry. The days of hiding are numbered.' "

And indeed the new prime minister, John Major, soon requested a meeting with McKellen, prompted by the Tory Campaign for Homosexual Equality (TORCHE). Douglas Slater says of Major, "I think he genuinely wanted to build a more inclusive society. He was of a different generation than Mrs. Thatcher and . . . he was attempting to make the Tory party a friendly place." The truth was that Major was in a very difficult position; while gay-rights initiatives were anathema to his Conservative party, which had proudly enacted Section 28, he wanted to extend an olive branch. McKellen, though flattered, recognized the dilemma and was wary of the encounter. "He had a very real fear, which I think was quite accurate, of going into a meeting with John Major and not getting anything out of it," Slater says. "Then people would say that Ian had sold out or that he let the prime minister off the hook—that this was just sort of a public relations exercise on the part of the Tory government." Still, it was an opportunity to present the prime minister with a broad roster of concerns, from arts funding to gay rights, and Slater urged McKellen to meet with Major, saying "Ian, just go in and be yourself." To which McKellen replied, "That is very difficult for me, to be myself. I'm an actor and I want to be someone else."

As it turned out, the meeting was more of a public relations coup for the homosexual community than for Major. Although no tangible benefit was accomplished, "It was a big moment for us," Slater says. "It was the first time a prime minister had taken any trouble to confer legitimacy on the movement. In a way, Ian got everything he was going to get out of [the meeting] when he walked into Ten Downing Street and the television cameras saw it. It was very well publicized." Angela Mason, by this time the director of Stonewall, concurs: "It was a very important sign of lesbians and gay men achieving visibility and respect in our society. It was the first time an openly gay man had gone down to Downing Street and had a chat with the prime minister about the state of the world. It was a major thing to have happened—it was extraordinary." Lisa Power recognized that the meeting gave the gay community its first foot in the door with the Conservative government: "It crossed the boundary that we had for a long time, that we were not allowed to talk to people like John Major. [But] you have to deal with the people in power if you want to affect their decisions." Indeed, Stonewall, with Ian at its helm, would soon engage the Tory government in a more effective dialogue than ever before.

The issue was the age of consent for same-sex contacts, which the 1967 act decriminalizing homosexuality had fixed at twenty-one, five years older than the heterosexual age of consent. The issue had long been a thorn in the side of the gay community, and Major had now proposed submitting it to the public for a vote. Stonewall lobbied furiously for a change in the law. Angela Mason says, "Ian was absolutely at the forefront of that campaign—talking to politicians, giving interviews to the media. It was at that time that we had the idea of doing what we call our *Equality Show*." Staged at Royal Albert Hall, the evening was conceived and directed by McKellen. "It was enormously successful," Mason says, "and attracted not only a wonderful galaxy of stars who've given very generously of their time and money, but also a large number of political guests. Over the years, it's grown to be a fabulously glamorous and I think politically significant occasion." Indeed, the annual *Equality Show* has become one of the most prestigious, lucrative, and well-attended gay and lesbian events in the world.

Owing at least in part to Stonewall's aggressive lobbying, the National Society for the Prevention of Cruelty to Children, psychiatric colleges, the Royal College of Surgeons, the Union of Headteachers, and nearly all the newspapers in the country, came out in favor of lowering the age of consent to sixteen.

As the vote neared, filmmaker Derek Jarman was on his deathbed with late-stage AIDS and had a friend deliver a conciliatory message to McKellen. "Derek sends his love," the messenger reported, "and he says he thinks you've done really well." Two weeks later, when the amendment was put to the vote in the House of Commons, a gay contingent kept vigil outside the Palace of Westminster, many holding candles in memory of the recently deceased Jarman. The amendment was passed, but to the gay community's dismay, the age was lowered only to eighteen, instead of sixteen. "Eighteen is not a compromise," argued Peter Tatchell of the group OutRage, "it's discrimination!" Furious at the outcome, the vigil keepers stormed up Whitehall Street in protest. "Derek would rather have approved of that," McKellen says with a hint of a smile.

It was not until 1997, when progressive Prime Minister Tony Blair came to power, that the gay community could hope for equality on the age of consent. Indeed, with Blair's support, the House of Commons voted for parity, only to see the measure thrown out by the House of Lords. The Archbishop of Canterbury spearheaded the fight against it, and Margaret Thatcher, now a peer, made one of her rare appearances in the House of Lords to vote it down, as did Lord Longford, an elderly peer who is playwright Harold Pinter's father-in-law. The ninety-two-year-old Catholic Conservative argued that the age discrimination was fair because no young girl who was seduced by a boy ever came to any harm, but any young man who was importuned by another would be blighted for life. The peer's ramblings prompted one journalist to quip, "Lord Longford speaks like a man twice his age."

Although McKellen's professional life was now fully split between activism and acting, neither suffered for the dichotomy. He continued to appear regularly onstage in such productions as Ibsen's *Enemy of the People* and Chekhov's *Uncle Vanya,* and even *Peter Pan*—the first play he ever saw—as well as in his new one-man show, based on his own life as a gay actor, called *A Knight Out.* And his film career, always on the back burner, suddenly began to skyrocket. "In my early fifties, after I came out, I was finally ready to act for the camera," McKellen told *Movieline* magazine. "Movie acting is easier than stage acting—you don't have to have trained your voice or your body. But I'd read enough reviews of my stage acting to know that what people liked about it was its flamboyance, and that won't work on film. What I had to do for the camera was to root the performance in my own feelings, so that it was as true and as real as I could make it. The camera may lie on occasion, but it doesn't lie when it comes to your feelings."

Roles in diverse films such as *Six Degrees of Separation, Restoration, Cold Comfort Farm,* and *Richard III* came in quick succession. When Sean Mathias was slated to direct the film version of *Bent* in 1997, he insisted McKellen be in it. Although now too old to play Max, "symbolically, he had to be in it," Mathias says. "He had brought life to the play; he had the courage to do it when many, many other actors wouldn't have done it. And he was quite big at that point, and lending his name to the film would also give it tremendous focus." It was decided that McKellen would play the small but flashy role of Max's uncle. "And I think he's really brilliant in the film, actually," Mathias says. "Really wonderful." Then when *Apt Pupil,* based on the Stephen King novella and directed by Bryan Singer, and *Gods and Monsters,* the story of gay film director James Whale, directed and adapted by Bill Condon, opened in 1998 within months of each other, suddenly Ian McKellen, at the age of fifty-nine, became one of the hottest actors in Hollywood. *Time* magazine even designated him its 1998 "film star of the year." After winning a slew of critics awards, McKellen was nominated for an Academy Award as best actor for *Gods and Monsters.* Although Ian lost to Roberto Begnini, Bill Condon won an Oscar for best adaptation. Mathias, who interrupted his busy schedule to again accompany McKellen to an award ceremony, says, "It was a major achievement for this film to have been seen by so many people and been nominated for a number of Oscars." Recalling a similar sentiment at the Tony Awards in New York nearly twenty years earlier, Mathias was struck by the journey. "For Ian to be sitting there with his ex-boyfriend and Bill and his boyfriend to be sitting there—it was a huge move in gay liberation."

Yet McKellen, anxious for more, knew that the biggest moves must be accomplished in the political arena. "You've got to be in there getting your hands dirty with the people who've got the power," he says, "and it isn't pleasant because reason doesn't always prevail, nor does right, and it's constantly frustrating." Frustration compounded in the

spring of 1999 when again the House of Commons passed a bill lowering the age of consent for homosexuals, and again the House of Lords
voted it down. With over 60 percent of the country in favor of parity,
Angela Mason rightly scoffed, "It is quite clear that the Lords are completely out of touch with modern Britain." McKellen, too, was getting
irate: "If I were younger and not privy to the sort of negotiations that
Stonewall is regularly having, I might think, 'What the hell is this
Stonewall doing? Why are they even talking to these dreadful politicians who are not doing anything to help us?' But if the Blair government doesn't very soon pull off a couple of changes in the law, my own
patience might begin to run out and I will be more out in the streets,
because it really won't do. The argument has been won, over and over
again.

"Why do we have to keep making it?"

As if on cue, at the Stonewall annual benefit dinner on May 20, 1999,
Cabinet Office Minister Jack Cunningham announced that Blair's government intended to finally scrap the twelve-year-old Section 28. "I
can say quite clearly that the government believes that Section Twenty-
eight serves no useful purpose," Cunningham said in a speech. "We remain committed to the repeal as soon as Parliamentary opportunity
arises. Section Twenty-eight was wrong in 1987. It is wrong in 1999.
And it will go." Immediately mobilizing, Angela Mason announced that
Stonewall would institute a series of "Roadshow Meetings" around the
UK as a focus for grassroots campaigners. "It will demonstrate to the
government," she said, "the great support that exists around the country for repealing Section Twenty-eight."

Yet in February 2000 legislation to abolish Section 28 was defeated
in the House of Lords—so Stonewall's fight continues.

"Britain is changing," McKellen says, undaunted. "I think we'll see
that gay openness—and the gay activism which has encouraged that
openness—is just a part of a bigger self-awareness appropriate to a nation that's proud of being law-abiding and socially responsible."

He remains personally involved in Stonewall, gratified that it has
grown into such an effective political force. "There's a bit of awe in the
office when he's here," says Matt Aston, Stonewall's young information

director. "But he's very friendly and puts everyone at ease—very warm, very jolly, very happy. It's so important to have someone of such stature to represent us here at Stonewall and the gay community at large. And people take great strength from what he's doing for us. And quite rightly, a lot of people love him for what he does."

Still, McKellen is always startled when people walk up to him and say, "Thank you for all you're doing." "And I think, 'What *are* they talking about?'" he says. "Then they'll say, 'With regard to civil rights . . .' and then you know that they're gay. And you begin to see how wide the closet door is and how big it is inside and how many people who don't appear to be in the closet actually are for the major part of their lives."

Ian McKellen's dual life, as actor and activist, has shown him that playing any part in life requires a simple prerequisite: rigorous honesty with oneself. "The big bonus of coming out," Ian says, "I don't think is necessarily the way you're perceived or the jobs you might get, but rather is self-fulfillment and self-contentment and self-awareness and self-confidence, all wrapped up together. It means taking pride in being able to say, 'I'm gay.' And out of that self-confidence has come an emotional freedom that directors and friends have detected in my work. There's nothing that I can't do, and I don't think that I could have felt that if I hadn't come out. Get out, say it, and having said it, you can get on with living your life. You won't be alone.

"The family I'm a part of, the nation I belong to, is the gay nation."

He had always found joy in playing a part. Now added resonance is found in being a part as well.

ROBERTA ACHTENBERG

A "Justice Thing"

THE FAMOUS CHERRY TREES had just finished their ceremonial cycle of flowering, and thousands of gardens were beginning to take their turns splashing color against the stark white of the city's monuments and edifices. The White House lawn was regaining its resplendent green; the Potomac River was again ice-free. The sun, in a brilliantly blue sky, had supplanted the winter chill with the clean, crisp briskness of April. Washington, D.C., was beginning anew. With a new president in power, William Jefferson Clinton, and a new crop of congressmen under the rotunda, the capital was now engaged in its own rites of spring: approval hearings in the Senate for new presidential appointees.

Just north of the majestic dome of the Capitol was the Everett Dirksen Senate Office Building, which houses the offices of the United States senators. Inside, in a labyrinth of dimly lit, dingy hallways, Senate pages dressed in navy blue careened around corners, a sense of urgency in their faces and footfalls. Secretaries and staffers, and even an occasional senator or two, darted back and forth. All hurriedly passed by the door to room SD-538, unaware of the drama unfolding inside.

There, at the head of the room, beneath a high, ornate ceiling with elaborate antique lighting fixtures, was a large, semicircular table peppered with thin microphones. A battalion of senators was positioned

behind it, perched on high-back chairs. Directly in front of the senators' table was the oak witness table. On the back wall, the plain clock
read 11:03 A.M.

It was April 29, 1993, and the eighteen-member Committee on
Banking, Housing and Urban Affairs, chaired by Senator Donald W.
Riegle, Jr. (D–MI), had three nominees on the docket. Quick approvals
were expected for two of them: Kenneth Brody as the new Chairman
of the Export-Import Bank, and Nicolas Retsinas as Federal Housing
Commissioner and Assistant Secretary of the Department of Housing
and Urban Development. It was the third nomination that had packed
the hearing room with TV cameras and filled the wooden benches behind the witness table to overflowing. An open lesbian, forty-two-year-
old Roberta Achtenberg of San Francisco, had been nominated by the
president for the position of Assistant Secretary of Housing and Urban
Development for Fair Housing and Equal Opportunity. For the first
time, a United States Senate Committee was being asked to confirm
the sub-cabinet appointment of an acknowledged homosexual. It was a
day for the history books, but the diminutive, tawny-haired candidate,
dressed in a handsome robin's-egg-blue St. John suit, seemed perfectly
unruffled and confident as she took her place at the witness table.

Chairman Riegle, a committed populist and defender of civil liberties, made it clear from the outset that he supported Achtenberg. "Certainly, this assistant secretary position plays a critical role in eliminating
discrimination in our nation's housing markets," he said, addressing
Achtenberg. "That is a problem that needs strong, confident leadership.
And I've studied your background. . . . You are superbly equipped by
your experience and your professional training and by what you have
already done in your life to step into this assignment. . . ."

Riegle's opening remarks were interrupted by the entry of Jesse
Helms, a Republican senator from North Carolina who was not on the
committee, into the chamber. Nemesis of the left and sometimes even
an embarrassment to the right, Helms was nonetheless a force to be
reckoned with, an entrenched and powerful elder statesman of the Senate. Taking a place at the back of the room, he folded his arms across
his chest and stared at the nominee. The chairman continued, "You're
crossing one of those invisible lines that we have in our society . . . with
respect to sexual orientation. I realize, though, there may well be peo-

ple who, for reasons of their own orientation or perspective or philosophy or whatever drum they may be beating, will want to take issue with you for reasons that are, I think, totally extraneous to your capacity to serve your country. . . ." Helms glowered, his eyes still trained on Achtenberg. Riegle, finishing up, smiled at her. "You won't be the last, you'll be the first, and someone had to be the first, and I'm glad it's you."

Spontaneous applause erupted from the audience. In the back, the elderly senator from the Tarheel state did not join in.

"Let me ask you to rise now," Chairman Riegle said, "and raise your right hand." The oath was administered, and then repeated by Achtenberg. With those words, she was officially sworn in to testify on her background and qualifications. She sat down at the witness table, took a deep breath, and pulled the microphone down toward her. Helms listened intently as she threw down the gauntlet to the Republican senator and his allies on the religious right: "I'd like to begin by introducing my family to the committee. My beloved partner, Judge Mary Morgan . . ."

When she was growing up in Inglewood, California, in the 1950's, Roberta had no idea she would end up in public office. "I wanted to be a lawyer," she says. "Lawyers righted wrongs and they advocated justice. I'm not sure where I got that—maybe it was watching *Perry Mason* on TV or something."

Her immigrant parents—Louis, from the Soviet Union, and Beatrice, from Quebec—ran a mom-and-pop grocery store in nearby Los Angeles, where they worked seven days a week. In 1955, they bought a brand-new tract home near the Los Angeles airport, with a large brick-fenced backyard that would be a playground for their four children: Jack, the oldest and only boy, Gail, Roberta, and Susan. Roberta—nicknamed "Birdie" by a young cousin who couldn't quite wrap her tongue around the name "Roberta"—shared a bedroom, first with older sister Gail, then with Susan. The sanctuary was a study in pink: frilly print bedspreads over pink dust ruffles, pink-and-white curtains at the windows, even ruffly pink trimming on the toy shelf above the beds. "It was very girly," says Susan Achtenberg Thomas, the youngest.

So were the glasses Roberta had to wear: "Plastic with little glitter sparkles over the top," Susan recalls. "Sometimes they were pink, sometimes they were blue. They were just awful."

Even in childhood, Roberta stood out—and not only because of her eyewear. "She was just so much smarter than the rest of the kids," according to Susan. "But Birdie was not only brilliant, she also had the kindest heart." That combination of intellect and empathy for others was a hallmark of the Achtenberg family.

Having had to leave school after eighth grade, Louis and Beatrice prized education, filled their home with books, and were determined that all four of their children would go to college. "There was never any question about it. It's just what was expected," Roberta says. "Because we were Jewish, education was very important."

It was not a traditional Jewish household, though the Achtenbergs were proud of their heritage and sent their children to religious school. To them, Judaism meant a strong ethical tradition: "We were for justice. We were liberal," Roberta says. "That's who we were." Fervent Democrats, they revered Franklin Delano Roosevelt and supported Adlai Stevenson twice against Dwight Eisenhower. Roberta took her first political stand at the age of nine, when she cut up a "John F. Kennedy for President" bumper sticker to fit on the rear fender of her Schwinn bicycle. "I rode all over the neighborhood so that everyone would know we were for Kennedy."

Today she says, "When I think of layers of identity, I think about Jewishness before I think about identifying myself as a female, and femaleness certainly preceded any self-conscious sense of myself as a gay or lesbian." She soon learned that in those days, being female often meant being discouraged from intellectual achievement. She was an exceptional student and also excelled at sports—in eighth grade she was named "Girl Athlete of the Year"—and was the first girl to be president of her class at Morningside High School. "It was no great surprise when she later went into public office," Susan says. "She was always the leader." Yet when she expressed her intention of becoming a lawyer to a school guidance counselor, the man replied, "Roberta, you're a straight-A student. You should be a teacher." Roberta remembers being astonished and asking, "Why should I be a teacher? I want to be a lawyer!" Although the counselor did not say it in so many words, it was quite clear to Roberta that she was not supposed to become an attorney because she was a girl. "But all it did was make me want to be a lawyer more," she says. "I had a 'justice thing.' I never had a chip on my shoulder, but I always had a big mouth. If I thought something was wrong, I usually didn't sit silently."

In 1963, Louis Achtenberg suffered a debilitating stroke and was confined to a nursing home for five excruciating years. While the family was still reeling from his incapacitation, tragedy struck again when Roberta's brother, Jack, then twenty-three, who was cycling in Switzerland, was thrown from his ten-speed racer and his spinal column critically injured. Without family permission, a neurosurgeon performed an operation—later determined to be an experimental procedure—that left Jack a quadriplegic, destined to spend the rest of his life in a wheelchair. While overseeing her husband's care and helping her physically challenged son, Beatrice Achtenberg still had to run the family store. The girls rallied to support her.

When the time came for Roberta to go to college, she was accepted at the University of California at Berkeley, where Jack and Gail had gone, but stayed home to attend UCLA because of her father's declining health. Midway through her first year of college, Louis Achtenberg died. Deeply saddened by her father's death but somewhat relieved to be freed from the daunting family responsibilities, she transferred to UC/Berkeley, where she began a lifelong love affair with the Bay Area. This was the time of the Vietnam War, and Berkeley was a hotbed of student protests—the Free Speech movement, sit-ins and love-ins—with hippies and Yippies promoting a counterculture of rebellion, drugs, and rock and roll. Roberta, however, preferring to concentrate on her studies, resisted getting involved in that brand of radical politics.

While in college, she began to date a young law student, David Chavkin, whom she'd met through her brother Jack. "I think my coming out experience was kind of atypical," she confesses, "but I didn't even have an inkling that I might be a lesbian. When I tell this to people, they don't believe me. It's actually true. I had no clue. I had no idea." Before long, Roberta and David had set a date for their marriage, and to earn money for the wedding expenses, she took a job as a waitress at the Lakeside Delicatessen in Oakland. Right before the wedding, while slicing some cold cuts, she cut herself deeply on, of all places, her ring finger. Laughing, she now says, "I should have taken it as an omen!"

Roberta and David were married in Live Oak Park in Berkeley. After she graduated with a Phi Beta Kappa key, Roberta attended Hastings Law School in San Francisco until David, also studying to be an attorney, received the Reginald Heber Smith Community Lawyer Fellowship from Howard University. The "Reggie," a distinguished fellowship that many law students tried to snag, sent Chavkin to Salt Lake City, Utah, where he was assigned to do class-action litigation at a legal services office. Determined to be with her new husband, Achtenberg transferred to the University of Utah Law School. There, besides participating in a challenging curriculum, she discovered extraordinary opportunities, including assisting Arvo Van Alstyne—the best constitutional law professor on campus—with research for his book. Consequently, at the end of her second year, when David had completed his fellowship and wanted to go home to San Francisco, Roberta balked. They decided that he would return to the Bay Area, while she stayed on to graduate from the University of Utah Law School in June 1975.

Not only did the separation put undue strain on the marriage, but during that third year of law school, Roberta found herself attracted, literally out of the blue, to a woman. "I remember thinking to myself, 'Oh, my God! I must be a lesbian!' Because it was just so qualitatively different than anything I had ever experienced before, and I thought of myself as happily heterosexual and pretty happily married, quite frankly." The realization threw Achtenberg into an agony of confusion. She found it hard to concentrate; she couldn't eat. "There have been very few times in my life when I have been so affected that I couldn't eat," she says, "but that was one of them." She knew that she still loved and greatly respected her husband, but feelings were developing that had to be addressed. She started reading whatever she could find on homosexuality but kept her sexual ambivalence to herself. And after graduating from law school, she returned to California and to David.

She became a teaching fellow at Stanford University in Palo Alto, an hour south of San Francisco. While she was there, law professor and activist Don Knudson, who was a visiting faculty member, came out in the school newspaper, *The Stanford Daily*. The announcement caused such a stir that it discouraged Roberta from further exploring her suspicions about her sexual orientation. "It's one thing to recognize you might be a lesbian. It's quite another to deal with all the things that have been constructed around you that have something quite opposite as their focus. First of all, I had a husband. I had a family, I had a mother—all kinds of things that had to be dealt with."

Sadly it was another series of family tragedies that made her realize that she had to face the truth. Her brother Jack, also in the legal profession, was teaching at the San Fernando Valley College of Law when he was struck from behind by a car and thrown from his wheelchair. He suffered brain damage and, after lingering for two weeks in a coma, died on Labor Day in 1976. Then Roberta's mother Beatrice, who had recently endured a coronary bypass, relapsed into serious heart disease and died not long after. While coping with these crises, Roberta and David decided that their marriage could not be saved. "We had been thinking about it and probably did the thing that you should never do, which is to make a final judgment about something so life-altering while you're in the midst of grief," she admits. The divorce took place early in 1977, and was so amicable that after David moved to Washington, D.C., remarried, and sought work in the Carter administration, Roberta gave the FBI an enthusiastic endorsement when it was checking him for a security clearance.

Roberta now faced decisions as to what her new life would be. "When David and I divorced, I began realizing that if I was going to live this out, it meant I would be spending my life with a woman," she says. "I didn't identify the particular woman; it's not that I knew I would be with this woman or that one for the rest of my life. But I had to discover if this was really me." She confided her ruminations only to her sisters. Ironically, her older sister Gail had just divorced her husband, who had revealed he was gay—"so I wouldn't say gay people were her favorite at the time," Roberta says with a smile. For her younger sister, Susan, Roberta's revelation was a decided nonissue. "We'd been through so many things as a family, this news seemed like nothing," Susan says. "I told Birdie, 'I don't want to know what you do in the bedroom, and you don't want to know what I do in the bedroom!' " Susan was dating a black man at the time, whom she eventually married, so the youngest Achtenberg was no stranger to controversy. "It just didn't matter," she says with a shrug.

However, when it came to telling people outside her immediate family, Roberta recognized that she would have to be discreet. She had gotten a new job in San Francisco as a professor of civil procedures and director of skills training programs at the New College of California School of Law, which had recently been founded to train community-oriented lawyers, primarily students of color and students from working-class backgrounds. The school was seeking accreditation at the time Roberta was named dean—becoming the youngest dean in America. As she says, "There were lots of things going on that I felt like I should not jeopardize." Thanks to her efforts, the school did win accreditation, and it still trains class after class of community-oriented lawyers. "And does a very good job of it," she says with pride.

The importance of concealing her sexuality at the New College brought home to Roberta the great inequities homosexuals faced in society: job and housing discrimination, hate crimes, potential prosecution under archaic sex laws, bias in adoption proceedings, unfair tax guidelines, and violations of privacy rights, among them. Now her "justice thing" kicked in, and she began to investigate the legal barriers that stood between homosexuals and first-class citizenship. Joining the National Lawyers' Guild in 1978, she got involved with its Anti-Sexism Committee, which developed a manual for lawyers representing gay and lesbian clients. With that primer as a starting point, Achtenberg assembled and edited a seven-hundred-page book, *Sexual Orientation and the Law.* Energized by becoming an expert on gay-rights law, she then looked to politics, joining the Harvey Milk Gay and Lesbian Democratic Club and then the Lesbian Rights Project, an advocacy group founded by lawyer Donna Hitchens, who would later become a dear friend. Downplaying her accomplishments today, she says, "We didn't really have goals back in those days. We just did the things we needed to do and the rest just sort of, well . . . happened."

In 1979, she attended a National Lawyers' Guild Conference, where an impressive lawyer did a demonstration examination of an expert witness in a lesbian-mother custody case. Mary Morgan, a remarkably pretty woman with a shock of black hair and azure eyes, had won an unprecedented number of such custody cases. Dazzled by her skill, Roberta secured an introduction through a mutual friend, Patti

Roberts. "She made a very big impression on me because she was very cute and very, very aggressive," Achtenberg admits.

A native of New Orleans, Louisiana, Mary Morgan had left the South to attend Smith College in Massachusetts. "I wanted to be a diplomat," she says, "and actually chose my college based on that." She spent her junior year abroad in Geneva, Switzerland, and returned to find America embroiled in the social tumult of the late 1960's, with the federal government cast as the villain of the piece. Abandoning the idea of diplomatic service, Morgan enrolled in New York University Law School and, after she graduated in 1972, packed all her things into a Volkswagen van and headed west to San Francisco, the epicenter of the counterculture. There she landed a legal services job and through it began doing groundbreaking work on lesbian-mother custody cases. She was so successful a champion that she rose to national prominence as the acknowledged expert on the issue.

Her high-profile work brought Mary into contact with some other powerful Bay Area lawyers who had formed a coalition and wanted to sponsor a worthy cause. They found that mission in 1980, when Governor Jerry Brown appointed two openly gay judges in Los Angeles— Steve Lachs to the Superior Court and Randy Schraeder to the Municipal Court—and made it known that he intended to make a similar historic placement in northern California. Many in the group, which Achtenberg joined, felt that the judgeship should go to the eminently qualified Mary Morgan, so they put Morgan in contact with the politically well-connected southern California attorney Sheldon Andelson, and he in turn brought her to the attention of the governor. One year later, in 1981, Jerry Brown appointed Mary Morgan judge in San Francisco. "We liked to say that she was the first lesbian ever appointed to the judiciary anywhere in the universe," Achtenberg says.

By now Achtenberg, still dean of the New College law school, had made a name for herself as a lawyer dedicated to social justice. She was also becoming known as a gay-rights activist through her work as a staff attorney for the Lesbian Rights Project, of which she eventually became director; as a cofounder of the gay Bay Area Lawyers for Individual Freedom (BALIF); and as the Executive Director of the National Center for Lesbian Rights. For all the recognition she was achieving for her work, she achieved something even more fulfilling in 1982, when she became romantically involved—and ultimately, committed to a life-time partnership—with Mary Morgan.

Before long, they decided that they wanted to have a family. Achtenberg had always longed to have children; in fact, one of the things that troubled her most about discovering her homosexuality was the belief that it precluded motherhood. But when she represented friend Donna Hitchens in an adoption procedure for Hitchens and her partner, Nancy, she learned to her delight that she could indeed have children. "In fact," Roberta says, "*we* were making it possible. Mary was the first one to do a lesbian custody case. I did the first second-parent adoptions. I did the first joint adoptions by a gay or lesbian couple. I got to create gay and lesbian families with my own hands. . . . In terms of validating my own life and making things possible not just for others but myself as well, it's been some of the most important work I've done."

They decided that Mary would bear their child through artificial insemination, and that Roberta would legally adopt the child. Hitchens would represent her, returning the favor Roberta had done her. Named for Achtenberg's late mother, Beatrice, Benjamin Alexander Morgan Achtenberg was born in 1986. Of all the satisfying collaborations the couple had done and would do together in the future, "Benjie," Roberta says with a mother's undisguised pride, "is the most important."

When Benjie was two, Roberta finally felt ready to take her gay-rights activism to a bigger arena—electoral politics. After so many years of arguing the law, she was fascinated by the prospect of effecting change directly by actually shaping policy. In 1988, California State Assemblyman Art Agnos was elected mayor of San Francisco, and a special election was set for April 12 to fill the seat he was vacating in the 16th District, which encompassed nearly a third of the city. While in the Assembly, Agnos had been a good friend to gays and lesbians, in the forefront on antidiscrimination legislation and supporting sensitive approaches to the AIDS epidemic, which had hit San Francisco especially hard. The homosexual community longed to have someone with similar views take his place.

But Willie Brown, Speaker of the Assembly at the time and himself a formidable political force, was intent on resurrecting the career of a popular former Democratic representative, John Burton. Brown's determination to anoint Agnos's successor was much resented by the gay community, as was the contention of certain members of the old-boy network that homosexuals were too politically green to govern. Brown himself had said to Roberta Achtenberg, "You people are not ready to represent yourselves." As Achtenberg told *The Advocate,* "That kind of arrogance—that kind of attitude exhibited toward the gay and lesbian community and our right to self-determination—was shocking." Achtenberg believed that it was time to change that view, and her many champions, including Mary Morgan, concurred. They convinced her to run for Art Agnos's Assembly seat herself. "I had the benefit of being naive," she says now. "We sort of thought, 'Why not?' The issues were very important."

In her campaign headquarters on the seventh floor of a Market Street high-rise, Roberta stood amid a sea of yellow-and-magenta campaign posters and announced her candidacy to the cheers of some sixty supporters. "The people of this city reject the notion that the only way to get things done is to leave it to the old boys," she said. "There must be a changing of the guard because the people of San Francisco are demanding it." Characterizing herself as a progressive candidate who would champion the causes of social justice and responses to the AIDS epidemic, she also reached out to mainstream voters, calling her political inexperience an advantage—she was an outsider unattached to special interests.

While still active on the California bench, Mary's job during the campaign was twofold: getting young Benjie off to day care while struggling not to transfer the stress of the race onto him, and issues research. And, as always, Morgan and Achtenberg would be there for each other in a myriad of support modes—emotional, intellectual, and tactical. "We're very good at consulting each other and trusting each other's judgment," Morgan states. "I think we have different *opinions,* but we have a lot of respect for each other's intellectual abilities. So I think both of us, regardless of what the project is, take comfort in knowing that each can consult the other."

It would prove to be a bruising campaign. Burton's loyalists spread the word that, although he was a straight man, he was a better feminist than Achtenberg and a better champion of gay rights. Roberta found such campaign rhetoric devastating. So the couple developed a strategy: Mary would be the one to get angry. "Somebody had to," Roberta says. "I would be completely incapacitated if it had to be me." In that vein, another one of Morgan's side jobs was to apprehend the morning newspaper first and scope it out to ascertain what her partner should and should not read.

Then came the day when one of those papers proclaimed in a head-line: ACHTENBERG GAINS ON BURTON. Still, Roberta knew better than to bank on even such a positive sign. "I knew all along I could lose, and I suppose a part of me probably thought I *would* lose since John Burton was so famous," she says, "and I was not known." By election day Achtenberg was so exhausted that she fell asleep before the returns were in. "Particularly toward the end, when you're running that hard, you don't think, you don't look, you have blinders on," she says. She had prepared two speeches—one for victory and one for conces-sion.

This time she would have to employ the concession speech. But by anyone's account, she had run an exceptional campaign. Through the efforts of her network of friends all over the country—people she had met through her activism, and some who knew her legal work on be-half of gays and lesbians—she raised more than $350,000 for the cam-paign coffers. "Nobody expected me to raise that kind of money or get that kind of validation, that kind of support," she says.

So in 1989, when five slots opened up on the San Francisco Board of Supervisors, her supporters urged her to try for political office once again. "There's no question that I was viable," Achtenberg recalls; she now had the name recognition she had lacked in the Assembly race. Furthermore, since there were five slots open instead of one, this race would very likely be less personally abusive and taxing than her last run. After much discussion, Roberta and Mary agreed that she should begin to test the political waters in January for the election to be held on November 6 of the following year.

For her campaign slogan, Achtenberg spun off the Christian Coali-tion's buzzwords "family values," which cast aspersions on nontradi-tional lifestyles, to claim that she represented "real family values." In keeping with that theme, she announced her candidacy that spring in the auditorium of her son Benjamin's grade school, standing onstage in front of a banner painted by Benjie and his classmates. She drew a parallel between "real family values" and governmental responsibility. "The way we treat our families is a measure of us as a city," she said. As the cameras rolled, precocious five-year-old Benjamin took the opportunity to make faces and steal a little of the spotlight from his mother.

From the outset, the powerful Democratic machine seemed bent on punishing Achtenberg for having challenged John Burton in the Assembly race. Indeed, the head of the party, former governor Jerry Brown, came out in support of Carole Migden, the charismatic chair of the local Democratic Central Committee, who was also running—and who was also a lesbian. Under the headline TWO LESBIANS BID FOR SUPERVISOR SEATS IN S.F., *The Advocate,* among other publications, tried to set up the race as a catfight.

In Achtenberg's view, apart from their gender and sexual orientation, she and Migden were very different—with different approaches, different styles, different opinions. Migden was known for her political connections and clout, while Roberta was perceived as a civil-rights lawyer with proven regional credentials in the fight for gay rights. Migden promised state and federal action on local projects, while Achtenberg alleged that power for reform lay within the city itself. One directed focus outward, the other inward. Moreover, the supposed rivalry was ultimately a nonissue because of the multiple slots available. "I don't think she and I ever saw it as canceling each other out," Roberta says. But as the race progressed, the mainstream press focused not only on the perceived competition of the two, but on the fact that the public would never vote for two lesbians. That especially rankled Achtenberg, for as she told the San Francisco newspapers at the time, "There is some level of shared experience, life experience, and some appreciation of history that you do have in common with other lesbians. . . . I think of that in terms of being Jewish. While I'm not much of a practicing Jew, I do feel some kinship with other Jews and some appreciation of our collective two-thousand-plus-year history. But it doesn't mean we all have the same view of solid waste disposal."

On election night, Achtenberg was at her campaign headquarters on Market Street when the Registrar's Office called around nine P.M. to report that the race was going very well for her. Although they could not guarantee where she would finish, it would be in the top five.

Before the evening ended, Mary Morgan would introduce her partner to the cheering crowd as "My son's other mother, your new supervisor, Roberta Achtenberg!"

Migden also won, for as Roberta says, "It was not the way the press liked to make it: 'Well, she's a lesbian and she's a lesbian, and the people couldn't possibly want two.' That's not the way the public thought about it." Indeed, the *San Francisco Chronicle* hailed that election night as "A Lavender Sweep"; with Achtenberg and Migden joining board member Harry Britt, three of the city's eleven supervisors would be gay. Also, gay schoolteacher and comedian Tom Ammiano, who took to referring to himself as a "Refugee from the Planet Mary," astonished the politicos and finished first for a seat on the Board of Education. Finally, Proposition K, the domestic-partnership ordinance, was resoundingly approved. Conservative candidates, many fueled with money from the city's chamber of commerce, experienced no victory celebrations.

The outcome reestablished San Francisco as the center for homosexual political advancement in America, highlighted the electability of lesbians in particular, and proved that gay candidates could appeal to mainstream voters. Roberta said to the gay press: "People learned in this race that our concerns go beyond civil rights to encompass the environment, affordable housing, and child and health care. This is a remarkable affirmation that people can be judged on their merits and the power of their messages." Urvashi Vaid, executive director of the National Gay and Lesbian Task Force, said it more succinctly: "Our time has come."

At her swearing-in ceremony in the Board of Supervisors chambers, Achtenberg spoke from the heart of her joy at having the chance to serve all the citizens of the city she cherished and also at the opportunity to set an example for her son. Tearing up a bit, she pointed with pride to Benjamin, saying how happy she was that he could be born and raised in such a great, liberal city, which was teaching America a lesson in tolerance.

Achtenberg began a three-year tenure on the board, a job and an honor she loved. One of the first pieces of legislation she got through the Board of Supervisors was a requirement that the city put into place more curb-cuts for wheelchair access. For a city with such a substantial pedestrian population—citizens and tourists alike—the legislation was much needed. For Roberta, it was also personally meaningful as a nod to her late wheelchair-bound brother, Jack. Before long, Supervisor Achtenberg established herself as an aggressive advocate for her constituents, battling to bar housing discrimination against families with children, fighting for tenant protection against wrongful eviction, and introducing bills to build affordable housing for low-income families and to guarantee small-business access to city contracts. When a community development block grant from HUD came through, she saw to it that a portion was set aside to support domestic-violence shelters. She also commandeered the effort to institute a children's budget for the city, which would allot millions annually to benefit underprivileged youngsters. Among her many duties, she was particularly fond of the occasional public hearings. "I liked the chance to show the public respect," she says. "I always thought those were very important opportunities."

Being in the spotlight, Achtenberg also found herself deluged with mail from homosexuals not only in San Francisco, but from around the country. "With all the nut letters you'd get—and those, of course, are the ones that stick out in your mind—for every one of those you'd get ten letters from people who express such *sincerity,*" she says, "letters from young people, from people in rural areas. You think, 'What am I doing this for?' and then you pick up one of those letters." Some especially heartwarming letters came from parents of gay children, expressing gratitude for Roberta's efforts that might enable their offspring to lead more satisfying lives. "Yes, some parents are homophobic, but for the most part, parents see homosexuality as diminished options, consigning their child to a life of unhappiness. And of course, no one wants that for their child," Achtenberg says. "The ability to be in public life has been enormously positive to our movement, for our people. And being able to contribute to that has been very gratifying."

Still, Achtenberg experienced a decided downside to the notoriety when she began receiving a series of alarming death threats, which were all the more frightening because she had her son's safety to consider. Throughout the crisis, the couple's overriding agenda was to keep an even closer watch on Benjie—he was never let out of their sight. As Roberta says, "There are some people out there who basically think you're a legitimate target, that you're not really a person, that your kid is not really a child; to them you're just objects." Roberta and Mary, however, refused to substantially alter their lives to accommodate such hatred—and, fortunately, nothing came of the threats. "San Francisco is a great place, maybe the best place on earth to be gay," Roberta said to the press at the time. "But that doesn't make it heaven."

By now the gay and lesbian press had taken to calling Morgan and Achtenberg "San Francisco's newest power couple," or, using Mayor Art Agnos's stronger words, "the city's most powerful couple." So when a crowded field of Democratic hopefuls—among them Paul Tsongas, John Kerry, Jerry Brown, Tom Harkin, a little-known governor from Arkansas named Bill Clinton, and Mario Cuomo, the patriarch of the Liberal wing—started jockeying for position to challenge seemingly unbeatable Republican President George Bush in November 1991, Roberta Achtenberg started getting phone calls. The first was from ex-nun Virginia Apuzzo, who in 1999 was to become the highest-ranking lesbian in the Clinton administration and who at that time was Governor Mario Cuomo's liaison to the gay and lesbian community in New York. "Mario's going to run," Apuzzo told her, describing her boss's good record, intellectual acumen, and pro-gay stance. "Would you be for him?" Achtenberg said without hesitation that she would be happy to support the governor. "Then," she reports, "David Mixner called me and said, 'I want you to meet with the Clinton people.' " At that point, Bill Clinton had barely 1 percent in the polls and desperately needed some kind of elected official's endorsement.

"Mixner went down the whole rap," Roberta says. " 'He's an old friend, he's good on gay rights, they're this modern couple, he's progressive on all these things—' and so on." Finally she promised that if Cuomo did not run, she would consider endorsing Clinton—but there were stipulations: If she was going to stick out her neck to endorse him, she had to have a visible position in the campaign; and if he won, she wanted a place in the administration.

After prolonged deliberation, Mario Cuomo decided not to seek the Democratic nomination. "The next day, Mixner's on the phone: 'Okay. Now I want you to consider Clinton,' " Roberta says. "And I said, 'Okay, fine.' " As with all projects undertaken in the Achtenberg/Morgan household, Roberta went home to discuss it with Mary, who was not pleased. "What are you talking about?" she cried. "Clinton's for the death penalty! I can't believe you got talked into this cockamamie deal!" She remained skeptical until Roberta took her to one of candidate Clinton's speeches much later. Impressed not only with the candidate's message, but also his palpable charm and energy, she, too, became an avid supporter.

Colleagues in San Francisco were also initially skeptical, because Clinton was perceived as a moderate, not as a true, hard-line Democrat. Although some local elected officials were envious of the press Achtenberg was getting with her early endorsement, most firmly believed the man from Arkansas was unelectable. Regardless, Roberta became a committed member of the campaign. "I thought it was important for us [gays and lesbians] to be visible in national politics, but I didn't want to be for somebody just to be for somebody. These people had good ideas. And they had a demonstrated record of accomplishment—both the governor and Mrs. Clinton."

Although less familiar with Hillary Rodham Clinton, Achtenberg got a crash course when she was recruited to accompany the first lady of Arkansas during her initial campaign trip to San Francisco. When they met at the airport, Achtenberg began to brief Mrs. Clinton on the events of the day ahead, but says, "She turned the tables on me immediately." Having read Roberta's dossier, committing much of it to memory, the governor's wife turned to Achtenberg in the limousine on the way into the city, saying, "Roberta, tell me about the New College Law School." Being on the Legal Services Corporation Board, "she wanted to know everything about it. Then she started asking more questions about this and about that," Achtenberg recalls. "Finally I said, 'Um, Hillary, I'm supposed to be briefing *you*.' Needless to say, it made a big impression on me. I liked her immediately."

A major Western state fund-raising dinner was planned for Clinton, to be held on February 28 at the Beverly-Wilshire Hotel in Los Angeles. The candidate was improving in the polls and had made the cover of several national magazines. It looked as if he might even have a chance of beating Paul Tsongas in the New Hampshire primary, which would be an impressive feat, considering Tsongas hailed from New England. Then disaster struck. First, lounge singer Gennifer Flowers told the tabloids she had had a long-term sexual affair with Clinton, and then Clinton's alleged avoidance of the draft in the 1960's became front-page news and the subject of an intense national debate. On February 18, the wounded Clinton lost the New Hampshire primary to Paul Tsongas, 25 to 33 percent. Editorials in newspapers throughout the country read like political obituaries for the beleaguered candidate.

Still, those involved in the L.A. fund-raiser were determined to make a good showing. The ballroom downstairs would hold a large dinner; the upstairs conference rooms would boast gatherings of four groups who had raised more than fifty thousand dollars—one of which was Access Now for Gay and Lesbian Equality (ANGLE), the advocacy group that had raised a stunning seventy-five thousand dollars. It was there at the ANGLE fete that Achtenberg first met Clinton in person, and she felt an instant rapport. "There is a genuine genius that he has for making people feel recognized and appreciated in the moment. It's not just charisma," she says. "It's really something—in Hillary, too—*substance*. Very smart, concerned about the right things." Although clearly exhausted by the month's events, voice raspy and raw, Clinton spoke to the group from the heart, gesticulating robustly, and using personal stories to illustrate his convictions. Initially dubious, the audience was dazzled by the end of the speech, and Clinton left Los Angeles with the gay and lesbian community in his pocket. As Tim McFeeley, executive director of the Human Rights Campaign Fund (HRCF), says, "He was the first candidate to see the community as a clear, desirable bloc that he wanted, and he knew he had to be up-front about it. It couldn't be a 'closet' courting. Clinton was very clear—he said, 'I'm going to do things for you and you're going to do things for me. And the world's going to know about it.'"

Achtenberg returned to San Francisco energized. A northern California for Clinton group was formed by her, Marsha Scott (later a presidential assistant), Martha Whetstone, Willy Fletcher, and Mike Kahn. Due to her closeness with the Clintons, when something needed to be accomplished quickly, the group usually turned to Scott, and she would attempt, many times with Achtenberg as coconspirator, to get to Hillary Rodham Clinton. When, for instance, there was a problem with the initial California campaign manager, who was widely perceived as a good person but not up to the task, Scott said to Achtenberg, "I'm going to get you in the car with Hillary, and you tell her what we think." Roberta did—and within days, the campaign manager was replaced.

With such determined campaigners in his corner, Clinton began to recover his momentum; and Harkin, Kerry, and Tsongas began falling by the wayside in subsequent primaries. To prepare for the important California primary in June, Clinton came to San Francisco, where Roberta Achtenberg arranged an outdoor rally at an unusual location, the crowded intersection of Twenty-fourth and Mission streets, where the Latino, Chinese, and gay neighborhoods conjoined. "On one corner there is a Chinese take-out, on another corner is an El Pollo Loco, and there's a beatnik coffeehouse up a ways," Achtenberg says. "The bus line and the subway crisscross. And you stand on the corner there and the people who walk by are every color and kind." When Clinton's advance team came out to build the stage, they got nervous and badgered Achtenberg to come up with a crowd estimate. She enthusiastically predicted two thousand people. Skeptical, the advance people admonished her, "Well, Roberta, you better produce or else!" She then upped her estimate to three thousand, based on her staff's reports. "I said, 'Don't worry, it's going to be fabulous. And there's going to be every kind of person there. Clinton's going to love it!' "

Nearly eight thousand people showed up. "It was huge. It was absolutely huge," she crows. "And I had it organized so that Clinton was the only one who went onstage. Nobody introduced him. I wanted him basically to arrive, walk up on the stage, and talk to the people." Clinton reveled in the informality of the event, and after his speech, took off his jacket, grabbed Achtenberg's arm, and said, "C'mon, Roberta," pulling her off the stage and into the crowd. "It was really a scene," she recalls. "I almost got crushed. It's not that it's not thrilling— you have the thrill for days—but he didn't just do it for the thrill of it. He was committed and he cared."

ANGLE had planned another fund-raiser for Clinton, to be held on May 18 at Hollywood's Palace Theater. Roberta flew down to attend. The southern California gay and lesbian community—seeing the evening as an invitation, finally, to sit at the table of national politics— turned out in force, raising over a hundred thousand dollars in campaign contributions. The most comprehensive fund-raiser ever attempted by the homosexual community for a candidate for President, the event saw the Palace packed with people primed to be true believers. Backstage, waiting to go on, Clinton turned to Achtenberg and said, "Roberta, if I go to Washington, I want you to go with me."

He made a speech that night remarkable for its clarity, insight, and compassion. Tackling every issue meaningful to the community—from gays in the military to AIDS to sexual orientation discrimination—he wove a spell that reduced many in the audience to tears. He ended by saying, "What I came here to tell you in simple terms is: I have a vision. And you are part of it." Two days later, *The Washington Post* described that night as not only a milestone for gay America but as a turning point for Clinton as well: "It seemed that his political and emotional sides converged to give his voice a deeper sense of conviction." In June, Bill Clinton won the California primary.

By the time July rolled around, Clinton seemed to be the most likely candidate to win the Democratic nomination, and many news stories pointed to the newly influential gay and lesbian community's role in his campaign—in fact, they had raised nearly four million dollars for Clinton. The Democratic convention was to be held at New York's Madison Square Garden. On Tuesday, July 13, Clinton's political platform would be presented, and among the speakers would be two HIV-positive leaders, AIDS activist Elizabeth Glaser and openly gay Clinton friend and environmental adviser, Bob Hattoy, introduced by Representative Pat Schroeder (D-CO). Onstage, alongside the party leaders and top elected officials from around the country, would be Roberta Achtenberg.

"I was one of the party platform drafters, which is why I was supposed to be up there," Achtenberg says. "I was defending the platform." She would be the first open lesbian ever to address a national convention of either major party. "We knew what I was going to be doing and what Hattoy was going to be doing were the first real manifestations of the Democratic party's commitment and our nominee's commitment to gay rights," Achtenberg says. "We knew that it was a big deal." She insisted on writing her speech herself, with the help of her City Hall aide, Alex Clemens, and spent every moment she could rewriting and revising the text. Due to timing matters, all speakers rehearsed again and again before the fateful night, ensuring not only a smooth show, but also relaxed participants. "The thing they tell you before you walk on is:'What goes on in the hall is not important.You're speaking to the television cameras. So, look right ahead and *don't yell.*' " By the end of the run-throughs, Roberta was confident of her speech and comfortable behind the podium.

When the night finally came, the Garden was humming with excitement. Standing backstage, listening to the rest of the rousing speeches, Achtenberg admits to a sudden attack of nerves. "Even though I knew the speech word for word, I stood back there, wondering how I was going to stack up," she recalls. Hundreds of homosexuals were there to witness the historic moment; gay and lesbian signs bobbed on a sea of red, white, and blue. When Roberta walked onstage, flash cameras popped like firecrackers and her supporters started chanting, thumping the floor, and climbing on chairs to see her—*their* delegate. Not only was the gay and lesbian community wildly ebullient, but the rest of the delegates, feeling pride at being part of a drive to end decades of discrimination, joined in.The din was ear-shattering; the decibel level deliriously high. Achtenberg was moved to tears. "It was a wonderful motivator," she says. "It put a smile on my face and it made my heart swell." It took a while for the hall to quiet, but when it did, there was absolute silence. For a luscious moment Birdie Achtenberg was frozen in time, an instant icon in history.When she spoke, she identified herself as a woman, a mother, a lesbian, and a Jew, tying each of those identities to a section of the platform and expressing her deep commitment to the Democratic agenda. She also spoke movingly of Clinton, who nurtured such diversity.Then, in what seemed like the blink of an eye, she was finished. Again, the crowd went wild, calling out, clapping, and crying.

Backstage, cameras and microphones were shoved into her face; a new star was christened in the Democratic party firmament.Yet what Achtenberg remembers most was some older Jewish women who approached her and thanked her for identifying herself as a Jew. Even though there were many Jewish people in the Democratic party, the women confessed to feeling invisible in the crush. "So," Roberta says, "it was a coming out for all different kinds of people."

The following evening, at the conclusion of the convention, Clinton won the Democratic nomination; and in his acceptance speech, when he listed all the constituencies that were threads in the tapestry of his America, he paused for a meaningful moment before pronouncing the last one: "gay." It was a word heard around the country and savored not only in the hall, but also in every gay and lesbian home in America.

In August, the Republicans held their convention in Houston, Texas, and renominated President George Bush. Pat Buchanan, who had run unsuccessfully against Bush in Republican primaries, gave a keynote speech so filled with hate and divisiveness that he alarmed thinking people everywhere. While the extreme right rose to applaud, the rest of the country recoiled in horror. The frightening rhetoric, though, was ultimately helpful to the voting public—it clearly delineated the differences in the two parties.

The buzz-phrase "It's the economy, stupid" resounding like a clarion call, the Democrats successfully exploited a sluggish economy and, bit by bit, chipped away at Bush's seemingly insurmountable lead. Realizing that the gay and lesbian community voting bloc might be the deciding influence in the tight race, Roberta worked tirelessly, spearheading the drive around the nation to sew up those votes for her candidate. Tim McFeeley of the HRCF says, "It was the first time the gay community really had a national political movement—political in the sense of being electorally focused on a national election. From Hawaii to Maine, from Florida to Washington State—everyone was on board with this."

On November 3, 1992, Bill Clinton was elected the forty-second President of the United States.

Mary and Roberta were in Little Rock, Arkansas, for election night, and Achtenberg recalls sitting in the hotel ballroom, watching the returns on television. "Party muck-a-mucks were saying, 'Oh, my God, it was the gays who put him over the top!' " It was the first time she had heard out loud what she felt in her heart. "They were officially crediting us with the President's election, or being a very important part of it."

Not since John F. Kennedy's election thirty-two years earlier had the nation's capital reverberated with such youthful energy and excitement. Being the first "baby boomer" to be elected President, Clinton was determined to have the young and idealistic aid him in running the government, with an administration that, he claimed, "looked like America." Gay and lesbian leaders from all over the nation converged on Washington to secure their ties to this new administration, knowing that it was a long way from well-meaning campaign speeches to the implementation of changes. The Human Rights Campaign Fund (HRCF) now approached Roberta to help define the agenda the gay community should work to achieve. For Achtenberg, the top-priority issues were appointments, legislation, and the military.

To push for appointments, William Waybourn, executive director of the National Gay and Lesbian Victory Fund, helped put together Coalition '93, a screening group that identified potential gay candidates for government positions and then lobbied the transition office, headed by Vernon Jordan, on their behalf. Roberta Achtenberg's résumé was at the top of the pile, given her close ties to the Clintons and the role she had played in delivering the gay and lesbian vote to the President-elect. Coalition '93 warned her that the Senate approval process would most certainly be grueling. Coalition adviser Mike Bento thought it likely that she would be asked about Benjie's parentage. "I told her she needed to think through sitting in front of a committee and being asked, 'Is he your son or Mary's? What are the circumstances of that child's conception?' " Roberta, however, was firm: "She said, 'I will not answer questions on this subject.' " Bento recalls. "It was absolutely essential to her that nothing happened in that confirmation hearing that would be scarring to her son. That was far and away her biggest priority, and I respect her a tremendous amount for that."

She would also have to face the prospect of being physically uprooted, of having to give up her beloved job as supervisor and, since Harry Britt had retired, leave Carole Migden as the sole homosexual on San Francisco's Board of Supervisors. Mary would have to leave the bench, an eventuality that didn't faze her. "I had been a judge for a dozen years. It was very interesting and I loved it. But I was ready to go on and do something different." Benjie, then seven, would be forced to leave his school and friends. But considering the great triumph Achtenberg's appointment would be for the gay and lesbian community, the family decided that it would be well worth the sacrifice.

Soon Achtenberg was told to be on the alert for a phone call from the President-elect. Consequently, she and Mary canceled the three tickets they had bought for a Thanksgiving vacation in St. Lucia and instead waited by the phone. The call finally came after the holiday, in the middle of a heated debate at the Board of Supervisors, and Achtenberg's aide tiptoed in to whisper excitedly, "Roberta! It's the President-elect!" Clinton offered Achtenberg the position of Assistant Secretary of HUD for Fair Housing and Equal Opportunity, which would make her the chief enforcement officer of the federal laws prohibiting discrimination in housing. She was asked to meet with Secretary-designate (and former mayor of San Antonio) Henry Cisneros.

Roberta was a little disappointed at first, having had her heart set on a slot in the Justice Department. "Since I was sort of a symbol of the gay community's vote nationwide, we thought that I should be given the highest award possible," she says. William Waybourn recalls, "There was some concern on her part on whether the position with HUD would be of sufficient stature for her to give up her job as supervisor. But we told her it was the best job she was going to get and that we wanted her to take it." Mike Bento agreed. "I thought it was a terrific job, an appropriate job for the first lesbian appointee—that she would be in charge of the administering of civil rights in the nation's housing system. I thought it was a great statement about our commitment to civil rights." Finally, Roberta and her advisers were satisfied that the appointment was appropriate and should be accepted.

Achtenberg now met with Secretary Henry Cisneros—a leader of the gay and lesbian community meeting a leader of the Hispanic community—and they got on exceedingly well. "He's just a fabulous, fabulous person and I thought it would be terrific to work with him," Achtenberg recalls. Cisneros returns the compliment: "Roberta is a person deeply and passionately motivated by what is right and what is wrong. It is so powerful with her that it simply overwhelms everything else. Injustice is just not acceptable to her, and that gives her the courage to face great odds. She is remarkable."

Having won acceptance by Cisneros, Achtenberg now faced a much harder test of her mettle: the approvals process of the U.S. Senate. The Constitution accords the Senate the power to confirm the major appointments of the President, such as his cabinet members, judges, commissioners, and ambassadors. Usually, the hearings are pro forma and the President's choices are confirmed without dissent. But sometimes—most often in the case of Supreme Court appointments—opposition to the President's candidates is fierce. Battles over Abe Fortas, Clarence Thomas, and Robert Bork had raged for days, as did the fights to seat

Senator John Tower (R-TX) as Secretary of Defense and Zoe Baird as Attorney General. Recently, Clinton's nominee for ambassador to Luxembourg, openly gay James Hormel, was refused to be even considered for confirmation by the Republican-run committee. Finally, in a rarely used tactic, a frustrated Clinton had to take matters into his own hands by anointing Hormel with a "Recess Appointment" while Congress was out of session.

Once the combat begins, a nominee can become the helpless pawn of the forces vying for political power. Often the factional lines get drawn so deeply in the sand that the nominee has no choice but to withdraw from consideration. It was in this arena that appointee Roberta Achtenberg's fate was to be decided.

Since she would be the first openly gay person ever to go through a Senate confirmation hearing, Achtenberg knew the odds were against easy approval. Not only were conservative Republicans making threatening noises, but the Christian Coalition was also mounting a fervent and mean-spirited opposition to her. A typical protest came from Reverend Lou Sheldon of the Traditional Values Coalition, an Anaheim, California-based evangelical group, who said of the nomination: "It fits into the homosexual agenda of overhauling straight America. What you have with this appointment is the continuation of Bill Clinton's big payoff to the homosexual community." Just as George Bush had wanted to be the "education President," Sheldon groused, Clinton "is becoming the homosexual President."

Facing such opposition, Roberta knew that she would have to prove herself unimpeachably qualified for the job. "I studied for months. At the Washington, D.C., Lawyers' Committee there were a number of people there who really wanted to help. And they put together a binder for me that was essentially a primer on the entire Fair Housing law, all of the regulations, all of the important Supreme Court cases that had interpreted the law, various initiatives that had been undertaken under prior administrations, things that were wrong with the process that they wanted me to consider, how much money had been spent doing this, that, and the other thing."

She would also have to undergo a rigorous background check. She called her ex-husband, David Chavkin, to warn him that he would be hearing from the FBI and to seek as glowing a recommendation as the one she had offered him in the past: "Guess what, honey? Now it's time to return the favor!" When she told her family about the background check, her sister Susan asked what would be the worst thing they could possibly dig up on someone as ethical as Roberta. Achtenberg jokingly replied, "Well, they might find out that this leading lesbian used to date men!"

Mary joined Roberta in Washington, D.C., to take part in the inauguration festivities, dubbed "An American Reunion," during the week of January 17, 1993. Despite the bone-rattling cold, there were outdoor performances at the Lincoln Memorial by Bob Dylan and Aretha Franklin, a televised inaugural celebration featuring Michael Jackson and Barbra Streisand, a splendid fireworks display, and a moving swearing-in ceremony followed by a boisterous parade. "As we stood on the Mall," Mary recalls, "we said to each other, 'Who would ever have dreamed?' We were very unlikely candidates for federal service." There was a spate of glamorous, star-studded gala balls, including one sponsored by the Human Rights Campaign Fund, and there, surrounded by their gay brothers and lesbian sisters, the two women really felt at home. "It was maybe the last time we felt the euphoria combined with the naiveté," Achtenberg recalls wistfully. "That was before the difficulty set in. We didn't appreciate it. We didn't understand it. But that night, we owned it. That's how I felt. I felt like we made this happen."

Following the inauguration, Achtenberg, with her fellow board members surrounding her, held a press conference at the San Francisco City Hall to announce that, subject to Senate approval, she would accept the $115,700-a-year HUD job, heading an office of seven hundred people. "It is a distinct honor and privilege to have received the President's vote of confidence," she said. The next day, the front page of the *San Francisco Chronicle* described the nomination as a "milestone for gay political clout." The *Los Angeles Times* printed the encomiums of Art Agnos, who said, "She is an outstanding American who is a role model for anyone who seeks to serve the public, because of her extraordinary standards of excellence and her high principles." The *San Francisco Examiner* quoted Achtenberg as saying, "We are going to revitalize that [HUD] division from top to bottom. There seems to have been a mandate in past administrations to dismantle that department." The article also carried this prophetic paragraph:

No openly gay man or woman has ever had to undergo Senate confirmation for a national post, and the forty-two-year-old Achtenberg could face tough scrutiny by conservative senators on the Senate's Banking, Housing and Urban Affairs Committee.

Shortly before the hearings were to commence, Achtenberg went to Capitol Hill to pay preliminary visits to senators on the committee, accompanied by Liz Arky of HUD, who had been assigned to shepherd its nominees through their confirmations. "Although she's many years my junior, Liz had a maturity and a presence that was very reassuring," Roberta says. They called first on the chairman of the committee, Donald Riegle. Riegle, an eighteen-year veteran of the Senate, had begun his career as a Republican congressman from Michigan but then, in a crisis of conscience over the Vietnam War, abandoned the GOP to become a staunch liberal Democrat. A passionate civil-rights advocate, he strongly supported Achtenberg's nomination and outlined his strategy for the hearings. Riegle planned to rely on Senator Barbara Boxer (D-CA), who not only was on the committee, but was from Roberta's home state. "It would be her job to carry me forward," Achtenberg says, "which she was happy to do and did brilliantly." Boxer would introduce the nominee, along with Senator Dianne Feinstein (D-CA) and Senator Joseph Lieberman (D-CT). "I had become acquainted with Joe Lieberman on the Democratic Platform Drafting Committee," Achtenberg says. "One of the reasons I wanted him to introduce me, if he was willing to—and he was more than willing to—was because I knew that as an intellectual in the Senate and as an Orthodox Jew, his introduction of me would carry some real weight." Before the meeting ended, Riegle broached the subject of Achtenberg's sexuality, the only senator on the preliminary tour to do so. "To his credit, he said, 'Look, I want to do what's respectful to you, and I want to make sure that I do it right,' " Roberta remembers.

Unable to visit every committee member, Achtenberg and Arky decided to concentrate on the Republican senators, whom they suspected would be harder to sell. Senator Al D'Amato (NY) "gave me kind of a rough time," Achtenberg recalls. The senator sized her up, saying gruffly, "I'm told that you're a good talker. They say you're a smooth operator." Achtenberg accepted the backhanded compliment and spent the rest of the meeting discussing the upgrading of HUD and what she would like to accomplish in her position there. When she finished, D'Amato showed her to the door, pledging his support. She had an equally successful meeting with Senator Robert Bennett (UT), who turned out to be a fellow alumnus of the University of Utah Law School. Senator Christopher (Kit) Bond (MO) was more challenging. "He was nondisclosing, very difficult to read and very aloof," Roberta says. They left Bond's office not knowing how he might vote. One senator flat-out rejected Achtenberg's request for a meeting: Lauch Faircloth (NC), who was a vocal opponent of gay rights.

Meanwhile, the opposition forces were gearing up for an attack. Before the week was out, North Carolina's other senator, Jesse Helms, would angrily accuse Achtenberg of misusing government resources in preparing for her hearings. Nominees are required to furnish their committees with copies of all their publications, but since *Sexual Orientation and the Law*, the book Achtenberg had edited, was out of stock and going into a new printing, she was unable to lay hands on enough books. She got clearance from the chief administrator of HUD to run off two additional copies of the seven-hundred-page book on the office duplicating machine; somehow Helms got wind of it, charging that Achtenberg had employed government resources "to proselytize her lesbian way of life." "I was very shocked and frightened," Roberta remembers. "I didn't really know what to do. And he demanded this document and that document and the other document by noon the next day—and this was a Friday night." In a panic, she called White House Chief Counsel Bernie Nussbaum. Nussbaum, calming her, dispatched his deputy, Ron Klaim (later chief of staff to Vice President Al Gore) over the next morning. After hours of work, all the information explaining the "incident" was forwarded to Helms, and the matter went no further. Still, it was yet another harbinger, as if Achtenberg needed one, of how the game was going to be played.

On April 26, three days before the hearing date, the monumental National Gay and Lesbian March on Washington took place. Thousands upon thousands lined the streets of the capital in numbers reminiscent of the March on Washington for Civil Rights in 1963. Achtenberg, now a national symbol to the community, was asked to appear but was prevented by Senate protocol. "I wanted to speak and they wanted me to speak, but I wasn't allowed to," she laments. She was given an award the same weekend by the Victory Fund but was allowed only a brief comment. "Basically, I got up there and said, 'Thank you very much. Can't talk now. Love you all.' It was very hard."

Roberta used the next two days to mentally and emotionally focus herself for the hearings. She knew she was prepared; she thought she was ready. But as Mary Morgan says today, "Who knew? Who could have imagined that the process was going to be like that? Not in your wildest nightmares could you imagine . . ."

On April 29, 1993, accompanied by Mary and a coterie of supportive friends, Achtenberg headed for the Everett Dirksen Senate Office Building feeling as if she were going to court. "That sort of nervous sensation. But I had studied so hard that there wasn't a question they could ask me that I didn't know the answer to." Even when Senator Jesse Helms walked in to view the proceedings, she says, "By the time it was my turn at the table, I was calm." The first senator to speak for her was Dianne Feinstein, an old friend from San Francisco politics, who detailed Achtenberg's accomplishments, the political offices she had held, and the many boards on which she had served. Feinstein did not broach the issue of Roberta's homosexuality, alluding to it only at the end of her speech: "This is an important appointment to a community that has often felt excluded from the decision-making process. . . . The doors of opportunity will open once again."

Next, Senator Barbara Boxer endorsed Achtenberg, making only an oblique reference to her sexual orientation by saying: "She knew what it meant to be discriminated against, to be told that you weren't wanted, that you were not the right type of tenant. . . . When we confirm Roberta Achtenberg . . . we will be saying that discrimination is unacceptable, and we will be saying that the promise of equal opportunity is alive and well." It fell to Senator Joseph Lieberman to address the issue head-on: "This is, I believe, an historic nomination because of Roberta Achtenberg's sexual orientation, but the point of it is that we are here advocating her nomination . . . because she is superbly qualified to serve this government and the American people." Representative Nancy Pelosi (D-CA) finished up the round by reading a supportive letter from the Democratic members of the California Congressional Delegation.

Now Chairman Riegle offered his own endorsement, which was greeted by a burst of applause. Senator Carol Moseley-Braun (D-IL) followed up by saying, "I am so firmly convinced that racism and sexism and all the isms that divide us and pit us against one another have no place in this society and quite frankly are evil, in my opinion. . . . I can think of no more highly qualified candidate to serve . . . than Ms. Achtenberg. I want to congratulate her." Senator Kit Bond reserved judgment until he could ask further questions. Only Lauch Faircloth took issue with Achtenberg, hinting at what was to come: "I'm all for diversity," he said. "Unfortunately, there are some people who are only for diversity when it fits their special agenda and comes out the way you want it to be. I will ask you a few questions to find out your opinion on the subject of diversity. . . . I look forward to your testimony."

Then it was Achtenberg's turn to speak. After introducing the family members, friends, and staffers who were with her, she embarked on a thoroughgoing assessment of public policy, fortified by statistics and case studies, charging: "We must recognize the ravaging effects of separation, not only on our cities, on our suburbs, and on rural America, but on our national fabric. . . . I will bring to this task . . . a fervent commitment to . . . make this nation's fair housing dream a reality for those who have been pushed aside and forced to live separate and apart." She ended her assured and sometimes stirring remarks by saying, "I have been a public-interest lawyer, a teacher of public-interest lawyers, a civil-rights advocate, a defender of the children of lesbian mothers and gay fathers, and an elected official. Should I be granted the opportunity to become an assistant secretary, I will do my best, with a deep sense of responsibility, to serve the nation that gave my parents and my family such boundless opportunity. It would be a remarkable privilege to do so."

Senator Faircloth came out swinging. Citing the recently adopted Colorado amendment denying "special rights" to homosexuals, he asked if Achtenberg thought the voters were entitled to pass such a law. Trying not to be thrown by the obtuseness of such a question, Achtenberg responded that the voters had the right to pass any law, but whether the law was upheld by the Constitution was another matter. Undaunted, Faircloth switched gears: "As a member of the United Way and the San Francisco Board of Supervisors, you supported expelling the Boy Scouts from public buildings and cutting off the United Way funding. . . ." Achtenberg immediately corrected the senator's statement, explaining that the United Way's board of directors, where she was one of over fifty members, voted unanimously to cut off funding for the Boy Scouts because they would not provide services to boys who were self-identified as gay or bisexual. As for their use of public buildings, no group with a stated discriminatory policy was permitted to use classrooms during school hours, but after hours, all kinds of groups—including the Boy Scouts—were welcome. She also provided documentation proving that the San Francisco Board of Supervisors had no jurisdiction over the school board and hence had no say in its decision to bar the Boy Scouts. When Chairman Riegle interrupted, asking Faircloth for the source of his information on the Boy Scouts, the senator admitted, "the Family Research Council," which elicited loud guffaws from the audience—the Family Research Council being a somewhat self-serving right-wing Christian conservative think tank.

After that, most of the committee's questions focused on housing. Senator Kit Bond asked whether Achtenberg would lobby to make "sexual orientation" a category protected against discrimination under federal housing statutes. Achtenberg replied that such legal revisions were the job of President Clinton and the Congress, adding wryly, "Should you see fit to amend the statutes further, it is my job to enforce." The session lasted for two hours, and when it was over, "Everybody recognized that I had done very well," Achtenberg modestly says. "I was very relieved." A week later, despite the last-minute lobbying of right-wing groups, Roberta Achtenberg was approved by a vote of 14–4. Only senators Phil Gramm (R-TX), Richard Shelby (D-AL), Faircloth, and Connie Mack (R-FL) voted against her, claiming that they had done so because she had dodged questions about the Boy Scouts. Senator Shelby said in a statement, "Ms. Achtenberg's action with respect to the Boy Scouts is indicative of her willingness to use her position to impose her personal convictions on others." This erroneous characterization would balloon beyond all logical credulity when the committee's approval of Achtenberg was sent to the Senate floor for confirmation.

"It was absurd," Achtenberg fumes today. "The Boy Scouts do harm to gay-identified boys. And they shouldn't, because everybody knows that the Boy Scouts build leadership. They teach you skills that you need to know; they build character. Why shouldn't something like that be available to all boys? And who needs support more than gay-identified boys? I wasn't intolerant of the Boy Scouts. I just think they should make their services available to all boys, not just some boys. You know, at one time the Boy Scouts was only for white boys, too. I thought I was standing up for gay youth. I thought I was standing up for inclusion."

The press was already predicting that her appointment would face a hostile delay in the Senate. The *San Francisco Chronicle* quoted a Capitol Hill Republican as saying that opposition to Achtenberg was part of "the plan to increase Bill Clinton's misery index." *The Washington Times* reported, "[Jesse] Helms said he will try to block the nomination when the full Senate takes it up 'because she's a damn lesbian! I'm not going to put a lesbian in a position like that. If you want to call me a bigot, fine.'"

Helms also sent his Senate colleagues a letter denouncing Achtenberg on the Boy Scout issue: "I want Americans to have a chance to decide whether they want to get into the business of having an avowed lesbian in a high government position who has insulted in the meanest way the Boy Scouts of America!" He was then quoted in the *San Francisco Chronicle* as saying: "She is not your garden-variety lesbian. She is a militant-activist-mean lesbian, working her whole career to advance the homosexual agenda. Now, you think I'm going to sit by and let her be confirmed by the Senate?"

The article went on to say that when the paper tried to contact Helms personally, a member of his staff said, "We don't talk to the homo San Francisco press." Some members of the press enthusiastically joined in on the Achtenberg-bashing. In *The Washington Times,* nationally syndicated columnist Samuel Francis wrote:

No other administration in American history has been so tasteless as to foist off on the country an admitted homosexual who boasts of her perversion and who was so repellently brazen as to show up at her confirmation hearings with her "lover"—"my beloved partner, Judge Mary Morgan"—in tow and introduce her to the committee.

But Miss Achtenberg's sexual preferences—or "orientation" or "choice" or "genes" or whatever excuse prevails this week—are not the only reason she should be sent back to the San Francisco stews from which she crept. Rather more dangerous to the republic than her lesbianism is her bigoted insistence on deploying the full force of the state against private groups that don't share her demand for "tolerance. . . ."

Eric Rosenthal, political director of the HRCF, now told executive director Tim McFeeley: "She's in trouble. This is not going to go. The White House is not helping. They nominated her; they feel that's all they have to do." At that point, the new administration was too overwhelmed by the sheer number of appointments it had made—virtually every major job had to be filled—to get involved in individual confirmation proceedings. McFeeley and Rosenthal approached Roberta, who at first was reluctant to accept their help, believing that the Senate would approve her on her merits and not because of political finagling. "I think she thought that pressure from gay political groups was exactly what she didn't need," McFeeley says, "that something like that would only hurt her." Soon, however, she came to see that the merits of her case had nothing to do with the kind of attacks she was getting. With her blessing, Rosenthal and McFeeley got to work.

To be Achtenberg's point person, they engaged Hillary Rosen, an HRCF board member who had known her personally ever since Roberta's run for the California State Assembly. Rosen soon identified their chief problem. "The White House and HUD had not had experience with gay and lesbian issues," she says. "The most important thing would be to first establish Roberta's credibility in the area she was going into at HUD. Secondly, it was clear that her enemies were painting her as this woman with horns, and I knew it was very important that she very quickly develop a personal connection with a core group of swing votes in the Senate. That was our strategy."

Rosen and Nancy Davis of the Equal Rights Advocates garnered positive characterizations of Achtenberg from straight business and community leaders, not only in San Francisco, but around the country, blitzing the media with them, and set up one-on-one meetings for Roberta with the senators who would constitute the swing vote. But the anti-Achtenberg camp was also moving into overdrive, as the *San Francisco Chronicle* reported:

> Senate aides have been looking in gay press archives for potentially embarrassing information. It is unusual for Washington to devote such time and attention to an assistant secretary nominee, but the conservative groups who pushed the senators to move against Achtenberg say her "dangerous status" warrants such attention.
>
> "This woman is motivated by her sexual orientation," said Andrea Sheldon, the government affairs director for the Traditional Coalition in Washington. "That is what drives her. She has not chosen to keep it quiet. She made her sexual orientation an issue herself."

Sheldon's father, Reverend Lou Sheldon, echoed his daughter, claiming that Achtenberg's "only rise to fame is her lesbianism; she's only interested in one percent of the population [those who are gay]" and warned, "There's going to be blood on the floor over this one." Then, the day before the Senate debate, some conservatives, spurred on by the Christian Coalition, showed a video of the 1992 San Francisco Gay Pride Day parade, in which Roberta Achtenberg and Mary Morgan rode with their son Benjie in a car bearing a placard that read: "Celebrating Family Values." At one point, Roberta gave Mary a quick peck on the cheek. "This was supposed to be the great offense, right?" Roberta says. Christian Action Network president Martin Mawyer said of the video, "We're not opposed to gays and lesbians holding federal office, but her performance in that parade is evidence she's a lesbian activist, not just a lesbian!"

The Senate debate on Achtenberg's appointment took place on May 19, 1993, and was broadcast in its entirety on C-Span. It made for rather dramatic viewing. From the outset, Senator Jesse Helms took up the cudgel against Achtenberg. "We are crossing a threshold," he announced. "This is the first time a homosexual or lesbian has been nominated for a position in the United States government. . . . They expect Jesse Helms to vote for her nomination. No, Bill Clinton, I won't!" He went on to accuse the nominee of using "draconian tactics" as supervisor and called her a "pushy, demeaning, demanding person . . . a mean person."

Senator Barbara Boxer met Helms eye-to-eye. "She is not pushy and she is not demeaning and she is not demanding and she is not mean," she countered. "And I am sure that the senator from North Carolina himself might be surprised at how many people think *he* is mean." Senator Donald Riegle then demanded to know whether Helms had been correctly quoted in *The Washington Times* as calling Achtenberg "a damn lesbian." Helms shot back that he couldn't remember using the word "damn" but that he very well may have, to which Riegle replied, "I find it a very disturbing statement . . . I think it's distasteful. It reflects poorly on the United States Senate." Helms then played foul, threatening to launch into a tirade about Riegle's alleged involvement in the Keating Five savings-and-loan scandal, and stormed out of the chambers.

Senator Carol Moseley-Braun rose. "It demeans our body to have a member taking credit for being quoted as a bigot," she said, referring to Helms. "I am frightened to hear the politics of fear and divisiveness raise its ugly head on this Senate floor." Senator Boxer joined her. "Character assassination will not hold, whether it is in the press or in this beautiful hall. People who don't know this woman and who admittedly don't like her private life would try to destroy her. . . . What we heard here from the senator from North Carolina saddens me deeply." She then read from a pile of letters supporting the nominee.

Senator Trent Lott (R–MISS) rose to claim he was not against Achtenberg's sexual orientation but instead wondered if she was "temperamentally fit for the position," saying that she was known for "intolerance, discrimination, and vendettas against those who do not share her beliefs. The Boy Scouts are not exactly a subversive organization," he declared, "yet Roberta Achtenberg used her public position to threaten and extort any organization that had ties with the Boy Scouts." He then proceeded to read from what he called a *San Francisco Chronicle* "editorial" on the subject that accused Achtenberg of possessing a "twisted mind." The *Chronicle* had never published such an editorial; what the senator was misrepresenting as one was an irate letter to the editor. Just then, in a bit of surreal timing, a troop of Boy Scouts was ushered into the visitors' gallery. Fidgeting and fussing, they looked confused as to why their organization was being referred to over and over on the Senate floor. The scoutmaster escorted them out before anyone could ask the reason for their seemingly cued presence.

Roberta and Mary were not present at the confirmation debate. As instructed by Hillary Rosen, they had sequestered themselves in a borrowed Washington apartment, avoiding the television and the newspapers. "It was a very emotional time for them and for Benjie," Rosen says. "They didn't need to hear it all." Instead, Roberta read the Senate transcripts every night to identify inaccuracies put forth by the Republicans. As William Waybourn says, "Obviously she couldn't respond. So we had surrogates who could talk to the press . . . people from all over the country who would respond after we alerted them to what went on that day . . . saying that it was a right-wing extremist attack on the credibility of Achtenberg. Roberta had no knowledge of that because we didn't want her closely tied to these kinds of activities."

Achtenberg also had important champions on the Senate floor. "I couldn't speak, but Barbara Boxer could speak and Don Riegle could speak and Dianne Feinstein could speak. . . . I will always be grateful to the people who carried the filibuster for our side." Achtenberg had accumulated a huge sheaf of supportive letters, from everybody from the president of the Pacific Stock Exchange to the dean of the Stanford Law School to priests and rabbis in San Francisco. To hold the floor, Roberta's supporters read the letters into the record, one after the other. "Each of our senators . . . had these notebooks filled with, 'If they say this, you say that. If you need to kill time, start reading from these letters,' "Achtenberg says. "So it's not like I was undefended. I was being defended." As Hillary Rosen recalls, "In those three days leading up to the actual vote, Barbara Boxer and Dianne Feinstein worked very closely with me. . . . We were prepared for the acrimony and we knew that the more outrageous it was, the more important it was to stay calm and strategic and focused."

The second day of the debate was just as acrimonious as the first. Senator Boxer read two statements: a pro-Achtenberg *San Francisco Chronicle* editorial and a statement from San Francisco Mayor Frank Jordan, taking Helms to task for his "bigoted campaign" against the nominee. Helms jumped to his feet to strike the statements from the record, citing a Senate rule against personal attacks on another senator.

"Call it gay-bashing if you want," he declaimed. "I call it standing up for America's traditional values!"

Then came yet another round of attacks based on the Boy Scout canard, with Senator Orrin Hatch (R-UT) scolding Achtenberg as "worse than intolerant. By using her position to attack the Boy Scouts, she brought the power of government to bear against a private association because that private association does not mirror her beliefs." Senator Gramm agreed and echoed Senator Lott: "I wonder about someone who engages in vendettas against people they disagree with," he said. "I have no doubt about her dedication, but I am concerned about her temperament." Senator Slade Gorton (R-WA) went so far as to say that with the Boy Scouts, Achtenberg "crossed the line from advocacy to misuse of government power." Minority Leader Bob Dole (R-KS) characterized Achtenberg as a "ringleader of an ideological crusade to remake the Boy Scouts in her image."

When Boxer moaned aloud that all this criticism was a "smokescreen for Roberta's private life," Helms shouted, "She sure wasn't private when she was hugging and kissing last year in that parade in San Francisco!"

Dole, with a nod to Helms, moved from the Boy Scouts to criticizing aspects of Achtenberg's gay-rights advocacy as too radical. "Showing tolerance and respect should not force us to endorse an ideology that most Americans do not embrace," he declared.

Exasperated, Dianne Feinstein could stand no more. "Because Roberta Achtenberg is a lesbian, she is being subjected to a barrage of nasty, unseemly, untrue allegations," she cried. "Enough is enough! When the debate moves away from Roberta Achtenberg's qualifications, it reflects poorly on the United States Senate." Senator Patty Murray (D-WA), weary of the dissension, agreed, saying, "This country is tired of people who view America as 'us' versus 'them.' "

Achtenberg's supporters outside the Senate also deplored the rancor of the second day. Achtenberg's sister Gail called to say, "Birdie, I just can't stand it! I don't care about the lesbian part and all, because everyone knows that, but they're saying you're mean! You're the nicest person in the world!" Younger sister Susan sat in her Oakland home watching the C-Span channel, furiously yelling back to the television set. Mary Morgan, too, was outraged. "To have the person that you not only love the most in the world but respect, who's never done anything but good—be ground up in a meat grinder, just seemed completely insane. It was like, 'Hello? Does anyone remember that we're the people giving up our lives coming here three thousand miles? Why are you trying to grind us into the floor?' "

Achtenberg would even get two consolation calls later on, from Senators Ted Kennedy and Donald Riegle. "I'm sure one was not prompted by the other," Achtenberg says, "and each of them basically said to me, 'Roberta, I've been in the Senate a long time, I've been in the Capitol a long time, and I have to tell you, I never had any idea it would be this way.' They were calls of apology."

The White House issued a tepid statement, expressing its "full confidence" in Achtenberg. "All the people in the White House were very nice," Roberta says charitably, "but they were involved in other things." Not only were there other nominees, but the administration spinmasters were being deployed to handle the backlash Clinton was getting for his stance on gays in the military. Instead of simply signing an executive order banning the discrimination as he had promised, because of a conservative outcry, the President had been coerced into forming a committee to investigate the ramifications of lifting the ban against homosexuals—a compromise that was pleasing no one. Coalition '93 was similarly preoccupied, Mike Bento says. "The timing was such that we were fighting on two fronts because gays in the military divided our resources."

On Friday, the third day, the debate seemed all but stalemated. Then tall, distinguished veteran Senator Claiborne Pell (D-RI) rose from his chair on the Senate floor. Pell was known on Capitol Hill both for his great eloquence and for his New England reserve, which he wore as a badge of honor. Now, in a rare moment of self-revelation, carefully measuring his words, Pell stated that he had a personal reason for supporting Roberta Achtenberg. "My daughter, Julia, is president of the Rhode Island Alliance for Gay and Lesbian Rights," he said. "I would not want to see her barred from a government job because of her orientation." In the spellbinding silence that followed, Senator Donald Riegle stood to commend Pell for his moving statement. "We can't entertain the notion that people ought to be denied service in our government . . . by virtue of some test that one or another person might apply," he said, "based on their personal orientation or values."

Throughout the battle, Senate aides had been scurrying back and forth with messages proposing compromise points that could end the debate and force a vote. Finally, Minority Leader Robert Dole huddled in the Democratic cloakroom with Majority Leader George Mitchell, and a deal was struck: The vote would be called Monday in exchange for the commencement of debate on Dole's pet issue, campaign reform.

Over the weekend, the Christian Coalition stepped up its anti-Achtenberg phone campaign to congressional leaders. Reverend Jerry Falwell dashed off cautionary letters labeling Achtenberg a threat to the American family, and was quoted as saying that her nomination "sets a terrible precedent for America." But the end was in sight—and through it all, Roberta Achtenberg had held up remarkably well. She never even considered withdrawing her nomination, for her "justice thing" demanded that she stay the course. As she says simply, "We don't give up." Still, as Henry Cisneros says, "Roberta showed extraordinary courage— the kind that we rarely see in American politics and government. She was no novice, having been through many political battles, but nothing could prepare her for the venom, the hate and anger directed not only at her, but her family. She fit the definition of grace under fire."

Monday dawned, and the Senate got ready to vote. Senator Helms warned his colleagues, "If any member of this Senate thinks this vote will go unnoticed by their constituents back home, they may find out otherwise!" Trent Lott went one step further and predicted that a vote for Achtenberg "could hurt a candidate for the Senate next year. This is a vote that will count. Any Southern Democrat who votes for this nomination and is up in the next two or four years is going to have to answer for it." But by the time the seesaw tallying was concluded, the vote stood at 58–31 in favor of Achtenberg's confirmation. Ten senators had not been present. Thirteen Republicans had crossed party lines to join the forty-five Democrats confirming the nomination; five Democrats, all Southerners, had joined twenty-six Republicans to oppose it. Homophobia, like Humpty Dumpty, had had a great fall.

"We were all crying," Hillary Rosen remembers, "and very happy." The jubilant Barbara Boxer would be quoted in the major newspapers as saying, "We did it! We stood up to Jesse Helms and we won." Greg

King, speaking for the HRCF, said, "Roberta Achtenberg has knocked down a wall and made it possible for future nominees to be judged on the merits" instead of prejudice. When Rosen slipped away from the emotional din in the Senate to phone Roberta with the news, all the new assistant secretary at HUD could manage as a reply was a timid, "Are you sure? Are you sure there wasn't a miscount?" William Waybourn says, "I never saw Roberta show any emotion until after her confirmation was confirmed. She had a small party that night, and it was the first time I had seen her acknowledge how hard it had been on her. But it didn't last very long, because she's a tough lady, and she's very, very appreciative of the individuals who helped her through that process." Relieved to be done with the battle, Roberta issued a spare statement to the press: "I am proud of the vote of confidence by the United States Senate."

Achtenberg says of everyone involved: "We were all just so proud of ourselves. There is a pervasive cynicism in the Congress, on the Hill, and the Senate staffers who worked on this—a number of them came to work for me later—felt this was such an optimistic victory. It was like, for a minute, the veil of cynicism and jadedness was pushed aside and people could experience more of the reason why they came there. It had a certain idealistic quality to it that we really, really enjoyed."

When she returned to San Francisco, she found a giant spray of yellow roses in her small office, fifty-eight blooms and thirty-one bare stems symbolizing the breakdown of the vote. She told the press, "It's been very difficult for a politician to keep her mouth closed for four months. That's been as big an ordeal as anything." But she acknowledged that when the fight got personal, "It was pretty brutal. I guess the first person who walks on the field gets spit on. When you put yourself forward, you recognize your entire life will be scrutinized, but I didn't realize they would mischaracterize me as much as they did. . . . To have the legitimacy of your family questioned, to have your partner maligned and vilified as if she were not a person, and to have my child even made reference to . . . I was surprised at all of that."

Because of her love for San Francisco, she rented out her family's Noe Valley home rather than selling it, and leased a house in Silver Spring, Maryland. As she said, "When I give my departing remarks at the board on Tuesday, I want to encourage my colleagues to cherish and protect this place and lay partisan concerns aside, because this is a special place on earth and we've got to take care of it." There was a grand send-off party for her on Castro Street on the evening of June 1. Nearly five thousand people jammed the district to cheer the battle that had been won and to say a fond farewell to a favorite daughter of the city. Former mayor Art Agnos said to the crowd, "This is someone who is a dear personal friend and a great San Franciscan. Her victory is for all of us a victory."

The next morning, the Achtenberg/Morgan family boarded a plane to Washington, and on Thursday, June 3, 1993, Roberta was sworn into her new position. As she started her tenure at HUD, Mary began to set up a domestic violence clinic at American University. Benjamin was enrolled in the Georgetown Day School, where many ambassadors and congress members sent their children. Given all the animosity directed at her in the nomination process, Roberta said, "It was important for him to be someplace where we would know that he would be safe, where they would watch out for the kids and not let anyone suspicious around."

Once at HUD, Achtenberg began an uphill battle to reinvigorate the office that had seriously languished in the Reagan/Bush years. "HUD represents the cities," Achtenberg explains, "and poor people and their housing." On the Republican watch, civil-rights enforcement had not been a top priority. The first big test of the fair housing office was the integration of public housing in Vidor, Texas. "Literally no African-Americans lived in the city, let alone lived in federally financed housing," Henry Cisneros says. "Vidor was a flashback to the small-town segregation of the 1960's." To launch what Cisneros describes as one of the most difficult battles HUD faced during his tenure, Achtenberg developed a strategy: "I had my staff down there for six months working with the community, interviewing people who said they wanted to go live in Vidor, working with the white tenants in Vidor to accept the black tenants, working with the ministers and others in Vidor and Beaumont communities—you just don't do these things instantaneously. There had been a lot of racial strife there, with the Klan and that kind of thing."

Having laid the groundwork, Achtenberg, Cisneros, and Assistant Attorney General Web Hubbell went to Texas to notify the Orange

County Housing Authority officially that it was being put into receivership. Achtenberg personally oversaw the relocation of the tenants. "She literally physically moved the African-Americans into the projects in Vidor at five A.M., to minimize the potential for violence," Cisneros remembers. "It was a tinderbox." He adds: "I had to smile. Here was this San Francisco lesbian in Vidor, Texas, protecting the rights of African-Americans being protected by federal marshals. She handled the situation without violence, with a great sense of justice and incredible dignity not only for herself but the new tenants. Her own oppression as a lesbian gave her the strength and wisdom to free others."

"We did an excellent job," Achtenberg says proudly. "The Justice Department supported us extraordinarily well; the U.S. Marshals and the Texas Rangers gave us total cooperation." Roberta was especially glad of the effect the success had on her staff. "They got to be the civil-rights workers that they had wanted to be. Many of them had been in the department for more than twenty years and had never really been allowed to do what it was they needed to do."

A triumph for HUD, the integration of Vidor in October of 1994 was also an important affirmation of the Clinton administration's commitment to civil rights. *The Washington Post* ran Roberta's picture over a glowing front-page story about HUD's refocusing. When Mary walked outside to get the paper that morning and saw Roberta's picture, she panicked, and without stopping to read the headline, ran inside, crying, "Oh, my God, Roberta!" Thinking that she was the latest in the long line of Clinton administration casualties, Roberta said, "Oh, no, don't tell me! We're going to have to go home."

Both women were very relieved to see that the story was positive, but the fact that they immediately jumped to the conclusion that Roberta was being fired reveals how beleaguered the Clinton administration had quickly become. "Maybe you had to be in Washington to feel this way, but everyone was looking around and wondering whether or not this whole thing would come apart," Achtenberg remembers. "They were predicting doom and gloom for the President." Pundits were calling his election with only 43 percent of the vote a feeble mandate, and then his much-heralded "economic stimulus package," designed to jump-start the economy, went down to ignominious defeat. The Pentagon was evincing outright insubordination to the President, its commander in chief, over gays in the military. An investigation had begun over "Travelgate," with a purge of the White House travel office. Many of Clinton's appointments, especially his choice for Attorney General, were shot down. The new President seemed so estranged from the political mainstream and even from his own party that there was doubt that he would get his first budget through Congress—ultimately, it passed by only one vote. "It was insane," Achtenberg says emphatically. "I mean, all this stuff led to Vince Foster committing suicide. The Beltway had a stranglehold on Washington. They were essentially trying to take the President down."

Through it all, Achtenberg remained a staunch Clinton supporter—and then the administration, desperate to halt congressional defections, caved in on the gays-in-the-military issue with the much-maligned "Don't Ask, Don't Tell" policy. The retreat angered Achtenberg, who as a politician nonetheless understood that the fledgling administration was struggling for survival. "Gays in the military," she says sadly, "had to be sacrificed." She chalks the President's early failures up to inexperience. "I think Clinton was naive. We all were. The Republicans had governed for twenty of the last twenty-four years. We were new to all of this. We hadn't run the White House. We hadn't conducted foreign policy. We hadn't led the troops. We hadn't put together a budget from the point of view of the executive branch. None of these things had been done within anyone's memory. So, mistakes were made, as they say."

The backlash against Clinton led to a Republican sweep of the congressional elections at the end of 1994, giving the party majorities in both the Senate and the House. This meant, of course, that they chaired all the committees, and as soon as they were seated in January 1995, the Republicans began to scrutinize all the executive departments. "We had to come up for all these hearings," Achtenberg says. "Constantly. We were constantly up in front of this committee or that committee." HUD, never a favorite of the Republicans, was a favorite target. But if their intent was to keep HUD from doing its job, "they weren't successful," Achtenberg says. She was instrumental in getting the President to sign the Fair Housing Executive Order of 1995, which created not only the President's Fair Housing Council, but gave HUD authority to fight discrimination in the home-finance and insurance industries.

But Republican badgering was not the only problem HUD faced. In the spring of 1995, Secretary Henry Cisneros came under investigation for lying to the FBI about the circumstances surrounding questionable payments to a former mistress while he was mayor of San Antonio, Texas. Fiercely supportive of her boss, Roberta was dismayed. "Talk about someone who didn't deserve any of it," she says. "His skill and his passion and his compassion were just enormous. I learned so much from him." A special prosecutor was appointed, and Achtenberg could see the handwriting on the wall. "Henry was in a precarious position and I didn't know how much more we could get done," she says sadly. "I didn't think that we had much hope of being able to repeat in the second two years what we had been able to accomplish in the first two years." Four years and ten million dollars later, Cisneros's case would end with an innocuous misdemeanor plea bargain—which the *Los Angeles Times* would derisively describe in an editorial as "a whimper of a result."

Meanwhile, San Francisco was gearing up for a mayoral race. The incumbent, Frank Jordan, had become so unpopular that he seemed destined for defeat. "The job was just way beyond anything he had the capacity to do," Achtenberg says. The prospect of running the city she loved, not to mention being its first gay mayor, was extremely attractive; so after lengthy discussions with Mary, Roberta decided to leave HUD and throw her own hat into the ring. While Roberta returned to San Francisco for the seven-month-long nonpartisan mayoral race, Mary, who had gotten a new job with the Justice Department, would remain in Washington, working to support the family. Benjie would stay with her, rather than be uprooted from Georgetown Day School.

On April 13, Achtenberg announced her decision at a HUD staff meeting. "She caught everyone by surprise," recalls Waite Madison. "It was an eight-thirty A.M. staff meeting and I had car problems so I arrived late. When I got there, I will never forget the somber atmosphere. Someone handed me a note that read, 'Roberta is leaving.' Everyone was sitting around moping, and I said, 'Say it isn't so. Say it isn't so.' It was a depressing scene." Secretary Cisneros and Achtenberg's full staff threw her a tearful good-bye party. "None of us wanted to see her go," Madison remembers. "She tried to give a good-bye speech, but she was too choked up. She was crying and very emotional." Of her staff, Achtenberg says warmly, "We were a team. I appreciated them, and their courage and their perseverance, because we were involved in a noble enterprise. And they appreciated my efforts, and that means everything in the world to me."

What impact her departure would have on Achtenberg's ultimate boss, the President, remained to be seen. *The Advocate*'s view was:

Roberta Achtenberg's departure from the Clinton administration leaves the President without his highest-ranking lesbian appointee, just when he needs to shore up support among disaffected gay and lesbian supporters for his reelection bid.

"With Achtenberg out of the administration, Clinton loses the most visible symbol of his support for gay rights," said San Francisco Supervisor Susan Leal, a lesbian who is the administration's coordinator of outreach to lesbian, gay, and bisexual elected officials. "She was proof of that image of the President getting out there on gay and lesbian issues," Leal said. "Her departure hurts him."

In the same article, Senator Lauch Faircloth was quoted weighing in with his opinion: "Obviously President Clinton decided that extremists like Roberta Achtenberg had no place in his campaign for reelection, and I am glad she is gone."

Back in San Francisco, Roberta ran up against her old adversary, Assembly Speaker Willie Brown, to challenge Mayor Frank Jordan in the mayoral race. Although Achtenberg had declared her candidacy first, Brown had been putting out feelers for months; and many of the city's gay politicos, including Tom Ammiano and Carole Migden, had already pledged him their support. Concerned that her candidacy might further polarize gay and black relations in the city, some gay and lesbian leaders had attempted to dissuade Achtenberg from running. She listened, but ultimately decided to stick to her gut feeling. For one thing, she knew that she was at the height of a popularity that she couldn't be sure would ever come again: "I thought if I was going to go forward, that this was the time." She also felt that her time away in Washington gave her "a perspective on San Francisco that I think San Franciscans lack." And more importantly, when it came to addressing gay concerns, she could not help but remember what Brown had said to her years before: "You people are not ready to represent yourselves." Furthermore, polls in the *San Francisco Chronicle* predicted that Achtenberg would get at least 47 percent of the gay vote, as compared to Brown's 29 percent. "It was a combination of that and thinking that I might be able to do it—I knew that I could lose, but it was also possible for me to win," she says. Soon, however, the press began to characterize the mayoral race as black (Willie Brown) versus gay (Roberta Achtenberg). Achtenberg rejected that characterization, pointing out that it was not merely a two-person race—Mayor Jordan and Supervisor Angela Alioto were also candidates to be considered. Yet she did recognize that the choice between herself and Brown gave liberal voters "a real conscience tug"—especially the African-American lesbians and gays who would draw the curtain in the polling booths.

As election day approached, Achtenberg had overtaken Brown in the polls, and it looked as though she was about to achieve another first: becoming the first lesbian mayor of San Francisco. The Achtenberg team had expected the race to wind up as a runoff between Roberta and Frank Jordan: "Our theory was that Jordan would hold his base and that Willie would be squeezed in the middle, basically. And it would have turned out that way if Jordan did not do the one thing we didn't think he could do, which was to lose his base." He lost it a week before the election, because he attempted a press stunt—taking a shower with two deejays on a radio show—that backfired. "He thought he would show what a regular guy he was," Roberta says, but what may have sounded funny coming over the radio looked tasteless when captured on film. A photograph of the stunt ran in all the San Francisco papers, and overnight the mayor's support evaporated. "That's what cost me the election," Roberta says, for Brown picked up the votes Jordan lost—and so was guaranteed the mayoralty.

Following her defeat, Achtenberg returned to Washington to be with her family and to work for a time behind the scenes as Henry Cisneros's senior adviser at HUD. She was successful in accomplishing a few more things for her old office, but the combination of a wounded Cisneros and a hostile Republican Congress made it clear to her that the heyday of HUD was waning. She and Mary decided to move their family back to San Francisco for good. "I liked working in Washington," Mary says, "but I didn't like living in Washington. I was very happy to come home." The entire family, in fact, was anxious to return to its supportive group of friends—"people who are interesting and not *completely* ambition-driven," Mary says with a laugh. By the end of 1996, the family was comfortably resettled in their Noe Valley home. Roberta took a job as liaison for the San Francisco Chamber of Commerce; Mary returned to private practice; and their son, Benjie, happily rejoined his old pals. His mothers braced for his impending step into adolescence—his bar mitzvah.

The sojourn in the capital, though heady and invigorating and satisfying, had made them all realize how much they missed the notion of family. That was never so apparent as it was on the memorable day of Benjie's bar mitzvah. Both friends and family looked on with pride as the exceptional thirteen-year-old made his way flawlessly through difficult Hebrew and then eloquently spoke of what the Torah meant to him. Thanking his teachers and rabbi, he turned to Mary and Roberta and said, "I want to say to my moms, I love you very much." "There wasn't a dry eye in the house," his aunt Susan says. "Everyone was a mess." Benjie closed by urging everyone in the synagogue to go out and do a *mitzvah,* a good deed. "God only cares about what you do and not what you say," Benjie insisted. "Prayers alone are not good enough."

The remainder of the day was filled with toast after toast, party after party. Looking around at the gathering of well-wishers, the friends, the supporters, and especially the family, Roberta couldn't help but think how fortunate she was. Her own *mitzvah*—the "justice thing" that directed young Birdie through the painful loss of her dear family members, sustained her through the trial of the Senate hearings, and enlightened her influential political life—had served her well. And because it had, she was able, in return, to serve others well.

Like her son, Roberta Achtenberg knows that virtue lies in action. Thwarting the bigots who would deny homosexuals high government office, she says, does not make her a hero: "The thing that's most important to me about Washington was not having been the first of anything. It was that I was asked by the President of the United States to enforce the federal Fair Housing Act. That is a civil-rights law passed in the wake of the riots that came after Martin Luther King's death—a very, very important part of the promise that America makes to its citizens. That I had the responsibility of trying to make that promise come true was an incredible honor, and a privilege, and something that I took very, very seriously every single day. It was my job to do that. Bill Clinton asked me to do that job, investing his trust in me, and I was confirmed by the Senate so that I could do that job.

"And I did that job."

"I'm Just Like You"

I N HALF-LIGHT, the studio seems veiled in a haze of blue; deep in the background there is a proscenium arch capped with a familiar logo spelling out ABC NEWS WASHINGTON. Beneath the bright white letters runs a bank of blinking television monitors, which in turn frames a cyclorama boasting an image of the Capitol dome etched in hues of magenta and pink. As the clock nears eleven-thirty P.M. EST, Lieutenant (jg) Tracy W. Thorne is escorted to a swivel chair, stage left, behind the desk at the center of the set. A top-gun pilot in the U.S. Navy, he is remarkably handsome with bold, piercingly blue eyes, strawberry-blond hair cropped military-short, and the disarming smile of the boy next door. Rather than his usual uniform, Thorne sports a dark gray-green suit; he is wearing a vivid print tie that will be roundly ridiculed back at the airbase tomorrow.

Usually guests on the program are sequestered in a sound booth off-stage—their famous interviewer, Ted Koppel, as most viewers know, works alone. But tonight, one of only a handful of times in the history of *Nightline,* Thorne, the main guest, is seated at Koppel's side. Given the personal drama that is about to unfold, the show's producers felt that the young pilot might be more comfortable if he was face-to-face with his interviewer. Or maybe, Thorne suspects, "They were afraid I was going to wig out in front of fifteen million people."

Now Ted Koppel's mellifluous voice kicks in and they are live, on the air, as he begins his introduction. "You're going to meet a young man tonight who could very easily have been a model for a Navy recruiting poster," Koppel says to the camera. ". . . smart, resourceful, clean-cut, and courageous. This young man, however, is also gay. So you can cut smart, resourceful, clean-cut, and courageous." He goes on to tell the audience that because of his gayness and his decision to go public with that information on a nationally televised broadcast, Tracy Thorne will almost certainly be dismissed from the Navy. "The Pentagon, unfortunately, will not participate in tonight's broadcast," Koppel says. He notes, "Last February, Chairman of the Joint Chiefs of Staff General Colin Powell told the House Budget Committee that homosexual behavior is inconsistent with maintaining good order and discipline in the military. So, that's where we begin. . . ."

Planes flew in the air above his bed, and ships floated on imaginary waves, suspended on nearly invisible threads. The model planes and battleships that Tracy William James Thorne had toiled to cement together, plastic piece by plastic piece, meticulously painted and adorned with military decals and insignias, were his passion—an entire battalion that protected him as he slept at night. He was the youngest child in the Thorne family, thirteen years younger than Martin, the eldest, and seven years younger than his sister Patricia. They lived in the humid clime of Tampa, Florida, on the edge of Lake Carroll, in a white brick Colonial-style house sheltered by a massive pine tree more than seventy feet tall. The house had a screened-in back porch that was Tracy's refuge from the hot sun and the vantage point from which he watched dramatic thunderstorms sweeping across the lake. He had, he says, "the ideal kid's life. We were just a real, down-to-earth, modern-day, Southern-cultured family. Regular childhood, regular parents."

During much of Thorne's early childhood, his father, Roscoe, was away at the hospital, completing his residency as an orthopedic surgeon, "so I spent a lot of my time mostly around my mom," Tracy says. His sister Patricia was also very involved in raising him. "She kind of treated me as her child. She took care of me, she changed my diapers, she fed me, she took me shopping with her." Although he could be a bit of a hellion, as they got older, they grew close. The thing that most troubled Patricia about Tracy was that he was always honest—to a fault. Once she even went to their mother complaining, "Mom, why doesn't Tracy lie once in a while?!"

Tracy enjoyed being outdoors—riding his bicycle, playing touch football on the lawn and baseball in the street—and especially loved being near the water. "It was such a great lake," Tracy says. "My two best friends were within five or six houses of me. Each of us had a little boat and every day we'd come home from school and go swimming or water-skiing together." Though officially Methodist—"My family was never really big on pushing church on me"—he attended a Catholic high school when his family moved to West Palm Beach. Besides being a good student, Thorne distinguished himself as an athlete, but not at the team sports such as football, hockey, and soccer that he longed to play. His father squelched those plans after a three-hundred-pound high school senior came to see him to set a broken wrist. When Roscoe Thorne had asked, "So you're a football player?" the gridiron star had replied, "Yeah—I like to hurt 'em!" Thereafter, Tracy was barred from contact sports. A charismatic bear of a man with a Mississippi drawl, Roscoe Thorne harbored a soft spot in his heart for his youngest boy— "He was a little overprotective," Tracy says with a smile. So instead, Tracy ran. He had always been fast as a child, and he trained hard to become a mainstay of the school's track and cross-country teams.

Running helped him keep troubling ruminations about his sexuality at bay. From the sixth or seventh grade on, he had felt a perplexing inclination toward boys rather than girls. "But I assumed at the time that everyone felt that way," he says, "that it was a normal, heterosexual thing." Still, deep down, there were nagging doubts; sometimes he would find himself stifling fantasies about one of the boys in his class. Yet, for many years, this was not an inclination that he would allow himself to examine. "There was absolutely nothing I was going to pursue there. I was far too repressed."

Not one for idols or heroes, Tracy did find something of a role model in *Star Trek*'s Captain Kirk. "I wasn't really a 'Trekkie,' " he insists. "I think *Star Trek* appealed to the military part of me, being part of a mission; being part of the community, serving the government." But when he was young, joining the military was never a strong ambition. "My father always stressed the importance of being independent and self-employed," he says, "and actually discouraged me from pursuing an ROTC scholarship in college." When he was sixteen, having long been fascinated with planes, he asked his father if he could take flying lessons. Roscoe Thorne wouldn't hear of it, claiming, "Only crazy people would let their kids learn how to fly." Then he had an epiphany: Mired in the usual maddening bumper-to-bumper traffic on the way to the family's weekend home in the Florida Keys, he looked up to see an airplane flying south, toward Key West. Suddenly he announced to his wife and son, "We need to learn how to fly." Almost immediately, he signed himself up for lessons, and soon decided, to Tracy's delight, that his son could learn to fly, too.

From his first time in the cockpit, from the moment he first put his hand on the throttle, Tracy was comfortable, secure, and adept. And, most importantly, he loved it—he loved the intricate detail, the freedom, the sensation, and the mythology of flying. At the age of eighteen, with only nineteen hours of flight time to his credit, he soloed for the first time. The Cessna roared off the runway and circled the field of the small West Palm Beach airport with the teenager practicing landings and takeoffs again and again, flawlessly. "It was a little scary, being in the plane for the first time by yourself, with just the roar of the engine, with nobody there beside you to take over if you started doing things wrong," he says. "But it was also pretty incredible."

In 1985, Tracy graduated from high school and left home for Vanderbilt University in Nashville, Tennessee. "Coming from a Southern family, I wanted to go to a good Southern school," he says. Once there, he immediately became active in a fraternity, Alpha Tau Omega, eventually becoming its president, and signed up for cross-country, track, and intramural sports. "The more I got involved, the less time I had to focus on being introspective about my sexuality. I was always organizing some fraternity event, or hanging out with the guys in a social setting as opposed to a private setting. Which always kept me from dealing with those urges." Occasionally he would force himself to date girls, usually with unhappy results. He recalls a mortifying incident at a fraternity party when he and a girl he had been seeing for a short time ended up in his room after an evening of determined drinking. Instead of getting amorous, Thorne passed out on his bed, prompting the frustrated girl to stumble out of his room and down to the main floor of the fraternity, moaning plaintively, "Why won't Tracy sleep with me?" The incident made its way into the fraternity-house lore and, though they often teased him, none of his frat brothers seemed to draw any conclusions from it.

While at Vanderbilt, Thorne discovered his true calling by sheer serendipity. A friend recommended that he read *Flight of the Intruder,* a novel about Navy pilots flying A-6 Intruder aircraft during the war in Vietnam, which would later be made into a movie. "And it was like, wow!" Tracy says. "This is what I want to do." Here was a career where he could meld two of the loves of his life: flying and the water. The next day, he found himself at the local recruiting station, applying for a place in naval flight school. Switching gears at Vanderbilt, he spent his junior and senior years in ROTC classes preparing for a life in the military. "I liked the independence of it, the service of it. I also think that, to some degree, being a repressed homosexual at the time, a huge part of me had accepted the fact that I would just be in the closet for the rest of my life," Tracy admits. "It's hard to imagine a better draw than the military for your typical closeted gay man, because you are put into an environment where you have close-knit relationships with men all the time—mostly men, at least," he says. "And it's an environment where you don't have to get married. And to some degree, it's a benefit not to be married."

At that point in his life, he had done very little sexual exploration. At Vanderbilt, Tracy would sometimes find himself drawn to a bar called The Underground that catered to a mixed clientele—straight and gay—and was the hangout of androgynous "club kids" with wild makeup and platinum hair. It had the best house music in town, and Tracy usually went there with straight friends and their dates to dance. But perhaps twice a year, usually fortified by a drink or two, he would summon the nerve to return to the bar alone. "I can still remember driving down the road in the middle of the summer with the heat on in my car. And I'd be shivering and shaking. That's how nervous I was. And afterward, I'd be so overcome with depression and guilt that six months would go by before I'd get up the nerve to do that again."

Remaining deep in the closet, he never forged any friendships with the gay clientele. He would just stand there, with a drink in his hand, nervously looking on.

Upon graduating from Vanderbilt with a degree in political science, Tracy Thorne reported for duty at the Pensacola Naval Air Station in Florida. Leafy green oaks surrounded the expansive white brick barracks, marked with a polished brass sign boasting, "Through these doors walks the future of Naval Aviation." Thorne reveled in the atmosphere—"From the first day, I felt like I fit right in"—and felt lucky to have been accepted into the extremely selective Aviation Officers Candidate School (AOCS). AOCS was notoriously grueling, both physically and mentally. "Anyone who's seen *An Officer and a Gentleman* pretty much recognizes what it's all about," Thorne says. A screaming drill instructor would rouse the cadets at five A.M. and within three minutes they were to be dressed and outdoors, standing in formation. They would endure a session of muscle-burning calisthenics, followed by a five-to-ten-mile run around the base, before they wound up back at the barracks, showered and waiting in line for chow at six A.M. "Every hour of AOCS is planned out for sixteen weeks," Tracy says. "The military is very regimented. It takes up all your time."

That, of course, was part of its appeal to Tracy, who was still burying his sexual urges in overwork. But it paid off. By the end of the sixteen weeks, the original seventy-two candidates in the class would be whittled down to thirty-four graduates—and Tracy made the cut. "A lot of the people couldn't take the regimentation. Sometimes someone would just not be cutting the mustard and the drill instructors would smell blood in the water and they'd be like sharks coming in, hammering the people who couldn't cut it, until they would drop out." The conventional wisdom at AOCS was that the best thing that could happen to a candidate was to walk up to the drill instructor at graduation, salute him, and have him ask, "Who are you?" Thorne kept his head down, but quietly distinguished himself by leading the G and X company battalions as a candidate officer, receiving outstanding achievement awards for academic and physical training, and managing to graduate fourth in his class.

Now he was eligible for the Naval Flight Program, which offered the benefit of an allowance that enabled Thorne to move off-base for the first time. He decided to share a beach condo on the Perdido Keys on the Gulf of Mexico, west of Pensacola, with Jim Cowan, a fellow survivor of AOCS. Cowan, previously a Coast Guard enlistee, was almost Tracy's physical double, another blond, blue-eyed Southerner with a slight Louisiana drawl. As a third roommate, they took on Todd Suko, a gregarious and easygoing former college wrestler who had recently gotten his ensign's commission and moved down from Norfolk, Virginia. "We hit it off with Todd right away," Tracy remembers. "He's just a great guy, had a great sense of humor, was really humble and never afraid to laugh at himself." Most of the condos in the complex were occupied by military personnel; three Marines lived on one side of the trio, and three other Navy men on the other. The student aviators spent their days on the base flying and then came home to Jet Ski on the gulf. "It was a really wonderful part of my life," Tracy says. "It was hard to believe they were paying me to do it."

For Thorne, his training always took top priority. If he was to realize his dream of flying the A-6 he had read about in *Flight of the Intruder*, he had to be on top of his game. In basic flight training, officers get the choice of flying either fixed-wing land-based aircraft or carrier-based aircraft—but a flier was guaranteed to receive his chosen assignment only if he was number one in his class. "So the only way to assure that I was going to get to carrier-based aircraft was by being number one," he says. "Then you go through intermediate training, where you're assigned to fighters or submarine hunters or attack aircraft, which could be either electronic attack or munitions attack. To get to choose, you had to be number one there, too. Then when I went into my final phase, I still had to finish number one to get to choose the A-6, as opposed to the other attack aircraft. So it felt like this enormous hoop-jumping contest where I continued having to be number one."

Class status in flight training is determined primarily by daily flight missions. In the air, the instructor evaluates the flier on navigation, running weapons systems, running communications, and dealing with emergency procedures, using a grading sheet with twenty categories and three boxes in each category: Below Average, Average, and Above Average. To secure the coveted number-one position in class, a student had to receive nearly all Above Averages and no Below Averages. Thorne had some advantage over novice aviators because he had been flying since the age of eighteen, but Todd Suko insists that there was more to his success than that. "Tracy was definitely one of the hardest-working guys," he declares. "But that by itself didn't get you all the way. You had to have some kind of natural ability. A lot of people don't make it through flight school. But Tracy was tough and always willing to help others. That was the greatest part of his leadership. He always lent a hand and was a great team player."

As dazzling as he was in the air, his personal land-based operations left something to be desired. While both Todd and Jim dated women regularly, Tracy never did, and his roommates never remarked on it. "I think they just saw me as being married to the Navy," he says with a shrug. "I would party with them, but there was never this insane pressure from them or from our other friends to try and set me up on dates." When he read in the newspapers of Midshipman Joseph Steffan, who was expelled from the Naval Academy for being gay, the story did not particularly resonate with Thorne. He never imagined that he would ever be involved in any such controversy, because he had firmly decided to deny his sexuality. "I had just kind of accepted the fact that I was just going to devote myself one hundred percent to a career and living my life as a Navy officer and a single guy who was not tied down to a woman," he says, then, chuckling a bit, adds, "like Captain Kirk."

He managed to maintain that focus 99 percent of the time, but the remaining 1 percent was sometimes a bit of a stickler. On one foray, Thorne tried out his first gay bar, The Office, in Pensacola. He drove around the place a number of times before getting up the nerve to park nearly half a mile away. Unfortunately, he arrived at eight o'clock on a Saturday night to find only a small group of professional drinkers left over from happy hour inside. "I figured that since there were only half a dozen people in the bar, that's all the gays there were in Pensacola. Little did I know that gay America doesn't come out of its disco-nap until eleven or twelve at night. So my first experience was a bit of a let-down." Nor did he know that at the beginning of every summer, Pensacola hosts Beach Week, perhaps the largest gay circuit party in the South. "I went through two years in Pensacola and never knew that on Memorial Day, the city turned into this huge gay mecca," Thorne says, laughing. "They never came to the naval base."

Every six months or so, he would venture out again, and the guilt

and self-recrimination he felt would put him off the prowl for yet another half year. Since childhood, he had always been honest to a fault,
so it troubled him deeply to lead a double life. Yet he felt he had no
other choice.

He continued to excel at his training, which he loved. While his skill
was breathtaking, it was his infectious, unbridled love of flying that set
him apart. He was especially fond of the sensation achieved while "flat-
hatting"—flying low to the ground. "Before we had stealth aircraft, the
way to evade radar was to fly so low that the radar can't see you because of all the ground clutter," he explains. "We would come in fifty
to a hundred feet off the ground at five hundred knots. To be coming
in that fast and that low, with the terrain all around you, is a pretty
amazing feeling."

Thorne graduated on the Commodore's List with Top Gun honors.
When the captain pinned on his wings and presented his Sea Command pin, he even told him that he hoped one day Thorne would
command the Navy. From there, he went to Attack Squadron 42, where
he would endure thirteen more months of training and would again
finish first in his class of bombardier/navigators.

Thorne was still in training when the Gulf War broke out, and he
was severely disappointed that he couldn't participate in Operation
Desert Storm. "There wasn't a much safer war to be involved in, because there was very little resistance," he says. "The U.S. enjoyed complete control of the air." He longed to turn his practice runs into reality.
"But, on the other hand, I can sleep a little bit better at night knowing
that I never had to drop a bomb on another human being."

Now, at last, his long-held dream of flying the A-6 was within his
grasp. For the training he was transferred to Naval Station Oceana in
Virginia Beach, Virginia, right after Christmas 1990. To his disappointment, Jim Cowan had elected to go to the West Coast, and Todd Suko,
who was a month and a half behind Tracy in school, would not join
him until early 1991. Still, he says with awe in his voice, "Showing up
the first day at the A-6 squadron and getting in that jet for the first time
was a pretty overwhelming experience. Finally I was doing exactly
what I had set out to do."

In the month of downtime before official training began, Tracy got
into a severe holiday funk. Alone in a strange place on New Year's Eve,

he was determined not to sit at home all by himself. Temptation reared its head, but Thorne was so new in town and so naive that he had no idea how to find a gay bar. So he started scanning the Yellow Pages, looking first under G for "gay" and then flipping ahead to the H listings. There he found a number for "Homosexuals Anonymous," which he called, expecting to reach a gay tip line. He didn't—Homosexuals Anonymous is in fact a religious organization. Tracy says, "I'm telling this guy, 'I'm calling to find out where the gay bars are in town.' And he's, like, 'Well, actually, no, we're not that type of organization. We promote your healing through abstinence from homosexuality.' And I said, 'No, you don't understand, I don't want to be healed, I want to go out!' " After a few minutes of unsuccessful proselytizing, the man from Homosexuals Anonymous finally relented and said with a sigh, "All right, I'll tell you where to go. . . ."

He recommended a bar called Charades, a lively place with festive holiday decorations and an intoxicating sexual energy. Tracy was exhilarated to see so many normal-looking men dancing together with total abandon. Across the dance floor, he spotted a tall, handsome, Nordic-looking blond with broad shoulders who seemed to radiate confidence and ease. After a few moments of playing the standard eye-tag, Thorne nervously approached the man. "I said something really stupid like, 'Is this the only club in town?' or 'You from around here?' " Nonetheless, the stranger responded, introducing himself as Scott Keeling, an English major from nearby William and Mary College. After they toasted in the New Year, they wound up spending the night and the next several days together—a first for the cautious Thorne. Before he knew it, he had fallen passionately in love. "It was the first time I realized I could have an emotional attachment to another guy. It wasn't like a lightbulb going off in my head," he remembers, "it was like a *lighthouse* going off! It was an epiphany. An awakening!"

Thorne's plan to lead a celibate, priestlike existence in the military—denying his sexuality so he could retire in thirty years as a contentedly repressed admiral—vaporized. With Keeling's help, he began to take his first baby steps out of the closet. "He was a great, great person to come out with. He was so comfortable with his sexuality. For six months he helped me through the process to where I could really become comfortable with the fact that I was gay and that's the way it's going to be,"

Tracy says. "For the first time in my life I recognized what I was, that it could be a perfectly normal thing. I thought, 'I can have a relationship, I can be happy, and you know what? I don't have to hide this anymore! And, goddamn it, if I can be happy with who I am, who the hell are the military and society to tell me that they can't be happy with it?' It's one thing to climb up a building and shout from the rooftops that you're gay; it's another thing to have to actively go around hiding it from people." Most importantly, that knot in his stomach was gone: He wasn't lying anymore.

Thorne bought his own house on the beach, away from the base, so he could pursue his brand-new private life, and with boyfriend Scott's encouragement, cautiously began to come out to other people.

The first was his mother. Patsy Thorne had traveled up from West Palm Beach one weekend to help Tracy settle into his new house. They spent a wonderful, productive day together, shopping for linens, kitchen utensils, and cookware; and by the time they got home, Tracy felt close enough to his mother to try to tell her. He sat on the cold tile floor, waffling for a while, until finally it just popped out. "Mom," he said, "I'm gay, and I think I need to tell someone about it, so I wanted to tell you." Patsy was thoughtful for a long moment, then she said simply, "Well, I love you," and hugged him—adding, "At least they can't kick you out of the military for it anymore." Little did she know . . .

Pleased with how well his mother took the news, Tracy decided to come out next to his buddy, Todd Suko, who had joined him in Virginia Beach for A-6 squadron training. "Todd was a really good friend to me and always had been. To hide this from him and always make up an excuse as to why I didn't want to go out with his girlfriend's sister or why I wasn't dating someone—I just thought it was important to tell him the truth," Tracy says. "I needed someone to talk to about it as well, other than Scott."

One afternoon, while they were on a long jog, Tracy did it: "When we got far enough away that I knew he wouldn't just run off and leave me—when I knew he'd have to stay there and deal with it—I said, 'Todd, I've got something really important to tell you . . . I'm gay.' " Suko stopped running and stared at his friend, then finally asked, "Are you sure?" Thorne started laughing. "Are you kidding me?" Todd pressed. When Tracy assured him he was not, Suko simply said,

"Whoa. . . ," and suggested they keep jogging. Confused, Thorne asked tentatively if Suko was going to slug him. Now it was Suko's turn to laugh. "No," he said, "why would I do that?" To Thorne's relief, "He was great with it. In the following months we would even kid about it."

Privately, though, Suko did feel rattled. "I never thought Tracy was gay," he says. "In fact, he was the last guy on the planet you would have picked." Todd was well aware that his friend could be discharged from the service if the news got out, so he kept it quiet. "I didn't know if anybody else knew and I didn't ask if anybody else knew." Finally, after holding it in as long as he could, he did tell one person—his girlfriend. "She was in complete disbelief," Suko recalls.

In the coming months, Tracy also came out to Mike Ward, one of Todd's roommates who had become a friend, when the three of them were on desert training in California. Ward, a laid-back, soft-spoken farm boy, was not at all fazed by the revelation. "He was, like, 'So?' " Thorne remembers. "That was his response." The acceptance he was getting so emboldened Tracy that he told Todd Suko, "You know, I really don't care. You can tell people if you want. If people find out, they find out. I'm not going to hide it." When Suko told his other roommate, who was also in a fighter squadron, the news went down without a ripple. As Tracy Thorne finished his final year of flight training, he was thinking, "Well, maybe I can have it both ways: I can be in the military and I can be out to my friends. And that will be enough for me."

Then came a shake-up. Each A-6 training class had eight carefully selected young men, four pilots and four bombardiers. Being so small and training so intensively, the groups developed deep bonds. So when one group lost a pilot, Rob Zouhar, in a crash in the mountains during a low-level, no-visibility training run, all the students were devastated— and none more so than Tracy. He had never imagined a crash, believing that the U.S. military's training and hardware were the best in the world, and now his blind confidence was shattered. "If Rob could get killed, then so could I," Tracy says. "I was no better than he was, or his bombardier, and I started recognizing that this is a very dangerous mission that we do." For the first time, he started paying attention to the statistics, noting that 25 percent of those in carrier aviation died before they reached twenty years in the service. That gave Thorne pause—and made him realize that, facing risks so high, he wanted to live out whatever life would be allotted to him truthfully and openly.

His homosexuality had also become more of an issue because, in his final year of training, Tracy had been moved into a combat squadron away from his protective nest of friends. He was by far the youngest flier in the squadron, and all but one of his older colleagues were married. The pressure to date women grew intense and Thorne recalls constantly being asked, " 'Why don't you come out with us next Friday, we're going to this event or that event and we could set you up with my wife's sister. . . .' And I'd say, 'No, no, that's okay.' " Still, none of the would-be matchmakers seemed to suspect anything. As Tracy says, "I think most people felt that anyone who was part of a macho naval aviation community just couldn't be gay."

Thorne's feelings of isolation in his new squadron increased when Scott Keeling started growing impatient with the constraints of military life and the secrecy of their relationship. Mike Begland, one of Scott's college friends, now says, "Scott was just being outrageously idealistic and unrealistic." He met them for dinner in Williamsburg one evening and felt that Scott was being too hard on Tracy. "I thought, 'Well, what else are you looking for? I mean, this is the type of man anyone'd want to spend the rest of his life with. I don't know what else you'd want.' " Tracy barely remembers even meeting Begland, for at the time, he says, "I was head over heels in love with Scott. Mike could have been Tom Cruise in a flight suit, sitting across the table from me, and I would not have noticed him because of Scott."

Ultimately, not even Thorne's passion could keep the relationship alive, and he and Scott split up two months later. The breakup brought Thorne to a Rubicon of sorts about hiding his sexual identity: "It propelled me to a point of, 'You know what? I don't know if I can continue to do this.' " That spring, while on a skiing vacation with his sister Patricia at her condo in Snowmass, Colorado, he happened to catch a TV movie, *Doing Time on Maple Drive*, about a college student returning home and coming out to his family. The unusually effective and sensitive film became the catalyst for Tracy to come out to Patricia as she was driving him to the airport. "Which in retrospect," he admits with a chuckle, "was not a nice thing to do—'I'm gay! Bye!' But I remember how empowering it felt to tell her." Patricia, though, was furious that he had kept her in the dark so long. As Tracy says, "She was really upset that I had lived with this secret."

He was tired of living with it now. On the flight home, he wrote a long letter to his ex-lover Scott Keeling, laying out what he had decided: "I'm not going to live in the closet anymore. I'm going to come out to my commanding officer and the officers in the squadron—in the ready room, the guys that I fly with. And I'm just going to take my chances. There's a good chance that they could just be, like, 'So?' and life will go on. And I'd be able to live my life, to some degree, as an 'out' military man. And if it doesn't work out, it doesn't work out. . . ."

He had made a plan: At the base's weekly "All Officers Meetings," after the business of the squadron was discussed, the commanding officer would always ask if there were any announcements. "And I was going to, well, have an *announcement,*" Tracy says, laughing now at his naiveté. Then, however, he did a bombing demonstration for his commanding officer, P. J. Ross, who had wanted a firsthand look at Thorne's reputed Top Gun wizardry. The difficult exercise on a target ship near the Barrier Islands came off without a hitch. "It was just excellent," Tracy recalls. "All our bombing runs were direct hits on the boat." Impressed, the CO called out, "Good shooting, Zipper," and tossed Thorne a congratulatory jawbreaker. "He always used to carry these things called Fireballs and I didn't know what they were at the time, so I just popped it in my mouth." Ross, renowned for being a bit of a jokester, enjoyed Thorne's discomfort at the fire-hot cinnamon candy. But the commanding officer's next joke was even more of a shocker, as slapping Thorne on the back, he said, "You know what, Trace? A man can build a thousand bridges, but if he sucks just one cock, they don't put 'bridge builder' on his tombstone." Thorne nearly gagged on his Fireball. "It was just the oddest thing for him to say—and he swears to this day that he has no idea why he said it," Thorne says. "It was not based on any suspicion that I was gay."

The joke was enough to convince Tracy that coming out at the officers' meeting was a bad idea—that his admission could have serious consequences. Deciding it might be wise to get some advice from a knowledgeable organization, he took up the matter with a homosexual political action group, the Human Rights Campaign Fund (HRCF) in Washington, D.C., which he heard had done a poll on gays in the military after the Gulf War. Through the HRCF, he met Karen Stupsky, a young officer who had recently been discharged from the Navy for admitting that she was a lesbian, and she in turn sent Thorne to the well-known Washington gay activist, Frank Kameny. Tracy recalls Kameny's response as unequivocal: "Well, they're going to throw you out on your ass! Just forget about any chance of you coming out of the closet and staying." Thorne tried to stammer a protest, but Kameny shot it down: "Absolutely no way! You need to call someone at Lambda Legal Defense Fund."

Tracy got on the phone not only to Lambda, but, on Karen Stupsky's advice, to the Gay, Lesbian and Bisexual Veterans of America (GLBVA), which invited him to attend its national conference. There he first learned that ABC News was looking for an officer to appear on a show about some new legislation, overturning the ban on gays in the military, that was being sponsored by Democratic Representative Pat Schroeder (D-CO), a member of the House Armed Forces Committee, along with Barney Frank of Massachusetts and Norman Mineta of California. The GLBVA asked Thorne if he would be willing to be that officer. "No," Tracy insisted. "I'm just looking for legal advice. I want to make sure that I'm not going to Leavenworth or something for telling them that I'm gay." While sympathetic to his position and careful to spell out the risks, the GLBVA, along with Stupsky and Tanya Domi of the National Gay and Lesbian Task Force (NGLTF), asked him to think hard about the option. Thorne left the capital more confused than before.

In April 1992, Thorne heard from the Lambda Legal Defense Fund that Representative Schroeder, by all accounts, was going to propose the new legislation in November. The far-off date was a comfort to Thorne, for it left him plenty of time to make up his mind about appearing on television. But less than a month later, the GLBVA called to inform him that Schroeder had suddenly decided to introduce the legislation sooner—on Tuesday, May 19. Would Tracy talk to *Nightline* about doing a show that night, even though it was just a week away? His mind reeling, Tracy replied, "Well, that's a lot faster than I ever imagined doing it. Let me talk to my family. . . . I really need to think about it."

He hurriedly put in another call to Lambda to see what they could do to protect him. Having already committed their resources to the recently ousted Army Colonel Margarethe Cammermeyer and Midshipman Joe Steffan, they couldn't take on another gay military defense campaign. However, they did set up a session for him with temporary counsel, who laid out the actions the military might take were Tracy to come out on *Nightline.* In his heart, however, Tracy had already decided that no matter what the lawyer said, it was time to take a stand. Through the GLBVA and David Versure, an aide from Representative Schroeder's office, he told *Nightline* he would appear.

In Ted Koppel's book, *Nightline: History in the Making,* Richard Harris, the show's booking agent, recalls his conversation with Tracy. "I said to him, 'You understand what this means. . . .' This was not one of those interviews where I had to convince him to do it. He had to convince *me* that he wanted to do this and that it was the right thing." Thorne assured him that he was fully prepared to face the consequences, so Harris could only warn him, "This is going to change your life in more ways than you know."

Events were moving quickly and Thorne found himself still without official legal counsel. Then, mere days before the television program was to air, he ran into a friend of Scott Keeling's, Christopher Farris, who was working for Crowell & Moring, a large, prestigious Washington law firm. Farris, upon hearing Thorne's tale, said, "You ought to call my law firm. I bet they'd be interested in this." Thorne talked to a partner, Patrick Lee, who after an informal poll agreed to take the case, pending the firm's official approval. He promised to call Thorne about the approval on Saturday in West Palm Beach, where Tracy was headed that weekend. Not only was he going to come out to his father; he was going to tell his family about his decision to also come out on national television.

Relieved by having made up his mind, and summoning his undisputed gift for calm under fire, Lieutenant Thorne went to his squadron and requested leave for the weekend and the following Monday, Tuesday, and Wednesday. Then he boarded a plane to Florida. Since his parents were living apart, he had the daunting task of confronting his father without the buffer of his mother. He and Roscoe were sitting at the table having breakfast together when Tracy dropped the bomb. Thrown by the news, his burly father got up from the table, walked

around for a few seconds, and finally said, "Well, that's . . . that's okay."
Then he offered a bit of comic relief. "He clutched his heart and did
his best Fred Sanford [the Redd Foxx character on the sitcom *Sanford
and Son*] imitation—'This is the big one! I'm dying! You're killing
me!'—and dropped to his knees," Tracy recalls with a laugh. But
Roscoe Thorne's playfulness ceased when his son told him that he was
going to announce his homosexuality to the world on *Nightline*. "He
didn't take that well," Tracy remembers. "He spent the morning pleading with me that I didn't need to tell anyone, that I could just go back
to the Navy and fly those jets, do my job, then in four years I could get
out and live my life however I wanted. But for now, I should do what
the military expected me to do."

In truth, the entire family opposed his television debut. When
Patrick Lee called Tracy on Saturday at his mother's house to say that
the firm was now ready to officially represent him, both Patsy and Patricia got on the phone, begging the lawyer to talk Tracy out of his
plan. "The whole weekend was spent with my father, my mother, my
sister, and my brother, Martin, all trying to convince me not to do it."
On Sunday, when he boarded the plane heading home to Virginia,
Thorne's last image was of his father, mother, and sister sobbing at the
airport gate, crying, "Please don't do it! Please don't do it!"

Saddened but undeterred by his family's reaction—"I'm pretty stub-
born," he says—Tracy now had to break the news about *Nightline* to a
few more people. One was his friend, Todd Suko: "I didn't advise him
either way," Suko says. "I just asked, 'Why are you giving up flying?' But
I understood what he was saying. I mean, everybody has to sleep at
night and I can imagine how living a lie can just eat at you, especially
if you try to live by a higher standard, as Tracy does. I can see why he
was really conflicted."

Another was Commanding Officer Ross, to whom Thorne wrote a
letter explaining that, as a courtesy, he was giving him advance notice
of the *Nightline* telecast and outlining what he would most likely say. To
have the letter hand-delivered the day of the broadcast, he approached
the pilot he usually flew with, and without specifically mentioning
Nightline, told him that he was coming out on a television program and
wanted to alert Ross. Thrown but sympathetic, the pilot agreed to deliver the letter while expressing regret. "He was basically resigned to the

fact that I was going to get kicked out of the Navy," Thorne remembers.

In Washington, Thorne was to meet Patrick Lee in person for the first time, along with cocounsel Luther Ziegler, and was to receive media training. The firm had hired public relations expert Michael Deaver, late of the Reagan White House, to coach Thorne; but when Deaver had to cancel at the last minute, they brought in retired Marine lieutenant Art Brill, who had been the chief spokesman for the Corps. A tough, no-nonsense military man, Brill did not mince words: "Well, kid," he said, "I don't believe in what you're doing, but for eighty-five dollars an hour, I'll teach you how to sell it." Thorne appreciated his candor, and they got to work. Tracy, it turns out, was a natural communicator.

That evening the *Nightline* booking agent, Richard Harris, met with him. "He really wanted to take care of me," Thorne says. "You know how you get this view of journalists as hungry for the story and they don't really care about what it does to people's lives? Well, Richard was, more than anything, concerned that I was doing this because I wanted to and not because they were pressuring me, and he wanted to make sure I was going to be okay. He wanted to assure me that ABC News and the network were going to be behind me all the way; that they were going to continue to cover the story after it happened. I wasn't going to be just some footnote that they forgot about."

Harris explained the structure of the broadcast and what kinds of questions Tracy might be asked. The show would open with some stock military footage; then correspondent Jackie Judd would present a five-minute pretaped piece framing the debate. The heart of the show would be Koppel's live interview with Tracy, with Representative Schroeder, sponsor of the gay-rights legislation, offering comments from a bureau studio. As always, the *Nightline* staff had tried to create a balanced show and so had invited the military to join the debate. The offer had been firmly declined.

After the briefing, Harris took Tracy to meet Ted Koppel in his office, outfitted with a large partner's desk and dark leather furniture. A sign on the wall proclaimed "Nobody Gets in to See the Wizard," but Tracy found Koppel "just the most down-to-earth guy. We sat on the sofa and talked for, like, twenty minutes and he said, 'Well, you know what we just did? We just did the interview. All you have to do is pretend it's just you and me.' " Nearly numb, Tracy nervously quipped back to Koppel, "So I don't pretend there are fifteen million people watching, huh?"

The stage was set. Then, unbeknownst to Thorne, the network attempted, on the day of the broadcast, to bump the show.

As sometimes happens with a news program, a breaking story can supplant a planned episode. Lawrence Welk, the orchestra leader and host of a long-running variety show on ABC, had died early that morning; network executives wanted to substitute a tribute to Welk for the gays-in-the-military program. Richard Harris, adamantly opposed to the last-minute switch, stormed into Ted Koppel's office. "You cannot do that to this kid!" he protested. "He has put his career on the line, he's already given his commanding officer notice that the show's going on tonight, he's flown home to tell his father. If we bump him, he's done it all for nothing." Harris even threatened to quit if *Nightline* backed out of its commitment to Tracy. Struck by Harris's passion, Koppel refused to accede to the network's demands. Tracy Thorne would appear as planned on Tuesday, May 19, 1992.

Ironically, as the hour of the telecast approached, the concentration skills Thorne had learned in the Navy helped him keep anxiety at bay. "I felt like an automaton in a sense," he says. "I just put the machinery in motion, I never second-guessed it, I never had any doubts that it was what I needed to do." Before he knew it, the military footage was rolling up on the monitor and Ted Koppel was addressing the viewing audience. "The men and women of the United States Armed Forces," he said. "Uncle Sam wants them. But not if they're gay." As Koppel's opening segment concluded, a graphic of the official Navy seal came up as he said, "Tonight, a unique disclosure from one of the Navy's elite . . ." The seal opened to reveal a dashing snapshot of Lieutenant (jg) Tracy Thorne in his flight suit aboard ship, standing in front of his beloved A-6. "Tonight, an officer and a gentleman reveals that he's also gay. . . ." Then the familiar *Nightline* theme music filled the airwaves.

Correspondent Jackie Judd's in-depth filmed report outlined the debate and took some decided digs at the military. "A report commissioned by the Defense Department but never released warned that the military cannot indefinitely isolate itself from society. A second report concluded that the fitness of homosexuals to serve was good, if not better than the average heterosexual's. Military leaders once maintained that gays were a security risk—that's been disavowed and replaced by issues of privacy and maintaining order. . . ."

Now General Colin Powell appeared on film, telling the House Budget Committee of possible privacy and morale issues that might arise should gays be admitted; then the footage cut to former Assistant Secretary of Defense Lawrence Kolb calling that argument a smoke-screen. "The military basically feels it would be against their self-image—that the macho man having gays and lesbians in the force would not be in keeping with the image they see in themselves." Veteran Charles Magnus, who came out of the closet after his discharge from the Army, was up next, saying: "It's the same argument: We can't mix because it will break down the good morale and discipline of the forces. And that isn't true. It didn't hold water with the blacks, it didn't hold water with women, and I don't think it will hold water with homosexuals."

Jackie Judd's segment continued, noting that tens of thousands of homosexuals were serving in the armed forces with minimal incident. As for the contention that the military should not engage in social experimentation, Judd pointed out that a similar argument was raised back when it was proposed that segregation of blacks in the armed forces be ended. Yet this was successfully achieved, as was a change in the policy of promoting women.

When she finished, Ted Koppel turned to the camera in the studio. "When we return, we'll talk live with a Navy officer whose opposition to the military policy on gays takes on a personal dimension tonight." As Tracy Thorne's camera light went on, he seemed a little startled at first. He looked to Koppel, then to the camera, then back to Koppel, then back to the camera again, trying to suss out the focal point.

During the first commercial break, Tracy had time to take a breath. He was still feeling remarkably calm, especially considering that not only was he throwing his public and personal life into disarray, not only was he taking the entire United States military complex to task, but he was doing it all on live television.

Round two began with Koppel listing the lieutenant's impressive credentials and awards and asking Tracy, "If you're gonna tell folks that you're gay, there are easier ways to do it than coming on a network news program. Why this way, Tracy?"

"Well," Thorne replied, "I've just seen too much discrimination. I see thousands of people a year who are kicked out of the Navy for something that is beyond their control. It's what they're born as, it's what they are; the core of their human being. And I feel that discrimination is wrong and it's time to change it."

Koppel commented that if Tracy had come out privately, he might have been able to stay in the Navy. Tracy pointed out that "by doing that you don't create any change. What I'm trying to do is show people that you can be gay, you can do your job, and your friends, you know, your fellow officers in the Navy have no problem with it. People I've come out to have no problem with my homosexuality. They back me up one hundred percent on this. And to live life in the closet doesn't accomplish anything. It's not showing Americans that the people they work with every day are gay."

Koppel stayed focused on the consequences—that, under current rules, the Navy was obliged to dismiss Thorne.

"Yes, sir, they sure are. I expect that, when I return tomorrow, my commanding officer will follow through with his duties and start Administrative Separations Proceedings against me."

"And what do you expect will happen then?"

"They may ask me to resign my commission, but I'm going to refuse that. There will be an Administrative Board convened when I request it, and at that time we'll proceed with a case . . . and hopefully, on my record and the record of several people before me, we can try and get this ban overturned."

"Is there any kind of blemish on your record at all?" Koppel pressed.

"No, sir, none that I'm aware of."

"On what basis, then, are you going to be dismissed? Simply because you're a homosexual and have announced it?"

"Yes, sir," Thorne answered flatly. "Not on anything I've done. It's going to be based solely on my declaration that I am a homosexual."

Koppel then sat back in his chair a bit. "You and I spoke in my office before, and you said you were under the impression that the Navy probably would like this to transpire as smoothly and easily as possible. And if you would go quietly, you'd probably get an honorable discharge—no problem in getting out of the service."

"Yes, sir."

"You don't want to go quietly."

"No, I'm not going to go quietly. I love the Navy and I have nothing bad to say about it. But I have to stand up on this issue."

After the commercial break, Koppel introduced Representative Schroeder as the sponsor of the bill to abolish the ban on gays in the military. He then asked her, "Is Lieutenant Thorne the young man to make a difference here?"

"I think so," she replied, pointing out Thorne's top-level ratings and exemplary behavior. The only issue was his sexual orientation, and she was blunt about the military's perpetuating the sexual stereotype that people can't control their behavior. Talk like this, from General Powell and others, was *"baloney!"* she charged. Banning discrimination on the basis of sexual orientation was entirely separate from issues of behavior; everyone, gay and straight, was subject to the behavior rules.

She expressed her anger about a memo that had circulated at the Pentagon during the Gulf War proposing that no action be taken against gays until the war was won. "Now I'm sorry, if we're saying that these people can be out there putting their lives on the line, but the minute the war is over, in peacetime, we can't tolerate them—that's absolutely backward from how the military's supposed to work! I think that's why the Pentagon isn't here tonight! They can't explain it!"

Koppel thanked Schroeder and then turned to wrap up with Tracy. "What is the thing you're most afraid of?" he asked.

"Well, it would be easiest to say I'm most afraid of going back to see my skipper tomorrow," Thorne said with a grin. "But what really scares me is the fact that I may not be heard on this—that people aren't going to listen and that nothing's going to get accomplished. Prejudice is wrong . . . no matter how many people believe in it. Prejudice can never be validated [even] by unanimous consent."

Then the show was over.

Before he was even out of makeup, Thorne had become a hero. In just thirty minutes, he had gone from being a cog in the military machine—albeit one who had performed with great distinction—to becoming the public face and voice of the tens of thousands of gays and lesbians who had remained hidden in the armed forces.

"I thought he was terrific on *Nightline,*" said HRCF Communications Director Greg King. "He was forceful, competent . . . and he helped our effort enormously just by being who he was. He became a living symbol of why discrimination in the military should end." David Smith, of the Campaign for Military Service (CMS), says, "There were a number of stereotypes the public had about gay people who were serving in the military. When Tracy came out on *Nightline,* he shattered those stereotypes in one fell swoop. He was the boy next door; he could be anyone's son. He conveyed a strong sense of purpose and pride and self-esteem." Even from a position on the political sidelines, Todd Suko had to agree. "We all watched *Nightline* and everyone was, like, 'Whoa!' He did very well." Tracy himself credits Ted Koppel. "He's a *professional,* he's a natural interviewer. He just asked me questions and it was honestly like having the same conversation with him on the sofa in his office. He is a master of making you feel comfortable. I just told it how it was."

Feeling high on the congratulations of his friends and the ABC News staff, Tracy nonetheless had an attack of nerves when he walked through the door of his house in Virginia Beach. His mother and sister had feared the worst: "They had ingrained in me this belief that my house was going to be firebombed and I was going to have my life threatened as a result of what I did." His answering machine flashed thirty-two messages, and he thought, "Whoops—lots of calls for a couple of days. I guess this is where the hate mail starts." However, after pressing the playback button, he heard message after message of enthusiastic support: "People I had not heard from in years who had seen it tracked me down because my number was listed in Information. . . . It felt really good to come back to that."

One of the people who tracked him down was Michael Begland, the college pal of his ex-boyfriend Scott Keeling. "I was lying in bed," Begland remembers, "and a friend calls me and says, 'Turn on your TV.' So I go into the living room and turn on the set and there's Tracy and I'm, like, 'I know that closet case! A year ago he was just coming out—what's he doing on *Nightline*?' But I watched it and was really blown away—I thought it was amazing."

Tracy marvels: "It was amazing how many people watched that show. I had never watched *Nightline* in my life—and hundreds of people we've run across have said, 'We never watched that show, but we saw it that night, for some strange reason.' "

Among the viewers, of course, were fellow airmen at the base. When Tracy arrived in the ready room the next morning wearing his dress uniform, some of them seemed a little flustered. Friend Eric Anderson would later describe the collective reaction as "shock and disbelief." But when Thorne greeted him, Anderson said warmly, "Hey, Tracy, great to have you back." The lieutenant commander working the duty desk jokingly added, "Yeah. You looked good on TV last night, but next time lose the tie!" They told Thorne that the commanding officer was waiting for him in his office. Stiffening a bit, Tracy walked the hallway to the CO's office suite. When Ross called him in, he stood at attention.

"Relax," the commanding officer said. "I understand why you did what you did. And I appreciate you giving me the 'heads up.' But it's a real shame that it happened, because I have to start the discharge process now." Clearly pained at the thought, he asked Thorne why he had gone public.

"I can't be dishonest anymore," Tracy replied. "Especially when people like you grow up with the stereotype of gays that's out there and the result is you say the type of thing you said to me a couple weeks back."

Reminded of his unfortunate "cocksucker" joke, the CO replied, "I'm so sorry I said that." After a few more awkward but not unpleasant words, he told him, "Well, they're waiting for you over at the legal department. Could you go over there?"

Walking another series of hallways, Tracy wondered what was in store for him next. How retaliatory was the Navy prepared to get? The first meeting with the legal officers was inauspicious. After being read his rights, he was informed that he was under investigation for a violation of the Uniform Code of Military Justice and that he was suspected of acts of sodomy and conduct unbecoming an officer. Then they handed him a form and said, "Please sign this and waive your rights." Thorne was aghast. "Are you *kidding* me? You want me to waive my *rights*? I'm afraid I'm not going to do that." Determined to end the conversation, he said, "Gentlemen, if you have any desire for further communication with me, you can contact my lawyers at this address." He handed them Patrick Lee's business card, got up, and walked out.

"I was a little shocked that they decided to play hardball, at first," Thorne says. But apparently the Navy was stung by the public drubbing it had taken on *Nightline* and had decided to punish him. It attempted to coerce Thorne into resigning immediately by offering him an honorable discharge, threatening that an in-depth investigation might well yield an embarrassing dishonorable one. "That was the stick that they were trying to use to get me to resign, and I just said, 'No, no, no, no, no,' and continued to push forward," Thorne says. "And surprisingly, not more than a couple weeks into that, the Secretary of the Navy's office sent down orders that I would receive nothing other than an honorable discharge. So at that point, I was in a no-lose situation. There was no way I could lose by proceeding with the discharge hearing."

In the meantime, the military packed up his locker and his security clearance was suspended. The legal department might well have revoked it altogether had not the Department of Defense just ruled against revocation in such cases. Thorne was transferred out of his squadron and into a desk job on the admiral's staff, where the top gunner's duties would include planning a chili cook-off and running a deer hunt on the base. "I don't ever recall it feeling like I was walking out for the last time," Tracy stresses. "To me, it was more like just going across the street, which was literally all I was doing. It never really hit me that I wouldn't be coming back."

"It was a huge deal back at the squadron," Todd Suko recalls. "It's kind of like he threw down the gauntlet on national television and said, 'I'm a member of this club and I'm also gay.' It really rubbed some people, especially the old guard, the wrong way and they took it personally." To make matters worse, he adds, "Instead of calling them the Flying Tigers, they called them the Flaming Tigers. I'm sure they got sick of it after a while and I'm sure they got sick of the press."

Indeed, Thorne was again booked on ABC, this time on *Good Morning America,* and NBC's *Today Show* featured him the same day. The show on ABC went without a hitch, but *Today* threw Thorne a curve:

Minutes before the show, as they were hooking up the microphone, the producers told him he would be interviewed in tandem with California Republican Representative Robert Dornan, a politician known for his rabid homophobia. Dornan, armed with what he claimed was extensive briefing from the Navy (which later the Navy could not confirm) immediately went on the attack. Thorne's attorney, Patrick Lee, who was standing behind the cameras, kept signaling Tracy to remain calm. "I had been handled with kid gloves up to that point," Thorne recalls. "It was the first time I had been attacked for what I believed and so I hadn't had time to really formulate my responses."

Tim McFeeley, then executive director of the HRCF, was also a guest on the segment, not in Washington but in the New York studio with interviewer Stone Phillips. "I was really champing at the bit to get on," McFeeley says. "Dornan was basically accusing Tracy of wasting taxpayer dollars by going through all the training and lying that he was straight when he was really gay, and who the hell did he think he was, why didn't he stay out of the Navy to begin with. 'I don't consider you a hero,' he said. 'I consider you a creep!' It was that kind of personal attack." Tim McFeeley finally couldn't stand it anymore and blew up at the pompous Dornan. "I think you've had too many Wheaties this morning, Mr. Dornan," he said. "Maybe you should just calm down, sir!"

Although he admits he was flustered, Tracy believes he and McFeeley could have sat there completely silent, because Congressman Dornan was his own worst enemy. "His theatrics and the insanity of some of his thoughts just brought his own argument down," he maintains. "Tracy later got very good at arguing with people like that," McFeeley says. "But that first time was kind of a setback. And it set me off because I had had many tangles with Dornan myself."

Still to come were *Crossfire* and *Larry King Live,* and Thorne continued honing his media skills with Art Brill. "The neat story about him," Tracy says, "is that we worked together on this over the following weeks and he came to me and said, 'Well, I hate to say this, because I'm a pretty strong-headed guy, but you've convinced me.' I said, 'Convinced you of what?' He said, 'That you're right.' So he ended up writing this op-ed piece for *The Washington Post.* That really helped—a tag line saying, 'Colonel Art Brill is a retired infantry officer who served in

Vietnam.' To have someone like that writing an article saying, 'What the hell is the military doing?' felt pretty good. I thought, 'If you can convince him, maybe you can convince them all.' "

As effective as Thorne was becoming, William Waybourn, head of the National Gay and Lesbian Victory Fund, knew that the lieutenant's lawyers had little experience dealing with media problems specific to gay issues. Waybourn took it upon himself to unofficially advise Thorne on those with whom he should and shouldn't speak, as well as to introduce him to people who could aid him in his battle. "William really had the foresight to see that, as a spokesman for the gay community, I could be chewed up and tossed aside as soon as the need for me was gone," Tracy says. "And he really wanted to make sure that I was protected, that I was not putting myself in a position where I was going to have no way to survive, no way to take care of myself." "I knew the media frenzy would be all over him," Waybourn says. "I mean, he would no longer be able to go out for a meal without people coming up to him. There would be great expectations and he would lose his privacy completely."

Tracy's discharge hearing was set for the end of July. While the lieutenant's lawyers were immersed in the mountain of research and paperwork that accompanies any trial or hearing, Tracy was concerned about his dad. Roscoe Thorne, who had not spoken to Tracy since the Sunday he'd left Florida to do *Nightline,* had already told his wife that he was not going to attend. Although he seemed supportive when his son first revealed his sexual orientation, in actuality Dr. Thorne was having a difficult time dealing with the fact that Tracy was gay. "He went into a deep depression," Tracy says. "He pretty much stopped doing surgery. His doctor even grounded him from flying." Then, two days before the hearing, Tracy got a poignant message from his father on his answering machine: "Son, I'm coming up there for your board of inquiry, because any father who doesn't stand by his son is not worth having."

Both his parents and his sister Patricia sat in on the strategy meeting Tracy had with Patrick Lee and Luther Ziegler at the Virginia Beach Omni Hotel. In the middle of the discussion, Roscoe Thorne came over to his son and gave him a fierce hug. "If we're doing this," he said, "I'm gonna be talking tomorrow." Meeting privately with Tracy's father, Lee and Ziegler tried to advise him on what the content of such a speech should be, but Roscoe Thorne would not get specific. Nor would he be dissuaded.

The official board of inquiry, held July 23, 1992, was presided over by Captain John Seddon; also on the board were Commander John Dolenti and Lieutenant Paul Tanaka. The legal adviser, Lieutenant Commander Henry Sonday, would rule on issues of law, since the board members were not attorneys. The recorder, or prosecutor, for the Navy was Lieutenant Julie Tinker. Thorne's civilian counsel were, of course, Lee and Ziegler, aided by Christopher Farris and Dolly Hauck. Military counsel for Thorne was Andrew Dryjanski, JAGC, who was personally against the ban and content to take a backseat to the esteemed outside counsel. Along with the military personnel and the lawyers, some twenty-five reporters seated on very small government-issue folding chairs were jammed into the room.

The day began with Lee asking for a postponement because several witnesses, including Colonel Margarethe Cammermeyer, were unavailable to testify, and because the defense was waiting for a reply from President George Bush, whom it had petitioned for a "captain's mast." A "captain's mast" is an ancient British naval tradition, during which the accused would stand literally before the mast of the ship to be judged by the captain himself. Since George Bush was a former Navy man and, as President, the ultimate commander of the Navy, Lee and Ziegler attempted to push the matter politically by requesting that the President himself hear the case. George Bush did not reply, and the motion for extension was denied.

Not surprised, Thorne's attorneys began the voir dire, the systematic questioning to determine how objective or biased each board member might be. None of them were challenged for cause. Lee then charged: "I think there has been some intimidation of the military witnesses with respect to their testimony here. . . . I think they should have the comfort of understanding that they are not out on a limb in standing up for their friend, Lieutenant Thorne." Todd Suko confirmed Lee's suspicion. "It got ugly when they began calling witnesses in and the investigator showed me a list of senior Navy people and said, 'This guy is gay, and this guy is gay . . .' She [the investigator] was trying to intimidate people from testifying on Tracy's behalf."

One of Lee's preliminary requests was that defense witnesses be permitted to attend the entire hearing, so that they could understand the context in which their testimony would be interpreted. The legal adviser ruled that Tracy's father could be present, but the rest of the witnesses could not. Lee also asked that the Navy confirm or deny its supposed briefing of Congressman Robert Dornan before the *Today Show* and was assured of a response. Then Lieutenant Tinker took the floor to deliver her opening statement: "You must decide whether or not the Navy has a policy regarding homosexuality and whether or not Lieutenant (jg) Thorne is in compliance with that policy. . . . What you need to decide today is whether or not Lieutenant Thorne is, indeed, a homosexual as defined by the insurrections that are applicable in this case, and whether or not he should be separated if he does fit the definition for homosexual."

Lee objected to viewing the videotapes of Thorne's television appearances, but he was overruled and the tapes, focusing mostly on the *Nightline* episode, were shown. Following a lunch break, Ziegler delivered the defense's opening statement, focusing not on Thorne's admissions but on the policy itself: "What this case is about is strictly sexual orientation. There's no suggestion here, there is no evidence, of sexual misconduct. . . . What this case is about is whether the United States Navy should force out of its ranks a very talented and valuable officer with enormous potential, on whom the United States taxpayers have spent a great deal of money, simply because of his sexual orientation, an immutable characteristic that he had no control over.

"Now, in framing the issue for you, Lieutenant Tinker suggested that your job is very cut-and-dried. She suggested that your task here is simply to find out whether or not Lieutenant Thorne has made an admission of homosexuality, and if he has, simply to apply the regulations mechanically and to direct separation. And we're here today to suggest to you, with all respect to Lieutenant Tinker, that the regulations are not so rigid, they're not so mechanical, and that there is room here for the exercise of judgment, for the exercise of common sense, and for a sense of fairness." Citing Thorne's spotless record of achievement, he focused on the innate unfairness of the military's ban. "This is," he said in conclusion, "at a minimum, a case where an exception ought to be made, if not a complete reexamination of policy."

Tinker immediately objected to the suggestion that board members could make recommendations on Navy policy, and therefore challenged nearly all of the defense's one hundred exhibits. The legal adviser ruled in her favor, so most of Tracy Thorne's evidence was thrown out. Tinker was equally aggressive in challenging the defense's proposed witnesses. Todd Suko was allowed to testify—"I always regarded Tracy as one of the finest Navy officers I ever met. . . . And since I found out he's gay, my opinion hasn't changed"—as was Eric Anderson, who was slightly less effusive in his praise; when asked, "If the two of you had to jump in an A-6 right now, go out on a mission to defend the United States . . . would you have any hesitation doing so?" Anderson replied, "I would have no doubt as to Mr. Thorne's copiloting skills, sir, but I must support Navy policy regarding homosexuals in the military, being a member of the Navy." On cross-examination, Anderson admitted that his relationship with Thorne had been strained since Tracy's admission; moreover, the media's depiction of Thorne's squad being fully supportive, in Anderson's view, was not exactly accurate.

But such witnesses as Andrew Humm of the Hetrick-Martin Institute for Gay and Lesbian Youths, who was to debunk homosexual stereotypes, and Dr. Lawrence Kolb, the former assistant secretary of defense, and Colonel Charles Magnus, a decorated gay veteran, who were to offer expert insight on why Thorne should be retained, were barred from testifying. The legal adviser insisted that such testimony had no bearing on the narrow, specific questions that the board was to consider—whether Thorne was a homosexual and whether Navy rules required that homosexuals be dismissed.

Lee asserted that the board, not the legal adviser, had an obligation, before enforcing the Navy's ban, to determine whether the ban was legal. He argued that it was not legal to ban propensity, as opposed to conduct. Conduct, he maintained, was "not what Lieutenant Thorne testified to when he appeared on *Nightline*. He talked about his sexual orientation, a capacity he was born with." Although a somewhat specious argument from the gay point of view—analogous to saying that it's not illegal to be black, since you can't help it, as long as you act white—it was the best the defense team could hope for at the time.

Day two of the hearing began with a report from Tinker on Dornan's assertions that he had been briefed by the Navy. The Pentagon reported that it could find no evidence that the representative had had contact with anyone in the Navy: "There was no briefing by the people they talked to or themselves, no documents, no requests for a briefing." Dornan, it seemed, had exaggerated. The revelation was buoying for Tracy, who that morning delivered his own statement to the board. "You saw a tape," he said, referring to the *Nightline* broadcast, "where I expressed my greatest fear. That fear is that I would not be heard . . . I was *not* heard. . . . I had hoped that you would listen to the attributes of a naval officer. And I would have hoped that you would have realized I was just like you. . . . This is not a game of big-city lawyers coming down here to take on the U.S. Navy. This is a human being just like you who wants to serve his country." Going on to chronicle his training and accomplishments in the service, he said ruefully, "My dream is now over, because I went on *Nightline* and told the truth, as a naval officer should. . . . This policy is in complete contradiction to the qualities of a leader the Navy advances—honesty, integrity, loyalty to self. All these the Navy finds important, yet they encourage me and others to lie to myself and to others.

"The Navy and Department of Defense say a homosexual is not qualified to lead. It says we destroy unit cohesiveness. It says we will take away the rights of privacy of others. I say being gay has nothing to do with that. The Pentagon says I'm not qualified to be a leader, that gays are untrustworthy, effeminate, predatory in nature, and unreliable. I say these are stereotypes. They're groundless and based in fears. . . . The way to change these fears is through education. All of you know the Navy is one of the greatest educational systems in the world. We have the teachers. We have the up-to-date training methods. We have a great capacity to educate. When the military decides to do something, they do it with vigor. They did it with blacks. They're doing it with women. They can do it with gays. . . .

"On September 13, 1988, I took this oath of office: 'I, Tracy William James Thorne, do solemnly reaffirm that I will support and defend the Constitution of the United States against all enemies, foreign and domestic.' And that is what we are dealing with—enemies that are tearing our country up from the inside. I am fighting for my constitutional rights. Under the Fourteenth Amendment to our Constitution, I am guaranteed equal protection under the law. You will not hear me. My

First Amendment right to freedom of speech has been used against me because you will not hear me. My right to a defense has been denied because you will not hear me.

"You are just like me. You are naval officers. You all wear rings of gold. You are leaders among men. You are not machines. And if you allow yourselves not to question a policy that is based on ancient hatred and bigotry, and not based on reality, you are allowing yourselves to be machines, and not leaders. Please make the recommendation that you can make, that is based in Naval regulations, to the Secretary of the Navy, to look at my case. To take the enormous amount of time that he will have to take and read this case, because too many people are hurt. We have to do the right thing. Make that recommendation to the Secretary. I'm just like you."

The impact of the heartfelt, bravura speech was such that Patrick Lee had to ask for a recess. Then, when the hearing resumed, Roscoe Thorne got up. "I guess it was about twenty-five years ago, a friend of mine took my wife into the delivery room," he said. "He came out and handed me a baby boy. I took him in my hands and into an examining room. I put a stethoscope on him, and looked at his arms and legs, and I thought he was just fine. But until I heard this man just now, I didn't realize what a great man was given to me by that doctor friend of mine, delivered of my wife twenty-five years ago . . . a man that has already proved himself beyond a shadow of a doubt as a leader, as a commander, as a superb individual. And I'm happy to say I'm his father. And I wish I could be like him. Forgive me for my emotions, but I wish I could be as good a man as Tracy Thorne is."

Being a Southerner from Jackson, Mississippi, Roscoe Thorne now told the board how from childhood on he had been educated in bigotry. As a doctor, he knew when you cut open an African-American or an Asian or a Jew or a Mexican, you found the same organs inside; and when you administered medicine, straight people responded the same way as gay people. Armed with this knowledge, he strove to change his response to his fellow man, which, given his conditioning, was a difficult, slow process—but it had to be done. His implication—that the military would have to do the same—was unmistakable. "America, great country that it is, is bleeding because of a lot of wounds, prejudices, that are still left over. . . . We as Americans have got to make some effort to close those wounds." But Roscoe Thorne was no starry-eyed fool: "I've been around long enough to know what kind of meeting this is, and I want you officers here to know that if you allow anything to happen that would interfere with this young man's ability to have his freedom to serve his country as he has so ably proved his ability to do—if you allow that to happen, then when you go home tonight, I want each of you to find a good friend, and I want you to sit down with that good friend, and I want you to tell him that you've allowed something to happen that, deep down, you don't feel is real good." Battling for composure, he wound up by saying, "But if you tell it to one person that you trust, he or she will have heard it and you'll feel better for it, and that person will have heard the truth. And if one person hears the truth, then you got a victory, and that's what America is all about."

Lee called another recess, and out in the hall, Tracy silently embraced his father. Pleased with both Thornes' performances, Patrick Lee jokingly cried, "God damn it, how am I supposed to follow that!" When they returned to the courtroom, Julie Tinker, reeling from the punch of the father and son speeches, insisted that the testimonies were out of bounds, irrelevant to the two basic questions: whether "there is an instruction against homosexuality and whether or not Lieutenant Thorne is a homosexual." Now, for the first time, the legal adviser declined to uphold Tinker's narrow focus: "I'm not going to draw that kind of distinction with regard to the unsworn testimony of Lieutenant Thorne or his father," Sonday said. "The members are able, I think, to . . . attribute to them whatever weight they deem most appropriate. It was Lieutenant Thorne's opportunity to say what he wanted to say and he said it very eloquently." Seemingly, Thorne and his father had touched a few hearts.

Now it would fall to Patrick Lee to sway minds with his closing statement, a compelling comparison of Thorne's case to the infamous Scopes trial. "About seventy years ago," he began, "there was a great debate on a great issue that occurred in a courthouse in Tennessee, involving the great lawyer Clarence Darrow and William Jennings Bryan. And it, like this issue, captured national attention. And it, like this case, involved a watershed issue." He went on to discuss the trial, at which the judge would not allow scientists to testify, so that John Scopes was convicted of the crime of teaching evolution. "But a funny thing happened," Lee said. "All you hear about now is evolution. You read about it in the paper every day—another bone, another skull, and details keep mounting and proof sticks and we all believe in evolution. Science won. John Scopes lost, but science won.

"I take comfort in this story . . . because I realize . . . that it doesn't make any difference when the truth is withheld in court. . . . This trial, this odd trial where no one testified because science was irrelevant, marks the end of military discrimination against homosexuals. That discrimination died here today, just as the Adam and Eve story, the direct creation of man, died in the Scopes trial. . . ."

Lee then described the views of the experts, many of whom had been barred from testifying on Thorne's behalf. He spoke of Dr. Richard Green, esteemed professor of psychiatry, who believes that homosexuality is an immutable characteristic; of Dr. Gregory Herek of the University of California, Davis, who holds that homosexuals have the same skills as heterosexuals; of Dr. Michael Carrerra, whose writings have been translated into seventeen languages, who concurs that heterosexuals and homosexuals have the same capacity for intelligence, competence, leadership, industry, loyalty, courage, and discipline; of Professor John Boswell of Yale, who charges that penalization of homosexuals is contrary to Western moral tradition, among others. This body of knowledge, Lee insisted, "demonstrates that homosexuals in the military—and there are homosexuals in the military, thousands of them—are able to control their sexual urges, just like you can. They're capable of exercising judgment in the exercise of authority, just like you are. And they're capable of conforming to organizational policies just like you do on a daily basis, and just like Lieutenant Thorne has done throughout his career in the Navy. . . . He's just like you. . . .

"What you do here today will unravel just like the victory in the Scopes trial unraveled. . . . There's a difference between this case and the Scopes case, however. After the Scopes trial, John Scopes . . . just disappeared. That's not going to happen to Tracy Thorne. Tracy Thorne, you're going to hear from again. This homosexual over here, who is not different from you. This homosexual over here, whom the Navy thinks is so insignificant that they can ignore and deny his constitutional rights . . ."

The room was deathly still. "You know," Lee concluded, "igno-rance . . . is an everyday problem. It's just a condition of living. But willful ignorance is something else. To choose not to hear testimony about what homosexual orientation is, when the basis for throwing this homosexual out of the military is the fact that he said on a television show, 'I have a homosexual orientation'—that is willful ignorance. . . . Willful ignorance is not a condition of life. Willful ignorance is morally wrong. . . ."

Recorder Julie Tinker had the difficult job of invalidating Lee's mas-terly summation. She had no choice but to attempt to dampen its emo-tional impact by reiterating the narrow purpose of the hearing and reassuring the board: "You should not be made to feel guilty in fulfill-ing your duties here as naval officers, and apply lawful regulations to the situation at hand," she told them. "And that's all you are required to do. That is your purpose here. It is not to debate policy. It is not to discuss whether it is right or wrong, but to apply the facts of this case to the lawful regulations that you're required, as naval officers, to follow. . . ."

Over the two-hour lunch recess, Tracy Thorne brazenly took his at-torneys and family to the base Officers' Club—he was, after all, still an officer and had the right to dine there. His presence caused a stir. "I think people were a little shocked that I would show up there with all of these high-powered D.C. attorneys," he says. "But that was their problem, not mine."

Then the hearing reconvened, and the presiding officer, John Sed-don, addressed Thorne directly, saying: "We have heard you here today, Lieutenant." Then he read the verdict aloud: "The board finds that Lieutenant Thorne has stated that he was a homosexual, and is a ho-mosexual, by a vote of three to zero. It is the recommendation of this board, by a vote of three to zero, that Lieutenant Thorne has failed to show cause for retention in the naval service, and that he is sepa-rated. . . . The board recommends, by a vote of three to zero, that this separation be characterized as honorable. . . ."

With those words, Tracy Thorne no longer had a home in the Navy. But he still had reason to hope. By now the military ban was constantly being challenged in the courts. Navy ensign Keith Meinhold was in the process of fighting his ouster in the Ninth Circuit Court of Appeals. Perry Watkins, dismissed from the Army after successive tours of

Vietnam, would actually win reinstatement when his discharge was ruled to be a violation of the equal-protection clause of the Constitution. Change was in the air, and gay leaders recognized what an effective spokesman for the cause Thorne could be. "All someone opposed to gays in the military had to do was spend ten minutes with Tracy and their opinions changed," remarks William Waybourn. Washington lobbyist Jeff Trammell seconds that opinion: "The community could not have gotten a better spokesman than Tracy Thorne." The Human Rights Campaign Fund took Thorne under its wing: "We wanted to make sure he would make a living," Greg King says. "He didn't have a job. His main function was to be a communicator. We had a full-time volunteer who would schedule Tracy on talk radio programs. He also traveled around the country and did press events." As he had said on *Nightline* months before, Tracy Thorne wasn't going quietly.

As Thorne's public presence grew, his personal life was also blossoming. His board hearings and activist work frequently brought him to Washington, where Mike Begland, Scott Keeling's old friend, had been living for a year; they encountered each other now and then. "I had gotten my gay adolescence out of my system," Mike recalls, "and really was at a point where I was ready to settle down." Then his thoughts at that long-ago Williamsburg dinner with Scott and Tracy echoed in his mind. *"This is the type of man anyone'd want to spend the rest of his life with. . . ."* Begland realized: "My God . . . what about Tracy?" He immediately got on the phone and made a date to have dinner with Thorne in Virginia Beach on Saturday night, October 17.

"When he opened his door, that was the moment," Mike says. "Violins were playing. Symphonies were playing. Fireworks were going off . . ." It was the same for Thorne. "I can remember everything about that night," Tracy says. "I mean, I can remember exactly what he was wearing. The smile on his face. Yeah," he recalls with a slow smile. "Everything. It's like a snapshot in my mind. Still."

They went into Norfolk to a restaurant, Café 21, where they talked nonstop through dinner, then took a romantic walk on the beach before returning to Thorne's house. "So we're kissing around and I said to him, 'You know, Tracy, you big stud, you better take me to bed now, or lose me forever.' It was one of the goofball lines one of the girls uses in *Top Gun,*" Mike says, laughing. That snippet of Hollywood purple prose, corny or not, apparently worked. From that night on, they spent every weekend together. "I think there's a Fleetwood Mac song, 'When I came in the door or when I came to your house, I knew I never wanted to leave . . .' " Mike says. "And that's exactly how it was. It was like walking into his life and knowing it was right."

A different Fleetwood Mac song, "Don't Stop (Thinking About Tomorrow)," was the campaign anthem of William Jefferson Clinton, who two weeks later would be elected President of the United States. Clinton was on record calling the military ban on homosexuals "a quaint little rule" that he planned to lift by executive order should he win the election. As one of his campaign advisers, openly gay Bob Hattoy, reported in *The Advocate*, "I remember telling him that I thought that the generals would go nuts if he lifted the ban. To which Clinton quickly replied, 'Yes, but it's the right thing to do.' "When Clinton was elected in November 1992, Thorne was elated. "All of a sudden, this enormous weight was off my shoulders," Tracy recalls. "I had hopes I could go back to my squadron. I had hopes I could go back to flying. . . . I remember sitting in my little beach house, with tears rolling down my cheeks as I listened to him say, 'I come from a place called Hope and I still believe in hope in America.' I bought into Bill Clinton's dream one hundred percent."

Within a week of the election, the dream seemed to be coming true. On November 11, the judge in the case of Petty Officer Keith Meinhold ruled that the military ban was unconstitutional and ordered the Navy to reinstate him. President-elect Clinton, in his first press conference, said that he approved of the Meinhold decision and that he intended to keep his promise to lift the ban by executive order. There was an immediate firestorm of opposition; new to the ways of Washington, the Clinton staff had clearly misjudged both public sentiment and how power was distributed on Capitol Hill. "They should have touched base and cleared this and figured out what they had to do to get the President's way before it got public," Tim McFeeley says. "Once it got public, then people's positions got locked in." The gay leadership, who could have told the Clinton camp what to expect, had not been briefed, nor had the Joint Chiefs of Staff, who were already mistrustful of the new commander in chief who had avoided the draft in the 1960's. Democratic senator Sam Nunn of Georgia, head of the Armed

Forces Committee, perhaps still smarting about being passed over for the position of Secretary of Defense, led the vitriolic fight against Clinton in Congress. "All of a sudden it became a national issue," Tracy says. "The mainstream press was focusing on it almost daily. . . . [Greta] Cammermeyer's case became much more public, my case took off . . . then, other soldiers and sailors started coming out of the closet and there was this snowball effect."

Initially dazed, Thorne rose to the occasion by becoming more vocal, more visible. As Tanya Domi of the National Gay and Lesbian Task Force told *The Advocate* about Thorne and Meinhold: "We used them to the hilt. It became an act of civil disobedience with tremendous impact, because the media just ate the story up." Jeffrey Schmaltz, a reporter for *The New York Times,* said, "These were not radical gay activists. These were people who were boys and girls next door, people almost everyone would be proud to have in their family. Even homophobes had to admit it took a lot of courage to come out like that. If you're an editor and are making a decision about whether you should cover a street activist screaming and shouting or a boy or girl who could be your own kid, the decision is pretty easy." Of his "regular guy" persona, Thorne remarked, "Sad as it is, the boy-next-door who's gay gets off a lot easier than the more flamboyant drag queen does," he says. "That's why some of my biggest heroes were the drag queens at Stonewall. They were the ones that had to face the ridicule and harassment, whereas someone like me, who was, like, the biggest fag in America for a few months, never had to face any of the hostility or violence."

Before long, the President set up a special task force on gays in the military led by John Holum. Holum met with Barney Frank, Gerry Studds, and other openly gay officials "trying to figure not whether they would do this, but how the whole thing would work," Tim McFeeley recalls. "Then, Barney Frank began calling me virtually every day, saying, 'We've got to do something. Politically, this is going to go the other way.' " Frank was also talking to the HRCF and NGLTF, advising them to organize and brace for a tough battle. "I begged them to get a letter-writing campaign going," he told *The Advocate.* "The groups were making a fundamental error. They thought that having a president on your side means you've won. Having the President on your side is a necessary condition, but it's not a sufficient condition." Jeff Trammell concurs, "We had a friend in the White House for the first time, and I think there was a certain naiveté in the community. All of us thought Clinton's election was the end of the struggle and not the beginning." William Waybourn says flat out, "The gay community kept thinking that somebody was going to fix it for us and that was just a total fallacy."

At that point, however, George Stephanopoulos, senior adviser to the President, had asked that gay-rights advocates retreat to the wings, allowing the administration to take center stage on the issue. Warily, gay leaders did—and watched their new champion in Washington get sandbagged by the cannier old politicos of the opposition. When the Senate considered the new administration's first bill, the Family Medical Leave Act, Minority Leader Bob Dole freighted it with an amendment barring the President from lifting the military ban by executive order. Desperate to get the bill passed, the Democrats turned to Senator Sam Nunn, who proposed a compromise: The executive order would be put off for six months, during which time Congress would discuss the issue of gays in the military. Clinton agreed and the bill was passed.

But now there was blood in the water. Secretary of Defense Les Aspin appeared on the CBS show *Face the Nation* to say that he doubted Clinton had enough backers in Congress to overturn the ban; the next morning the outlines of his confidential memo to the President, aimed at preventing an embarrassing congressional overturn of the executive order, appeared on the front page of *The New York Times*. The article cited General Colin Powell's opposition: "The Joint Chiefs of Staff, headed by Colin Powell, contend that repealing the ban would wreck morale and discipline, undermine recruiting, force devoutly religious service members to resign, and increase the risk of AIDS among heterosexual troops."

"Once the proponents of change signal that we don't have the votes," Tim McFeeley says, "then it's all over." The Religious Right now moved in for the kill, mobilizing its vast network to place half a million antihomosexual phone calls to Capitol Hill in a single week. "I couldn't figure out how they could generate so many calls," William Waybourn says. "I later found out that they had these patch-through phone banks that were completely new at the time, and they were able to randomly call people up and ask what they thought of gays in the military. If they said they were opposed, the right-wing groups would patch them through to their congressman on a one-eight-hundred number at no cost to the individual."

With Congress calling for hearings by the Senate Armed Forces Committee, on January 29, nine days after his inauguration, President Clinton announced that he would not issue an immediate executive order but would suspend enforcement of the Pentagon's ban. He was proposing a compromise:

> The debate over whether to lift the ban on homosexuals in the military has, to put it mildly, sparked a great deal of interest over the past few days. . . .
>
> I have asked the Secretary of Defense to submit by July 15 a draft executive order, after full consultation with military and congressional leaders and concerned individuals outside of the government, which would end the present policy of exclusion from military service solely on the basis of sexual orientation and at the same time establish rigorous standards regarding sexual conduct to be applied to all military personnel. . . .
>
> In the meantime, a member whose discharge has been suspended by the Attorney General will be separated from active duty and placed in standby reserve until the final report of the Secretary of Defense and the final action of the President. . . .
>
> This compromise is not everything I would have hoped for, nor everything that I have stood for, but it is plainly a substantial step in the right direction.

The announcement was a personal blow for Tracy, who was officially still in the Navy, with his paperwork on hold at the Pentagon pending new legislation on the ban. But he'd known which way the wind was blowing, having received a heads-up call from Congressman Gerry Studds: "Hey, kiddo," he'd said. "I wish I had good news for you, but I don't. It looks like the President is going to have to back down on this, and there's no way we can keep you in the military in the meantime." All Tracy could say was: "That's all right."

Many gay leaders took a harsher view, insisting that Clinton should have embraced his position as commander in chief and ordered Colin

Powell and the Joint Chiefs of Staff to fall in line. They believed the new President had seriously failed his first test as a leader. Greg King, who did front-lines battle for the HRCF, was more pragmatic: "We should have been politically astute and recognized that Presidents don't have the power to make sweeping changes without having the cooperation of the military and of Congress. There was no way that a President with the military baggage Bill Clinton had was going to be able to make this change within the first hundred days of his administration without facing opposition. And we deluded ourselves into thinking he could."

Chastened, the White House approached the gay and lesbian community for help. Stifling recriminations, William Waybourn recalls, "We finally decided to respond collectively on the issue and we formed the Campaign for Military Service (CMS)." For the first time ever, all the national gay-rights organizations banded together to wage war on a single front: the crisis of gays in the military.

Under the leadership of Tom Stoddard, executive director of the Lambda Legal Defense Fund, CMS went immediately to work. "It was high-pressure, twelve- and sixteen-hour days," says David Smith, its communications head. Before long, they found a new way to approach the fight: "The problem was that the issue was framed by the national groups as a gay-rights issue," says Waybourn. "It wasn't until CMS was formed and some poll research was done that they recognized that the issue of job rights resonated far more with the American public. That everyone had a right to a job in this country and that included people in the military." David Smith came up with a Tour of Duty bus, modeled on the effective Clinton/Gore campaign buses, on which "out" military personnel toured fifty cities in twenty states to beat the drum. "It actually was a great success," Smith says. "It garnered a lot of media attention."

Yet, it still wasn't enough. "Nunn was controlling all the images," Waybourn remembers. In one memorable gambit, Nunn and Republican Senator John Warner of Virginia, along with a peeping-tom camera crew, toured a Navy aircraft carrier, poking into the private areas, bunks, showers, and latrines, to demonstrate graphically that homosexuals did not belong in such close quarters. "So," Waybourn continues, "I called the networks and said, 'You're killing us on this.' And they said,

'Give us somebody to talk to.' Tracy helped fill this vacuum." Having served on an aircraft carrier, Thorne could counter Nunn with authority. Still, a lot of damage had been done, according to Chris Bull of *The Advocate*: "When Clinton was elected, the images shifted from Tracy Thorne on *Nightline,* which was the dominant image during the campaign, to Colin Powell threatening to resign or Sam Nunn showing bunks on battleships. It got to be much more about homosexuality [than] about Tracy Thorne. Nunn was brilliant about making that shift. Clinton had already started compromising by the time CMS started getting people like Tracy back on the news. It was too late. The polls had already reversed."

But Thorne kept on pushing: "A lot of it was the military training I had. I mean, they trained me to get bombs on target on time and we did it over and over and over again and practiced until we were perfect at it. Doing 'gays in the military' was the exact same thing. It was something that was immensely personal to me, and I found out what I did wrong and tried to improve on it, and I continued to keep coming back and beating the same drum over and over and over again."

Through it all, William Waybourn says, Tracy's support network was Mike Begland. "It was through Mike that Tracy was able to express a lot of his frustration about what was happening to him. If Tracy is 'Commander Cool,' Mike is 'Mr. Emotions.' They complement each other quite well, especially in a time of great duress." The two had grown committed to each other so quickly that less than two months after their first romantic night, Mike brought Tracy home to his parents' house for Thanksgiving dinner. "My parents had never met anyone I'd dated," Mike says, "and by this point Tracy had some notoriety. 'Gay activist' brought up a whole lot of connotations. . . ." Thorne laughs. "They expected me to show up in a leather harness, I guess." Then, thirty seconds after Tracy walked into the Begland house, all the electricity went out. The family had to repair to a local restaurant for the holiday meal, and Tracy was sure the rattled Beglands were thinking, "The evil homosexuals are destroying our lives!" But they all made it through in fine shape. "His family was incredible," Tracy now says. "All I knew was that Mike's dad was a retired colonel from the Rangers and an infantry officer in Vietnam. So I'm expecting this Art Brill–type colonel, spitting nails. But he was a lot more warm and fuzzy than you would expect, and Mike's mom is the sweetest woman on earth. Just this warm Italian mama always shoving a plate of lasagna in front of you and saying, 'You've got to eat more.' " It was clear to the Beglands that Tracy and Mike truly cared for each other. "They realized that I could be happy in a gay relationship, which had always been their biggest concern about me being gay—that I couldn't have a fulfilling, happy gay relationship. They came around very quickly and were real supportive."

For Christmas Day, Tracy reciprocated, and now it was Mike's turn to feel intimidated at the prospect of meeting Roscoe Thorne. He'd heard that Roscoe was still struggling to accept his son's homosexuality, as well as the notoriety that accompanied it. "So I'm gonna be the first guy he's met who's dating his son, and I was half expecting to walk in and get my jaw broken," Begland recalls. "But he was awesome. He walked in and gave me a hug and it was really wonderful."

Mike Begland had become a kind of copilot for Thorne on his speaking tours. "When Tracy was asked to go to a speech or a fundraiser, he wouldn't take any honorarium, but he would just ask if they would pay for two plane tickets, one for me, one for him," Mike says. During Tracy's appearances, Mike would jot down the notions and images that resonated with the audience so that every speech thereafter could be revised for maximum effect. "I would help him perfect his message and make sure he stayed grounded." He also ran interference for Tracy. "If he was talking with someone or he had a fan that just didn't want to leave him alone, I'd kind of intervene." There was tremendous stress. "There were definitely days when I felt I'd given up all my privacy," Tracy says. "There were a lot of reporters, straight and gay, who thought I owed them an interview." But on the whole, Begland sees the time as positive. "To be two young gay guys caught up in a really exciting campaign, to be around the country in different parts of the gay community at rallies and fund-raisers was just really exciting," he says. "There was such an overwhelming sense of enthusiasm and hope and adrenaline."

There was one function at which Waybourn engineered a meeting between Thorne and Vice-President Al Gore. "Tracy was dressed in full military regalia, and I knew he would have no trouble getting past the Secret Service," Waybourn recalls. "Al and Tipper Gore were sitting at this large, round table with about ten people when Tracy approached him. Now, at the time, Al Gore had a broken leg, so he was a captive audience. Making small talk, Gore complimented Tracy on his uniform. Tracy responded by saying, 'You should know that today is my last day wearing this uniform.' 'Why?' the Vice-President asked. Tracy said, 'I'm getting kicked out tomorrow. The Navy's getting rid of me because I'm gay.' If Gore could have gotten away, I'm sure he would have, but he couldn't find his crutches," Waybourn says with a chuckle. "To his credit, as second to the commander in chief, he stayed there and talked to Tracy and learned more about his situation." A few weeks later, Gore's staff called Thorne and asked for more information about his case. "Clearly that personal contact and Tracy's ability to persuade had an impact on the Vice-President."

The President, meanwhile, was sending mixed signals. Clinton invited some gay leaders, including Tom Stoddard, Tim McFeeley, and William Waybourn, to the Oval Office. "He absolutely convinced me that he was still with us and he was going to sign the order," McFeeley says. "He charms you and assures you. We couldn't criticize him and say 'Why aren't you doing more?' because he kept saying, 'You're right, I'm with you, we're gonna win this thing.' "

Soon the public would have a chance to weigh in on the issue. In spring of 1993, the Senate hearings on the ban were officially convened and were broadcast on the C-Span channel. There were some ugly moments. The senators were shown a video called *The Gay Agenda*, a crude propaganda piece put out by the Christian Coalition, that was an assemblage of images of drag queens, leathermen, Dykes on Bikes, and the like, overlaid by an inflammatory narration warning that such homosexuals were "out to recruit others to their deviant lifestyle." Generals Colin Powell and Norman Schwarzkopf came before the Senate to predict dire consequences should the ban be lifted; and a Gulf War hero, Colonel Fred Peck, testified that, while he loved his gay son, Scott, he did not believe that the boy belonged in the military. Disgusted, Thorne told *Time* magazine that the entire affair should be labeled, "Sam Nunn's Dog-and-Pony Show."

Then the time came for Tracy himself to testify.

He would appear at Norfolk Naval Base in Virginia, the largest base in the world, where the Senate committee had set up shop in a two-thousand-seat amphitheater. The base commanding officers had all been instructed to send whatever personnel they could spare to sit in the audience. By the time the hearings commenced, the theater was overflowing with rowdy sailors and Marines. "It was like the Roman Coliseum with the Christians being thrown to the lions," Thorne says. Senator Nunn had called for seventeen people to testify on the ban—fifteen for and only two, including Tracy Thorne, against. He had stacked the deck: "He handpicked every witness," Thorne told *Our Own Community News.* "I have had at least a dozen soldiers and sailors call me up and say, 'I called the Senate Armed Forces Committee and told them that I was a straight sailor or a straight officer who wanted to testify on behalf of lifting the ban on gays in the military and was told that I was not needed.'"

With his mother and sister watching in the audience, Tracy was badgered by the committee members, demanding to know why he had shoved his homosexuality in other servicemen's faces, as the audience heckled him and hooted approval. When Thorne asked the panel if it was "shoving it in faces" if a person wore a wedding ring or kept a picture of his wife on his desk, the sailors and Marines in the stands shouted protests. "It was the first time that I really felt uncomfortable with where I was and what I was doing," Thorne admits. "I was in a room with two thousand people who were booing me."

When the jeering got too loud, Chairman Nunn would bang his gavel and in a token attempt to quiet the room, say, "Now, now, that's not appropriate. These people are here to give testimony and we should treat them with respect." Senator Strom Thurmond (R-SC) asked Thorne if he had sought psychiatric help to change from homosexuality to the normalcy of heterosexuality. "I wanted to tell him that some people don't think that it is normal for ninety-year-old men to marry thirty-five-year-old women, but *he* decided to do it," Tracy quipped later to the gay and lesbian press. "I'm not going to judge him on that. He sure as hell shouldn't judge me on what *I* do." Unfortunately, the zinger did not occur to Thorne until he left the auditorium.

By the end of the day, it looked depressingly clear to Thorne that the hearings were a sham. "The fact that Congress said they were studying this policy was just a line of crap," he says vehemently. "Everything was preordained. They were looking for pieces of the puzzle that were necessary to make the picture come out the way they wanted. It was a totally created media circus playing to the most basic fears of the American public."

The Department of Defense, armed with the results from hearings, meetings, and political polling, was beginning to formulate its position on gays in the military. Tom Sheridan and Chai Feldblum of the CMS were briefed by Les Aspin's staff on the proposed position—the first time that "Don't Ask, Don't Tell" was revealed. The hackneyed and convoluted proposal deemed that military officials would be prohibited from asking prospective enlistees about their sexual orientation but were still allowed to ferret out closeted gays and lesbians and place them on standby reserve, suspending their pay and benefits. Shocked, Sheridan and Feldblum reported back to David Smith, who responded, "We've got to blow this up. We've got to leak this." Smith says now, "We needed one last chance to derail this train, because the train had left the station. And it had 'Don't Ask, Don't Tell' on it." The next day, it was front-page news in *The New York Times,* and the White House and Pentagon were furious—"primarily because we leaked it and they didn't," Smith maintains.

Barney Frank, who according to *The Advocate* feared that Congress would soon codify the "Don't Ask, Don't Tell" policy, proposed yet another compromise in *USA Today.* Dubbed "Don't Ask, Don't Tell, Don't Investigate," it would prohibit officials from asking recruits about their sexual orientation and bar military personnel from declaring their homosexuality on base, but would allow them, off base, to pursue whatever lifestyle they chose. Horrified, the gay-rights organizations immediately denounced the compromise as an unacceptable retreat. The head of CMS, Tom Stoddard, was especially critical: "Barney has created the impression . . . that we can't possibly get what we want on this issue anymore, and that leads to a sense of despair," he told *The Advocate.* Frank countered that the gay groups were overmatched by those upholding the ban—that his proposal was better than anything else gays were likely to get. Greg King, one of Frank's few supporters, maintains, "Barney Frank understands what is doable in politics more than most of us. I think we would have been better served paying attention to political realists such as Barney and seeking his guidance."

Tracy Thorne was one of those who vehemently opposed Frank.

"You don't go out there saying, 'I want equal rights' and then settle for half a cup. Half of equal is still unequal. Barney should have known better. There are certain things you don't compromise on and civil rights is one of them," he says, still angry today. William Waybourn concurs. "I'm not going to characterize what Barney does as being right or wrong," he says. "He did it for whatever reasons he had to do it. But it was, in the minds of about sixty people involved with CMS, an act of betrayal. There was no advance notice and suddenly it was out there that Barney supports 'Don't Ask, Don't Tell.' It pulled the plug on our efforts. It ended right there."

Thorne went so far as to say that, if he escaped discharge, he would not return to his beloved Navy job on any sort of "Don't Ask, Don't Tell" basis. "If the policy is changed to treat me just like anybody else, then I am going back in as soon as the Navy will allow me to," he said. "But if the policy is changed to some kind of compromise where I am treated as a second-class citizen, then I don't want any part of it. I don't think the government has any place regulating people's private lives. If you want to legislate morality, well, you can move to another country where they don't have separation of church and state." But on May 19, exactly one year after he appeared on *Nightline,* Tracy's discharge was officially signed by President Bill Clinton.

Even knowing which way the political tides were shifting, Thorne hoped against hope that a directive would be issued on the July 15 deadline that would allow him to return to flying. Until then, since there was no reason for him to remain in Virginia Beach, Thorne moved in with Mike Begland in Washington, D.C., and began working full-time as a lobbyist for CMS and HRCF. When July 15 finally came around, President Clinton announced his administration's official policy on gays in the military—and "Don't Ask, Don't Tell" became a reality.

The proclamation fell on the capital like a shroud: The White House felt seriously damaged by its attempt to support gay rights, and the homosexual community felt seriously betrayed by a President they had championed. "I had no illusions that Bill Clinton could have signed this policy on day one of his presidency and made it all disappear," Thorne maintains. "But the bottom line is, Bill Clinton said, 'I'm giving this to the gay community. You take care of it. You've got six months to get two hundred and something votes in the House of Representatives and fifty-one votes in the Senate and you take care of it because I'm not going to deal with it.' And for six months, everything he could possibly do wrong, he did wrong. As a result, the moderate members of the Republican and Democratic parties abandoned any efforts to change it. It was left to a few liberals like Ted Kennedy and Pat Schroeder, and an incredibly disorganized gay community, to try and run this thing through. So while I recognize that Clinton couldn't have done it no matter how well he had lobbied, I really, really was hurt and insulted by his lack of commitment. When you have the power to influence so many people, you shouldn't hold out dreams to people that you can't fulfill." Thorne sadly shakes his head. "As President of the United States, Clinton signed into law one of the most hypocritical pieces of legislation this country's ever seen."

Ironically, in early 1994, United States District Court Judge Stanley Spork ruled that Thorne be reinstated in the Navy in a noncombat capacity while awaiting a second board hearing. Assigned as a branch officer at Naval Air Systems Command in Arlington, Virginia, Thorne managed a team of forty military and civilian personnel who were developing a Department of Defense prototype computer network. Again—this time on the ground—he distinguished himself, prompting his commanding officer, Craig Luigart, to rank him number one of all the lieutenants he'd dealt with in the naval service. It was a tremendous validation for Tracy. "It really saved my whole Navy experience," he says. "I was treated very, very, very well. I was given a lot of responsibility. I had a super commanding officer who ended up awarding me a Navy Achievement Medal."

When the date July 11, 1994, was set for the second board of inquiry, Roscoe Thorne wanted to fly up to support his son again. "Let's get those sons of bitches, Tracy," he said. "We're gonna win this." But he never got the chance. Two weeks before the hearing, Tracy was shopping with Mike and Mike's mother at a giant antique market in Pennsylvania when an announcement came over the public address system that Judy Begland should report to the office. It turned out, Mike says, that "Tracy's family had contacted mine because they couldn't get in touch with him." The small plane Roscoe Thorne was piloting had experienced engine failure upon takeoff, and he was killed in the resulting crash. "My mom actually had to tell Tracy and that was really hard."

Immediately, they drove back to Washington, and from there Mike accompanied grief-stricken Tracy to Palm Beach, Florida. "His family included me in everything," Mike says. "I was a part of every decision that was made in terms of funeral arrangements. To have to go through this together really strengthened Tracy's and my relationship."

On July 11, the second board of inquiry convened, presided over by captains Douglas Cook, Robert Smith, and Eben Barnett. The legal adviser was Major R. J. Stutzel; the recorder was Lieutenant Peter Dutton. Luther Ziegler and Patrick Lee again served as Thorne's civilian counsel.

This time Thorne's CO in Arlington, Craig Luigart, appeared, calling Thorne's work for him "absolutely exemplary" and saying that his "biggest administrative nightmare right now is trying to figure out how to replace him in about six weeks, depending on how proceedings and everything else go. My chances of randomly being assigned a lieutenant of his strength are essentially nil." Todd Suko was up next, and again testified about the unparalleled strengths of his friend. Upon cross-examination, both Luigart and Suko were asked about Michael Begland—Did they know him? Did they know that Thorne had named him on his life insurance policy? Were they homosexual lovers?—in an effort to expose "inappropriate" sexual behavior. Dr. Lawrence Kolb, barred from the first hearing, testified that statements made by Lieutenant Thorne about his homosexual orientation did not demonstrate a propensity to engage in homosexual conduct, nor were statements about his sexual orientation sufficient grounds for separating him under the new "Don't Ask, Don't Tell" regulations. When asked by Ziegler, "Does what you know of Lieutenant Thorne's record lead you to believe that he has the kinds of characteristics that would warrant trust and loyalty?" Kolb replied, "If I were young enough to go back on active duty, I'd love to serve with him."

Then Tracy Thorne spoke for himself. "I've had what many might describe as a unique opportunity for a junior lieutenant, that is that I've served in the Navy twice. . . . The first time I served my country as, to all appearances, a heterosexual, a person the Navy expected and wanted, a person they were willing to spend millions of dollars to train, a person they praised over and over again. . . .

"Now, the Navy has a different Tracy Thorne. I am still devoted to my country, I still love the U.S. Navy and am committed to its goals and the values that it fosters. I still achieve, I still receive praise from my superiors and still get high marks from those who work for and with me. The only thing that is different now is that I'm honest with myself and honest with you. . . .

"I joined the Navy because I believe in three things: I believe in duty. I believe in honor. And I believe in country. I am here today as Lieutenant Tracy William James Thorne. I'm a proud American, I'm a proud naval officer, and I am a proud gay man. I have earned my wings of gold, and the rank I wear upon my shoulders. I wear it with pride, just as you do, and I have earned my rightful place in the United States Navy."

In his closing statement, the recorder, Peter Dutton, used Tracy's own words to attack him: "He stated in one context, too, that they threw away millions of dollars spent on his flight training. 'I graduated number one. I was a top student.' The Navy spent that money but it is of no benefit to the Navy. It's a benefit to Lieutenant Thorne and is being used at this point for nothing more than to forward a personal political agenda. He is a political activist, who he said, suspected in high school his homosexuality, was pretty sure in college—well before entering the Navy. . . . He paints himself as a victim, but it is the Navy that has been used as the tool of this man to advance his political agenda."

In his summation, Luther Ziegler countered by saying, "The sad irony of this case is that we're here today not because Lieutenant Thorne failed to live up to qualities like personal integrity and honesty, but precisely because he did live up to them. It would have been, as he poignantly pointed out, a far easier course for him to have lied about himself and about who he is by pretending to have a heterosexual orientation. But he didn't do that. He didn't do that because he believed that the virtues of honesty, personal integrity, and courage—the virtues that the Navy has instilled in him—required that he candidly acknowledge who he is. And having done that, the government would now tell you he cannot serve. We do not believe that that is what the regulations require. We do not believe that that is what justice or common decency require. . . . We urge you to recommend that Lieutenant Thorne be retained in the United States Navy."

On July 14, at 11:30 A.M., Captain Cook intoned the verdict: "By a vote of three to zero, the board recommends Lieutenant Thorne has failed to show cause for retention in the naval service and he should be separated with an honorable discharge. These proceedings are adjourned." By 11:33 A.M., the inquiry was officially over.

With that pronouncement, in the span of three minutes, Thorne's two-year public David-and-Goliath battle against the U.S. Navy came to an end. He was no longer a lieutenant—and he was no longer encumbered by the notoriety of being what he called a "professional homosexual." Soon thereafter, Thorne and Mike Begland moved from Washington, D.C., to Richmond, Virginia, where they bought a home. Both enrolled in law school, and they now work as attorneys. As Tracy says, "The biggest contribution I can make is just to continue living my life as an 'out' person. I think the gays-in-the-military debate, more than anything prior to it, brought the everyday homosexual into America's living rooms. That was the thing that was really the most important. Sure, we didn't change the policy, but we raised the visibility of your everyday gay and lesbian American—bankers and lawyers and auto mechanics who just happen to be gay—to a new level. And I was damn lucky to be part of it."

On October 19, 1998, attorney Christopher Farris presented an appeal of the "Don't Ask, Don't Tell" policy to the United States Supreme Court on behalf of Tracy Thorne. Maintaining that the policy was based on "bigotry" and "invidious and irrational prejudice," the appeal went on to state, "Gay and lesbian service members who want to serve their country while living an open and honest life are the victims. This victimization will continue, absent guidance from this court." It noted that, although the policy was formulated to ease discrimination against homosexuals in the military, figures showed that gays and lesbians were being discharged at a markedly higher rate than before the policy's implementation—the most recent Pentagon report showing that 67 percent more homosexuals were discharged in 1997 than had been drummed out in 1994.

The highest court in the country, however, rejected the appeal, turning away the challenge without comment.

When the Pentagon released the official homosexual discharge figures for 1998, it revealed that the firings had jumped yet again—to a record 1,145—a whopping 92 percent increase since the policy began six years earlier. C. Dixon Osburn, co-executive director of Servicemembers Legal Defense Network, said, "These numbers are shameful. Military leaders have turned a blind eye to the continued asking, pursuit, and harassment of gays, lesbians, and bisexuals serving our country. What will have to happen before the Pentagon turns its ship around?"

Then, on August 12, 1999, the *Los Angeles Times* reported that the Pentagon had issued new guidelines designed to curb abuses in its much maligned "Don't Ask, Don't Tell" policy. The newspaper reported:

> The guidelines . . . will require that troops receive anti-gay-harassment training throughout their careers, beginning with boot camp.
>
> The guidelines will also require that when an investigation is opened into the sexual orientation of a soldier, the inquiry will be handled at a senior level of the military justice system.
>
> Abuses in the past have often been attributed to low-level, poorly trained investigators who have turned their investigations into virtual witch-hunts for homosexuals in uniform.

On October 6, 1999, President Clinton signed an executive order to allow tougher sentences under the military criminal code for hate crimes motivated by sexual orientation, ethnicity, gender, or disability. The day after, at a speech to gays and lesbians at Empire Pride Day in New York City, he expressed regret over the policy, labeling it "that awful battle that I waged and didn't win."

Tracy Thorne, now working in the Richmond, Virginia, prosecutor's office, notes the climate, saying, "It's just a matter of time. When it does change, I look forward to being the oldest lieutenant in the Navy. I absolutely would reenlist." Although he is cognizant that he would not be on flight status or doing the same work as before, he says, "I have always loved the Navy and still want to be a part of it—any time they will let me come back. I don't think it will be tomorrow or next year. But I will see that day when I am in uniform again."

When he does, then the country will truly have a military comprised of people who can say, honestly and straightforwardly, "I'm just like you."

DIANNE
HARDY-GARCIA

Relentless

A T THE John Thomas Gay and Lesbian Community Center in the Oak Lawn section of Dallas, Texas, a group of nearly seventy-five has gathered in the parking lot. In the steamy evening, each holds a candle, the flames flickering in the gathering breeze. Lobbyist Dianne Hardy-Garcia, in town from the state capital, has seen all of this before. Too many times. The pretty, compact woman with large, soulful eyes cannot count the occasions she has held a candle to honor a slain gay person. To Hardy-Garcia, they all blur together. She shakes her head, smiles sadly at her partner, Mary Anne Messina, and closes her eyes.

To the west, a bank of ominous thunderclouds has gathered, laced with heat lightning. While the sky roils and rumbles, the group moves underneath a covered walkway as community activist David Taffett, board member of The Foundation for a Compassionate Society, begins to speak in a quiet voice. "We're here to remember Matthew Shepard," he says. "Today was his funeral. His father said at the service that the amount of love that was shown around the country and around the world is something that would have amazed Matthew. . . ."

The tragic story of twenty-one-year-old Matthew Shepard had started out buried, like most of the others, in the back of the first section of the nation's newspapers a week earlier. On October 6, 1998, two high school dropouts, Aaron McKinney and Russell A. Henderson, also twenty-one, had lured the slight University of Wyoming student from a campus hangout, the Fireside Lounge, in Laramie, Wyoming, telling him that they were gay and wanted to get "better acquainted." Once all three were inside his pickup truck, McKinney pulled out a .357 Magnum and announced that they were not gay and that Shepard was being "jacked." When they discovered their victim had only twenty dollars in his wallet, the two assailants beat him with the butt of the gun as they drove across the flat plains east of town. Reaching a deserted area, they threw Shepard out of the truck and, as he pleaded for his life, smashed the base of his head so severely that his skull cracked open. Then, lashing him to a deer fence, they left him hanging there, like a bleeding scarecrow, to die in the freezing weather. Eighteen hours later, he was discovered, alive but barely breathing, by a passing mountain biker. When the sheriff's deputies arrived, they had to struggle to pry him off the fence because he had been bound so tightly. They noted that his blood-encrusted face was streaked with what appeared to be tears.

Hooked up to life support, deep in a coma with his brain stem severely damaged, Shepard became front-page headlines and led the nightly news broadcasts. His family stood vigil at his hospital bedside as Americans around the country joined them in spirit, expressing collective dismay at the savage assault. Wayne Besen, spokesman for the homosexual community's Human Rights Campaign (HRC), said, "Matthew became a symbol because the boy next door was hung up like a scarecrow. People saw him as their son or little brother."

On October 12, five days after he was cut down from the fence on the lonely plain outside of Laramie, the son, the little brother, died.

There was a nationwide outpouring of sorrow and horror. The Reverend Jesse Jackson expressed the anguish of many when he stated: "We must stand against a perverse use of our Bible that justifies hatred and killing. All Americans should be protected from hate crimes." President Bill Clinton went still further, saying, "I hope that in the grief of this moment for Matthew Shepard's family and in the shared outrage across America, Americans will once again search their hearts and do what they can to reduce their own fear and anxiety and anger at people who are different. In our shock and grief, one thing must remain clear: Hate and prejudice are not American values." Then he added, "There is something we can do about this. Congress needs to pass our tough hate-crimes legislation. It can do so before it adjourns, and it should do so."

Shepard's funeral was held in his hometown of Casper, Wyoming, north of Laramie. Mourners filled St. Mark's Episcopal Church, and a large spillover crowd stood outside in a blinding snowstorm—many near tears, holding on to each other for comfort and support and solace. Across the street, Religious Right picketers held up signs saying, "God Hates Fags," "Matt in Hell," and "AIDS Cures Fags." The Reverend Donald Spitz, director of Pro-Life Virginia, wrote in a letter to the editor in *Time* magazine, "For all the media attention surrounding Shepard's death, the fact remains that he has passed into eternal hellfire. The Bible is clear: Homosexuals do not inherit the kingdom of God."

As he was laid to rest, Shepard's accused murderers were held without bond and charged with kidnapping with intent to commit bodily injury, aggravated robbery, and first-degree murder. They would later both be found guilty and sentenced to two consecutive life sentences each.

That night, there were more than a hundred impromptu marches and candlelight ceremonies all over North America. "There are Matthew vigils everywhere, in cities as small as 60,000," wrote San Diego journalist Rex Wockner, who chronicles gay-related news and funnels it to on-line services. "Suffice it to say, this would seem to be the biggest gay news story of all time." More than five thousand marched in New York City, and eight thousand gathered on the steps of the Capitol in Washington, D.C. Boston, Los Angeles, Toronto, Miami, Seattle, and San Francisco joined the group in Dallas in the communal cry of pain.

In Dallas, David Taffett turns to acknowledge the colleague to his left. "Tonight, we have with us Dianne Hardy-Garcia. Dianne is the Executive Director of the Lesbian and Gay Rights Lobby of Texas, and working on hate-crimes legislation in Austin is something that has been Dianne's passion for nearly six years now." Taffett, having formerly been a board member of LGRL, knew firsthand of Hardy-Garcia's expertise, focus, and unflagging dedication. "This will be the third session that she will be banging her head against the wall, talking to legislators who just fear her sight," he continues. "I'd like Dianne to say a few words about hate crimes and the effect that they have on all of us."

Hardy-Garcia lifts her eyes and takes in the faces looking toward her. "All week I've been watching the candlelight vigils across the country and I think they're all very touching," she says, her words slow and measured. "But at the same time, I've got to be honest with you, I'm angry about them. Because we have seen too many candlelight vigils. We've had twenty-seven gay men murdered in this state in hate-related murders. So hate crimes are nothing new to us. And I know that candlelight vigils are not enough." Hardy-Garcia feels protective of the twenty-seven Texans murdered; their deaths were just as horrific as Matthew Shepard's. However, it is Matthew Shepard's story that has caught the nation's attention. And Dianne knows that there is a chance that now, after all these years of knocking her head against legislative walls, Shepard's senseless death and the anger surrounding it might be the catalysts that finally wake up the lawmakers.

"How many Matthew Shepards will there have to be before we get government action on this issue?" She surveys the crowd illuminated by patches of candle flame. "The only true and fitting memorial to Matthew Shepard and to the twenty-seven gay men who have lost their lives in Texas because of hate crimes is stronger hate-crime laws. We *deserve* that."

The wind begins to extinguish some of the candles; many listeners dip their wicks to catch a flame from their neighbor. "Governor George W. Bush has never said a thing about hate crimes. And he knows, he *knows,* about the deaths." As the rain begins falling in earnest, the group moves closer together. Hardy-Garcia pushes her glasses up her nose a bit. "We've got to hold our legislators accountable for the votes against this law," she continues. "We have to bang on their doors and let them know that their constituents care about these laws. I think that will be a fitting memorial to Matthew Shepard." Around her, people are nodding in agreement. Dianne has seen the sympathetic, well-meaning gestures before. Wondering now if this time it will be different, wondering if this time she won't be a lone voice in the Lone Star State, she ends by simply saying, "Thank you."

David Taffett gestures toward Hardy-Garcia. "The week Governor George W. Bush was elected, his first statement about the gay and lesbian community was that Dianne and the rest of her board were a bunch of extremists." The crowd chuckles appreciatively as the lobbyist nods her head in mock acknowledgment. The wind is now whipping through the parking lot; candles are being extinguished more quickly than they can be relit. "You know," Taffett continues, "I've heard about each of the hate crimes across the state of Texas. When I heard about this one, I just . . . I just started crying. This one, I think, for some reason, has affected everybody across the country. And I think we needed to be together as a community for this. . . ."

Everyone raises a candle, lit and unlit. "To Matthew Shepard," the group intones. Then all the flames go out.

A native daughter of Texas, Dianne Hardy-Garcia was born in San Antonio on July 10, 1965. She was the oldest of three children, with a sister, Kristina, two years younger, and a brother, Kenny, six years younger. Since her grandfather was in the military, her father, Kenneth Hardy, grew up primarily in Guatemala and Chile but, says Dianne, "He never really had a home—he always longed for that." After attending San Francisco State University, he entered the Air Force, and it was at Brooks Air Force Base in San Antonio that he met Mary Jane Garcia, a sister of a coworker. Darkly pretty Janie, a sweet Texas twang to her speech, was the youngest of the three Garcia daughters. "Her mother didn't much like me at first," Ken Hardy admits. "Not only was I a GI, but I'd gone to school in California, which was considered a wild place then." And he was Anglo. Jane's mother would voice her complaints to her daughter in front of Ken in a stream of uncomplimentary Spanish, not realizing he was well versed in the language and understood every remark. A lively, outgoing, and outspoken girl, Jane liked what she saw in the gentlemanly, reserved, and very smart Ken Hardy, and despite her mother's reservations, they began dating seriously. After three years together, in 1964, they decided to marry. By then, Ken was on his way to becoming a nuclear physicist and Jane was an elementary school teacher working in predominantly Hispanic schools. "They had had tumultuous childhoods in different ways," Dianne explains. "Both of them are products of bad marriages. So they both wanted stability in their marriage."

Their children grew up conscious that they were the result of two very different cultures, which Dianne calls a distinct advantage. "Being biracial has had a big impact," she says firmly. "It was a real gift to my sister and my brother and me." However, it was a realization hard won. As a child, in the race category on school forms, she would check "other" because she felt as if she really did not belong squarely in one group or the other. She also recalls being perplexed by San Antonio's segregated neighborhoods, with blacks living in one area, Latinos in another, and the whites in still a third. She witnessed even more confusing social stratification on family visits to Mexico, where she saw people living in shacks. Dianne asked her father, "Why do the white people live differently? Why do the Mexicans have to be so poor?" He replied, "It's not fair, honey. And it's not right." Jane remembers, "Every time we came back to the United States, we thanked God for where we lived. It makes you very patriotic."

The Hardys raised their children in a solidly middle-class San Antonio neighborhood of ranch-style houses and well-kept lawns. "Little pink houses, real neat, all in a row," Dianne says of it, "like that John Cougar Mellencamp song, 'Pink Houses.' " For a while, Dianne and her sister shared a bedroom. "It didn't last too long," Ken Hardy recalls. "Kristy and Dianne were the original Felix and Oscar." Or, as mother Jane puts it, "Kristy was very neat, very analytical; everything had to be color-coordinated and just so. And, well, Dianne was a slob." When the two sisters bickered, their parents refused to be referees. "My mother would say, 'You guys need to handle this yourselves!' " Kristy recalls. "And we'd have to stay in our room until we did." The battling ended when a bedroom was added to the back of the house and Dianne, by then a teenager, moved in alone. "We got along so much better when that happened," Kristy says with a laugh. Happy to be on her own, Dianne would sit in her messy room for hours listening to recordings of Janis Joplin, Cat Stevens, and Joni Mitchell. "I was so out of step!" she says. "I liked all of the early seventies songs about revolution. I never really got into any of the eighties music like everyone else my age." Amid the tumble of everyday adolescent living, she kept stacks and stacks of books. "Of all the kids," Ken Hardy says, "Dianne was the reader."

Their house, on a cul-de-sac with the unlikely name of Tally Ho, was situated directly behind their church, Holy Spirit, and the Hardy children could simply climb over the fence to attend its grade school. "Our backyard went into the rectory's backyard," brother Kenny remembers. "The priests used to come over all the time for dinner. We knew them all." They lived in the shadow of the church not only literally but figuratively, for Ken and Mary Jane Hardy were devout Catholics and known for their neighborhood activism on behalf of the poor. "They both had a heavy social consciousness," Dianne says. "I watched them get involved with a lot of activities and work really, really hard on those issues. They were constantly giving, all throughout our childhood." With the assistance of like-minded friends, the Hardys organized and built a summer camp to aid underprivileged children, as well as conducting food and housing drives to help disadvantaged families. "Our parents instilled good values in us," Kenny notes. "We think the best of people and hope for the best in people."

"My parents really sacrificed to make sure that we all went to Catholic schools," Dianne says. "They gave up a lot of vacations." The children, in turn, helped out by always having summer jobs. All three also excelled scholastically, served on student councils, and became class presidents. Dianne also became adept at sports, especially soccer. The Hardys found themselves in the stands, game after game, cheering on their sports-enthusiast daughter. When Kristy, especially skilled at ballet, performed in recitals, the family was there. When son Kenny began expressing an interest in acting, they went to see him in all the school plays. Whatever their children sought, the Hardys supported. Still, in this family of diversity and accomplishment, Jane maintains, "Even from a very early age, Dianne was the leader. She was always the chief and insisted her brother and sister be the Indians."

When Dianne went on to her Catholic all-girl private high school, Ursuline Academy, she found herself going head-to-head with the nuns. "There were girls who went there who had money, and there were girls there whose parents were struggling like crazy to put them through, and then there were girls like me—middle-class. And each group would be treated differently. Certain things the nuns did started to bother me, and I would openly challenge them." One of her battles was over the yearly school trip to Europe. Given the expense, only the wealthy girls were usually able to go, so Dianne organized a campaign to raise enough money to pay the way of the entire class. The nuns, however, did not appreciate her efforts, for they wanted any fund-raising the girls did to be devoted to improving the school or support-ing the church. "They got really angry and we had a big fight about it," she says. "I just thought it was wrong for a school to sponsor an event that only the rich kids get to go to."

Another run-in came after Dianne wrote a paper, knowing the nuns would squirm, that promoted bisexuality as the most authentic and democratic sexual orientation. "Oh, my God," she recalls, laughing, "I was threatened with suspension for that. I got into *major* trouble. It was not the time to explore ideas like that in parochial school." Nor was this the only time she was threatened with suspension. Ken and Jane Hardy were constant visitors to the Mother Superior's office, where they would hear that, while their daughter was a gifted student, she was a disciplinary nightmare. Ken Hardy continually tried to reason with his headstrong daughter, admonishing her not to "ruin your future over these issues." Her mother thought that Dianne was letting school chums take advantage of her natural leadership skills. Being a teacher herself, she saw the dynamic played out many times in her own classes. "They would all convince her to stand up for things, push things, and then Dianne would walk up there alone," she says. "And she would be the one to get into trouble. We were never called down for her school-work. It was always the other things, the outspoken side of her." Jane Hardy sighs, admitting, "Which she gets from me, I suppose . . ." Di-anne grudgingly agreed to temper her politics. "In retrospect, I proba-bly should have just been expelled," she says. "I should have just gone and I would have been freer. But I stayed. I stuck it out." Upon gradu-ation, her class voted her "Most Radical."

When the time came, Dianne decided to *really* go away for college—to South America, to the University of Colombia in Bogotá, where she could explore her Latino roots. However, over the summer, a letter came from the father of the host family, explaining that he would act as her male guardian the entire time she was in Colombia, and insist-

ing that she was to spend every weekend with his family. Dianne panicked. "He sounded like a really macho-shit guy," she says. "And I
thought, 'I'm not going to go down there and have this guy telling me
when I can and when I cannot go out! What a nightmare! No way!' So
I decided I wasn't going."

However, with her first semester in college a mere two months away,
she had no time to apply to other schools. Concerned, Jane Hardy got
on the phone to her alma mater, Incarnate Word in San Antonio, and
pulled some strings. Dianne was accepted despite the short notice, and
to help persuade her to attend a school she was not particularly eager
to attend, the Hardys bought her a car. "Believe me, my parents are not
the 'buy-you-a-car' kind of parents," Dianne says. "They were just really afraid I wasn't going to go." Though having the Honda Accord
would have allowed her to commute to school from home, Ken Hardy
insisted that Dianne live on campus so she could have the full college
experience.

Incarnate Word, the second-oldest college in San Antonio, boasts a
small but picturesque campus featuring redbrick and white limestone
Victorian-style buildings. At the time Dianne attended, the enrollment
was just over 1,500; five dormitories, a hundred rooms in each, housed
the students living on campus. Although she initially fought the whole
idea of going to Incarnate Word—another Catholic school, taught by
more nuns—Dianne soon realized that it was a good decision: "There
was a lot of individual attention there." She chose a double major, English and psychology, and to her surprise, actually came to like the Sisters of the Incarnate Word, who were less restrictive and more spirited
than the nuns at Ursuline.

Although she had always had fulfilling friendships with other girls—
some of them even lesbian—Dianne dated men. "I never had a bad relationship with a guy," she recalls today. "I had really sweet, wonderful
friends that I would go out with. But I never fell massively in love with
them." She thought that she simply had not met the right one yet. She
had some gay male friends who were going through the difficult
process of coming out, but she didn't identify with their plight. "I didn't
ever think it applied to me," she says, expressing astonishment that they
knew they were gay as far back as grade school. "I was in pigtails playing in the dirt then," she says with a laugh. "I wouldn't even have

known what they were *talking* about!" But then, in her junior year, she met a diminutive and vibrantly attractive woman, Mary Anne Messina.

Mary Anne Messina grew up between two brothers, Joe and Frank, in an Italian Catholic family in the New York City suburb of Merrick, Long Island. Because her father, Frank, Sr., came from an impoverished immigrant family, Mary Anne says, "He was a very frugal, by-the-book kind of guy. He was an accountant, and he had that certain personality that goes with people who are CPAs." Her mother, Louise, a writer and an artist, was less of a traditionalist, although quite religious. "My mother doesn't go to church because she has to," Mary Anne says. "She wants to. My dad went to church every Sunday because that's what you had to do. He followed the rules." Like Dianne, Mary Anne attended parochial school all her life, but unlike Dianne, she had taken the nuns' teachings to heart. When she arrived at Incarnate Word, she says, "They built it into the schedule that any individual could attend mass, thirty minutes, and also have thirty minutes for lunch, and then you could run to your one o'clock class," she recalls. "I did that for maybe two years straight." Pursuing a degree in psychology, she worked with severely disturbed children, as well as abused and neglected youngsters confined to psychiatric hospitals or group homes. When, at the age of nineteen, her younger brother Frank was diagnosed as schizophrenic, her commitment to helping the mentally ill grew even stronger.

Mary Anne, too, dated men in college, even becoming engaged for a time in her sophomore year, and then experimented a bit with women. Given her religious convictions, the idea that she might be a lesbian was initially "totally devastating to me. I felt like somebody had pulled my roots out of the ground. I was wobbly, I didn't know my footing anymore." When she met Dianne Hardy, the scenario became even more complicated.

A year behind her at school, Dianne had known Messina from afar. "By then she was more involved in the lesbian community on campus," Dianne recalls. Even though she was familiar with the group and would occasionally hang out with them, Dianne was dating a boy named Patrick, of whom she was very fond. Still, she found Messina an unusually bright, attractive, and fun girl, and before long they had formed a potent friendship.

They quickly discovered that they shared a highly developed intuitive sense about other people. "It's like sonar," Mary Anne claims. "Dianne's even higher than me in some respects. She can be in a room full of people and she'll know what certain people are feeling. Even if they don't know how they're feeling. She's like a psychic. I have that, too." When they were together, their intuition became almost symbiotic. It still is. "She'll pick up on things on certain people that I may not," Messina says. "And I'll pick up on certain people that she won't. Sometimes we freak ourselves out." Yet, despite feeling so psychically aligned, for a long time their friendship remained purely platonic.

Then, Dianne found herself in an awkward situation saying her good nights to Mary Anne. At first, the ritual did not concern her. "Everyone in San Antonio kisses hello and good-bye. Everyone. It's no big deal." But when the friendly good-night kisses became longer and more intense, Dianne became conflicted. "That kiss was a little too long," she said to Messina one night. "This is not how friends kiss. What does this mean?" Mary Anne replied, "What's the problem? Don't worry about it. Everything will be fine." "That's always how our relationship went," Dianne says. "I have to find out what everything means, and Mary Anne always says, 'It's going to be okay.' " After a year of back-and-forth questioning, they finally relented and became physically involved, but they kept their relationship a secret. Eventually the subterfuge began to weigh on Dianne, and she told Mary Anne, "There's no way I can live a closeted life like this. This lying thing, it's not working for me. If this is what it is to be gay, I don't know if I can do this. We've got to find another way to be."

Deciding that a separation might clarify their feelings, upon graduation Dianne signed on for a year with the Jesuit Volunteer Corps, which was a Catholic version of the Peace Corps, though it welcomed people of all faiths. As they planned it, while Dianne was doing her stint with the corps in Nashville, Tennessee, Messina would continue her psychology studies. When the year was out, if they still felt committed to each other, they planned to reunite on the East Coast, where Mary Anne had enrolled in graduate school at Seton Hall University in New Jersey.

Through 1987 and 1988, in the rocky green foothills of Nashville, volunteer Dianne was instructed to observe four precepts—to work for social justice, to live in the community served, to commit to a spiritual life, and to live simply—while performing service in a field new to her. She chose the penal system, helping men in jail with their parole petitions and, once they were freed, with housing, employment, and adjustment problems. The work was difficult and frustrating, but also richly rewarding. Once, when her parents came to visit, Dianne introduced her mother to some of her convict clients. Wary but fascinated, Jane smiled politely at the reformed criminals, shook some of their hands, and listened to them praise her daughter. She and her husband left Nashville telling each other, "Well, she is one gutsy girl. . . ."

Through it all, Dianne and Mary Anne kept up a constant stream of phone calls and letters and, by the end of the year, determined that they did indeed want to be together. Messina was living in Hoboken, New Jersey, and Hardy was looking forward to being on the East Coast, well away from the possible raised eyebrows of people back home, and doing social work. Finishing her stint in Nashville, she flew north and moved in with Mary Anne in Hoboken. There, directly across the Hudson River, Manhattan beckoned.

It was 1988, and the New York City gay population was energized and focused. The AIDS epidemic, which had hit urban centers like San Francisco and New York very hard, was at its height. Radical activist groups such as Act-Up were gathering clout. While Mary Anne stayed in New Jersey, immersed in her taxing graduate work, Dianne went through the Holland Tunnel daily to Manhattan. Enthralled with the city, Dianne went into high gear. She worked in a domestic-violence shelter, as well as with ex-offenders on parole, homeless families, and people with AIDS. For a while, she worked with a branch of the Red Cross. "I was shocked when I went up there to visit her," Ken Hardy says. "The Red Cross was in the Brownsville section of Brooklyn because it had literally been declared a disaster area. And it *was*. And Dianne was working down there." Although he was proud of her courage and drive, for the first time, Ken began to be a little concerned for his daughter's safety. Dianne finally settled into a social-work position at the Gay Men's Health Crisis (GMHC), which was trying to refocus its AIDS counseling program. "It was no longer just about gay men," she says. "They had to start servicing people of color and women and drug addicts, and it was creating a culture clash at GMHC." The only nonlicensed social worker there, she was hired because of her previous work with homeless families, battered women, and intravenous drug-users.

In tandem with her work, Dianne became deeply involved with the gay and lesbian community. "I *loved* it. I would go to rallies and watch all these gay activists speaking up so brilliantly," she recalls. "Such outspoken and proud and smart people. Every time I'd hear them speak, I'd just sit there and cry. It was so moving to me." She was also fascinated by the decidedly "un-Southern" confrontational stance of the activists. "They never worried about offending each other. It was about the essence, the *idea*," she says. She now vowed to hone her already impressive speaking skills. "You couldn't just say something and not expect that it was going to be challenged," she says. "In the South you can't, because you don't challenge to the face. It's rude. It's *damn* rude. We don't express our feelings openly."

Eventually, Dianne persuaded Mary Anne to move to Manhattan. It was no easy task. "Mary Anne's parents had this whole 'the city is bad' philosophy," Dianne says. "Long Island, where she grew up, was okay, but the city was dirty and full of crime. And she kind of had that feeling, too." The deciding factor was the proximity of Messina's part-time job as assistant manager of a residence for chronically mentally ill adults in Riverdale, just north of the city. She would end up working there for the entire three years she was pursuing her master's degree. For a thousand dollars a month, they found a one-bedroom apartment over a fish market just below Greenwich Village. "All the New Yorkers who saw our place thought it was the best deal in the world," she recalls. "It actually had a *bedroom*—people would come in and think it was palatial." Visiting friends from Texas, however, were appalled. "They thought it was disgusting," Dianne says with a laugh. "They all said, 'You can't open your windows! It stinks! It's dangerous!' And they hated walking everywhere. Texans don't walk. They never have comfortable shoes. So they always ended up with blisters when they came to visit us."

Hardy loved the tiny apartment, and now, being in Manhattan, she became even more involved in gay and lesbian activities. "She was coming out and going to gay-pride marches and doing all this stuff," Messina remembers, "and I was like, 'Wait a minute. I can't handle this right now. . . .' I wasn't on her timeline at all. So we fought a lot and it was very stressful." Although in Texas Mary Anne had been the one more comfortable with gay life, the roles were now reversed. "Those are the growing years, you know," Dianne says. "Those post-college years when you change a lot. The essence of your person emerges—you become your values. We didn't know how we were going to end up as people, so we had a rough couple of years there, trying. We didn't know if we would make it."

Slowly, Mary Anne warmed to the gay community in New York. "She kind of reached a plateau with it," Dianne says. "She became much more active and got more into what her beliefs were." One evening, when they were sitting around an apartment with some Queer Nation activists, the issue of coming out was raised—and all ten people present had to confess that they had not yet told their parents about their sexuality. That seemed absurd, considering the fierceness of their gay political affiliations, so they made a pact that over the Christmas holiday they would all go back to their hometowns and formally come out to their families.

Dianne and Mary Anne had already told most of their siblings. Messina's older brother Joe posed no challenge, for he was homosexual, too, although he was not yet out to their parents; Frank, schizophrenic, paid the news little heed. Dianne's sister, Kristina, had stumbled upon the information in some personal letters during a bit of kid-sister snooping on a New York visit, so only brother Kenny remained in the dark. Dianne decided she would tell him first, then her parents.

Since the Messinas now lived in Albuquerque and the Hardys were headed to nearby Taos for a skiing trip, Dianne and Mary Anne could cover the two families in one trip. Both fully intended to tell their parents face-to-face, but should that prove too difficult, they had written them letters, which they packaged with copies of a book, *101 Questions About Homosexuality*. It was designed as a "Plan B"—an in-absentia tactic that would be used only if necessary.

The Hardys met them at the airport. Dianne had insisted on renting an extra car for the ski trip; she wanted an escape hatch should she need to speed away after the grand revelation. The two cars drove to the Messina home to drop off Mary Anne. Because the temperaments of traditionalist Frank Messina and outspoken Jane Hardy clashed, there would be no dinner out together, no overnight stay. Mary Anne and her brother Joe would join the Hardys later in Taos to ski.

With Dianne, Kristina, and Kenny in one car and Ken and Jane in another, the Hardy family crept through a steady blizzard to their planned ski trip. At one point on the journey, Dianne, who was driving, turned down the radio and looked in the rearview mirror at her brother in the backseat. "I need to talk to you about something," she said. Immediately Kenny stiffened, thinking somebody had died. Kristina, sensing what was coming, sat silently, staring ahead at the snowy highway. Dianne explained that she was a lesbian and Mary Anne was her partner. After she let the information sink in, Dianne asked her brother, "How do you feel about that?"

Kenny had had a vague suspicion that his sister was gay, but he had never broached the subject with her. "I want you to be happy, but I'm sad," he said, "because I know it's not going to be easy for you. People can be so cruel." Dianne told her siblings that she was going to come out to their parents during the vacation, and that Mary Anne was going to do the same. Kristy and Kenny shuddered. "I just didn't think it was a good idea," Kristy says. "I knew my parents wouldn't take it well." They braced themselves for a very tense Christmas holiday.

As the vacation wore on, the tension did not subside. "I had a feeling my parents knew something was up," Dianne says. Then Mary Anne and her brother Joe met up with the Hardys. Although happy to be together, the two young women suddenly got cold feet about their planned coming out. There, on the snowy slopes of Taos, they decided to abort Plan A and opted for Plan B—and the backup letters were mailed back to their parents' homes. At the end of the vacation they sped to the airport. "We wanted to get on that plane and take off," Dianne says. "It was a really chicken-shit thing to do, but at the time we were just so afraid of what the reaction was going to be. We felt like we needed them to sit on it for a while."

Back in San Antonio, when the coming-out package arrived, Kristina placed it on her parents' bed. She and Kenny did not want to be around when the missive was read, so she left the house to be with her fiancé, Gary, while her brother went to morning mass at Holy Spirit. When he returned, he found his father working on the car. Tentatively, he approached him. "Did you get the package?" he asked his father. "Yes, we did," Ken replied evenly, not taking his eyes from the engine. "We'll always love your sister, but we're not really pleased with it. We don't think it's right." Dianne had told Kenny in the car that she thought their father was the one who was going to be angriest about the revelation, but Kenny suspected it would be their mother. "I walked in and Mom was pretty irate," he recalls clearly. "She said, 'I don't want to speak about this. Ever.' "

Back in their Manhattan apartment, Mary Anne got a tearful phone call from her mother, who, although not angry, did not handle the news well. "My mom is half old-world, half progressive," Mary Anne says. "Whereas my dad was just like a straight shot—you knew where he stood on issues. You didn't have to agree with the guy, but at least you knew where he stood." And, because Mary Anne knew very well where he stood on this subject, she had addressed the coming-out letter solely to her mother. "My dad always totally adored me, but his spiel on homosexuality was that it's against God and the church—almost like rhetoric," she says. "He would say gays are sick and need to be treated. He thought men should be men, be the breadwinners, and women should take care of the kids—that traditional old-world way of thinking. He was eighty-one. He was a few generations behind me." But Frank Messina had his suspicions and one day he asked Mary Anne on the phone, "What is it with you and Dianne? You're like husband and wife." Steeling herself, Mary Anne said, "Do you really want to know?" Her father replied, "Yes, I want to know." When she told him, he shouted, "You mean you're *lesbians*? Don't tell your mother!" Mary Anne was well aware that her mother was listening on the other line; her parents were always on the line together during long-distance phone calls. She sighed. "Dad, Mom knows." "Then don't tell your brothers," her father shot back. When Mary Anne told her father that the boys had known for quite a while, he said, "What am I, a dog? I'm the last to know! Is that it?" Angry and hurt, he hung up. Mary Anne's mother, who remained on the line, told her daughter that she had to give her father a little time to become adjusted to the idea. And loving his daughter too much to cut her off, Mr. Messina got back on the extension for further discussions on the subject. Attempting to be open-minded, he still could not quite restrain himself from warning that this "thing," Mary Anne recalls, "would cause me to go to hell or whatever. That fire-and-brimstone garbage . . ."

In the meantime, Dianne heard nothing at all from her parents. Ken and Jane Hardy, heavily influenced by the Catholic Church's rigorous condemnation of homosexuality, were having a very difficult time with their daughter's revelation. "It was just something we could not accept," Jane says. When the telephone call was finally made to Dianne in New York, the Hardys were terse. Ken told his daughter that love wasn't always unconditional. They not only expressed their disappointment and displeasure, they admitted that they would be uncomfortable should Dianne ever bring Mary Anne to San Antonio again. Dianne flew into a rage and receivers slammed down at both ends. Kenny, the family peacemaker, was heartsick about the rift. "It was almost two years of angry fighting," he says sadly.

Dianne threw herself into her family of friends in New York and her challenging work at the Gay Men's Health Crisis center. As her job there grew more demanding, it became clear that she needed to attend graduate school for accreditation if she was to go any further in her chosen profession. Mary Anne, longing to return to Texas, pointed out that the University of Texas in Austin would be much less expensive than New York colleges. Furthermore, she noted, Austin, the state capital, the most progressive and vibrant city in politically conservative Texas, had a substantial gay population. It also had the advantage of being only a seventy-mile drive from San Antonio, where Dianne's family lived. Perhaps the proximity would give her a chance to work out the differences with her parents. Torn, Dianne agreed, but she made herself a promise: She would enter a sixty-hour graduate studies program, be there for two years, and then she and Mary Anne would get back on a plane and return to New York permanently.

Relocated in Austin and armed with her master's degree in psychology, Mary Anne went immediately into assisting disturbed children and working in psychiatric hospitals. Dianne, on the other hand, found herself homesick for New York. Her extensive class load at the University of Texas helped in the rocky transition; so did occasional trips home to San Antonio. Ignoring her parents' admonishments about not welcoming Mary Anne in their house, Dianne insisted on bringing her partner home with her whenever she came. "We love Mary Anne," Jane Hardy still insists. "But we cannot condone their relationship." This caused a great deal of discomfort for Messina, but she realized it was the only way they could successfully present a united front. "It just forced us to interact more," Dianne recalls. "But we had tumultuous fights about them never wanting to talk about what we did or who we were." Finally, following yet another major confrontation, Jane, who was trying her best to adjust, sat her daughter down. "Look. I've only had a year and a half to get used to this," she said. "You've had five years. It isn't fair to expect me to be up to par or where you are!" Dianne saw her mother's point, realizing that, all things considered, her parents were doing the best they could. "On a scale of one to one hundred, my parents are in the top ninety percent," Dianne admits. "They went to every PTA meeting, they did everything, they put everything they could into raising their children, they gave us every opportunity. So when you look at that, compared to what others got growing up, I'm truly privileged and blessed. From their perspective, to feel like and be told they've failed, that they did something wrong when they put so much effort into raising us—it makes me angry for them. I feel bad that they've been hurt by homophobia as well."

In 1992, as part of her second-year graduate program, Dianne began an internship with Democratic Texas State representative Elliott Naishtat. The tall, lanky Naishtat was to become a great advocate and mentor for Dianne. "Elliott is such a good technical legislator," she says. "He taught me the technical side of passing bills. He showed me that everything is not how you see it—it's not about what's said publicly. I learned a great deal from him."

Democratic representative Glen Maxey, the first openly gay member in the Texas legislature, who occupied the office next to Naishtat, was immediately impressed with his colleague's new aide. "Dianne was an extremely hard worker and very committed to the causes that she worked on," he says. "From her first day, she jumped in with a vengeance."

Maxey was the sponsor of one of the first bills Dianne would see debated, a measure for the repeal of the state's archaic sodomy laws, which, although recently ruled unconstitutional by a Dallas judge, remained on the books. The state Senate had already voted—by a very close vote, 16–15—to repeal the laws, but much more of a fight was expected in the rough-and-tumble House, with its one hundred fifty members representing every niche culture in Texas. Among them was a powerful champion of the laws, Republican representative Warren Chisum, president of the Texas Conservative Coalition, who wanted to uphold them expressly because they were punitive to homosexuals.

When it became clear that he couldn't muster the votes for repeal, Glen Maxey resorted to some legislative sleight of hand. If he proposed the bill and it was voted down, he would not be able to resurrect it, because House rules prohibited introducing the same bill twice in the same legislative session. So he now revoked his introduction of the bill. That left Chisum unable to shoot it down with his planned diatribe on the evils of sodomy. Furious with Maxey's gambit, Chisum quickly got his aide to write an amendment to the laws making sodomy illegal for everyone—heterosexual as well as homosexual. He knew that it would be removed and changed; any time there is a difference between the House and Senate on a piece of legislation, the wording is revised. But Chisum figured this would allow him his bully pulpit.

Just as the hastily penned, quite explicit amendment was introduced, a group of fourth-grade students on a civics class outing entered the visitors' gallery above. As they quietly took their places in the chairs, a hot and colorful debate began over Warren Chisum's amendment prohibiting anal or oral sex between consenting adults. Democratic representative Debra Danburg, whose Montrose district in Houston includes a substantial gay population, stood to face Chisum and said in her honeyed drawl, "Mr. Chisum, what if it . . . slips?" Chisum, wondering if he heard correctly, said, *"What?"* Danburg, enjoying the tweaking, elaborated. "What happens if my husband's penis accidentally touches my anus?" she said with a straight face. "Is that a crime?" Amid titters below, the teacher escorting the fourth-grade class in the gallery gasped, rose, and quickly ushered her charges out of the building. The old sodomy laws remained on the books as a Class C misdemeanor.

Besides Maxey, Naishtat, and Danburg, Hardy would soon encounter other gay-friendly representatives—among them, Democrats Steve Woolens, Senfronia Thompson, Scott Hochberg, and Harryette Ehrhardt—who would become important allies. Under Naishtat, she would even handle a bill herself—and learn another lesson about legislative tactics. Dianne's bill proposed that residents of housing projects be given a stake in their communities by having two of their residents sit on each public housing authority board. Not only did the legislation plug directly into her social work expertise, but it also mirrored her passion for the disenfranchised and disadvantaged. To lobby for the bill, she canvassed the entire state and rounded up housing-project residents to come to Austin to testify in person before the House. Because she had no transportation budget, the residents would have to travel to Austin at their own expense—and many did, including poor Mexican families who arrived in battered station wagons packed with eight and nine passengers. "This whole crowd of them came in," Dianne recalls, "and this is when you know that they are really poor—they were *enthralled* with the Capitol. How clean it was, how large it was, and the biggest thing—how clean the bathrooms were. They had never seen bathrooms that nice. *Ever.* And they were so psyched to testify. . . ."

However, when the chairman of the committee saw the ragtag battalion of people who had come to testify, Dianne says, "He took one look, told his aide they were not going to have the hearing that day, and walked out and played golf." Furious, Dianne marched up to the chairman's aide, shouting, "I'm going to call every reporter friend that I have and I'm going to get someone to do a story on this! You tell him I said that!" Then she stormed in to tell Naishtat, who calmed her down. "You know, Dianne," he said, "maybe there's another way to use this." He called the chairman himself to make a show of apologizing for his aide's outburst and to reassure him that she would not call the press "because we both know what would happen if this got out. . . ." Nervous about the implications, the chairman not only passed the bill out of his committee and over to the House floor, but even spoke eloquently for its passage. Despite substantial opposition, the bill passed, because, Dianne says, "the chairman had blown it with us, and Elliott knew how to use it. That's the thing about Elliott that I loved. He's not the flashiest, he's not the most outspoken, he doesn't like to get up and debate. But he passes the most legislation—just steadily. The day my bill passed, I was crying because it showed that laws had the power to effect substantive change. I got addicted to that."

Dianne marked the end of graduate school by adopting her mother's maiden name and becoming Dianne Hardy-Garcia. Her siblings had already done this, and brother Kenny pointed out that her hyphenated name made a political statement: "They never think of a Latino as gay." But more than that, Dianne wanted to acknowledge the cultural dual citizenship that was the source of her identity. Armed with her new name and a new Master of Science degree in social work, she took stock of events swirling around her. "I was watching the gay issues being played out and the social issues and I thought, 'Maybe I could combine my skills.'" To that end, she became cochair of the Austin Lesbian/Gay Political Caucus. There she used her acquired legislative skills to spearhead the effort that established Domestic Partnership benefits for city of Austin employees.

As she and Mary Anne headed into 1993, the timetable for returning to New York was looming. Yet, much to her chagrin, Hardy-Garcia found herself questioning the return. State activists continually pointed out to her that there were hundreds like her in New York City—and only one of her in Texas. "Why go there," they said, "when we need you so badly here?" Mary Anne gently made it clear that she was not keen on going back to New York—she wanted eventually to open her own practice in Austin. Dianne was beginning to agree that perhaps the most effective work she could do was in her home state.

Glen Maxey encouraged her to apply for the position of executive director of the Lesbian/Gay Rights Lobby of Texas (LGRL), an organization that lobbied the Texas legislature and state governmental agencies to eliminate social, legal, and economic discrimination based on sexual orientation. "She had that fire in the belly about making change and being dogged about it," Maxey, a former director of LGRL himself, says. "She was intent on achieving the goals she set out after."

An initial stumbling block was the fear of further alienating her parents. "Accepting the job meant not only was I 'out' to them," Dianne recalls, "but I was 'out' to *everyone*." However, she knew that the position presented the chance of making a substantial difference in the lives of gays and lesbians all over the state. After much soul-searching, she abandoned her plan of returning to New York City and, when it was offered, accepted the job at LGRL.

Founded in 1978, the Lesbian/Gay Rights Lobby was a statewide organization by 1993, with a twenty-seven-member board of directors representing the major cities of Texas. Sustained by member donations, it has offices in a converted yellow stucco house on the corner of Seventh and Nueces streets in the shadow of the Austin capitol. Inside, the atmosphere is decidedly low-key, even funky. "People think it's some kind of high-rise, fancy-ass office with leather chairs and twenty-line phones," says Messina. "Well, they've got another think coming." But the shabby setting belies the organization's effectiveness. "The amount of work that comes out of there is enormous," she adds.

However, from the very first week of Hardy-Garcia's tenure, something besides lobbying efforts grabbed her attention, focus, and breath—and the next seven years of her life: murder.

In organizing the office, Dianne came across a bulging folder on anti-gay hate crimes in Texas, which she was stunned to see had increased a full 70 percent between 1992 and 1993—a single year. The stories in the folder—harrowing tales of men who were brutally attacked solely because they were homosexual—had striking commonalities: Virtually all of the perpetrators were teenage boys; many lured their marks with the promise of sex; some of them described getting high on the fear of their prey; and nearly every attack was an act of savagery, leaving its victim riddled with bullets, perforated with stab wounds, or beaten beyond recognition. Picking up on conventional street wisdom that gay men were rich, too nelly to fight, and too ashamed to report attacks to the police, the youthful assailants realized that they had found the perfect victims. What began as a robbery would escalate into beatings and often—too often—it would balloon into murder. "The dehumanization that has been done—by preachers and law enforcement officials turning the other cheek to it, or by lawmakers not speaking—all comes into play," Hardy-Garcia says. "And that rage comes out and it's like a dog-pack mentality."

What stunned Hardy-Garcia almost as much as the brutality of the crimes was the "recreational" view many murderers took of gay-bashing. In 1991, Paul Broussard, a young Houston banker, had been approached by two cars full of teenagers who said they were looking for a gay bar. When Broussard directed them toward Heaven, a popular night spot, all ten young thugs jumped from the cars, wielding pipes and nail-studded boards, and beat Broussard to death right on a city side street. When apprehended, the teens told the police they were just out to "beat up some queers." As Broussard's mother, Nancy, said bitterly, "They thought it was a sport. Like bowling."

Hardy-Garcia was also appalled by the fact that, to many, a proposition from a homosexual was grounds for homicide. A popular Midland/Odessa hairdresser, Tommy Musick, was shot four times in the back of the head by an eighteen-year-old who explained that he had no choice but to kill him because Musick had made a pass at him. One Texas judge, Jack Hampton, had no compunction about telling the *Dallas Times Herald* why he had sentenced Richard Lee Bednarski to thirty years instead of life for murdering two men: "The victims were homosexuals who were out in a homosexual area picking up teenage boys. Had they not been out there trying to spread AIDS around, they'd still be alive today. . . . I don't care much for queers cruising the streets picking up teenage boys. I've got a teenage boy." He went on to say that he "put prostitutes and gays at about the same level. I'd be hard put to give somebody life for killing a prostitute."

Hardy-Garcia's shock turned to fury. "Why isn't anyone screaming about this?" she asked her staff and friends in the homosexual community. "Why aren't we *all* screaming about this?"

Then, before she was even able to make it through all the material, Dianne got a call from Tyler, Texas, an isolated city southeast of Dallas, near the Louisiana border. There, Donald Aldrich, a twenty-nine-year-old petty thief just recently released from prison, had made a practice of calling his girlfriend from a public phone in Bergfeld Park. He struck up an acquaintance with Henry Dunn, Jr., nineteen, and David McMillan, seventeen. Sharing their resentment of the cars and clothes and apparent affluence of the gay men they saw in the park, he joined them on several "fag-bashing" sprees. Then Dunn and McMillan targeted a darkly handsome medical records clerk, Nicholas West, twenty-three, because of his sleek, late-model red Mazda truck, trying repeatedly to lure him deep enough into the park to rob him. One night, just after Thanksgiving of 1993, West happened to stop the coveted truck near Aldrich's phone booth, and the three men, armed with a .410 shotgun and a .357 Magnum, seized the opportunity to kidnap him. They drove him to a desolate stretch outside of town, where Aldrich ransacked the Mazda and the three stripped West of his wallet, jewelry, pants, and shoes. Finding a ten-dollar bill concealed in his shoe, Aldrich beat him in the face with the .357. To the boys' delight, they saw that West had become so terrified that he had soiled his underwear. "I thought it was hilarious," Aldrich later told investigative reporter H. G. Bissinger, who was preparing an article for *Vanity Fair.* "When you scare a man so bad that he literally shits on himself, that man is *scared.*" He described the sensation as "an adrenaline high. I enjoyed it. I really did."

Buoyed by West's fear, they walked him up a long corridor of scrubby pines to a red clay outcropping called The Pits, where Dunn challenged him to a fistfight. He threw punch after punch into West's abdomen, chest, and face. When his fists got too raw, Dunn resorted to kicking. But Nicholas West would not fight back. Enraged, Dunn grabbed Aldrich's pistol and shot West in the stomach. Then the three assailants took turns shooting him in the arms and hands and fired four bullets in a straight line up his back, as if stitching a seam. But Nicholas West was still not dead. Finally, weary of the game, Dunn took the shotgun and fired the last shot, the ninth one, point-blank at the base of his skull. When West's riddled remains were discovered nearly a month later, the local coroner would describe the body as a "pincushion."

After hearing the grisly account over the telephone, an enraged Hardy-Garcia realized she had to do something. She decided to use the resources of her lobbying office to make certain that people would know about Nicholas West and the horrible, senseless way in which he died. She got into her car and drove north to Tyler.

Hardy-Garcia expected the local police to resist labeling the murder a hate crime. "Sometimes the police are bigoted," she explains. "Sometimes it's because they don't have any training in hate crimes, and sometimes it's because they're trying to 'protect' the gay people and their families because this is 'so embarrassing.' " However, the Tyler police not only recognized the case as a bias crime but also had the perpetrators in custody. Donald Aldrich, it turned out, had tried to win the sympathy of the detectives in the Smith County jailhouse by claiming that West had propositioned him and, vividly recounting the murder, boasted that there was now one less pervert in Tyler, Texas. As further justification, he told them that one of his friends had a daughter who had been "raped by some homosexuals." He had developed this strategy, Aldrich was to explain to H. G. Bissinger, because "I thought it might help me get a lesser sentence or a lesser charge." Bissinger quoted Jason Waller, one of the detectives, who said of Aldrich, "He thinks he's a good guy. He's not perceiving he's doing anything wrong, because this was a fag. This is not a store owner or a preacher. This is a fag."

Since the police seemed to be on top of the case, Hardy-Garcia decided that the best thing she could do was to get the word out—to raise a tide of public outrage high enough to show the Aldriches and Dunns and McMillans of America that the country would not tolerate their virulent strain of hatred. She telephoned a reporter at the *Austin American-Statesman* with whom she was friendly, and asked her to write a detailed story on the murder. She then put her staff to work firing off press releases and, to make sure the story got the widest possible coverage, decided to give the media a news peg—an antiviolence rally. Thinking it was appropriate and would have a powerful impact to hold the event in Bergfeld Park, Dianne went down to the park offices to register for a permit. The hapless clerk filling out the form had difficulty writing out the word "lesbian." "That's when I *really* knew where I was," she says. "They were, like, 'Lesbene? Ma'am, how do y'all spell that?'" Getting local people to attend the rally would be difficult, she knew, for the gay population in Tyler lived deep in the closet and, terrified by the murder, had retreated even further into hiding. So, with the help of co-organizer Wesley Beard, founder of the East Texas Gay and Lesbian Alliance, she started pulling in favors from all over the state. "I called everybody," she says. "I got hold of every activist I could, saying, 'These people have nothing and they're scared to death. If you guys don't show, we're going to be standing out there by ourselves.'" Commitments to attend soon streamed in.

She had a much more difficult time attracting the support of area straight politicians. "I called every one in East Texas," she says. "Not one would come." At a loss, she turned to Democratic state senator Rodney Ellis, a black legislator from Houston who not only had always been a friend to the community, but was also considering sponsoring stronger hate-crimes legislation. "She said, 'I recognize that there's really no political upside for you to do this,'" Ellis recalls. "'And I also recognize that it's a hell of an inconvenience to go to Tyler, Texas, of all places. . . .' But she was persuasive because she was sincere. And having watched her over the years, I knew it was important to her." Nonetheless, Ellis gave Dianne only a tentative yes, for he was hesitant to appear at such an inflammatory event in Tyler, which was renowned as redneck country. In fact, a black man had been killed there two years earlier in a race-related hate crime. His anxiety was warranted, it turned out, for when Ellis informed the state police of his possible plans, they insisted that he travel with an escort of no fewer than six uniformed officers.

Desperate to ensure his attendance, Dianne asked Ellis's aide in confidence, "What do I have to do to make sure the senator gets there?" The aide shrugged and said, "I don't know. Maybe get him on national TV." Hardy-Garcia was at a loss as to how to accomplish such a feat, when, out of the blue, the booking agent from *Larry King Live* on CNN called. Having caught articles in *The New York Times* and *USA Today,* as well as Dianne herself on a local TV talk show displaying Nicholas West's photograph, the booker wanted Hardy-Garcia to appear on a program King was planning about hate crimes. "Sometimes God intervenes for you," Dianne says with a grin. "A lot of times, Providence just follows me around." Sacrificing a personal stint for the cause, she offered him Rodney Ellis, who ended up appearing on the show and making an eloquent appeal for hate-crimes legislation to Larry King's vast audience.

At two P.M. on Saturday, January 8, the "Stop the Hate" rally began in a chilly, windswept corner of Bergfeld Park and drew more than a thousand protesters. Among them were representatives Glen Maxey and Garnet Coleman (D), several members of the Tyler City Council, and Dr. Mel White, then dean of the Metropolitan Community Church's Cathedral of Hope in Dallas, the largest gay church in the world. Reverend David Galloway, pastor of Tyler's Christ Episcopal Church, delivered an impassioned speech: "I say it again to anyone who claims a Judeo-Christian background—if you say you love God and hate your brother, you are a liar. Tyler is a diverse community reflective of our wider American society, and we must at the very least learn how to tolerate one another. At best, we can come to understand each other." Reverend White led the crowd in an emotional prayer urging, "Let love triumph and let hate die." But it was Rodney Ellis who moved the crowd to tears. In a ringingly clear voice, he spoke about the heartbreaking nature of hate crimes, and how they affect everyone—black, gay, straight, male, and female. Surrounded by his half-dozen state trooper escorts, he pointed out the sad fact that a black man such as himself could still have fears about traveling to a place like Tyler, Texas. He argued that effective hate-crimes measures could and should change that. "Senator Ellis has a really great presence," Dianne says. "He was just excellent. Because of him, we got national coverage and a lot of attention."

Hardy-Garcia knew she had to affect Ellis beyond the rally, for he was the hope for hate-crimes legislation in the Texas Senate. "I needed for him to feel the depth of the gay and lesbian pain around the issue," Dianne says, "because I needed him to fight for us." She knew that the coalition between blacks and gays had to be solid in Texas; they were arguably the two groups most discriminated against in America. "When I got there," Ellis says, "it made me really embarrassed that I had had any second thoughts about going—I really didn't want to go because of the inconvenience; I was doing it for Dianne—but it was one of the most moving experiences of my life. There were local officials, the Right Wing, the Left Wing, the Religious Left, the Religious Right, people who were both gay and straight. Dianne did an excellent job of gathering people across the political spectrum; she pulled together a broad-based coalition by persuading people it was the right thing to do. The park was packed. Just packed."

The day after the rally, Dianne learned that a verdict had finally been reached in the case of the murdered Midland/Odessa hairdresser, Tommy Musick, whose case she had found in the hate-crimes file when she came to LGRL. Ramsey Blake Harrell had been convicted of the crime, but was sentenced to a mere twelve years in prison and could be eligible for release in as little as three. Buying the so-called "gay panic defense," the jury explained that they had not sought a stiffer sentence because the evidence suggested that Musick had made a sexual advance to Harrell. Appalled, Hardy-Garcia traveled west to Midland/Odessa to help organize another protest rally, only to find that, as in Tyler, the gay population was too fearful to risk exposure—and worse, that intolerance was exacerbated by the poverty of the erstwhile oil town. In Odessa, there were two bars where gays were tolerated, The Mining Company and Nite Spot, but because Midland is dry, the only place homosexuals could assemble there was a makeshift, windowless church fashioned from an old gas station. A small group met with Hardy-Garcia under the cover of night, and sat in the unventilated room, furiously smoking Marlboro Reds and nervously shifting in their seats. Tommy's devastated lover, Jerry, sat in the rear. Hardy-Garcia proposed a rally in Midland that would get reporters engaged, much like the one in Tyler had, but with the mention of national exposure, the group balked. They were so fearful that some even asked Dianne if they could come to the rally with paper bags over their heads. Realizing she wasn't going to get much of an attendance out of the locals, Hardy-Garcia once again put out the call to her activist friends across the state.

This time, however, the response was less than eager. Her lesbian activist friends felt that they were already devoting too much energy to such "male issues," and the gay men's organizations, with their limited resources already overtaxed by the fights against AIDS and discrimination, did not feel able to marshal a major demonstration every time a homosexual was murdered. They simply didn't see hate crimes as a priority issue. Hardy-Garcia was dumbfounded.

Help came from an unlikely source—Tommy Musick's straight female clientele, who were angered not only by their hairdresser's death, but by the jury's acceptance of the killer's excuse. As one of the women said to Dianne, "Honey, if women went around killing every man who'd ever made an unwanted pass at them, there wouldn't be any men left in West Texas!" The women conducted a telephone campaign and on the day of the rally turned out in force, alongside the gays and lesbians Dianne had managed to pull in from nearby Lubbock, Amarillo, and El Paso, and a smattering of brave Midland/Odessa homosexuals. Hardy-Garcia learned just how brave these local attendees were when Musick's lover, Jerry, insisted on lodging her entourage, including Mary Anne, in his trailer home—with caveats: "At night, you don't want to stand in front of the windows. Bend down or turn the light out or pull the shade, because someone could take a shot. And don't answer the phone because it could be a crank call. Close all the shutters and lock the door." Dianne's friends were apoplectic. "We didn't get much sleep," she admits. "We heard every little noise."

That night, every single car in the parking lot of the Nite Spot gay bar in Odessa had its tires slashed. Fortunately, the rally itself came off peacefully and effectively, generating plenty of press coverage. "Midland/Odessa is as conservative as Texas can get," Representative Glen Maxey says, "and Dianne took this obscure crime that was pretty much thrown away in the general public's mind—nobody paid attention to it—and developed it into a major news story. It's just remarkable the kind of things she has done, again and again, in that context. Making it very visible, making people understand, bringing varied people to the table."

Although Hardy-Garcia was coming to be recognized as an authority on hate crimes in Texas, her principal job at LGRL was to lobby the state legislature for gay-rights initiatives, such as barring mandatory HIV testing and other anti-gay ballot measures, creating AIDS funding, and appointing openly gay and lesbian people to state commissions. Recognizing her potential, two of the most influential lobbyists in Austin, Bettie Naylor and Nancy Molleda, mentored her, despite the fact that, as Molleda says, "Lobbying is pretty scary, and also it's a very secret and closed profession. People don't help you—it's dog eat dog." Molleda, openly gay and known not only for her designer wardrobe and vast resources of self-confidence but also for her aggressive, take-no-prisoners battles on behalf of her corporate clients, showed Dianne how to collar legislators. "When she first got hired by the LGRL, she was like a deer caught in headlights," Molleda says with a laugh. "I showed her how to walk in there like she had every right to be there. *More* than a right. I taught her to look for what the legislator responds to"—to get her way, whether by being straightforward or by acting like "a sweet l'il ol' girl from West Texas." Public interest lobbyist Naylor, known for her gentle but insistent cajoling, helped Hardy-Garcia with planning and strategizing, warning her to be guarded in her dealings with the media. "I stay much further ahead in the game if I don't talk to the press," she maintains. Dianne was very grateful. "They are such fabulous women," she says. "I learned so much from them." Her mentors, in turn, are effusive in praising her. "She has a wonderful aura and presence," Molleda says. "She's not pushy, she's steady. And stable. She listens to what they have to say, she's respectful of their right to believe whatever damn stupid thing they believe." Naylor agrees. "She's a grand grassroots organizer, she's tireless, she's bright and has a lot of vision. She has proved her mettle to me over and over and over. She is the best thing that's ever happened to the gay community of Texas."

Hardy-Garcia would be all the more appreciative of their expert tutelage when she mounted a lobbying effort for the issue that had become her passion—strong hate-crimes legislation that recognized bias on the basis of sexual orientation. The battle for such laws in Texas had begun in 1991, when Glen Maxey and others finally managed to compel the Department of Public Safety to maintain statistics on hate crimes. Yet to get the measure through, they had to water down its language so much that even the words "hate crime" did not appear. "We had to say 'any kind of crime reported under federal law,' " Maxey explains. Then, near the end of 1993, armed with two years' worth of collected data, they attempted to push through an actual statute punishing crimes committed because of a victim's race, religion, disability, gender, ethnicity, or sexual orientation. Unfortunately, conservatives in the legislature again demanded that the bill avoid mention of any specific group and refer only to people "historically discriminated" against. Later, the U.S. Supreme Court ruled that such laws had to be specific to be enforceable, leaving prosecutors in Texas hesitant to invoke the hate-crime statute for fear of being overturned on appeal. According to *The Dallas Morning News*, prosecutors' estimates indicated that less than one half of 1 percent of the hate crimes documented by police were actually tried using the hate-crime statute. "From the beginning," Maxey says, "it was clear that we could pass better legislation if sexual orientation were dropped. So Dianne and I and others had to forge a coalition refusing to enact any hate-crimes bill in Texas unless all people are protected."

It was a tough position to maintain, for many legislators and law enforcement officials had come to believe that Texas would be better off with an enforceable hate-crimes bill, even if explicit protection of gays and lesbians had to be added later. Hardy-Garcia, however, knew she couldn't allow that to happen. Recognizing that there would always be fierce opposition to incorporating the sexual-orientation language—that, in fact, it might prove impossible to ever add it—she decided that she had to make an unarguable case for its inclusion by presenting the legislators with all the data she could accrue on bias murders of homosexuals. "She systematically, through anecdotal kinds of things, through section-B-in-the-newspaper accounts, searched out the examples of the cases, met with communities, and brought visibility to what basically Texas thought was 'just another' murder that occurred," Maxey says. "Nobody, until Dianne, ever picked up on the fact that the murders were committed because of sexual orientation."

Sadly, she would find a frightening number of Texas anti-gay hate crimes to document. There were two throat-slitting cases, one in the Dallas suburb of Irving and the other in San Antonio. Another San Antonio man was thrown over a bridge to his death on the rocks below by a sixteen-year-old who justified his actions by claiming that he had been propositioned. In White Oak, a man was shot to death by a quartet of teenage boys who told authorities they had been "queer hunting." In Houston, four teenagers forced a gay man to withdraw four hundred dollars from an ATM and then executed him with a gun blast to the back of the head. The ringleader, a nineteen-year-old football scholarship recipient, bragged that he had felt "like a judge." Down in Harlingen, near the bottom tip of the state, no fewer than four gay men had been brutally killed.

Not only were the murders constant, they were beginning to *escalate*.

Zigzagging her way across the state in her battered Chrysler LeBaron to investigate reported hate crimes, Hardy-Garcia kept hitting the same brick wall of noncooperation thrown up by terrified small-town gay communities that she had encountered in Midland/Odessa. In one especially heartrending case in El Paso, a good-sized city, even the victim's family was too intimidated to fight back. His siblings called Dianne for help because, given the fact that their brother—who had been strangled and bludgeoned, with "faggot" written in his blood on the wall above his body—was not only gay but Hispanic, they believed that the police would not take the case seriously. Indeed, Dianne recalls, by the time she arrived, the police had warned them: "Look, we don't want to deal with this as a hate crime, because, in this area, we don't like gays. If this was some kind of gay issue, then your brother's murderer will get a lighter sentence. So lay off on all the gay stuff." The confused family was leaning toward suppressing the truth, as the police had advised. "They wrestled with it a lot," Dianne recalls. "They felt horrible that he had never told any of them he was gay; they felt like they had not been good siblings to him. At the same time, they wanted to protect their mother. They had all this guilt based around maybe it was their fault, that their brother shouldn't have been so isolated. It was horrible." Finally they decided not to go public with the murder, and Hardy-Garcia respected their wishes.

The attitude of the El Paso police was all too common. On her travels, Dianne saw firsthand a bullet taped to a gay man's door with an accompanying note that said, "Die, faggot, die. A bullet like this will one day kill you." The local police dismissed the death threat with the comment: "Well, kids will be kids." She remembers the phone call she got from a terrified, effeminate-sounding man in Liberty, Texas—"I thought that was pretty ironic, 'Liberty,' " she says—whose trailer had been shot up. Hardy-Garcia calmed the man, and then, in her official capacity, called to demand action from the local police. "Hell, ma'am," the sheriff told her, "they're just foolin' around. It wasn't nothin' but a damn pellet gun." Dianne was aghast. "There is a huge, gaping *hole* in his house," she said firmly. "Obviously it could have hurt him!" She tried to convince the sheriff that harassment was often just the opening salvo in a fight that could turn deadly. "When the murders happen, it's over," she explains. "We know that hate-crime murderers have prior hate-crime offenses, for the most part. And perhaps if we had hate crimes taken seriously at the misdemeanor phase—the vandalism, the assault phase—if we could intervene there, we could prevent the murders."

She was now coming to appreciate how unusually enlightened the small-town Tyler police had been in their approach to the murder of Nicholas West. Among Texas's big-city police departments, Houston was becoming the most knowledgeable and sensitive about hate crimes. As police sergeant Lawrence Newcomb, who had investigated the Paul Broussard murder in 1991, told *The Dallas Morning News,* the department hadn't recognized the extent of anti-gay violence until undercover officers posed as gay couples in the Montrose neighborhood where Broussard was killed. There, just like the gay residents, the policemen were pelted with beer cans, Maced, punched, and struck with baseball bats. Fifteen teenagers were arrested in the sting—and an entire police squad got a lesson on the wages of prejudice. "You don't know there's a problem," Newcomb said, "till you become a part of it."

As awareness of the prevalence of hate crimes grew, many gay and lesbian leaders pointed to the radical right's Christian Coalition, charging that its demonization of homosexuals granted bashers license to commit their acts of violence. Indeed, Gary Bauer, Family Research Council leader and would-be Republican presidential candidate, speaks of his intent to ". . . wage the war against the homosexual agenda." Pat Robertson of the Christian Broadcast Network stated, "The acceptance of homosexuality is the last step in the decline of Gentile civilization." From a decidedly different pulpit, gay minister Mel White says, "They say we molest, we recruit, we abuse . . . we're not fit to be in the military. All this rhetoric goes on and on, and they wonder why kids are beating the shit out of us." To address the issue head-on, in October of 1999, White would call a summit meeting with his old estranged employer, the Reverend Jerry Falwell, to modify some of the vitriol. Falwell acquiesced to his former speechwriter's plea to soften his diatribes, but he would not change his position that homosexuality was sinful and an abomination before the eyes of the Lord.

In August of 1994, Hardy-Garcia traveled back to East Texas for Donald Aldrich's trial for the murder of Nicholas West nearly a year before. Although Henry Dunn and David McMillan had also been charged, Aldrich was the first to go to trial. Dianne, sitting with co-activist Wesley Beard, stayed for the entire week of the judicial proceeding; she was attempting to experience a sense of closure because Nicholas West had been the first victim for her in this long, gruesome journey.

Facing the jury, prosecutor David Dobbs said, "This is about as senseless a killing as you're going to find. Nicholas West, who is dead and gone, was selected as a victim by Mr. Aldrich and his buddies because he was a homosexual." Describing Aldrich as "cold and remorseless," Dobbs said the key issue in the case was whether "it is okay to kill somebody just because they are different from you." Walking up and down the length of the jury box, he told them that when Aldrich shot West, "he was betting on you all saying it was okay. He was betting on twelve people saying to themselves, 'Because the victim was a homosexual, this crime is just not as serious.' " The State then presented four days of testimony, including a portion of Aldrich's confession to the Tyler police.

Given his turn, defense attorney Bill Wright said, "I'm not going to come up here and tell you Donald Aldrich is an angel—that's just not true." However, he explained, Aldrich just meant to rob West, not kill him. He said his client panicked and fired two shots after Henry Dunn opened fire on the victim. The defense called no witnesses.

After the closing arguments, it took the jury of seven men and five women only thirty-one minutes of deliberation to come back with a guilty sentence. When the verdict was read, Wesley Beard burst into audible sobs. Dianne said at the time, "As sad as this whole situation has been, it seems as if justice has been done. What is also important about this case is that people find out that this murder happened and why it happened. As long as some otherwise legitimate people continue to dehumanize gays and lesbians, they are going to be made targets of such crimes."

That Friday, Aldrich was sentenced to death. McMillan and Dunn would eventually follow him on death row.

Brutal murders of homosexuals were occurring like clockwork in Texas, nearly once a month. Yet, even though the constant travel and her daily diet of horror and heartbreak began to take their toll, Dianne refused to let up. She suffered through bouts of insomnia and two instances of walking pneumonia to persist in her relentless drive to build support for an inclusive hate-crimes law. The LGRL offices went into a compressed timetable dubbed "Crunch Time." In addition to the daily tasks of opening, answering, and filing away half a tub of mail, depositing any checks that came in, staffing the phones, and dealing with everything from answering legal questions to acting as an emotional outreach center, they called in volunteers to do mailings and work the telemarketing banks. Mary Anne Messina took some time away from her practice to organize the volunteers, a particular forte of hers. "I'm a pretty good motivator," she says. "I figure out why they're there and then use them as fast as I can." A massive mailing campaign was mounted to urge voters to pressure their politicians, while legislators were plied directly with accounts of the ever-increasing gay-bias murders. In January of 1995, Dianne drew national attention to the issue of anti-gay violence when she appeared on the ABC News program *Prime Time Live,* which devoted an entire segment to the hate crimes in Texas, and when she shared her findings with H. G. Bissinger, who used them for an article for the February 1995 issue of *Vanity Fair* magazine.

Hardy-Garcia was also drawing attention to herself, welcome and unwelcome. "People started coming up to her and saying, 'I've been following your career. . . .' " Mary Anne says. "And Dianne would turn to me and joke, '*What* career? Do I have a career?' " But they also had to contend with threatening phone calls from the unhinged, and unmarked envelopes with used condoms inside. "It goes from one end of the pendulum to the other," Messina says with a sigh. "People who respect and admire her, and those who are kind of fanatical and a little strange." When she and Dianne were interviewed and photographed for a "Coming Out Day" profile for the *Austin American-Statesman,* Mary Anne asked that their address be cropped out of a shot taken of them holding their cat, Romeo, on their front porch. "This is Texas, this is the Bible Belt," she says. "You never know." Yet Dianne and Mary Anne would not adjust their lives for the lunatic fringe. They would continue to be openly together; they would devote their energies to LGRL.

One day, to dispel the oppressive air of exhaustion and anxiety in the LGRL offices, Dianne and Mary Anne went out and bought Day-Glo paints and rollered the walls into a kaleidoscope of vibrant colors. When Andy Delony, a fresh-faced, nineteen-year-old University of Texas student first walked in as a volunteer, he noted the gaudy walls and said to himself, "Oh, my God, do I really want to work here?" But he stayed on, eventually moving up to the position of events coordinator, and now sees the vivid colors as morale boosting. "Especially in the winter," Andy says. "It can get pretty dark and depressing—not much light comes in. The bright colors really help keep our spirits up."

Delony claims that Hardy-Garcia's flexible approach with her employees is a big reason that the office runs so smoothly. "If there's ever a problem, you can always talk to her about it," he says. "No one's afraid to go up to Dianne." Her leadership has inspired loyalty that rarely occurs in the corporate world. Other than their annual fund-raiser, the Texas State Pride Festival, all the money to run the office comes from member support. And sometimes the funds run dangerously low. "There've been a few times that I've delayed my paycheck for a few days," Delony says. "There are other times where I won't fill out a time sheet for a few days, to give more leeway." Hardy-Garcia has skipped taking paychecks herself every so often, hoping and trusting that she will get paid back in the future.

With her professional life so full and her life with Mary Anne so fulfilling, the only cog out of place, as far as Dianne was concerned, was her strained relationship with her parents. She was, however, at a loss as to how to bridge the chasm. Then, the February 1995 issue of *Vanity Fair* featuring the hate-crimes article hit the stands. Although they knew it was coming out, Ken and Jane Hardy had not read the piece. Son Kenny, the never-confrontational family mediator, uncharacteristically took his parents to task for their reticence. "Look at the phenomenal things this woman is doing!" he shouted. "If it wasn't about being a lesbian, any parent would be glowing. This is a national magazine and you haven't even *read* the fucking article! You should be ashamed of yourselves!" The Hardys were shocked at the outburst, and Kristina angrily rebuked her brother for scolding their parents—dividing the family into hostile camps.

When Ken and Jane finally did read the twelve-page article, entitled "The Killing Trail," they came away with renewed admiration for their eldest daughter. Eloquently describing many of the murders and the tragic aftermath the victims' families faced, as well as indicting Texas for its indifference to gay rights and a strengthened hate-crimes bill, the extensive account concludes by saying:

> It has been a wrenching time for Dianne Hardy-Garcia, because each of the killings that she has looked at brings layers upon layers of sorrow that can never be healed. . . . She has spent more than a year on the killing trail across Texas. She knows the uncomprehending horror of it and the basic indifference to it. She knows she must have a rest from it, get away from it, and then comes a plea in an unmarked envelope as tiny and poignant as the whisper of a frightened child. . . .

The *Vanity Fair* piece marked a thaw in Dianne's relationship with her parents, and it now has a permanent place of honor on the Hardy living-room coffee table. "Actually we're kind of glad we didn't know the extent of what she was doing around the state," Ken Hardy says. "We would have been so worried about her." Kristina, too, was impressed by her sister's journey: "I thought, 'Wow—she really has done some amazing things.' " Kenny says of his oldest sister, "Words cannot describe how proud I am of her." Inspired by her, he made a point of phoning state representatives himself, urging their support in the hate-crimes battle. In April of that year, he walked beside Dianne in the Hate-Crimes March she had organized. Two years later, their parents would join them.

Although Dianne's publicity efforts cast an embarrassing spotlight on the vexed state of hetero-versus-homosexual relations in Texas, anti-gay political initiatives were proliferating. The Galveston County Republican Party passed a resolution espousing the quarantining of HIV-positive people; and the state Republican Party platform was revised to include the statement: "Homosexuality should not be presented as an acceptable alternative lifestyle in our public schools. No person should receive special legal entitlements or privileges based on sexual preference. We oppose marriages between persons of the same sex and homosexuals obtaining the right to adopt or obtaining child custody." Austin voters repealed domestic-partner insurance benefits for the partners of unmarried city employees—the policy that Dianne had been instrumental in implementing when she was with the Austin Lesbian/Gay Political Caucus. Even the student government at Austin State University canceled funding for the Gay and Lesbian Association on campus because its members are "sodomites" under Texas law.

It was against this daunting backdrop that the LGRL, armed with Dianne Hardy-Garcia's data, began to push for passage of a hate-crimes bill when the legislative session began in January of 1995.

Dianne knew that it was going to be a grueling fight—that legislators with progressive attitudes, such as senators Rodney Ellis and John Whitmire, and representatives Harryette Ehrhardt, Steve Woolens, Glen Maxey, Debra Danburg, Elliott Naishtat, and Senfronia Thompson, were in the minority. "No matter what television show we got on, no matter how much national news coverage, no matter how many times we rallied, the politicians would not act," Dianne says. "It just made me more and more enraged." Ehrhardt says, "It's very hard to press on in the state legislature when we have so much animosity and so much hatred," but she believed that Dianne was equal to the task.

LGRL board member Steve Atkinson agrees that Hardy-Garcia, having made the LGRL a force to be reckoned with, could mount a formidable challenge to the entrenched legislative conservatives. "Dianne really established a reputation for herself in Austin of being an effective, sensible lobbyist," he says. "And people view her that way—even people who are very much on the other side of the fence on our issues. She's not viewed as a crazy queer. She's viewed as a very sensible businesswoman who knows what she's doing."

The Christian Coalition cast the first stone against the hate-crimes measure by dubbing it the "Protect the Pedophiles" bill, but Dianne made a conscious decision to not lash back. "I think that we get to sounding just as intolerant," she holds, "when we become overly critical of religious beliefs." When attacked by the Religious Right, her tactic was to offer an olive branch. "We live in the world together and we've got to figure out how to get along," she would say to them. "And surely you've got to agree with me that violence shouldn't settle our differences. We can't have hate crimes terrorizing people because we're different." Concentrating on the lawmakers, she worked to apply external pressure by assigning a lobby captain for each of the 181 legislators; these captains would rally the politicos' constituents to press for passage of the bill. When the debate began, she planned to create internal pressure as well—to touch the legislators' hearts and minds by showing them concretely the evil that hate crimes had wrought, through the testimonies of the victims' families. Persuading those families to testify would not prove easy; most, she learned, were loath to relive the horror. Many parents who had been on good terms with their murdered offspring blamed themselves, in the mistaken belief that rejection might have turned their sons away from homosexuality and kept them alive. Parents who had censured their sons felt equally guilty for having abandoned them. "There was no way to win for them," Dianne says. "They were devastated."

In the end, however, she managed to enlist a good number of families to present their heartrending stories to the state legislature, beginning with the senate. The torrent of pain these tales unleashed left many of the testifiers crying—and moved the legislators listening to tears as well. Senators who had already decided to vote against the bill were so shamed by the families' suffering that they had to leave the chambers. "They couldn't sit there," Dianne recalls. "They couldn't stand it. It was so emotional."

Still, it didn't seem likely that the bill would pass. In the course of the tumultuous week, Bettie Naylor recalls, "A couple of senators had yelled at Dianne and one conservative Republican, Drew Nixon, had really given her a hard time, doing all this dastardly stuff behind her back. She was very distressed. I said, 'Dianne, we've done everything we can possibly do. The only thing left is to pray for divine intervention.' " In a last-ditch effort to save the bill, Dianne made one last round of visits to the senators' offices, hoping to find some sympathetic ears.

Early the next morning, Naylor recalls, Hardy-Garcia came running up to her, breathless. "Bettie! Bettie! Bettie!" she cried excitedly. "We got divine intervention!" One of the senators she had visited late the night before, Democrat John Whitmire of Houston, Chair of the Criminal Justice Committee, had listened as Dianne morosely described her fear for the bill and her frustration with senators like Drew Nixon. Whitmire smiled devilishly and said, "You know what, Dianne? I am going to be able to give you a Christmas, birthday, wedding, and christening present combined," and pulled out a just-released police report. The moralistic Senator Nixon had just been arrested for alleged prostitute solicitation. Asked to resign, Nixon would refuse; but eventually pled guilty to the charges.

The first week of April, the hate-crimes bill, sponsored by Senator Rodney Ellis, resoundingly passed, 22–8, in the Senate.

The measure would be a much tougher sell in the House, Hardy-Garcia knew. Before it even got to the floor, the bill had to pass muster with the Criminal Jurisprudence Committee, a nine-member body that already had four votes committed to and four votes against the bill. The swing vote would be cast by Dallas Democrat Sam Hudson, who was notorious for his poor attendance record. "He had a historical thing of being here, but never coming to the floor," Glen Maxey says. " 'Where's Sam Hudson?' had been the battle cry for years." Maxey recalls telling Dianne, "If he's not there, we're screwed," and Dianne replying, "I'll have him there." Determined to win the critical vote, she appointed a volunteer to be Hudson's full-time shadow—sitting through lunch with him, watching television with him in his office, even following him to the door of the men's bathroom five times— since the committee could be called to the House floor at a moment's notice. Thanks to Hardy-Garcia's bird-dogging, Hudson made it to the floor and cast the yea vote that sent the bill to the House for general debate.

From the beginning, Dianne knew that Representative Warren

Chisum, familiar to her from her internship with Naishtat, was going to be their nemesis. The deceptively elfin-looking Chisum was on record as being opposed to any legislation that would benefit homosexuals by giving them what the right wing referred to as "special rights." In the *Vanity Fair* article "The Killing Trail," he was quoted as saying, "I don't agree with their lifestyle. . . . Homosexuality is demeaning to the natural nature of man. I mean, animals don't do that."

Attempting to put her personal reservations about Chisum aside, Hardy-Garcia bearded the lion in his den, eloquently pleading for the hate-crimes bill, and attempting to rouse his sympathy by recounting the barrage of murders of gay men. "I was a lobbyist, and I can tell you it would be a cold day in hell that I would want to talk to Warren Chisum," says Glen Maxey. "But Dianne's method of operation was to talk to Warren Chisum *every day.* You can neutralize people by making sure they understand the issue. I don't think Dianne thought up front that this would be a strategy to soften Warren Chisum; it's just that Dianne doesn't think that anybody in the legislature is a lost cause. I would look at her and just shake my head." Indeed, the representative from Pampa was polite but unmoved. He informed her that not only would he not vote for the measure, but that he would vigorously lead the forces against its passage.

Debate on the bill, carried in the House by Democrat Scott Hochberg, began in late April. As in the Senate, grieving parents and siblings rose to testify, most choking back tears as they described in horrifying detail the suffering their murdered loved ones had endured. Again, as in the Senate, many legislators openly wept. Seeing the effect, Glen Maxey, who had been polling the legislators, allowed himself a moment of optimism. Estimating that they could count on eighty votes in favor of the bill—ten above Dianne's tally of seventy—he told her, "We're going to win." Dianne replied, "Glen, you're sweeter than I am. You need to deduct ten for liars from your list. And I need to deduct five for liars from mine. Somewhere in between is the truth. That means I've got sixty-five and you've got seventy. We've got sixty-eight votes."

On the day that the bill was put to the vote, the Religious Right turned out in force. The Eagle Forum, the Christian Coalition, and the conservative wing of the Republican party stationed dozens of supporters at the House doors to collar legislators who entered and threaten them with political revenge should they endorse the bill. Undaunted, Dianne stood right next to them, greeting each legislator by name and personally encouraging each to follow his or her conscience and do what they knew to be the right thing.

The final tally was 68–70, exactly what she had predicted. The bill went down to defeat. "It was so hard," she recalls bitterly. "It was in front of all of the families. It was like their kids didn't matter. It was the worst kind of slap; it was just utterly cruel." Dismayed and furious, Hardy-Garcia approached a conservative legislator from East Texas who was rumored to have a lesbian daughter. The LGRL had targeted him early to plead for his vote, but nervous about his constituency, he waffled and on the day of the vote just bolted. Now Dianne confronted him, saying, "I cannot believe you weren't there!" Unable to look her in the eye, all he could do was stammer, "Dianne . . . I'm sorry. . . ." Then she approached a Republican who was for the bill but felt he couldn't vote—he had proposed a compromise with her, pledging that he would "walk" instead of voting nay. But at the last minute, he opted to stay and vote against the bill. "What happened?" she demanded. "I'm deeply ashamed of myself," he replied. "But there's too much pressure." The Religious Right, sensing that he was on the fence, had been calling him every day. Tears welling up in his eyes, he said, "I know, I know I'm wrong." And he walked off. "Those are the ones that get you," Hardy-Garcia says. "The ones who *know* it's wrong." Had the legislators done what they had promised, the stronger, more specific hate-crimes initiative would have passed and become law.

To have come so breathtakingly close and yet not win was shattering. Glen Maxey was too distraught to comment to the waiting press, so it fell to Hardy-Garcia to put up a brave front and address the media. "I'm disappointed," she said evenly, "but this is more votes than we've ever gotten before. We're not going to give up. We're going to keep fighting. We will be back until this becomes law." Privately, she was comforted by Representative Senfronia Thompson, Chair of the Judicial Affairs Committee, a feisty black woman who occupied the seat once held by the late, great Barbara Jordan. "Listen, honey," the plain-spoken Thompson said, "don't let the motherfuckers get you down. We have made some giant strides. Not long ago a little brown gay thing like you wouldn't've been walking around these halls organizing left and right. We'll get that bill passed yet."

Numb and exhausted, and having gone through her third bout with pneumonia, Dianne knew she desperately needed a break. At the same time, Mary Anne, usually excellent at boundaries, found herself taking the burdens of her patients home with her. Coupled with her continued volunteer work for LGRL, she, too, needed a vacation. The couple decided to head to the Texas shore. Mary Anne issued an edict: While there, they would not, under any circumstances, work or even *talk* about work.

Not long after arriving, Dianne was sitting poolside, her eyes closed, when she heard a timid voice say, "You're Dianne Hardy-Garcia, aren't you?" She cocked open an eye to see a young man sitting near, his feet dangling in the cool, rippling water. She nodded, knowing what was coming next. "I've been watching your hate-crimes stuff and following what you've been doing," he said hesitantly. "I lived in Laredo, and there were three guys murdered there. I knew and I got the hell out. Did you know about those?" Hardy-Garcia sighed and said, "I heard. . . ." That, however, did not stop the man from telling her all about them in vivid detail as they sunned by the pool. There she was, in the middle of nowhere, hearing yet again how another person was murdered simply because he was gay.

It never ended.

It was relentless.

As 1999 began, a gay couple, Laaron Morris, twenty-eight, and Kevin Tryals, thirty, of Texas City were discovered on a rural road. They had been shot to death and their car had been set on fire. Their deaths marked the sixth year that Hardy-Garcia had been consumed by tragedy, spending much of that time on the road documenting the grisliest and most vicious of murders, comforting fearful and anguished families, and battling hostile or indifferent public officials. Yet thanks to her dedicated work, hate crimes against homosexuals had begun to jar the nation's conscience, and other activist groups had come to join the fight. With the Matthew Shepard murder galvanizing renewed talk of a national hate-crimes law—the Hate Crimes Protection Act (HCPA)—she was no longer the lone voice. "Maybe the growing shock and horror are a good sign," she says. "Maybe now people are saying, 'This is too much. This is it.' "

Every year, like clockwork, hate-crimes legislation had been introduced in the Texas legislature, and every year it passed in the Senate and failed in the House. The vote was close, the issues were debated more freely, but the state still had no effective hate-crimes legislation on the books. When the proposed bill—renamed the James Byrd, Jr., Hate Crimes Act after the Jasper, Texas, black man who had been dragged to his death in 1998 by white supremacists—resurfaced in 1999, Rodney Ellis, the sponsor again in the Senate, made certain that it would be debated first in the House. "He told me he couldn't bear to go through yet another year of fighting for the bill only to have it die in the House," Dianne says. Representative Senfronia Thompson, who was to carry the bill there, cornered Dianne and asked for her preliminary tally. Dianne told her that, due to some recent Republican converts, she had a personal count of 78 for and 72 against the legislation. "You know that's not good enough," Thompson countered, "if you take the liars into account." Dianne knew that was true. She also knew that Governor George W. Bush, who was preparing to run for President, had had meetings with all the Republicans in the House, urging them to stop the bill. Bush was opposed to the legislation, and many maintained he did not want to be in the unpopular position of having to veto it while under the glare of the national spotlight. Despite the statistics—2,700 Texans had been the victims of hate crimes in the past seven years, an average of one a day—and the fact that 72 percent of the state supported the legislation, the Republican governor would not budge from his stance. At a loss as to how next to proceed, Hardy-Garcia suggested to Thompson that the representative call Warren Chisum. Looking blankly at the lobbyist, Thompson said, "Are you nuts? I've done enough ass-kissing for you, girl . . ."

In fact, Hardy-Garcia had come to grudgingly respect her old nemesis, Chisum. Although they had fought each other vehemently the previous year over his failed bill that would have barred gays and lesbians from adopting in the state—a bill Dianne was instrumental in squelching—she always found the Pampa representative willing to listen.

"Sometimes we just have to walk in and talk to the people carrying anti-gay legislation," she insists. When she had met with Chisum on the adoption bill, pointing out how it would hurt so many gays and lesbians who wanted children, he had replied with sincerity, "If I have hurt anyone, I am truly sorry. That was not my intention. I just have strict religious beliefs."

Thompson relented, said with a sigh, "Okay. My lips are chapped anyway," and got on the phone to Warren Chisum. With Dianne sitting in her office listening, Thompson wheedled and cajoled Chisum, asking what it would take for him to support the bill. "Take the gays out," he flatly replied. Thompson refused. Citing the recent Matthew Shepard case and the public outcry against anti-gay violence, she said, "They are the second most targeted group in hate crimes, Warren. We cannot morally take them out." Finally, Chisum said that perhaps if the wording was changed from "sexual orientation" to "sexual preference," he might vote for the bill. Elated, Thompson agreed, but insisted that with the change there would have to be a clear definition of that phrase—and it would be gay, lesbian, bisexual, and transgendered people. "We're not talking about folks who fuck dead people or pigs here, Warren," she said tartly. Chisum replied that even if he were to vote for it, he would probably sway no more than four or five votes with his, thereby acknowledging that there were now legislators even further to the right than he was.

The passionate debate on the House floor went on for three hours. "Senfronia was amazing. She wrangled so many legislators," Dianne says with admiration. To everyone's astonishment, on April 27, 1999, the House, for the first time in Texas history, passed the toughened hate-crimes bill, 84–63—including the five votes promised by Warren Chisum.

A concerned Governor Bush met with Senate Republicans, determined to keep the bill from coming to a vote there. This time his efforts worked. The bill stalled in the State Affairs Committee, when Republican Florence Shapiro, the chair, would not allow it to come up for a vote. Shapiro, who had voted for the bill in the past, did not want to go up against the will of George W. Bush. Dianne says, "Every Republican who had voted for it before told me, 'Dianne, I'm on George W's team.' "

A frustrated Hardy-Garcia suggested to Ellis that the Democratic senators filibuster. "No, we're not going to do that," Ellis insisted. "We've come as far as we can." But Hardy-Garcia would not let it drop. She could take losing, but she wanted to go down scratching and biting. "Y'all need to fight like girls!" she cried. "I think that it's important that people know that George W. Bush stopped this bill. We have to keep fighting even though we aren't going to get the vote!" Spurred on by Thompson, who loved a good fight, too, Dianne devised a flamboyant plan to draw attention to the battle. Knowing that filibustering required constant standing, she went out and bought tennis shoes for all the Democratic senators and had them delivered to the Senate floor. The newspapers got wind of the inventive gesture and reported that the idea of a filibuster was being floated around the Senate hallways.

Late that night, Thompson and Hardy-Garcia had joined Ellis in his office when a phone call came in from Senator John Whitmire, inviting them all over to the Austin Club, where legislators gathered to relax, chat, and raise a drink. At two A.M., the three found themselves in the company of a group of senators, led by Whitmire, who proposed that they indeed filibuster. "I don't want to be out there by myself," Ellis moaned. The rest assured him that not only would they be beside him, but since the session the next day—which would begin in less than four hours—was the last day for bills to be passed, the gambit had to be done then. Thompson turned to Hardy-Garcia and said, "Well, honey, you got your wish." Before the late-night caucus adjourned, the group told her they needed a rabbi and a few ministers to conduct a prayer vigil at eight in the morning, before the session. And could she also see to it that there were at least three hundred supporters filling the rotunda, cheering the filibuster on? Dianne looked at her watch, which now read three A.M., gulped, and answered, "Okay." She left the table and started dialing the phone, tears streaming down her cheeks, cheered because these champions were going to the mat to fight a grand battle, not caring that the war had already been lost.

On May 6, 1999, Democratic senators, true to their word, shut down the Senate for the entire day with a ringing filibuster. Surrounded by a full gallery and hordes of press, the speeches went on from morning until evening. John Whitmire, the architect of the plan, was perhaps the most stirring. "You know what this is about," he said to his colleagues.

"This is about homophobia and a person who is running for the presidency of the United States not wanting to support a bill because gays are in it!" He looked around the ornate room. "You *know* gays and lesbians. They're in this room; they work on your staff. How can you do this to them?" Other bills died throughout the day as the filibuster progressed. As it stretched on and on, both sides went into secret negotiations. "We almost got somewhere," Dianne says. "But every time they would run the revising of the bill by George W. Bush's staff, they wouldn't accept it." The last gasp at the end of the day didn't see the bill come to a vote, but a moral victory had been claimed all the same. "That and the House win were the highlights of my career," Hardy-Garcia says firmly.

As if only to further underscore the opposing sides, President Bill Clinton, by coincidence, came to Austin that very night for an unrelated speaking engagement. All through the hate-crimes fight that year, Dianne had befriended Renee Byrd, the daughter of murdered James Byrd, Jr. Renee was on hand in Austin for the vote in the legislature. When they learned that Clinton was coming to town, the activists asked if he would possibly consider meeting with her. Within a matter of hours the White House agreed to the request. The President's attitude was a sharp contrast to that of Governor George W. Bush. "It took forever for Bush to agree to meet with Renee," Dianne says. "He kept stalling; he claimed he hadn't read the bill—even though I had personally made sure he had it in front of him." When the governor finally did agree to see her, it was a strained meeting, with a frustrated Renee breaking down into tears at one point.

President Clinton listened intently to Renee Byrd as she recounted her life since her father's gruesome murder. As he comforted her she innocently asked, "Can you help us? Can you call George W. Bush?" Clinton said he would indeed try, but that he didn't believe it would do much good. "He doesn't like me too much," the President told her. "I beat his daddy." That night, when Clinton gave his prepared speech at Bergstrom Air Force Base, he again mentioned the importance of passing the Hate Crimes Prevention Act.

Yet despite the President's continuing endorsement of the HCPA, it has not passed. And although statewide legislation to increase penalties for hate crimes against homosexuals was introduced in twenty-six states by 1999, Missouri alone passed the law. Only twenty-one states and the District of Columbia have laws that include sexual orientation; nine, including Texas, have no existing hate-crimes laws at all.

The National Coalition of Anti-Violence Programs (NCAVP) reported that the total number of anti-gay incidents in America in 1998 was 2,552. The number of anti-gay murders had skyrocketed by 136 percent, from fourteen in 1997 to thirty-three in 1998. LGRL reports that in that same year, the total of reported victims of hate crimes in Texas was 351, up from 299 the previous year; of these, sexual orientation was the motivation for 21.2 percent, up from 17.8 percent in 1997. Sexual orientation was now the second most common reason for a hate crime, after race.

Although she will never give up the fight, Dianne Hardy-Garcia feels the toll; she knows the burnout. "One of the things that's hardest about AIDS is that we've lost our institutional memory in a way," she says. "A lot of gay men who had been doing this work for a long time could be guiding us along. I miss them. So I know I have an obligation to be around so I can train another generation so they can carry on and have that memory. I've got to balance it and I've got to try to be better and go home sometimes. But the hard part is that the work never ends. It's *endless*. I feel bad about not being able to do more for all the people that call in. I feel like my office needs caseworkers to handle the cases and referrals. I feel like there need to be more lobbyists like me in every state. There need to be more—just in Texas—organizers and money. And I've got to raise it. So I'm trying. Because I know I can't do it alone. I can't be the lone voice.

"We've all got to fight like girls."

ACKNOWLEDGMENTS

As authors, we felt very privileged to profile the achievements of these seven heroic individuals. We are grateful to have the support and energies of so many people. Their time, wisdom, and effort gave us the words to bring alive these stories of courage.

Most important are the heroes and heroines who graciously gave us unlimited access to their lives: Phyllis Lyon and Del Martin, Elaine Noble, Sir Ian McKellen, Roberta Achtenberg, Tracy Thorne, and Dianne Hardy-Garcia. There is no way we can thank them enough for opening up their hearts and minds to two writers wanting to tell their tales of bravery. Their patience, understanding, returning of calls, answering of repeated questions, and support of this project has meant a great deal to both of us.

Special thanks must go to Bantam publisher Irwyn Applebaum for originating the idea for this book and entrusting its writing to us.

Ann Harris at Bantam Books is every writer's dream editor. Her devotion to excellence, attention to detail, and commitment are amazing. With the assistance of Elisa Petrini, she has guided and taught us. She gave us confidence, while at the same time demanding more from us. We are grateful for her experience, wisdom, and truthfulness.

Our agent Todd Shuster once again was there for us every step of the way. Quite simply, he is the best in the business. He held our hand, gave us needed support, and provided invaluable advice.

A dedicated research team is imperative in putting together a book of this nature. Special thanks to Carla Pack Bailey, Michael Bailey, Clare Fields, Wayne Besen, Jennifer Pawlitschek, and the talented and capable Neil Miller. Their diligence and hard work were herculean.

Many people allowed us to interview them, provided materials, and shared their history with us. We are especially grateful to the following: Benjamin Morgan Achtenberg, Terry Anderson, Matt Aston, Steve Atkinson, Andrew Barrer, Michael Begland, Michael Bento, Wayne Besen, Brian Bond, Ivy Bottini, Chris Bull, Michael Cashman, Henry Cisneros, Andrew Delony, Representative Harryette Ehrhardt, Senator Rodney Ellis, Santa Fareri, William Dudley Gregory, Kenneth Hardy-Garcia, Kenneth and Mary Jane Hardy, Tom Henderson, Gail King, Greg King, Joel Lawson, Ann Lewis, Waite Madison, Ann Maguire, Joe Martin, Angela Mason, Sean Mathias, Armistead Maupin, Representative Glen Maxey, Tim McFeeley, Mary Ann Messina, Nancy Molleda, Mary Morgan, Bettie Naylor, Sarah Porch, Lisa Power, Hillary Rosen, Bob Ross, Douglas Slater, David Smith, Todd Suko, Susan Achtenberg Thomas, Jeff Trammell, Kristina Voelkel, and William Waybourn.

Dennis wishes to thank his friends who provided such a great support system, including Beth Broderick, Gary Bankston, Dinah Manoff, Mary Gutzi, Jeff Marcus, Dean Pitchford and Michael Mealiffe, Dale Davis, Harris Spylios, Donna Murphy and Shawn Elliott, Kathryn Cordes, Dan Davis, Nathan Haas, Russell Lewis, Ralph Bruneau, Judith Ivey, Denny Sevier, Pam Braverman, Ginger Lawrence, Glen Fretwell, Hank Stratton, Allison Kingsley, Alex Mustelier, and Willy Hall. Love and gratitude go to his entire family, especially his parents, John and Shirley Bailey, who have always been unconditionally and enthusiastically supportive.

David is grateful to all of his family and friends for their support and love in this process. They maintained their humor, showed endless patience, and were great caretakers. A few who were exceptional in their support of this book include Jeremy Bernard, Marylouise Oates and Bob Shrum, Herb Hamsher and Jonathan Stoller, Judith Light and Robert Desiderio, Scott Hitt and Alex Koleszar, Roberta Bennett, and too many others to name in this limited space. They have his eternal love and gratitude.

We give our thanks to Patrick Marston, who kept us organized, helped us to meet our deadlines, and provided crucial support.

Finally, there are thousands upon thousands of heroes and heroines in the gay, lesbian, bisexual, and transgendered community. We only wish we could have told all of their stories. We are proud to be part of them.

INDEX